Evaluating
Educational
Performance

A SOURCEBOOK OF
METHODS, INSTRUMENTS,
AND EXAMPLES

EDITED BY
Herbert J. Walberg

College of Education
University of Illinois at Chicago Circle

McCutchan Publishing Corporation
2526 Grove Street
Berkeley, California 94704

The editor and authors
dedicate this book to the memory of
Dr. Robert J. Coughlan
Professor of Education and Management
at Northwestern University
and coauthor of chapter 16

FOREWORD

In the Report of the Committee on Educational Research of the National Academy of Education appears the following brilliant and forceful paragraph.

> We start with the premise that inquiry into educational matters is essential but extremely difficult. We therefore are particularly concerned with the impediments to excellence in educational research. To discover and propagate new mechanisms for conducting research and new research styles will require changed attitudes within the academic community. These must grow; they cannot be legislated. (Cronbach and Suppes, 1969)

To get to the new mechanism, new styles, and changed attitudes, we need a continuing dialogue with constructive criticism in the larger educational community. In the book you are about to read the authors take a large step in starting the necessary dialogue. They give examples of new attacks on real problems. They open several doors into methodologies seldom used in disciplined inquiry in education. Case studies are presented of inquiries into areas of education that are extremely difficult to investigate. Furthermore, the work is presented with humility and an obvious desire for criticism. The editor speaks for the other authors and himself in the first chapter when he states that this is not a handbook of routine solutions but is a source book of "beginning efforts to offer useful instruments and procedures to our colleagues in universities and schools."

In the Report edited by Cronbach and Suppes it is stated that "disciplined inquiry is conducted and reported in such a way that the argument can be painstakingly examined" (p. 15). The authors of this current volume reveal a disposition and an ability to do just that. They are cautious regarding the immediate implications of their findings in the evaluation of teaching effectiveness, in assessment of affective learning, and in describing the conditions of use of their instruments and procedures. Through this book they submit their "thinking to the skilled and assiduous review of [their] colleagues, who have special training in such criticism" (Cronbach and Suppes, pp. 268-69).

About six years ago I published a hortative paper directed to the educational-measurement community (Hastings, 1969). The main theme was one to which others have spoken: those of us in educational measurement must cease to depend solely upon the methodologies of psychometrics, and correlation; rather we must adapt and adopt procedures, instrumentation, and logic from sociology, economics, history, and elsewhere if we are to understand better the complexities of education today. I do not believe that the paper I refer to had any effect on the authors of this book; however, the chapters in this volume do give flesh to the bones of my exhortation. In these pages you will find careful adaptation of concepts and methods from social anthropology, from history, and from geography. Although they do not deal extensively with economics in such terms as cost-benefits, the authors do open the way to collecting more complex and meaningful data with which to do such studies.

Many excellent books and articles have been published concerning various models and methods for evaluation of education. This book, far more than most in my opinion, takes one into the classroom and the school system for attacks on real problems. The methods and instruments presented in chapter after chapter have grown out of the serious and difficult work of attempting evaluations which will be of help to decision makers in educational settings.

Accountability, evaluation of programs, and teacher performance are loud words and phrases in educational literature today. Unfortunately, many of the prescriptions for handling the issues suggested by these topics are so oversimplified that the results of their use would be disastrous. Boards of education and administrative personnel are being pressured to use some highly touted but little researched prescriptions. This book, with its careful regard for complexity, is much needed by the whole educational community. Although it is directed primarily at evaluation and research personnel, I hope that its message—especially on complexity—will be transmitted to our decision makers. Clearly, this collection of reviews and studies is needed today.

J. Thomas Hastings

Notes

Cronbach, L. J. and Suppes, P., editors. *Research for Tomorrow's Schools: Disciplined Inquiry for Education.* Report of the Committee on Educational Research of the National Academy of Education (New York: Macmillan, 1969) 3.

Hastings, J. Thomas. "The Kith and Kin of Educational Measures." *Journal of Educational Measurement* 6 (1969): 127-30.

CONTRIBUTORS

GARY J. ANDERSON is Assistant Director of the Atlantic Institute of Education, Halifax, Nova Scotia, Canada. After receiving his Ed.D. from the Harvard Graduate School of Education in 1968, he held positions in the Faculty of Education and the Centre for Learning and Development at McGill University. In addition to his extensive work on classroom climate, his research has included studies of teacher education, early childhood education, and educational planning.

JAMES R. BARCLAY received his Ph.D. from the University of Michigan in 1959. He coordinated the School Psychology Training Program at California State University at Hayward, and presently chairs the Department of Educational Psychology and Counseling at the University of Kentucky. His interests include the philosophy of counseling, classroom climate assessment, social and academic problem prevention, and school psychologist training. He has published over fifty books, monographs, and articles, including *Controversial Issues in Testing* and *Foundations of Counseling Strategies*. In the last dozen years he has developed the Barclay Classroom Climate Inventory.

MARK BARGEN studied at Wichita State University. He was employed until September of 1973 by the University of Illinois at

Chicago Circle as an Assistant Educational Specialist in the Office of Evaluation Research, during which time he collaborated on articles on the social status and sibling constellation correlates of mental abilities and urban spatial models. Since that time he has been at the University of Connecticut Health Center, where he is performing research in health education. With Herbert J. Walberg, he has co-authored articles that have appeared in the *American Educational Research Journal* and the *British Journal of Clinical and Social Psychology*.

JERE E. BROPHY is Associate Professor of Educational Psychology at the University of Texas at Austin, where he has been since receiving his Ph.D. from the Committee on Human Development at the University of Chicago in 1967. He has also been Staff Development Coordinator for the Early Childhood Program of the Southwest Educational Development Laboratory. In addition to writing numerous articles and research reports, he has coauthored *Looking in Classrooms* with Thomas Good, and is writing a textbook for early education and child care workers with Thomas Good and Shari Nedler. In collaboration with Carolyn Evertson, he is also preparing a book on the research described in his chapter.

JAMES S. COLEMAN is University Professor in the Department of Sociology at the University of Chicago. His previous positions have included Professor of Social Relations at Johns Hopkins University, and Assistant Professor of Sociology at the University of Chicago. He received his Ph.D. in Sociology from Columbia University in 1955, and has authored, with others, *The Adolescent Society* and *Equality of Educational Opportunity*.

ROBERT A. COOKE is a Survey Research Center Study Director at the Institute for Social Research, University of Michigan. His Ph.D. work is in organization behavior with minors in educational administration and social psychology at Northwestern University. His research has focused on the organizational behavior of educational systems and innovation in education. He has authored papers and monographs on collective decision processes and structures in schools, interorganizational temporary systems, and educational research, development, and diffusion.

ROBERT J. COUGHLAN was Professor of Education and Organization Behavior in the School of Education and Graduate School of Management, and Coordinator of the National Program for Educational Leadership, at Northwestern University. Prior to his association with Northwestern, he was Director of Program Development at the Industrial Relations Center of the University of Chicago. He received his Ph.D. in Educational Administration from the University of Chicago. His teaching and research interests were in the areas of organization behavior and development in schools. He served frequently as a consultant to educational systems in programs of organizational improvement, leadership development, and in-service training. He authored numerous articles, research monographs, training manuals, and educational materials in the areas of organization, leadership, communication, and work attitudes.

MAURICE J. EASH is Professor of Education and Director of the Office of Evaluation Research at the University of Illinois at Chicago Circle. He has been active as an evaluator of social and educational programs, both state and national, and has written articles and papers on the problems of program design and evaluation in field settings.

GENE V GLASS is a Professor of Education and is associated with the Laboratory of Educational Research at the University of Colorado. He received his Ph.D. from the University of Wisconsin in Educational Psychology in 1965. He is coauthor of *Statistical Methods in Education and Psychology* (with Julian C. Stanley) and *Design and Analysis of Time-Series Experiments* (with Victor L. Willson and John M. Gottman). Dr. Glass is a member of the Executive Board and Association Council of the American Educational Research Association, and is past editor of the *Review of Educational Research*.

J. THOMAS HASTINGS, Professor of Educational Psychology, is Director of the Center for Instructional Research and Curriculum Evaluation (CIRCE) in the College of Education, University of Illinois at Urbana-Champaign. After teaching mathematics and science in secondary schools for five years, he earned his Ph.D. (1943) in measurement and evaluation at The University of Chicago. He has taught courses in measurement, statistics, and evaluation, and was Vice President of the Division of Curriculum and Objectives of the

American Educational Research Association in 1965-67 and President of the National Council on Measurement in Education in 1968. He recently coauthored (with Benjamin Bloom and George Madaus) *Handbook on Formative and Summative Evaluation of Student Learning.*

ARTHUR R. JENSEN has been on the faculty of the University of California at Berkeley since 1958. He is now Professor of Educational Psychology and Research Psychologist at the Institute of Human Learning. A graduate of U.C. Berkeley, and Columbia University, he was a clinical psychology intern at the University of Maryland Psychiatric Institute and a post-doctoral research fellow at the Institute of Psychiatry, University of London. He was a Guggenheim Fellow and a Fellow of the Center for Advanced Study in the Behavioral Sciences. His research has been concerned mainly with the experimental psychology of human learning, measurement and structure of individual differences in mental abilities, genetic and environmental determinants of intellectual development, and causes of individual and group differences in scholastic performances. He has contributed more than 150 articles and chapters, many of them frequently reprinted, to psychological and educational journals and books. His latest book is *Educability and Group Differences.*

DAVID W. JOHNSON is Professor of Educational Psychology at the University of Minnesota. He received his Ph.D. in Social Psychology from Columbia University in 1966. He is the author of six books on effective interpersonal relationships and social psychology, and he has published over thirty articles on his research on conflict resolution, interpersonal interaction, and group dynamics. He has recently received a national award from the American Personnel Guidance Association for his outstanding research. His books include *The Social Psychology of Education* and *Reaching Out: Interpersonal Effectiveness and Self-Actualization.*

NANCY KARWEIT is an Associate Research Scientist at The Center for Social Organization of Schools, Johns Hopkins University. She is coauthor, with James Coleman, of *Information Systems and Performance Measures in Schools,* and is interested in developing and studying the uses of information systems in schools. She is currently implementing school attendance accounting procedures and is analyzing factors related to absence from school. She has had previous computer and research experience with the Rand Corporation, IBM, and the Applied Physics Laboratory, Johns Hopkins University.

DIANA H. KIRK is a doctoral student and research assistant to Alex Inkeles in the School of Education at Stanford University. She has previously been a research analyst at Stanford Research Institute and has served as a consultant on survey research methods to various government projects. She received an M.A. in the Sociology of Education from Stanford University in 1971. Her research interests include a number of areas: decision making in nonegalitarian groups, multicultural education, learning environments, desegregation, and causal models of human behavior in nonexperimental research.

DONALD N. McISAAC is Associate Dean of the School of Education and Professor of Educational Administration at the University of Wisconsin—Madison. He is also Director of the Wisconsin Information Systems for Education on the Madison campus. He holds a Ph.D. in Education from the Claremont Graduate School.

H. DEAN NIELSEN is a doctoral student and a research assistant to Alex Inkeles at Stanford University's International Development Education Center (SIDEC). He has been involved in educational research in Brazil, and has taught at the Federal University of Brazilia. He received his M.A. in Politics and Education from Columbia University's Teachers College in 1972. He is currently doing research on the relations of education and political socialization, with emphasis on the connections between learning environments and attitudes toward political dissent.

DANIEL POWELL is Associate Professor of Education at the University of Illinois at Chicago Circle, and teaches in the Department of Curriculum, Instruction, and Evaluation. He received his M. A. from Columbia University's Department of Public Law and Government. He was a John Hay Fellow at the University of Chicago in 1960-1961, and a clinical professor at Northwestern University. Mr. Powell is educational consultant for Scott, Foresman and Company in the field of secondary school social studies. He is the author of

Ideas in Conflict, The John Hay Fellows, and joint author of *Education and The New Teacher.* For some years he has served as committee member, reader, and consultant for the Advanced Placement Program of the College Entrance Examination Board. He has also served as an evaluator for the North Central Association and the National Council for Accreditation of Teacher Education.

KENNETH J. RABBEN is an award-winning journalist covering education from a national perspective in his weekly column, *Education Notebook,* distributed by Copley News Service. He has worked as an investigative specialist and writer for Rep. John M. Ashbrook of Ohio. Rabben won the International Reading Association's top award for outstanding reporting and writing in 1970, and a special award of excellence in 1971. He holds a B.S. in elementary education from Temple University, and is a member of the Johns Hopkins University chapter of Phi Delta Kappa. Rabben's freelance articles have been published in several periodicals.

ROBERT M. RIPPEY, currently Professor of Research in Health Education at the University of Connecticut Health Center, began his career as a high school teacher. After receiving his Ph.D. from the University of Chicago in 1964, he joined the faculty of the University of Chicago, Department of Education, where he was also Director of the Center for the Cooperative Study of Instruction, and Dean of Students of the Division of Social Sciences. Subsequently he moved to the University of Illinois at Chicago Circle, where he taught courses in evaluation and change and evaluated several educational innovations through the Office of Evaluation Research. He has contributed to two books and authored over sixty papers on evaluation, instructional theory, and educational change.

DENNIS W. SPUCK is Assistant Professor of Educational Administration at the University of Wisconsin—Madison, and serves as Assistant Director of the Wisconsin Information Systems for Education. He received his Ph.D. in Education from the Claremont Graduate School. His current research interests and writings are in the areas of evaluation for administrative decision making, computer applications related to the management of educational institutions, and the application of mathematical decision-making models to educational problems.

HARRIET TALMAGE, Professor of Education, is Head of the Department of Curriculum Instruction and Evaluation, and a Staff Associate of the Office of Evaluation Research, of the College of Education, University of Illinois at Chicago Circle. Her interests include teacher education program design and instructional materials design and evaluation. She received her Ph.D. from Northwestern University in 1967.

ERIK A. VAN HOVE is presently Professor of Social Science Research Methods at the University of Antwerp, Belgium. In 1972, as a Lecturer in Sociology at the University of Surrey, England, he did an analysis of school performance, to be reported shortly in a volume edited by M. Janowitz. His main interest is in mathematical sociology. He received his Ph.D. in sociology from the Johns Hopkins University in 1971.

HERBERT J. WALBERG, Professor of Human Development and Learning and Research Professor of Urban Education at the University of Illinois at Chicago Circle, was formerly at the Educational Testing Service, Harvard University, and the University of Wisconsin. He received his Ph.D. from the University of Chicago in 1964. Since then he has served as consultant to a wide variety of private and public institutions and agencies in the areas of program and curriculum design and evaluation research. He is author of more than eighty research papers on developmental and social psychology, social environments of learning, multivariate analysis, and other topics, and has contributed as author or editor to fifteen books, several of them on evaluation.

WAYNE W. WELCH is Assistant Dean for Research and Development at the University of Minnesota, a position he has held since 1970. His research interests include program evaluation and measurement, as well as research on science teaching. His current projects include a study of the relative role of values, information, and constraints in the decision process, and a four year evaluation study of diffusion projects funded by the National Science Foundation. As an Associate Professor in the Department of Educational Psychology, he teaches courses in the methodology and philosophy of evaluation.

ACKNOWLEDGMENTS

The editing of this book and the writing of Chapters 1, 6, 8, 12, 13, 14, 19, and 20 were generously supported by Van Cleve Morris, Dean of the College of Education of the University of Illinois at Chicago Circle; George C. Giles, Jr., Associate Dean and Acting Director of the Urban Educational Research Program; and Maurice J. Eash, Director of the Office of Evaluation Research.

Chapter 2, by Gene V Glass, is adapted from "Statistical and Measurement Problems of the Stull Act," a paper presented at the Conference on the Stull Act at Stanford University in October, 1972.

The research in Chapter 3, by Jere E. Brophy, was supported by the Research and Development Center for Teacher Education at the University of Texas at Austin (Oliver H. Brown and Robert F. Peck, Co-directors). The author thanks Edmund Emmer, Carolyn Evertson, Thomas Good, Earl Jennings, Kathey Paredes, Kathleen Senior, Jon Sheffield, and Donald Veldman, who were involved in planning and executing the project.

The research in Chapter 5, by H. Dean Nielsen and Diana H. Kirk, grew out of a Stanford University research project on school environments directed by Alex Inkeles and funded by the Southeast Asia Development Advisory Group (SEADAG) of the Asia Society in New

York. SEADAG supported the preparation of prior versions of this chapter and of Chapter 6, by Gary J. Anderson and Herbert J. Walberg, for a conference on educational environments held at the Institute for Humanistic Studies, Aspen, Colorado in May, 1972.

Chapter 8, by Wayne W. Welch and Herbert J. Walberg, is reprinted from the *American Educational Research Journal,* Vol. 9, No. 3, pp. 373-383. Copyright by American Educational Research Association, Washington, D.C. The research in Chapter 8 was supported by the Carnegie Corporation; Harvard University; the National Science Foundation; the Sloan Foundation; and the U.S. Office of Education. The data reported in this paper were presented at the National Academy of Education meeting in Chicago, 1972.

Chapter 9, by Maurice J. Eash, is reprinted by permission of *Curriculum Theory Network,* Ontario Institute for Studies in Education. An earlier draft of this chapter was prepared for the American Educational Research Association Annual Conference, Division B, Minneapolis, Minnesota, March 1970. Development of the instrument was performed pursuant to a grant from the United States Office of Education to the New York State Network of Special Education Instructional Materials Centers, Hunter College of the City University of New York. Acknowledgment is extended to Professor Gloria Wolinsky and her staff, who assisted at various stages of its development, particularly in arranging for the initial field testing. The author acknowledges the invaluable assistance of Richard Smock and Edward Kelly in analyzing the data.

Chapter 11, by Arthur P. Jensen, is reprinted from *Educational Research,* 1971, Vol. 14, pp. 3-28. Copyright 1970 by Arthur R. Jensen. All rights reserved.

Aspects of Chapter 12, by Herbert J. Walberg and Mark Bargen, were presented at a public lecture series on equality of educational opportunity co-sponsored by DePaul University and the University of Illinois at Chicago Circle during the spring of 1972.

An overview of Chapters 12-16 was presented by Herbert J. Walberg at the annual meeting of Professors of Curriculum in Minneapolis and at seminars at the Medill School of Journalism and School of Education at Northwestern University and the Department of Geography of the University of Chicago in 1972.

Chapter 19, by Herbert J. Walberg, is a version of a section of a book on geographical perspectives on urban problems being edited by Brian Berry for the University of Chicago Press and the American Association of Geographers and supported by the National Science Foundation. The present research was supported by the Office of Evaluation Research and the Urban Educational Research Program at the University of Illinois.

Chapter 20, by Herbert J. Walberg, was presented at a symposium, "Educational Implications of Zero Growth," at the annual meeting of the American Association for the Advancement of Science, Washington, D.C., December, 1972.

CONTENTS

1. EVALUATING EDUCATIONAL PERFORMANCE
Herbert J. Walberg

The words in the title—*Evaluating Educational Performance: A Sourcebook of Methods, Instruments, and Examples*—are intended to reflect my purpose in soliciting and editing the original writings for this book. "Evaluating" suggests a more active process or technique than does the static abstractness of the word "evaluation." The contributors to this book are engaged in programmatic research efforts, many of which they expect to extend for several years and to result in book-length monographs. In this research they are discovering what is effective in natural settings of learning and are finding constructive leads to what may work better; they are also discovering pitfalls, and speak from practical experience. While most of the authors are conducting basic educational inquiry, at my request they here address themselves to problems of practical evaluation for policy formulation, decision making, and planned change.

The word "Educational" in the title indicates my belief that education should ideally be a unique theoretical discipline and profession with a core of ideals, concepts, and tested methods. Evaluation can help attain this goal, make the practice of education more effective, and raise it out of its quasi-professional status. Of course, psychology, sociology, economics, anthropology, philosophy, and history have much to contribute to the evaluation process, but concepts and methods from these fields are better carefully adapted to educational problems than uncritically adopted. Similarly, medicine,

1

law, business, and social work offer insights useful for educators, but these also need critical screening and empirical testing.

The word "Performance" suggests the comprehensive measurement of educational needs, processes, and outcomes. To be sure, the testing industry provides a great number of reliable standardized tests; indeed, school systems often equate evaluation with student testing programs, and some educators in universities and school systems limit evaluation to the narrow range of student performance measured on standardized achievement tests. In this book, we turn from the evaluation of the student on these tests to the evaluation of the system and its effectiveness in the organization and provision of environments, personnel, services, and materials to promote student learning. Progress in attaining expressed goals of education such as growth in creativity, integrity, and democratic ideals cannot be measured accurately and comprehensively with existing tests. Valid measures of such progress would be helpful but their development has encountered great technical difficulties that are still unresolved. Consequently, evaluation of the system must often focus not on the standardized student outcomes or ultimate results but on the qualities of the educational environment that are thought likely to promote such learning. Qualities of the educational environment that are consistently associated with growth on standardized cognitive and affective outcome measures are valid to some extent. But we must avoid the error of equating what is most often measured or most conveniently measurable with what is most important in the environment and outcome domains. Thus, the contributing authors enlarge both domains; specify procedures and tools for measuring aspects of this enlarged conception; caution us concerning their use; and reaffirm our need for humility, intuition, and judgment in evaluating educational performance.

The words "A Sourcebook of Methods, Instruments, and Examples" describe the authors' beginning efforts to offer useful instruments and procedures to our colleagues in universities and schools. The remainder of this chapter is an overview of how the authors have attempted to do this and how their contributions fit together.

The first two chapters concern teacher evaluation. Glass, in "Teacher Effectiveness," reviews the work in this field and reanalyzes data from several studies. He is highly critical of proposals to use standardized student tests or simulated assessments, and recommends systematic observation and ratings of teacher behavior in regular classrooms and student assessments of their classroom environment. Though we do not yet have a clear understanding of teacher effectiveness, state legislatures and school boards are beginning to require evaluation of teachers for tenure and merit pay. Glass's critical summary of the state of the art of teacher evaluation provides useful guidance for school systems that are now planning and implementing such evaluation.

Brophy, in "Achievement Correlates," shows how classroom research can improve teacher evaluation. Working with a large battery of longitudinal assessments in the early elementary grades, he identifies four qualities of teaching that are related to the cognitive growth of students: task-oriented, businesslike manner; abundance of structuring comments; variability in the use of methods and materials; and provision of student opportunity to practice tasks on which he will be tested. Brophy is cautious regarding the immediate implications of his findings for evaluating teachers, but his chapter shows how sustained, programmatic evaluation research in the schools can develop valid teacher-assessment instruments and procedures.

In "Needs Assessment," Barclay, whose experience as a school psychologist led to ten years of research on psychological diagnosis of classroom social structures, describes instruments for collecting children's self-reports, peer-sociometric choices, and teacher judgments to characterize the individual child, the class, and administrative units such as schools and districts. His computer programs generate a quantitative and verbal diagnosis of the child and the social setting that may be used by consultants and school personnel to formulate ameliorative programs based on identified needs.

Chapters 5, 6, and 7 describe a variety of observation and rating instruments designed to assess processes of teaching and learning. A number of uses for these instruments other than teacher evaluation are suggested, including troubleshooting school-organization problems; detecting changes brought about by innovations; and employing variables such as group cohesiveness and fairness as indicators of conditions likely to foster student growth toward goals that are important but difficult to measure.

Nielsen and Kirk, in "Classroom Climates," review observation and rating scales for assessing school and classroom climates. They also specify the qualities of climates tapped by the more comprehensive, validated instruments. From their overview, evaluators can select instruments that measure climate characteristics of greatest utility for a particular evaluation or combine scales selected from the various instruments to construct a new tailor-made instrument. The authors emphasize the criteria of reliability and validity in selecting or constructing climate instruments.

Anderson and Walberg, in "Learning Environments," describe the conception and uses of environment inventories. They summarize research that suggests factors determining the learning environment and relating qualities of the environment to cognitive and affective learning. A number of uses of environment inventories in evaluative research are cited.

Johnson, in "Affective Outcomes," defines affective learning and shows its relation to values, cognition, and behavior. He then describes the Minnesota School Affect Assessment, an instrument that has been administered to the children of an entire school district. It is being used in an extensive three-year program to assess affective learning in the schools; to provide quantitative information on this assessment to the school staff; and to formulate organizational and instructional innovations on the basis of this information.

Chapters 8 and 9 focus on the evaluation of instructional media. Welch and Walberg, in "A Course Evaluation," describe an extensive psychometric evaluation of Harvard Project Physics, a new high school course that emphasizes the history and philosophy of science as well as the humanistic aspects of physics. This evaluation, the first national true experiment in education, illustrates the multiple effects of the course on cognitive and affective learning.

Eash, in "Instructional Materials," describes the development and field trials of an instrument for assessing instructional materials. Based on theory and research on instruction, the instrument guides the user in gathering data to make critical judgments and informed decisions when selecting educational media and planning for their use. Rather than accepting publishers' advertising and claims for effectiveness, educators can employ the instrument to compare the strengths and weaknesses of competing products.

Chapters 10 and 11 describe large-scale statistical studies of educational performance and equality of opportunity. Van Hove, Coleman, Rabben, and Karweit, in "Urban System Performance," describe the relative performances of public school systems in six of the largest cities in the United States. In all-white schools, for example, Baltimore scored lowest in the early grades but scored highest in the later grades. Chicago, on the other hand, showed the greatest declines from the early to the later grades among both white and minority students. The authors also assess the effects of racial composition in the urban school systems sampled.

In "Equality for Minorities," Jensen reports on an analysis of personality and ability measures on a large sample of elementary school children in California. When background factors were controlled, there were no significant differences between majority and minority children in scholastic achievement. Nor was there any evidence for a cumulative deficit in minority children. Jensen concludes that although the schools do not cheat minority children, they might be redesigned to optimize the learning of children with different ability patterns.

Chapters 12 through 16 describe the coordinated efforts of four teams to exploit, for system-wide evaluation, routinely-collected data on the several hundred public elementary schools and secondary schools in Chicago. While the data are usually employed to trace achievement patterns of individual students or to allocate funds commensurate with the number of students in each school, the teams use the data to provide answers to questions such as: Are effective resources as well as expenditures evenly distributed throughout the system? Do resources on which most school funds are expended relate to reading achievement (with other factors held as constant as possible)? Are there any distinguishing characteristics of schools that appear highly effective or ineffective in promoting reading achievement (see cautions above regarding standardized tests), given student quality and educational resources?

Walberg and Bargen, in "School Equality," specify six concepts of educational equality, none of which lead to completely acceptable operational measures of equality. They analyze national, state, and local research on equality and show how existing data on the Chicago schools can be used to evaluate equality of expenditures, resources, and achievement throughout the city, as well as for schools with different ethnic compositions. Compared with majority children in Chicago, minority children have less well qualified teachers, which may affect their achievement.

Bargen and Walberg, in "School Performance," use the same data to lay the statistical groundwork for chapters 14, 15, and 16. On a school basis, they relate "teacher quality" (education and years of experience) and class size—resources on which the bulk of school operating funds are expended—to reading achievement at given grade levels (with achievement at prior grade levels held constant). They conclude that teacher quality is probably causally associated with achievement but that class size is probably not. Also, teacher quality appears to benefit some ethnic groups more than others at certain grade levels.

From the last analysis, a number of schools were identified that had exceptionally high or exceptionally low reading achievement in a given grade, considering achievement of earlier grade students in the school, teacher quality, and class size. Three teams, with extensive educational experience, visited these two types of schools (without being informed of which type each school was) and administered instruments, conducted interviews, and made observations to characterize each school. They were then given the performance data on each school that enabled them to relate their characterizations to the performance findings.

Talmage and Rippey, in "Elementary School Cases," found no consistent differences between the two types of schools. While a larger replication of their methods may turn up distinguishing qualities of effective elementary schools, their results should humble those who believe they can visit a school for a day or two and make conclusions about its effectiveness, especially when their methods are less extensive and systematic than those of the authors.

Eash and Powell, in "Secondary School Cases," reveal some characteristics that appear to distinguish high from low reading-performance secondary schools. High-performance schools are better organized and concentrate their resources on cognitive growth. Though the staff is in command, students are treated with respect, and instruction is adapted to their abilities and needs. In one of the low-performance schools, the modern building and facilities failed to attract students from the surrounding slum, despite "official" records and the principal's claims of attendance (allocation of state funds and principals' salaries are based on attendance records in Chicago). On the other hand, in the two high performing schools, one of which was in a very depressed area of the city, the principals seemed able to organize community and school resources and to create a spirit of achievement among their staffs, parents, and students.

In "Work Attitudes," Coughlan and Cooke, using teacher morale scales, identify three factors that significantly distinguish effective school performance: techniques of student evaluation, developmental program emphasis, and perceptions of educational effectiveness. School-community relations, supervisory practices, and teacher participation in school policy also distinguish these schools. The authors describe how their instrument can be used to assess morale and work attitudes in the school and how programs may be formulated to improve the organization of school personnel and services.

In chapters 17 and 18, McIssac in "Trend-Surface Analysis" and Spuck in "Geocode Analysis" illustrate spatial analyses of educational data in a geographic area. Trend-surface analysis refers to contour mapping of computer-fitted aggregate values such as the mean student achievement in each school of a district. Geocode analysis pertains to unaggregated point values, such as student age coded by home address, that can be aggregated and mapped in various ways for different sorts of decisions. Either of these spatial analysis techniques can provide displays of information organized for policy and decision making in the form of maps of school achievement and resources, votes on bond issues, the distribution of student population within a district, or the pattern of educational needs within a state.

In "Urban Spatial Models," Walberg and Bargen trace some historical and social trends leading to hypotheses that levels of educational achievement in northern cities are distributed according to three classic models: concentric, sector, and status. The hypotheses are confirmed for Chicago by means of polynomial regression analysis. Computer-drawn maps reveal that the most experienced staffs tend to be in schools with the highest first grade reading readiness, where they are least needed.

In the final chapter, "Optimization Reconsidered," the editor reviews research on the standardized test correlates of heredity, home environment, and schooling. It is held that all three factors have continued to raise ability and achievement levels of American school children during this century. However, the recent controversies between hereditarians and environmentalists, both radical and moderate, may have harmed education by focusing too much attention on the limited factors measured by conventional tests. Thus, in addition to the other cautions regarding evaluation expressed in this book, the limitations of educational measurement must be kept in mind. In reading the chapters, it would be well to heed the physician's advice: "When in confirmation, to doubt; when in doubt, to refrain." At the same time, it is necessary to evaluate, to formulate policy, and to make educational decisions. It is our hope that these chapters, by making evaluation efforts explicit and open to criticism, can help others to improve on our work in subsequent evaluations.

In concluding this overview and introduction, three matters should be mentioned that are part of, or related to, educational evaluation but which are not systematically described in the rest of the chapters.

First, such matters as analyzing cost-benefit ratios and translating research and evaluation findings into policy are not treated here because they are covered in textbooks on educational administration, economics, finance, and decision making. Our main purpose is to show how data can be collected and analyzed for evaluation, not how it can be used to determine policy. The authors indicate how their instruments and procedures have been or could be used to provide organized information about school conditions and classroom learning environments for school boards and staffs. But just as it is difficult to draw distinctions between policy and its execution in superintendent-school board relations, the separation of evaluation from policy and practice remains ambiguous and variable. For example, a superintendent or school board can predetermine evaluation findings by picking outside or inside evaluators with known points of view or by awarding contracts or promotions to those who produce pleasing findings. Similarly, an evaluator can knowingly or unknowingly predetermine his findings in choosing his methods and analyses. Thus, in considering and using evaluation for decision making, we must avoid the extremes of cynicism and the true believer's naiveté by tempering our judgments with open-mindedness and skepticism.

Second, there are many excellent works on experimental design, survey research, questionnaire development and test construction, statistics, and data processing, but one design method deserves emphasis here—true experiments, the random assignment of individual students or educational units such as classes or schools to alternative educational programs or conditions. Experiments are expensive and difficult to carry out in natural educational settings, and they may lack generalizability if they are done in special settings, but they are the best way to detect probable causality. Most of the work in this book is correlational and subject to several causal interpretations. For example, good teachers may cause high student achievement, or high achieving students may attract good teachers to their schools, or more likely both of these factors may affect one another and causally interact with other factors. To sort out these causal relations, evaluators are urged to use the instruments and procedures described here in true experiments.

Assuredly, educational conditions present special difficulties in the measurement of causal constructs. Unlike the agricultural field research that has served as its statistical model, quantitative educational inquiry does not deal with several distinct varieties of subjects all starting the experiment at the same stage of growth and development. And the other model often followed in educational research, laboratory psychology, may be inappropriate in several respects. Deep educational questions concern processes that are more like those of economics in that they usually treat ill-defined conditions better observed over months and years rather than minutes and hours; clinical psychology, psychiatry, and medicine in that symptoms must be expertly perceived and judged; meteorology and sociology in that large masses of data must often be obtained and then reduced to a few major forces; and genetics and developmental psychology in that later environmental variations often bring about only small perturbations in growth curves characteristic of the individual organism determined by heredity and early environment. Moreover, educational inquiry resembles philosophy and history more than chemistry and physics in that ideology and values determine purpose, method, evidence rules, and sometimes even the results of inquiry.

Finally, this book concentrates on practical, technical issues of research methodology in the schools as they are presently organized, and not on the philosophy of education or an evaluative reconceptualization of immediate or ultimate goals of learning. Although the authors enlarge our conception of the domains of needs, processes, and outcomes, none would claim even the beginnings of a systematic philosophical reconstruction of educational means and goals. The evaluation techniques suggested here are aimed at amelioration and reform rather than at discovering breakthroughs or creating a revolution in the schools.

2. TEACHER EFFECTIVENESS
Gene V Glass

Three separate means for evaluating teacher effectiveness are discussed here, each for a different reason: the first—standardized testing—because its use for teacher evaluation would be an egregious error; the second—controlled, simulated assessment of teachers' impact on pupil performance—because it has been vigorously urged on schoolmen; and the third—observation and rating of teacher behavior and students' evaluation of teacher performance—because it is the method of choice under current circumstances.

Pupil Gains

Although few evaluation experts would defend the practice, there is still danger that some school districts might use pupil gains on standardized achievement tests to evaluate teachers. The danger is sufficiently real that such attempts at evaluation deserve attention here. Evaluating teachers by measuring their pupils' gains from September to June on commercially available standardized tests is patently invalid and unfair. Standardized tests will uncover gross educational deficiencies in basic skills, but such instruments are not designed to reveal the variety of ways in which teaching and learning can be creative, favorably opportunistic, and uniquely meaningful to students. The inadequacy of standardized tests for evaluating school learning has become a favorite theme of several contemporary educational researchers (Stake, 1971; Bormuth, 1970; Anderson, 1972).

11

Aside from the irrelevance of much of the content of standardized achievement tests, their use in evaluating teachers is unjust. Nonrandomly constituted classes give teachers of brighter pupils an unfair advantage. This remains true whether the statistician calculates simple gains, residual gains, true gains, true residual gains, or covariance adjustments. Nothing short of random assignment of pupils to teachers as an ironclad administrative necessity would ensure that the teachers were in a fair race to produce pupil gains.

Even if the validity and fairness objections to using standardized tests could be met, available evidence indicates that teachers' effects on pupils' gains in knowledge across one year is not reliably measured by such tests. Assume that teachers' true ability to teach traditional subject matter is a stable trait which fluctuates little from year to year. We shall measure this ability by administering a standardized test to many teachers' pupils and correcting for the initial status of the class by partialing out that portion of the end-of-year mean score which is linearly predictable from the beginning-of-year mean score (a procedure which has everything in its favor except logical good sense; see Cronbach and Furby, 1970). How stable from one year to the next will this "residualized" measure of the teacher's effect be? How subject is it to the vagaries of the shifting composition of the class across years, the fallibility of the test scores on individual pupils, and the compounding of measurement errors in the calculation of "gain scores?" In Table 2-1, I have integrated the findings from three unpublished studies which provide some answers to these questions. In each study the investigator calculated residual gain scores across September to May for two successive years of each teacher's class. The correlations of these gains across two years are "stability-reliability coefficients." They tell us the reliability with which we can measure what we assume to be teachers' true ability to teach their pupils what standardized tests measure. The low reliability of such measures should eliminate any temptation to evaluate teachers with standardized tests.

If the reader is still unconvinced of the inadvisability of attempting to evaluate teachers by means of pupil gains on standardized tests, he need only consider some predictable results of such a policy. Teachers would teach the "safe" topics, possibly at the expense of the elusive but important ones. Teachers would not be permitted to administer their own standardized tests; an expensive

Table 2-1. Summary of one-year stability coefficients of teacher effects (residual mean gain-scores) on standardized test performance

Nature of Subtest	Average r for the row	Bennet (1971) Grade level: 1 Test: Metro. Ach. Covariate: Metro. Readiness No. of teachers: n=34 r's	Harris (1966) Grade level: 1 Test: Stanford Ach. Covariate: Stanford Ach. No. of teachers: n=30 r's	Harris (1966) Grade level: 2 Test: Metro Ach. Covariate: Metro. Ach. No. of teachers: n=24 r's	Brophy (1972) Grade level: 2 Test: Metro Ach. Title I Schools		Non-Title I Schools		Brophy (1972) Grade level: 3 Test: Metro. Ach. Title I Schools		Non-Title I Schools	
					n=26	n=22	n=42	n=36	n=24	n=20	n=44	n=42
Reading	.23	.05b	.32	-.08	.31	.00	.40*	.42*	.54*	.39	.26	-.07
Arithmetic	.30	-.01b			.24	-.12	.35a	.39a	.34a	.42a	.51a	.56a
Spelling	.49	.73*	.52*	.21								
Word Knowledge	.38	.23	.53* (Word reading) -.01 (Vocabulary)	.19	.49*	.18	.41*	.42*	.52*	.78*	.39*	.45*
Word Discrimination	.36	.69*		.26	.26	.28	.63*	.42*	.28	.19	.30	.26

*Significantly different from zero at the .05 level (two-tailed test).

a Average of stability coefficients for arithmetic computation and arithmetic reasoning.

b An "outlying" case more than four standard deviations below the mean was removed before calculation of the correlation.

external proctoring system would be required, and its cost in terms of trust might even exceed its cost in dollars.

The Popham-McNeil-Millman Method

W. James Popham and John D. McNeil pioneered in the study of teacher effectiveness by means of the direct measurement of teacher impact on pupil behavior (knowledge, skills and attitudes). Recently they have been joined in these endeavors by Jason Millman, who has teamed with Popham to offer school districts in California and across the nation their techniques for evaluating teachers.

With the Popham-McNeil-Millman method of assessing teacher effectiveness (the PMM method), a group of teachers is given advance notice of a few hours or a day or more that they are to teach a particular topic to an unfamiliar group of pupils. The teachers are often prepared by being allowed to study reference materials, instructional objectives, and even test items comparable to those which will be used as posttests. Frequently, the topic to be taught is one with which the teachers have had little prior experience. Ad hoc groups of six to thirty or more pupils are randomly formed from a large pool of pupils available for the assessment. The pupil group is taught for a period of thirty minutes to an hour. Because of the random assignment of pupils from the large pool, all teachers begin the instructional period with pupil groups randomly equated with respect to knowledge of the topic, ability, motivation, etc. Hence, the posttest pupil performance is an unconfounded measure of the teacher effect; "simple gain," "residual gain," "percent gain," and gain scores are unnecessary. Teacher effects can be further studied by randomly reconstituting the ad hoc pupil groups, by changing the topic of instruction, etc.

Logical Arguments Advanced for the PMM Method

This basic technique underlies the system of measuring and evaluating teacher effectiveness which Popham has advanced as the preferred technique of teacher evaluation. As he wrote in *Designing Teacher Evaluation Systems,* "Another possible valuable augmentation of our appraisal techniques is the use of a teaching performance test or, as it is sometimes called, an instructional minilesson." (Popham, 1971, p. 36).

The major logical arguments advanced by Popham and Millman for the superiority of their conception of teacher evaluation are 1) that the PMM method of appraising teachers is "objective," whereas other methods (notably rating scales and observations schedules) are "subjective," and 2) that the changes in pupil behavior like those which teachers produce during the simulated instructional periods are "the real thing" about schooling.

The hobgoblin of "subjectivity" can still be invoked to threaten the lay audience, even though it has been a dead issue in the philosophy of science for decades.

> All measurement yields, not a property, intrinsic to the object being measured taken in isolation, but a relation between that object and the others serving as standards of measurement. When the relation is to other human beings, or even to the observer himself, it is not therefore a subjective one. As always, everything hinges on the controls which can be instituted, and on the sensitivity and reliability with which the discriminating judgments are being made. (Kaplan, 1964, p. 212).

Every act of measurement, experimental design, hypothesis formulation, or data interpretation in scientific inquiry involves human judgment; indeed they may even involve aesthetic and, particularly, value judgments. In this sense, all science is subjective. The only "subjectivity" one need fear—both in science and in educational evaluation—is capricious and unsubstantiated opining. In this pejorative sense, the PMM method in its selection of instructional topics, statement of objectives, and selection of test items could be used as "subjectively" as the worst rating scales and observation schedules.

Second, is the teacher's ability to produce behavioral changes in pupils "the real thing" about schooling? Hardly. Education is many "real things." Changing children's behavior is just one of them. Permitting children to grow in supportive and interesting environments is another. Simple custodial care is a third "real thing" about schools that sounds trivial until one begins to contemplate the economic and social consequences of deschooling society.

Changing pupil behavior is one of the teacher's many responsibilities. However, we can currently conceive of and recognize in particular instances many more types of behavioral change than modern techniques can reliably measure. In spite of their commendable success in measuring even complex cognitive processes, measurement specialists have ample cause for humility. So far, practical measurement of many affective behaviors and personality characteristics is more hope than reality. Measurement of an educational goal as basic as creative (or at least "original") writing skill is still enormously complex and expensive. Teachers affect children's assessment of personal worth which are closely linked to the children's feeling of satisfaction and dissatisfaction with themselves. Yet few children trust the adults they deal with in school enough that they will disclose their true feelings about themselves.

Empirical Evaluation of the PMM Method

The testimonies for the empirical validity of the PMM method have been imprudent and immodest. Justiz (1969, p. viii) claimed no less for his study than that it had produced " . . . the first reliable measure of general teaching ability." Connor (1969, p. 16) wrote that his study not only "validated" the teacher performance assessment technique but also verified "the construct of instructional proficiency as a measureable variable." Popham (1971, p. 116) cited Justiz and Connor as having "recently reported high positive correlation between teachers' achievements on two different short-term performance tests. . . . " McNeil (1972, p. 622) considered such performance tests to be an "answer to the problem of identifying the effective instructor."

In the face of this partisan enthusiasm for the PMM technique, I wish to examine the following anti-thesis: The technique has not been shown to possess reliability adequate for measuring individual differences among teachers. The very data which are said to establish the reliability of the PMM method are consistent with the claim that the method has near zero reliability for generalizing across factors for which it must show stable measurements. A careful examination of the data obtained by Connor, Justiz, Popham, McNeil, and others will reveal no evidence to disprove the assertion that the teacher's effect on pupil performance is measured with near zero reliability across both topics taught and different groups of pupils by the PMM techniques. In short, I shall argue that the PMM technique has yet to pass the minimum requirement for measurement utility.

To be useful in teacher evaluation, the PMM method must show substantial reliability across different topics and different groups of pupils. The construct "good teaching" forces the issue of "topics" generalizability. "Good teaching" means more than the ability to teach isolated curiosities of the curriculum. If "good teaching" is not evident in the same teacher's consistent impact across a reasonably broad range of topics (even within a domain itself as narrow as secondary school social studies, for example), then "good teaching" is not actually being measured. For practical reasons, the PMM method must yield stable measures across different (possibly randomly constituted) groups of pupils. If teachers produce highly unstable effects when teaching the same topic to several different pupil groups, then fair comparisons among teachers can be bought only under two conditions, the first fatuous, the second cumbersome and impractical: 1) all teachers in a group (a school district, perhaps) about whom decisions are to be made must teach the same standard groups of pupils or, 2) each teacher's effect must be measured by averaging his or her effects across many randomly different groups of pupils. The PMM method either shows reliability across topics and pupil groups or else it remains a laboratory technique, useful for teacher training and research, perhaps, but not up to the standards of utility, economy, and fidelity required of a teacher evaluation technique for individual diagnosis or determination of merit.

Critique of Related Research

The Rosenshine Review

Rosenshine (1970) compiled the results of several studies of the short-term stability of teacher effect on change in pupil behavior which used methods like those of the PMM technique. Twenty stability coefficients from five separate studies were reported by Rosenshine (1970, p. 659). The twenty correlation coefficients, correlating the teacher effect on two separate (but closely related) topics on two distinct (but randomly equivalent) pupil groups, range from a low of -.45 to a high of .87; only two of the coefficients are statistically significantly different from zero at the .05 level (two-tailed test). Rosenshine (1970, p. 660) concluded that "when teachers taught different topics to different students, the direction of the correlations were [sic] . . . erratic, and few correlations were significant."

The Justiz Studies

Justiz (1969) conducted two studies in two different high schools. In School A, ten student-teachers each taught a group of about twenty pupils a half-hour lesson on "news story structure"; the pupils taught by each student teacher were randomly drawn from a pool of available pupils in the school. (The only compromise with complete randomization was that no teacher was assigned one of his own pupils.) After the lesson, the pupils were given a fifteen-minute test on the content of the instruction. The pupil groups were reconstituted, again nearly at random, and the student teachers instructed their new pupils on "concepts of the computer punch card." A fifteen-minute posttest was given, as before. The study was completed within two hours.

Justiz reported a Spearman rank-order correlation of .64 for his data, which I have confirmed. A Pearson's r seems equally appropriate, or even more so; its value for the data is 0.58, which is just barely statistically significant (alpha = .05, two-tailed test). But the 95 percent confidence interval for $r = 0.58$ with $n = 9$ better reflects how accurately the teacher-effect stability coefficient has been determined in this study; the interval extends from .08 to .89, an extraordinarily broad range. Thus we learn that the teacher effect is somewhere between nearly completely unstable and perfectly stable across two topics.

One of the ten student teachers was dropped before the end of the study. The reason given was that this student teacher ". . . refused to teach the Punched-Card Computer Concepts subject for lack of preparation" (Justiz, 1969, p. 47). Presumably if the teacher had been required to participate in the study then we could have expected some discrepancy in the performance of his pupils between the "news story" lesson, for which he felt prepared, and the "punch card" lesson, which he refused to teach. To assess the potential influence on the stability coefficient of having dropped this teacher, I assumed that his pupils would have achieved an average score on the "news story" lesson and the poorest score on the "punch card" lesson. The value of Spearman's rank-order correlation coefficient for this plausible set of complete data is 0.47, which is nonsignificant even for $\alpha = .10$, two-tailed test. One missing case can have a marked effect in such a small sample.

In the second high school, School B, Justiz repeated essentially the same procedures with the same topics, one exception being that the seven teachers in this sample instructed the same group of pupils on the two topics. Two of the student teachers were dropped before completion of the study because of irregularities in posttesting. Justiz reported a Spearman rank-order correlation of .90, "significant at the .05 level of confidence." The calculations and conclusion deserve closer scrutiny. For $n = 5$, an $r_s = .90$ is significant at only the alpha = .10 level for a two-tailed test; the two-tailed test is justified in this instance in view of the frequency of negative stability coefficients in similar studies (Rosenshine, 1970).

But a more fundamental problem exists here (if the reader is unimpressed with quibbles over .05 versus .10 levels of significance). Justiz broke a tie on one variable between two teachers in favor of a higher correlation. If the tie is broken in the other direction, the value of r_s is .80, which with $n = 5$ is nonsignificant at any reasonable alpha-level. The best resolution of the tie is to assign a rank of 4.5 to both student teachers, which yields a third nonsignificant r_s of 0.87.

Conclusion: disappearing subjects, miniscule sample sizes, errant correlation coefficients, and nonsignificant statistics hardly add up to ". . . the first reliable measure of general teaching ability" (Justiz, 1969, p. viii).

The McNeil Study

McNeil (1972) reported data which bear on the question of the reliability of the PMM method. Teachers were randomly paired with groups of three elementary school pupils. A topic such as code breaking was taught, the pupils were excused for a short recess, and a second group of three pupils randomly constituted for the second instructional period. In some cases the instructional topic changed between the two instructional periods, and in some cases it did not.

McNeil's (1972, p. 626) results section was brief and is reproduced below.

McNeil refers to the correlations which he has computed as being "positive." The one instance which he reports in detail (between Tests 3 and 4 with ten weeks intervening) produced an r of .39 ($n = 30$); the 95 percent confidence interval is .03 to .62. Unfortunately, we don't know whether the one instance reported was the most favorable finding among the "positive" correlations McNeil calculated, or whether it is genuinely representative of all the coefficients.

McNeil's table (Table 2-2), reproduced below, first appears to be based on the r of .39 to which he referred in the text of his paper.

... correlations between teachers' performances on the different tests given ten weeks apart with different kinds of pupils were positive. For instance, thirty teachers took Test 3 at the end of their methods course and completed Test 4 ten weeks later after a student teaching assignment. Their scores showed a Pearsonian r of .388 (p $<$.05). As indicated in Table 1 ... one could have made a probable prediction about the likelihood of high achieving teachers (top 25 percent and bottom 25 percent) making a similar showing on a second test weeks later.

Table 2-2. Chi squares for high and low teacher performance on tests of ability to teach two different tasks of reading

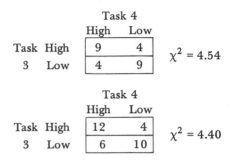

However, the situation is unclear, principally because the original sample contained thirty teachers, and the table, which is said to contain half of the teachers ("top 25 percent and bottom 25 percent") is based on twenty-six and thirty-two teachers instead of fifteen. We must presume that Table 2-2 contains data from studies independent of the study which yielded the r of .39.

Both contingency tables in McNeil's table are said to yield statistically significant associations (chi-square test, alpha = .05) between high and low teacher effectiveness across the two topics. My calculations show otherwise. I obtain a χ^2_1 of 3.85 without the continuity correction—a figure which should have corresponded exactly to McNeil's 4.54—and a χ^2_1 of 2.46 with the correction. The continuity correction is clearly in order due to the small sample size; the χ^2_1 of 2.46 is nonsignificant even at alpha = .10. (Fisher's exact test similarly failed to reject with alpha = .10.) For the lower half of McNeil's Table 1, the value of χ^2_1 corrected for discontinuity is 3.17, nonsignificant with alpha = .05. (However, Fisher's exact test yields a probability of .04 of a more extreme occurrence under the null hypothesis of no association.)

The import of McNeil's data is uncertain. The confidence intervals are broad, the nonsignificant findings also need to be reported, and some of the results reported as statistically stable appear not to be.

The Connor Study

Connor (1969) arranged for seventeen experienced male teachers to instruct subgroups of seventy-seven high school pupils in the topics "propaganda techniques" and "chance (probability)." A systematic, but probably nearly random, method of assigning five pupils to each teacher was employed, with the condition that no teacher was assigned to a pupil with whom he was acquainted.

Pupils in each teacher's "class" were tested on "propaganda techniques" before a fifty-minute instructional period. A comparable posttest followed instruction. Later in the day, the pupils were reassigned to teachers and the new ad hoc classes were taught "chance" for fifty minutes; pretests and posttests were again administered. A pretest-to-posttest gain score was calculated by subtracting the pretest number of items correct (times the number of pupils) from the posttest number of items correct (times the number of pupils) and dividing by the difference between the highest possible score and the pretest score. Thus, "gain as a percent of possible gain" was used as the measure of each teacher's effect on pupil performance.

Connor did not report either the value of r or r_s, Spearman's rank-order coefficient. However, I have calculated both using his raw data (Connor, 1969, p. 14). They are small ($r_{xy} = .26$ and $r_s = .35$) and statistically nonsignificant. Clearly, Connor's data give no evidence of nonzero stability across topics. Instead of reporting either of the above two coefficients, Connor reported a coefficient "corrected for attenuation," r'_{xy}, of .72. He applied an inappropriate significance test to this value, testing it as one would test a typical Pearson's r on seventeen cases. Appropriate inferential tests (Rogers, 1971; Forsyth and Feldt, 1969) reveal that even Connor's corrected coefficient is statistically nonsignificant at any reasonable α-level.

Moreover, the correction for attenuation procedure was inappropriate. Test reliabilities were estimated from internal consistency coefficients and do not embody a meaningful definition of measurement error for the purposes of the correction. More important, although correlations corrected for attenuation may have conceptual meaning, they are seldom useful in practice. There is small comfort in the fact that true scores on X and Y are highly correlated if one is considering making decisions about individuals with the only available data, namely the fallible observed scores.

The Belgard, Rosenshine, and Gage Study

Forty-three teachers taught two fifteen-minute lessons on the economic, political, and social conditions of Yugoslavia and Thailand to their regular classes on successive days. Class sizes varied from ten to thirty-one students. One week before the study, each teacher received copies of the instructional materials and half of the items from the posttests to be administered to pupils after each lesson.

To equate the abilities of the nonrandomly constituted classes, Belgard, Rosenshine, and Gage (1971) administered a tape-recorded lesson on Israel to all classes on the third day. Pupil's performance on a subsequent posttest was then used as a controlling variable for equating the forty-three classes. Essentially, residual "gain scores"—the difference between the class mean on the Yugoslavia test, for example, and the regression estimate of this class mean from the Israel class mean—were computed and correlated across the two topics to measure the reliability of the teacher effect. At this point, two fundamental questions can be raised. Pupils were not randomly assigned to teachers; instead, an ex post facto attempt was made to control statistically for pupil differences. The equivalence sought may not have been achieved. The classes may still have differed to a nonrandom degree on variables (e.g., some aspect of learning ability or motivation) not controlled statistically. Also, observation of the control variable (the Israel test) was made after the two instructional periods. The possibility exists that the statistical equating removed stable variance in the teacher effect present in the variance of the Israel class means because of positive transfer effects, motivation carry-over effects, etc., from the previous lessons. It would have been preferable to observe the control variable (Israel test) before the teacher-directed instructional periods. The first influence (lack of complete equating of classes) may have spuriously inflated the stability coefficient; the latter influence may have deflated it.

Belgard, Rosenshine, and Gage reported a correlation of the Yugoslavia and Thailand residual class means of .47 ($t = 3.37$ with $df = 40$; $p < .01$). The investigators recognized that this coefficient was based on different topics taught to the same pupils. To correct for this condition, the investigators divided the data in each class in half by designating even- and odd-numbered pupils. The correlation of Thailand residual means for the even-numbered pupils with Yugoslavia residual means for the odd-numbered pupils (or vice versa) is then a measure of teacher stability across both topics and pupil groups. The authors report the following two stability coefficients:

Yugoslavia residual means for odd-numbered pupils with Thailand residual means for even-numbered pupils: $r = .16$ $(p < .01)$

Thailand residual means for odd-numbered pupils with Yugoslavia residual means for even-numbered pupils: $r = .38$ $(p < .01)$

The authors then applied the Spearman-Brown formula to estimate the size of these two coefficients for classes twice as large as the "half-classes" on which they were derived. The resulting stability coefficients equalled .28 and .55—a very large discrepancy. The investigators averaged the two figures and settled on a stability coefficient of .41.

Belgard, Rosenshine, and Gage's (1971, p. 185) conclusion seems most appropriate: "The correlations were not high enough to indicate that the effectiveness of individual teachers can be measured with adequate reliability with only two lessons, ten-item tests, and classes of about twenty-one students. For such reliability, higher than about .40, additional lessons, longer tests, and larger classes would be needed."

The Popham Studies

Although Popham's (1971b) comparisons of the effects of experienced and inexperienced teachers on pupil performance were not addressed directly to the question of the reliability of the measurement techniques, they provide collateral evidence on the question.

Popham arranged for groups of experienced teachers, college students, and laymen to teach various topics to groups of high school and junior college students. A variation of "randomized blocking" insured equivalence of the student groups taught by the teacher and nonteacher groups. Popham (Table 2-3) presented three comparisons of teacher and nonteacher performance in terms of the average "percent items correct" earned by the students.

Popham (1971b, p. 601) wrote that "there appear to be no readily available (methodological) loopholes by which we can explain away the nonsignificant outcomes. A more strightforward explana-

Table 2-3

Topic	Comparison Groups	No. of Instructors	Average Percent Items Correct
Social Science Research Methods	a) Experienced teachers	13	67%
	b) College students	13	65%
Auto mechanics (carburetion)	a) Experienced teachers	28	49%
	b) Garage mechanics	28	47%
Electronics (basic power supplies)	a) Experienced teachers	16	52%
	b) TV Repairmen & electronics workers	16	50%

tion is available. *Experienced teachers are not particularly skilled at bringing about specified behavior changes in learners."*

However, there does exist an alternative explanation which is both consistent with the available data concerning the reliability of the PMM method and more generous in its assessment of teachers. Zero reliability measurement techniques can not show statistically significant discriminations among any groups; at least such differences will not be found at a rate greater than the size, α, of the significance test. Nonzero measurement reliability is a necessary condition for discriminating among groups on a measure. A test of "heads flipping ability" in which one's score is the number of heads tossed in one hundred flips of a fair coin—a test with zero reliability in the stability sense—will not show consistent, significant differences among streetcar conductors, waitresses, bank cashiers, or men-on-the-street.

Concluding Assessment of PMM Studies

The PMM group may have stacked the cards against demonstrating reliability for their technique. In most cases, the teachers taught new material, such as the computer punch card or news story structure, so that no teacher "had an advantage" over the other teachers because of familiarity with the material. In fact, the use of novel materials may have taken away from teachers the very "advantage" which makes one teacher better—and consistently better—than another. Teachers' knowledge of their materials is certainly a stable characteristic and may, particularly at higher grade levels, play a part in determining their effectiveness. Perhaps PMM and others (Fortune—see Rosenshine, 1970, Belgard) systematically eliminated from their studies an important stable variable related to teacher effectiveness. On the other hand, a few studies (McNeil, 1972, for example) used material more familiar to the teachers (e.g., teaching multiplication of two-digit numbers or pronouncing initial vowels in words with a silent final "e") and failed to produce convincing evidence of stability of teacher effects.

But fine points about naive versus knowledgeable teachers can do little to brighten the dismal composite picture presented in Figure 1 of the results of the available short-term stability studies. Presented in Figure 1 are the 95 percent confidence intervals on the twenty-one relevant coefficents that can be found in the published literature (principally the 1970 Rosenshine review and the studies reviewed here). Only four of the intervals fail to span zero. All but one span .15.

In theory, low reliability problems are among the simplest measurement problems to solve. Given that in its present form a measurement procedure has nonzero reliability, no matter how low its reliability may be, it can be made more reliable by lengthening it, that is, by duplicating and averaging repeated measurements from the procedure. Assume that from the dismal picture of the reliability (across topics and pupil groups) of the PMM technique, one draws the most generous possible conclusion, namely that the technique has a reliability in the region $\rho_{XX} = .20$ to .30. These estimates are based on the conditions which obtained in the studies reviewed above, the most important condition for our present purpose being that the entire procedure per teacher measurement involved at least one hour of about a dozen pupils' time, at least three or four hours time per teacher, and several hours of professional time for development and administration per episode. If the PMM method actually has initial reliability .30, it would have to be lengthened by ten times to achieve a composite reliability of .81 according to the Spearman-Brown formula for the reliability of a lengthened test. In other words, the simple methods typical of the studies reviewed above would have to be repeated across ten different instructional topics with ten different pupil groups before the average score for a single teacher attained a reliability above .80. Net costs of reliable PMM testing? Staggering, if we even bothered to pause and calculate them.

Add to this gloomy picture the developmental costs of devising new topics and tests each year (obviously the topics are "consumable" year in and year out), the administrative costs of shuffling pupils around (the procedure is unfair unless the pupil groups are randomly equivalent across *all* teachers about whom differential decisions are to be made from the measurements), and we behold an enormously expensive evaluation system.

In a 1929 study of teaching behaviors, A. S. Barr concluded that instability of teachers' behavior from one lesson to another is the dominant source of unreliability in the effect of teachers' actions on student learning. The contemporary studies reviewed above prove Barr's conclusion beyond reasonable doubt.

No conclusion is more fitting for this section than a quotation of Popham's own prudent remarks:

> "It now appears, in light of the grossness of the measurement devices likely to be available in the near future, that we shall be pleased even if the performance tests are suitable for use only with groups. In other words, it will be a sufficient advance to develop a reliable *group* criterion measure which could be used in myriad educational situations such as to assess the efficiency of teacher education programs." (Popham, 1971b, p. 116) (Italics added.)

An Observational-Judgmental System

The observational-judgmental system envisioned has three principal elements: 1) trained observers' ratings of teachers' specific classroom behaviors; 2) students' evaluation of teachers; and 3) collateral data.

Observation of Teachers' Classroom Behaviors

The word "specific" distinguishes the first component of this observational-judgmental system from our pathetic history of attempting to rate teachers' "openness," "professional manner," or "sensitivity." Past failures to rate teacher behavior reliably stemmed largely from vague, general definitions of the behaviors to be rated and lack of rater training. When these two defects are remedied, ratings reach surprisingly high levels of consistency and long-term stability (Medley and Mitzel, 1963, p. 292, for example). I would propose that no characteristic of teaching be incorporated into the rating scales until research has established both that it can be reliably

Figure 2-1. Summary of estimations (95 percent confidence intervals)
of the stability of the teacher effect across
instructional topics and pupil groups

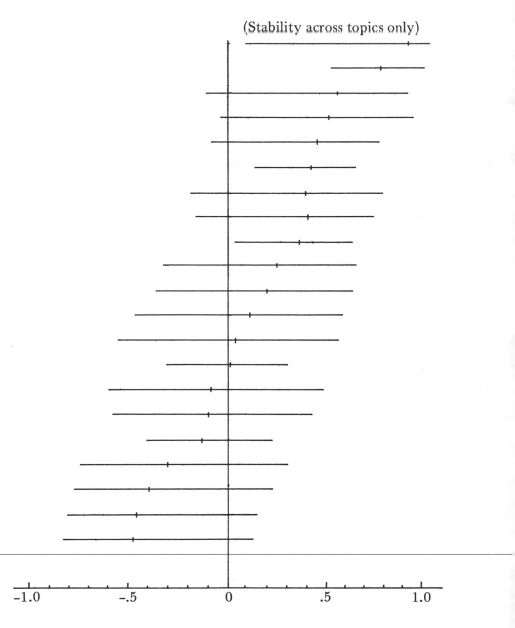

(Stability across topics only)

observed and that it bears some significant relationship to desired pupil cognitive and affective states. Research evidence (Rosenshine, 1971) currently justifies observing and judging the following teacher behaviors: clarity of presentations and explanations, enthusiasm, variety in use of instructional materials and techniques, task orientation and "businesslike" behavior, and provision of ample learning opportunities. This same research suggests observation of many other potentially important teacher behaviors: teacher use of students' ideas, use of multiple levels of discourse, absence of negative criticism, and "probing." Each characteristic can be precisely defined and can be reliably measured by trained observers.

Pupils' Evaluation of Their Teachers

The second element of the observational-judgmental system involves the collection of pupils' evaluations of their teachers. The data collected from students may be of several types; at the least, it should include information to corroborate outside observers' ratings of teacher behaviors.

Second, the system could include students' judgments of the learning environment, as defined and studied by Walberg and Anderson (1968); Walberg (1969), for example. Walberg and Anderson's work on the "Learning Environment Inventory" seems particularly promising and immediately useful. Their inventory, to be filled out by the students, gives class mean scores on fourteen factor-analytically derived dimensions of learning environment, each score being derived from individual pupil responses to seven items. The names of some of the dimensions and their internal consistency are: Intimacy (.78); Friction (.78); Satisfaction (.80); Difficulty (.66); and Apathy (.83).

Third, pupils' contributions to the observational-judgmental system could include their reports on the state of basic human decency that prevails in the classroom. McClellan (1971) reminds us that all teaching is simultaneously a "saying, doing, and making." We must judge what teachers "do" to children as well as what they "make" of them. Even if their actions had no visible residual effects on the pupils' adult behavior, teachers' rudeness, bad manners, and ill-tempered repression would be contemptible in themselves.

In proposing teacher evaluation based in part on pupil and outside-observer judgment, I am not recommending a ragtag system of uncritically collected data of dubious validity. The properties of the data should be studied periodically by means of the various statistical tools available for examining the reliability and validity of measurements. If two independent observers looking at adequate samples of teachers' performance can't agree on their judgments of teachers' "use of appropriate illustrations," then work needs to be done with the judges, the rating scales, the methods of sampling teacher behavior, or all three. Finding that principals' ratings of teacher rapport with pupils do not correlate with pupils' expressions of rapport with the teachers casts doubt on the principals' ratings, the pupils' ratings, or both—and something must be done about the situation.

Collateral Data

I have omitted from this teacher evaluation system any data of the type upon which teaching credentials are typically awarded, namely preservice credit hours, degrees, grade-point averages, inservice credit hours, etc. The omission is intentional and is based on the judgment that such factors are not valid indicators of teacher effectiveness. (Gutherie's 1970 review revealed weak, but consistent, correlations of "credential-type" variables and student outcomes; but the relationships may be due to uncontrolled variables such as socioeconomic status.) The lack of validity of "credentials" data stems from two sources: 1) nearly all teachers have been selected on such variables, hence in the selected group the restricted ranges of the variables work against their showing any correlation with effectiveness (e.g., intelligence and income are virtually uncorrelated among the alumni of the Harvard Graduate School of Business, though they are not uncorrelated in the general population); 2) many such "credentialling" factors have no direct effect on teaching effectiveness. Rosenbloom et al. (1966, p. 108) concluded from a study of high school mathematics teachers that

> The effectiveness of teachers using the SMSG materials and measured by student learning is not influenced to any significant degree by the length of the teachers' experience in teaching mathematics, his undergraduate and graduate courses and grades, and his participation in professional mathematics organizations. Apparently, if a teacher meets acceptable qualifications in these respects, higher qualifications do not make a difference.

One exception to the ban on "credentialling" data seems justified. It seems obvious—particularly at the high school level—that there are minimum levels of subject matter knowledge below which teachers are incompetent to teach. There may be arguments for the instructional value of having ignorant teachers, but even when such arguments can be made to stick, it's hard to justify paying high wages to ignorant teachers. Infrequently, a teacher's own grasp of the subject he is teaching drops below one of these minimum levels, as in the case of the football coach covering Algebra II who can't graph a linear equation, or the choral music teacher who can't read music. Such instances are, no doubt, so rare that correlational studies of teacher knowledge and student learning continue to show zero relationships. Nonetheless, they are present in the personal experience of each of us, and are sufficiently repugnant that they deserve attention in a teacher evaluation system, provided the costs are reasonable. Costs for this kind of evaluation can be held to a reasonable level by centralizing the knowledge testing of high school teachers, perhaps in the state education agency. Such an exam could be administered every other year or less, instead of only once at entrance into the profession. Thus some control would be exercised over shifting teaching assignments that make for administrative convenience but for no academic sense. Once again, the purpose of the testing would be to detect the one in a thousand egregiously indefensible teaching assignments, not to grade or rank teachers on their subject matter knowledge. The program would have a very modest goal; if its costs per teacher per year exceeded ten cents, it probably wouldn't be worth maintaining.

References

Anderson, R. C. "How to Construct Achievement Tests to Assess Comprehension." *Review of Educational Research* 42 (1972): 145-70.

Belgard, M.; Rosenshine, B.; and Gage, N. L. "Exploration of the Teacher's Effectiveness in Learning," in *Research into Classroom Processes: Recent Developments and Next Steps,* edited by I. Westbury and A. A. Bellack. New York: Teachers College Press, 1971.

Bormuth, J. *On the Theory of Achievement Test Items.* Chicago: University of Chicago Press, 1970.

Connor, A. Cross-Validating Two Performance Tests of Instructional

Proficiency. Mimeographed. Los Angeles: University of California, U.S.O.E. Project No. 8-I-174, 1969.

Cronbach, L. J., and Furby, L. "How Should We Measure Change—Or Should We?" *Psychological Bulletin* 74 (1970): 68-80.

Forsyth, R. A., and Feldt, L. A. "An Investigation of Empirical Sampling Distributions of Correlation Coefficients Corrected for Attenuation." *Educational and Psychological Measurement* 29 (1969): 61-71.

Gutherie, J. W. "Survey of School Effectiveness Studies." In *Do Teachers Make a Difference?*, edited by A. M. Mood. Washington, D.C.: U.S. Government Printing Office, 1970.

Justiz, T. B. "A Method of Identifying the Effective Teacher." Ph.D. dissertation, University of California, Los Angeles, 1969. (University Microfilms No. 29-3022-A).

Kaplan, A. *The Conduct of Inquiry.* San Francisco: Chandler Publishing Co., 1964.

McClellan, J. "Classroom-Teaching Research: A Philosophical Critique," in *Research into Classroom Processes: Recent Developments and Next Steps.*, edited by I. Westbury and A. A. Bellak. New York: Teachers College Press, 1971.

McNeil, J. D. "Performance Tests: Assessing Teachers of Reading." *The Reading Teacher* 25 (1972): 622-627.

Medley, D. M., and Mitzel, H. E. "Measuring Classroom Behavior by Systematic Observation. In *Handbook of Research on Teaching,* edited by N. L. Gage. Chicago: Rand McNally, 1963.

Popham, W. J. *Designing Teacher Evaluation Systems: A Series of Suggestions for Establishing Teacher Assessment Procedures as Required by the Stull Bill (AB 293), 1971 California Legislature.* Los Angeles: The Instructional Objectives Exchange, 1971a.

_____. "Performance Tests of Teaching Proficiency: Rationale, Development, and Validation." *American Educational Research Journal* 8 (1971b): 105-117.

Rogers, W. T. "Jackknifing Disattenuated Correlations." Ph.D. dissertation, University of Colorado, Boulder, 1971.

Rosenbloom, P. E. et al. "Characteristics of Mathematics Teachers that Affect Students' Learning." Cooperative Research Report, University of Minnesota, 1966. ERIC #ED 021 707.

Rosenshine, B. "The Stability of Teacher Effects upon Student Achievement." *Review of Educational Research* 40 (1970): 647-62.

————. "Teaching Behaviors Related to Pupil Achievement: A Review of Research." In *Research into Classroom Processes: Recent Developments and Next Steps,* edited by I. Westbury and A. A. Bellack. New York: Teachers College Press, 1971.

Stake, R. E. "Testing Hazards in Performance Contracting." *Phi Delta KAPPAN* 52 (1971): 583-88.

Walberg, H. J., and Anderson, G. J. "Classroom Climate and Individual Learning." *Journal of Educational Psychology* 59 (1968): 414-19.

Walberg, H. J. "Predicting Class Learning: An Approach to the Class as a Social System." *American Educational Research Journal* 6 (1969): 529-42.

3. ACHIEVEMENT CORRELATES
Jere E. Brophy

Although teacher effectiveness research attempting to link teacher behavior to student achievement measures produced generally disappointing results for a long time, recent reviews (Flanders and Simon, 1969; Rosenshine and Furst, 1973; Rosenshine, 1971; Dunkin and Biddle, 1974) provide greater cause for optimism, concluding that teaching behaviors related to teachers' general effectiveness are being identified more consistently in recent studies. One reason has been the use of better observation systems. Much early research used systems developed by psychologists to study group dynamics. Except under certain circumstances, these systems were not very appropriate for teacher effectiveness research. They were not developed for use in the classroom, and usually were not constructed specifically to determine whether a teacher met specified objectives, either in his teaching behavior or in the learning of his students. The outlook for process-product research in teacher effectiveness has improved of late with the appearance of new systems, and with improvements in some of the older systems (Flanders, 1970).

Despite these signs of progress, a new threat to the search for effective teaching behavior arose with the publication of Rosenshine's (1970) review of stability across time in teachers' abilities to produce student learning gains. After reviewing a large body of literature, Rosenshine could locate only five studies which contained data on stability in teacher effectiveness in producing student learning gains over long time periods. Of the five, only two seem immediately generalizable to the typical school situation. One of the five involved Air Force instructors teaching eight-hour airplane hydraulics courses to recruits, and two of the others involved experimental studies in which teachers were not using their typical methods of instruction. Thus only two of the five studies involved ordinary school teachers teaching in their normal ways. One of these two studies did not give an exact coefficient but noted that stability from one year to the next was quite low, while the stability coefficient from the other study was .09. These figures obviously suggest that teacher effectiveness in producing student learning gains is not a stable "trait," that a teacher who produces large gains in his students this year is not necessarily going to do the same the next year. Such results, if they accurately reflect the general case, threaten the validity of process-product teacher effectiveness research.

The Present Study

The research described here is a large scale attempt to address several of the problems mentioned above. Using several methodological innovations, it has been established that stability in teacher effectiveness, at least in certain teachers, is more evident than previous studies suggest. This information has led to a long-term and multifaceted attempt to identify the behavioral correlates of teaching effectiveness in a sample of teachers known to be stable in their relative effectiveness in producing student learning gains.

Teacher Selection

This study involved 31 teachers selected from a group of 165 elementary teachers in an urban school district. Teacher selection was predicated upon two assumptions: 1) In evaluating the impact of schooling on student learning, teachers, not schools, are the effective causal mechanisms producing student learning gains; therefore the individual teacher is the appropriate unit of analysis. 2) Because stability in teacher effectiveness is vital to process-product effectiveness research, teachers known or thought to be unstable in their classroom behavior should be avoided; therefore the study was restricted to teachers who had been teaching at the same grade level for at least five consecutive years, avoiding student teachers and brand new teachers.

Resource limitations demanded that the study also be restricted to two grade levels. Partly out of an interest in early education, and partly on the assumption that teachers probably make a greater difference in the learning of younger students than of older ones (because the younger ones are less capable of overcoming the effects of inadequate teaching through their own learning efforts), the decision was made to work at the early elementary grades. The first grade was rejected for lack of an adequate pretest. The children did take readiness tests at the beginning of first grade, but these are known to be unreliable and heavily influenced by the child's preschool experience, and especially by the stimulation he receives at home (Hess, 1970). Thus the second and third grades were selected for study.

Of 275 teachers working at grades two and three, 88 second-grade and 77 third-grade teachers met the selection criteria. The district administered the Metropolitan Achievement Tests each fall, and these data were used in determining teacher effectiveness. A second grader's scores from the test he took at the beginning of third grade the following fall were used as his postscores. A similar procedure was followed for third graders. Each student took three language arts subtests (word knowledge, word discrimination, and reading), and either one or two arithmetic subtests. Depending on which Metropolitan battery had been administered and on how the data were recorded in the school records, a given child's arithmetic data might contain an arithmetic computation subtest only, a combination score reflecting both computation and reasoning, or two separate scores, one for computation and one for reasoning.

Two sets of computations of residual gain scores were made for each grade, because of differences in the test batteries used. For each of these four data sets, residual gain scores were computed for each student within sex and within each of the three years on each subtest, using the student's prescore as a covariate. These residual gain scores for students were then collated by classroom, and a mean residual gain score was computed for each teacher for each subtest for each of the three years included in the study (Brophy, 1973). Intercorrelations among these mean residual gain scores were then computed.

The data show moderate to high correlations across subtests within each year, and low to moderate stability across years within subtests. The three language arts subtests correlate highly with one another (median = .64, range = .37 to .92), and usually also correlate highly with arithmetic reasoning. The same is true of the two arithmetic subtests (median = .71, range = .53 to .83). Correlations across the total set of five subtests were lower (median = .54, range = .03 to .92). The latter figure reflects the generally low correlations between the three language arts subtests and the arithmetic computation subtest (Brophy, 1972).

Stability coefficients reflecting teachers' relative effectiveness in producing gains on a given subtest were mostly insignificant in one of the data sets, but mostly significant in the other three. In the first set (N's = 22 to 26), these ranged from -.12 to .49, with a median of .25; in the second set (N's = 36 to 42), they ranged from .33 to .63, with a median of .42; in the third set (N's = 20 to 24), they ranged from .19 to .78, with a median of .39; and in the last set (N's = 42 to 44), they ranged from -.07 to .65, with a median of .40. Although still relatively low, these stability coefficients compare quite favorably with those reported in the two long-term studies reviewed by Rosenshine (1970). Thus, when the sample is restricted to teachers who have had several years of experience at the same grade level, the stability coefficients obtained are higher than those previously reported.

Analyses of each teacher's individual pattern across subtests and years revealed additional information. First, the vast majority of teachers were relatively equally successful with boys and girls; only 4 of 165 consistently produced higher residual gains in one sex than in the other (although girls generally outgained boys, as usual). Teachers' patterns were also analyzed to see whether gains on a given subtest were linear or nonlinear across the three years. Overall, 28 percent of the subtest patterns showed linear constancy, with very similar average residual gains on the subtest for each of the three years. An additional 13 percent showed linear improvement across three years, while 11 percent showed linear decline. The remaining 49 percent were nonlinear patterns (Brophy, 1972). Thus, teachers showed some form of linear consistency across three years about half of the time. Furthermore, many teachers showed constancy across subtests within years as well as within subtests across years, so that teachers who produced generally consistent gains across subtests and across the two sexes could be identified. The 31 teachers included in the process observation study were selected from this consistent group.

Studying Consistent Teachers

Since the teachers studied have already demonstrated consistency in their ability to produce student achievement gains, and since they have all had several consecutive years of experience teaching at the same grade level and have probably therefore attained a stable pattern or "style," research designed to identify the behavioral correlates of teaching effectiveness seemed particularly promising on such a sample. Naturalistic observations in these teachers' classrooms were therefore undertaken. At this writing, one year of naturalistic research has already been conducted, and a second is underway.

The teachers were divided roughly evenly between grades two and three, and the socioeconomic status of their schools' students spanned the spectrum. The data included process measures of classroom behavior, and personality and attitude data from pencil and paper tests. The process measures included both low inference behavioral coding and high inference ratings. Each teacher was observed for two mornings and two afternoons during the spring semester, for a total of about eight hours. The main coding instrument used was based on the Brophy-Good Dyadic Interaction System (Brophy and Good, 1970). This system picked up such variables as teacher versus student initiation of contacts, types of interactions (academic, procedural, or behavioral-disciplinary), difficulty level of teacher questions, quality of student responses, quantity and quality of teacher feedback and evaluative reactions to student responses and student work, and the teacher's methods and general effectiveness in handling classroom management and disciplinary problems.

A second coding instrument (created by project staff member Nancy Moore) was used on a subsample of ten teachers, five high effective and five low effective, who were observed twice during group instruction. This instrument was specially constructed to measure group instruction methodological variables, such as lesson composition, sequence, clarity, teacher questioning patterns, and handling of seatwork assignments.

Two sets of high inference ratings were also used. The first was a set of twelve classroom observation scales developed by Emmer (1973) to get at interaction variables common to several of the more widely used behavioral observation systems. These were five-point rating scales which were used several times during each of the four observations by coders using the expanded Brophy-Good system. In addition, following their last two visits to each teacher's classroom, observers also filled out forty-one high inference rating scales and fifteen high inference checklists and percentage estimates. The items on these ratings and checklists were culled from a variety of sources. Our intent was quite literally to measure "anything" which previous research or our own experience suggested as possible correlates of teacher effectiveness. These instruments included many variables measured in a different form on the low inference coding systems (to provide internal validity checks), but for the most part they dealt with variables not included elsewhere. Since observers worked in pairs, interobserver agreement data were available.

The pencil and paper attitude and personality measures were those included in the COMPASS battery developed by the Research and Development Center for Teacher Education (Veldman, 1972). These measures deal with the levels of teacher concern about teaching (Fuller, 1969), the teacher's general self-concept and concept of herself as a teacher, her coping style, and other aspects of her personality.

Preliminary Results of the First Year's Data Analysis

At the present writing, only certain analyses linking teacher measures to student gain measures are available, and only for the high inference ratings and checklists and the group instruction coding system. These are correlations between teacher process variables and student gain criteria for the five subtests. The criterion scores for each teacher on each subtest are the means for her classes for four consecutive years (data on a fourth year were gathered after the original study of stability across three years). These correlations reveal several interesting findings. With few exceptions, significant correlations between process variables and gain scores typically involve only one or two of the subtests, despite the fact that teachers had been selected because of their general consistency in producing student gains across all subtests. Thus it appears that certain teacher behaviors are more important for student gain in some areas than in others.

Also, the data contain several surprises. Many variables which correlated significantly with student gains in previous studies did so in these data also, but many did not. For example, teacher warmth, cognitive level of questions, enthusiasm, amount of student talk, peer tutoring, solidarity with students, and patience all failed to show significant correlations with student gains. On the other hand, a long list of process measures showed at least one significant correlation with student gains, and many showed several.

Among the latter are the following: pupil attention; presentation of information through lectures and demonstrations (as opposed to discussions or silent work); teacher spends much time introducing new material and supervising children as they practice it; teacher works with individuals frequently (rather than with groups or the whole class); teacher has classroom rules and the willingness to back them up if necessary to maintain order; appropriateness of seatwork assignments; time spent in games and free time arts and crafts activities in addition to lessons; teacher direction of a variety of classroom activities, rather than student free choice; high teacher expectations regarding student performance and independence; patterned rather than nonpatterned recitation turns; teacher always gets attention before starting to say something; teacher is well organized and prepared; room is attractive; room is uncrowded; teacher monitors class while working with small groups; teacher achieves smooth, efficient transitions between activities; teacher often does two or more things simultaneously; teacher usually waits for quiet without saying anything as a method of gaining attention rather than using a gimmick or shouting; teacher sees that children who need help get it, but does not allow them to interrupt her work with other groups; teacher gives good demonstrations and/or diagrams when explaining things or making seatwork assignments; teacher uses many materials created by herself in addition to the standardized materials provided her; and teacher spends less time in review than in direct presentation and practice.

Rosenshine and Furst identified nine variables that have emerged from previous research as likely correlates of teacher effectiveness. The present data confirm previous findings for four of these (task oriented, businesslike manner; use of structuring comments, variability in methods and materials; student opportunity to learn). Positive but nonsignificant trends were observed for a fifth variable: teacher clarity. A sixth variable, teacher enthusiasm, was completely uncorrelated with the criteria. Contradictory results were obtained for teacher indirectness, which was *negatively* correlated with effectiveness; and mixed results appeared for various measures of teacher criticism, although, as expected, it was mostly negatively correlated with gain scores. No data are available yet on the final variable (multiple levels of questioning or discourse), although they will be available when data from the dyadic system are analyzed.

The findings regarding indirectness probably reflect the grade levels studied. In the early grades, when most instruction is geared toward teaching children fundamental knowledge and skills to the point of overlearning, direct teaching is probably optimal. Later, when students draw on these skills to deal with abstract content, indirect teaching may be more effective. Even within the present data, measures of direct teaching (lectures, demonstrations, explanations) were more highly related to verbal knowledge measures (word knowledge, word discrimination) than to measures of skills acquired largely through practice (reading, arithmetic computation and reasoning). The latter criterion variables were more highly correlated with measures of teacher variability in presenting material, use of games and other special devices for providing practice, and amount of lesson time devoted to practice of newly learned skills.

The strongest correlations were for three major types of variables. Two of these, student attention level and uncrowdedness of room, are probably related to what Rosenshine and Furst call "opportunity to learn." The children learned more when they and their classmates paid good attention to the teacher, and when their room was uncrowded (not necessarily thinly populated, but uncrowded given the size of the room). The third set of strong predictor variables includes measures of the teacher's managerial skills stressed by Kounin (1970): smooth transitions, monitoring the class, doing more than one thing at a time, general "with-it-ness." Again, these teacher behaviors seem to be particularly important in the early grades.

These results are notable because they come from a teacher sample selected especially for its appropriateness for process-product research and because they come from naturalistic teaching observations. However, the data are quite tentative and in need of replication, for several reasons. First, the probability values used to gauge statistical significance cannot be taken very seriously, because only thirty-one teachers were studied on over one thousand variables. This obviously violates several assumptions underlying the use of significance tests. Second, data were based on only two to four observations per teacher. These frequencies are dangerously small, given the probable teacher variability from one observation to the next and the effects of situational factors operating on a given day (weather conditions, introducing versus finishing a unit). Third, partly because of the low number of opportunities to observe the teachers, the observers' high inference ratings and checklists show evidence of considerable halo effect and logical error, so that some of these variables remain suspect despite high observer agreement. Fourth, the data are only for the sample as a whole, without taking into account grade or socioeconomic status (SES) differences. (Preliminary analyses show that SES differences are important, and that, although there will be considerable overlap, many variables will be positively related to teacher effectiveness in high SES schools but will be unrelated or negatively correlated in low SES schools.) Fifth, the data are simple Pearson r's which reflect only linear relationships and do not take into account possible curvilinear relationships between predictors and criteria. It is known or suspected that some of the predictors will show curvilinear relationships with the criteria. Sixth, we need to take into account the confidence ratings that accompanied the observers' high inference ratings, as well as the distributions of the predictor variables, especially in evaluating the variables which do not show significant correlations. If the distributions on some predictor variables show little or no variance, this factor alone would explain the lack of significant correlations with criteria. Also, observers indicated their confidence when making high inference ratings. Sometimes they were not able to make a rating at all, and at other times they made one only with great reservations and low confidence. The latter are likely to be heavily influenced by halo effect and logical error. Finally, it should be remembered that the data are only partial and do not include the variables from the test battery or from the expanded Brophy-Good Dyadic Interaction Observation System, which was the major low inference data gathering instrument used in the study.

Given that the pattern of significant relationships frequently conflicts with the preconceived ideas of most observers (including those in this study) concerning effective teaching, it seems likely that most of the significant findings reflect true relationships which will be replicated. Also, there is reason to believe that many other relationships will be uncovered when grade, SES, and possible curvilinearity of relationship are taken into account in the data analysis and when the data are replicated with a larger number of observations on each teacher.

Follow-up Study

A follow-up study is presently under way to collect the replication data needed to complement the first year results. The same low and high inference measures will be used, with a few minor variations. However, each teacher will be observed fifteen to twenty times rather than two to four times. Thus the low inference coding measures will be much less affected by situational factors operating on a given day, and high inference ratings should be more differentiated and more accurate because coders will have seen each teacher many more times. A teacher interview also will be added during this second year. Parts of it will cover the same variables measured elsewhere, to provide additional internal validity checks. Most of the interview, however, will deal with variables which are not easily measured through periodic classroom observation (classroom rules and procedures and how they are instilled in the children; teachers' methods of dealing with children who get through with their work very quickly or cannot keep up and need some kind of adjustment or extra help; teachers' methods of dealing with children who have missed school due to illness; teachers' attitudes toward different methods of teaching language arts and mathematics; teachers' attitudes toward team teaching, open classrooms, learning centers, etc.; and teachers' methods of dealing with particular kinds of problem children). These interview data will help fill in some of the gaps which exist in the present data bank. Most of the teachers in the first year study are involved in the follow-up study, so that stability across years can be analyzed. New teachers, selected on the same basis as those in the first group, have also been added. Comparisons of data from this new group with data from the first group will allow us to make sure that findings are generalizable and not unique to a particular sample of teachers. The findings for both years will be reported in a monograph to be written by myself and my colleague Dr. Carolyn Evertson, the project director.

Implications for Teacher Evaluation

The project is not yet far enough along to allow us to draw many clear-cut implications for teacher evaluation, but a few statements can be made with confidence at present. First, although the Brophy (1972) teacher stability data were encouragingly higher than those previously reported, and although they allowed identification of consistent teachers to be included in the observational studies described, the stability coefficients for the sample as a whole were not high enough to justify the use of standardized achievement tests for evaluating teachers. Thus, in an unselected sample there is simply too much variability from one year to the next in teachers' production of student learning gains on these tests. Second, the Brophy data show that a yearly "class" or "cohort" effect is noticeable even when residual gain scores which are supposed to eliminate such effects are used. Residual gain scores from different subtests in the same year intercorrelate more highly than scores from the same subtest correlate from one year to the next. Such yearly variability might be due to rather obvious causes such as teacher and student health or personal problems or changes in curricula, but they may also be due to factors which are more difficult to identify, such as year-to-year differences in class leadership, class morale and motivation, or the general tenor of teacher-student relationships. Third, and probably most important, the standardized achievement tests do not necessarily measure the skills that the teacher is attempting to teach. Thus if teachers are to be evaluated via tests of student gain, I would use criterion referenced rather than standardized, norm referenced achievement tests, and would also use an I.Q. test or some other ability measure as a covariate to control for student ability differences.

Furthermore, given the Brophy findings that even the usual statistical controls may not be enough, I would make every attempt to control all known operative factors through matching procedures rather than relying on statistical controls. Thus I would make sure that each teacher at a given grade was assigned equal numbers of boys and girls, equal numbers of children at various levels of ability, classrooms of equivalent size, equipment, and general attractiveness, etc. Also, given that certain variables which many think are important teacher qualities did not correlate with effectiveness in producing learning gains, some may wish to consider using measures of these other variables in addition to measures of student learning gain in evaluating teachers.

For the reasons mentioned, the findings of the present study remain too tentative at this point to provide a solid basis for evaluating teachers through process observations. However, after two years of data have been collected and all of the planned statistical analyses have been completed, we should be able to identify teacher behavior that is related to the production of student learning gains with much greater confidence. The results will remain correlational, although those that replicate over two years and show up consistently on several different types of measures are very likely to be causes and not mere correlates of student gain. Following the second year of naturalistic study, we will move into a series of experimental and quasi-experimental studies in which teacher behavior that appears to be related to student learning will be systematically varied to see if predicted effects on students are observed. In these studies the teachers will be the experimenters and we will be the data collectors, using observation instruments to link teacher and student behavior and demonstrate causal mechanisms where they exist. These data, and those produced by other investigators in similar studies, should result in the development of observation scales that can be used to evaluate teacher behavior (Good and Brophy, 1973).

Before such process evaluation can be done with confidence, however, and certainly before it should be used for teacher accountability purposes, two advances in the state of the art must be made: 1) we must identify teacher process variables which show stable and reasonably high correlations with criteria (whatever criteria are used); 2) teachers should show high stability on the process variables themselves, in the absence of intervention or treatment designed to change their behavior on these variables. Where these conditions are met, teacher evaluation through process observation would be quite valid and defensible. Even here, however, process observation instruments should not be used for evaluation purposes only. Training modules designed to optimize teacher behavior on each variable should be developed and used with the teachers, and where accountability is involved, teachers should be rewarded for making gains on these variables or for maintaining a high level of performance. It would be tragic and wasteful if process evaluation data that had such obvious implications for in-service teacher training were used solely for accountability evaluations.

References

Brophy, J. "Stability of Teacher Effectiveness." *American Educational Research Journal* 10 (1973): 245-52.

———— "Stability in Teacher Effectiveness." Report Series No. 77, Research and Development Center for Teacher Education. Austin: University of Texas, 1972.

Brophy, J., and Good, T. "The Brophy-Good Dyadic Interaction System." In *Mirrors for Behavior: An Anthology of Observation Instruments Continued, 1970 Supplement,* Vol. A, edited by A. Simon and E. Boyer. Philadelphia: Research for Better Schools, Inc., 1970.

Dunkin, M., and Biddle, B. *The Study of Teaching.* New York: Holt, Rinehart and Winston, 1974.

Emmer, E. "Classroom Observation Scales." Research and Development Center for Teacher Education. Austin: University of Texas, 1973.

Flanders, N. *Analyzing Teacher Behavior.* Reading, Massachusetts: Addison-Wesley, 1970.

Flanders, N., and Simon, A. "Teacher Effectiveness." In *Encyclopedia of Educational Research,* 4th ed., edited by R. Ebel. New York: Macmillan, 1969.

Fuller, F. "Concerns of Teachers: A Developmental Conceptualization." *American Educational Research Journal* 6 (1969): 207-26.

Good, T., and Brophy, J. *Looking in Classrooms.* New York: Harper and Row, 1973.

Hess, R. "Class and Ethnic Influences upon Socialization." In *Carmichael's Manual of Child Psychology,* 3d ed., Vol. 2, edited by P. Mussen. New York: John Wiley and Sons, 1970.

Kounin, J. *Discipline and Group Management in Classrooms.* New York: Holt, Rinehart and Winston, 1970.

Rosenshine, B. "The Stability of Teacher Effects upon Student Achievement." *Review of Educational Research* 40 (1970): 647-62.

_____ *Teaching Behaviours and Student Achievement*. London: National Foundation for Educational Research in England and Wales, 1971.

Rosenshine, B., and Furst, N. "The Use of Direct Observation to Study Teaching." In *Second Handbook of Research on Teaching*, edited by R. Travers. New York: Rand McNally, 1973.

Veldman, D. "Comprehensive Personal Assessment System for Teacher Education Programs." Research and Development Center for Teacher Education. Austin: University of Texas, 1972.

4. NEEDS ASSESSMENT
James R. Barclay

A major problem in implementing new learning strategies in the schools is that learning is influenced by student, teacher, curriculum, parental, and other environmental factors. The school psychologist, counselor, teacher, or administrative policy-making group must allocate limited resources to maximize educational effects. This requires evaluating behaviors that relate not only to achievement, but also to self-competency, self-management, group interaction, motivation, and other affective and social variables. If the school is to prevent rather than respond to problems it should consider evaluation as a routine as well as an important function of its program. The purpose of this chapter is to describe an assessment system that utilizes the child's self-report as well as his peer group and teacher expectations, and offers a description of his characteristics in the classroom group and in grades, schools and other units.

From 1956 to 1959 I served as a school diagnostician in a suburban Detroit school district in which there were many problem children who defied attempts at diagnosis and remediation. Consequently, I began a series of studies designed to use peer and teacher judgments in ascertaining the characteristics of individual children in the classroom.

In one study, the interest patterns of 1,777 elementary and junior high school students were related to a sociometric device and teacher ratings (Barclay, 1966a). The subjects were asked their preferences in a variety of classroom interests, including watching television, listening to music, vocational planning, and the like. Results of the study showed that teachers' ratings and peer ratings differentiate between interest patterns, and that these patterns are associated with a broad extroversion-introversion continuum. A follow-up study (Barclay, 1966b) indicated that both the sociometric predictor and teacher ratings identified subsequent dropouts. It was found that 54 percent of the female and 64 percent of the male dropouts had sociometric and teacher ratings below the median on the data from four years earlier.

On the basis of these studies and several others (Barclay, 1966c, 1966d), a rationale was advanced that social desirability and social skills are related both to motivation to achieve and to survival in the elementary classroom. Because the assessment of the social climate of the classroom is a first step in introducing procedures designed to enhance learning, a new inventory was designed, based on interviews with elementary school children and on Holland's (1966) theory of personality-vocational choice. The new inventory, the Barclay Classroom Climate Inventory (BCCI), included self-report items, peer nominations, and teacher judgments. The skill areas encompassed in the inventory were related to artistic-intellectual, social-conventional, realistic-outdoor, and enterprising skills. Items related to reticent and disruptive behavior were also included. Children were asked to respond "yes" or "no" to items such as whether they could run fast, whether they liked to listen to others, and the like. The peer group was asked to nominate who, in that classroom, could do each of these skill items best. In addition, there were some vocational interest items, and some scales relating to reinforcers—activities enjoyed by the child. The teacher rating section was composed of a number of adjectives relating to both positive and negative adjustment, effort, and motivation.

The BCCI has been used in a number of traditional and novel studies of social interaction in the schools (Barclay, 1967; Barclay et al., 1972; Tapp, 1972). In these studies, internal consistency and test-retest reliabilities range from .40 to .80. Sociometric judgments and teacher expectations of students remain very consistent over a one-year period, while self-competency estimates and vocational-behavioral interest show more fluctuation (Barclay et al., 1972). On the basis of both principal axis and multi-method multi-trait factor analyses, a number of factors were obtained that represent the convergence or discriminant judgment of self, peer, and teacher inputs.[1]

On the basis of these studies a computer processing format has been developed. An answer sheet is optically scanned and the scores are converted to computer tape, analyzed, and reported in narrative output form. The programming consists of several steps. First the computer scores the various scales. Then it interprets high and low values in accordance with a set of rules designed to interpret the scale in relationship to the standard deviation from the mean. After differences among self, group, and teacher inputs are reported, a more complicated process begins in which combinations of scores are analyzed, chiefly through the guidelines of the multi-method, multi-trait factor analytic studies, to determine characteristics. For example, if a child is seen as impulsive, acting out, and uncontrolled by the teacher, is viewed by his peers as disruptive, sees himself as alienated from school, and is reinforced chiefly by same-sex peer activities, a statement relating to unstable extroversion is indicated. Scores on various scales tend to cluster in a broad extroversion-introversion continuum, and within that continuum modes of stable and unstable behavior are identified.

Using the convergence of these multiple-input scores, combinations of scaled scores are related to eight deficit areas in the school: self-concept or self-competency, group interaction, self-control or self-management, verbal skill, physical-manual or outdoor skills, vocational development, cognitive task-order motivation, and attitude toward school. A computer-constructed table reports suspected problems in each area. In addition, the proportion of boys, the proportion of girls, and the total class proportion of problems are indicated. Figures 4-1 and 4-2 provide examples of the data output on an individual child and his class. In this instance, boy #18 is a sixth grader who reportedly has deficits in self-concept, group interaction skills, verbal skills, vocational development, and attitude toward school. Obviously, these inferences should not be accepted uncritically. They are based on the logical convergence of scores from several inputs, but need to be verified with additional clinical and educational data.

The utility of the BCCI system for evaluation in the elementary school from grades two to six has been illustrated in a number of school districts. Differences between grades, between schools, and

Figure 4-1

EXPLANATION OF SUMMARY TABLE NO. 2
IN THIS TABLE THERE ARE EIGHT SUSPECTED PROBLEM AREAS. THESE AREAS ARE DERIVED FROM THE TOTAL PATTERN OF SCORES OBTAINED ON THE INDIVIDUAL STUDENT. THE NUMBER AND PERCENTAGE OF CHILDREN WITH PROBLEMS IN CERTAIN AREAS ARE INDICATED BELOW THE TABL

POSSIBLE TARGET AREAS FOR PROBLEM INTERVENTIONS

STUDENT AND SEX	SELF CONCEPT	GROUP SKILLS	SELF-CONTROL SKILLS	VERBAL SKILLS	PHYSICAL SKILLS	VOCATIONAL DEVELOPMENT	COGNITIVE DEVELOPMENT	ATTITUDE TOWARD SCHOOL
1/M						*		
2/F	*						*	
3/F	*				*			
4/F				*				
5/M							*	*
6/M						*		
7/F	*				*			
8/M								
9/F	*	*			*		*	
10/F								
11/F		*		*				*
12/M	*							*
13/F	*				*			
14/F						*		
15/M								
16/F	*				*	*		*
17/M								
18/M	*	*		*		*		*
19/F								
20/F					*			
21/F	*							
22/M	*	*		*				*
23/F								
24/M			*					
25/F								
26/M	*			*				*

SEE PROFILE ANALYSES OF BCCI CLASSIFICATIONS IN USER'S MANUAL PP. 59-108 AND SUMMARY OF STUDENT TARGET SKILLS AND ALTERNATE STRATEGIES P. 111.

MALES	4.	2.	1.	3.	0.	3.	1.	5.
PCT	36.	18.	9.	27.	0.	27.	9.	45.
FEM.	7.	2.	0.	2.	6.	2.	2.	2.
PCT	47.	13.	0.	13.	40.	13.	13.	13.
GROUP	11.	4.	1.	5.	6.	5.	3.	7.
PCT	42.	15.	4.	19.	23.	19.	12.	27.

Figure 4-2

STUDENT NUMBER 18 IS A BOY IN THE 6 GRADE.

THE FOLLOWING ARE IMPRESSIONS OF HIS SELF-COMPETENCY SKILLS:

LOW GLOBAL ESTIMATE OF SELF-COMPETENCY SKILLS. LOW SELF-ESTIMATE OF ARTISTIC-INTELLECTUAL SKILLS. ABOVE AVERAGE SELF-ESTIMATE OF REALISTIC-MASCULINE SKILLS. LOW SELF-ESTIMATE OF SOCIAL SKILLS. AVERAGE SELF-ESTIMATE OF ENTERPRISING SKILLS.

THE FOLLOWING ARE IMPRESSIONS OF HIS KNOWLEDGE OF THE FIELD OF WORK, AS A FUNCTION OF ACQUAINTANCE WITH THE ENVIRONMENT:

APPEARS TO EXPRESS AN AVERAGE AWARENESS OF VOCATIONAL ALTERNATIVES IN THE FIELD OF WORK. SHOWS LITTLE OR NO INTEREST IN MANUAL AND OUTDOOR OCCUPATIONS. SHOWS LITTLE OR NO INTEREST IN SCIENTIFIC, TECHNICAL, AND INTELLECTUAL-ORIENTED OCCUPATIONS. SHOWS LITTLE OR NO INTEREST IN SOCIAL OCCUPATIONS CALLING FOR INTERPERSONAL SKILLS. SHOWS AVERAGE INTEREST IN ARTISTIC AND CREATIVE OCCUPATIONS.

THE FOLLOWING ARE IMPRESSIONS OF HIS PERSONAL AND INTERPERSONAL SKILLS AS JUDGED BY PEERS:

PERCEIVED GLOBALLY BY PEERS AS POSSESSING FEW PERSONAL OR SOCIAL SKILLS. PERCEIVED BY PEERS AS POSSESSING SOME ARTISTIC AND INTELLECTUAL SKILLS. PERCEIVED BY PEERS AS LACKING REALISTIC AND MASCULINE SKILLS. PERCEIVED BY PEERS AS POSSESSING SOME SOCIAL COMPETENCIES AND SKILLS. NOT PERCEIVED BY PEERS AS MANIPULATORY OR POSSESSING INTERPERSONAL LEADERSHIP SKILLS. PERCEIVED BY PEERS AS BEING SOMEWHAT RETICENT, SHY, AND WITHDRAWN. IS NOT PERCEIVED BY PEERS AS DISRUPTIVE WITHIN THE CLASSROOM.

THE FOLLOWING ARE IMPRESSIONS OF HIS PERSONAL AND SOCIAL ADJUSTMENT AND EFFORT AND MOTIVATION AS RATED BY THE TEACHER:

MANIFESTS SOMEWHAT INCONSISTENT PATTERN OF PERSONAL ADJUSTMENT. MANIFESTS OCCASIONAL POOR SOCIAL ADJUSTMENT. MANIFESTS OCCASIONAL POOR EFFORT AND MOTIVATION.

SUMMARY:

THIS BOY IS IN GREAT NEED OF HELP IN THE DEVELOPMENT OF PERSONAL AND INTERPERSONAL SKILLS. THIS BOY'S BEHAVIOR BASED ON SELF, PEER AND TEACHER JUDGMENTS DOES NOT APPEAR TO BE VIEWED CONSISTENTLY AS EITHER EXTROVERTED OR INTROVERTED, CONTROLLED OR IMPULSIVE. HE APPEARS TO MANIFEST A BLEND OF TEMPERAMENT AND RESPONSE MODES.

THIS CHILD SHOWS HIGH INTERESTS IN PEER GROUP MALE REINFORCERS AVERAGE INTERESTS IN SELF-STIMULATING, ESTHETIC, TASK-ORIENTED, FAMILIAL, CONVENTIONAL, PEER GROUP FEMALE REINFORCERS AND LITTLE OR NO INTEREST IN THE REMAINING REINFORCERS.

THIS CHILD'S JUDGMENT OF THE SCHOOL ENVIRONMENT IS SOMEWHAT UNFAVORABLE.

STUDENT NUMBER 18   CLASSIFICATION CODE (B5)

SELF-RATED SCALES		GROUP NOMINATION SCALES			VOCATIONAL PREFERENCE SCALES			TEACHER ADJECTIVE SCALES			BEHAVIORAL SCALES	
SAI	0-	GAI	2	GR	1	REAL	0-	ENTR	0-	ST	2	PA+	0	SAO	7	MEL	6*	SSF	13	CNV	17
SRM	4	GRM	2	GD	2-	INT	0-	ARTS	0			SA+	0	EFFO	6	CHL	5*	ESF	14	PRM	33*
SSC	1-	GSC	2	GTOT	6-	SOC	0-	CONT	8*			EFF+	0	TR7	0-	PHL	19	ITF	15	PRF	19
SE	4	GE	1-			CONV	0-	MF	7*			PAO	6	TR8	19*	SAN	0	FRF	18	CCI	7-
STOT	9-							VTOT	17												

between districts can be obtained by comparing the frequency of problems observed. Recently I have analyzed the output of three school districts and 143 classrooms (Barclay, 1973). A multivariate analysis of problems between grades, sexes, and predominant racial groupings was obtained. Although differences between grades and between races were obtained on cross-sectional rather than longitudinal data, it appears that teachers' evaluations of children gradually decline from the second grade to the fifth grade, with a gradual upswing noted in the sixth grade. This evidence suggests that the ratio of positive descriptors applied to children by teacher ratings is much higher in the second grade than in the fifth grade. At the same time that teacher expectations appear to decline in favorability, the proportion of cognitive-motivation deficits increases from the second through the sixth grades. Attitude toward school gradually worsens. Though some progress appears to be evident in group interaction and self-management problems over the same time span, self-competency declines and seclusiveness increases.

Through the use of discriminant analysis it becomes possible to ascertain both the distinctive characteristics of schools and grades within the district, and differences existing between districts. For example, of the four schools located in a southern university city district, one tends to be somewhat low on teacher judgments and has a high incidence of poor attitude and self-concept deficits. Another tends to be very well controlled, but has poor cognitive-motivation task-orientation. Still another possesses high teacher evaluations but much disruptive and acting-out behavior. A fourth school shows marked differences between boys and girls, both in teacher judgments and in kinds of problems. These examples provide some information as to how the inventory can be used by a school district to ascertain the proportion of specific problems relating not only to a given classroom, but also to grade comparisons between schools and districts.

Effective educational change will have to be focused on both the individual and the classroom. Assessment techniques must integrate both traditional and impressionistic achievement data with a host of personal and social interaction data. Policy making at the highest levels of the school organization must reflect a decentralized but coordinated effort to involve heuristic criteria for performance goals, and alternate intervention procedures that maximize the interactions among subjects, methods, and evaluation feed-back mechanisms. Specifically, this means that if, within a given district, school A shows a very low teacher evaluation and a large proportion of students with poor attitudes toward school, as well as many behavioral problems, then it may be relevant to aid this school through a behavior-modification or structured-curriculum approach. If school B has many deficits in self-esteem and group interaction, it may be relevant to develop a curriculum or counseling procedure that accents the development of self-skills and verbal interaction.

In the past, we have been all too ready to test each new curriculum vehicle on the entire school district. However, it seems evident from the literature that no single set of approaches works best with all children. Some children may learn reading best through a kinesthetic approach, and others through a visual modality, while still others may do better with an auditory approach. It is probably true that all students will gain something from each of these approaches, but individuals can profit and accelerate their own learning potential by maximizing a specific approach. Moreover, I believe that the tentative conclusions of Cronbach and Snow (1969), regarding the interaction of personality types with learning modalities and methods, is a potentially important contribution to assessment for curriculum and guidance alternatives. They suggest that structured instruction may be better for the anxious, compulsive child, while structured and unstructured methods appeared to be about equally effective for the child who was neither anxious nor compulsive.

It seems logical to begin with a multiple-needs assessment of individuals and move on to groups such as classes, grades and schools. This kind of assessment provides information specific enough for dealing with individuals in a prescriptive manner and with groups by designing specific curriculum or psychological treatments. Moreover, a school district might reasonably want to know where its problems exist, as well as how its schools compare with those of other districts. The BCCI techniques show how it is possible to take the summary data of all kinds of individuals and obtain special analyses of groups to which they belong. Suppose a district wishes to see how the children of the military are faring, or children who live in foster homes, or children who have been in trouble with the law, or children with suspected learning difficulties. Or suppose a district wishes to evaluate the consequences in affective and social interaction of bussing, or a new curriculum, or the use of performance objectives. In each of these cases it would be possible to ascertain some important information about these target groups via inter- and intradistrict analyses.

The second step is logically dictated by the first. Once the characteristics of the district and groups within the district are known, this information should be disseminated to various problem-solving and skill groups for their discussion and action. From this process local targets, criteria, and resources can be determined. Obviously, the designing of specific procedures and treatments can be time-consuming and requires planning work. I do not believe that any specific set of procedures is applicable to all schools or groups, but through relevant data analysis it should be possible to provide school personnel with diagnostic clues. From that point on, teams of learning-development personnel can examine the resources of the district, the desired goals and performance objectives, and possible methods of implementing change.

With the determination of specific objectives, criteria, and methods of intervention, the district can design evaluation procedures that will enable it to examine both the quality and the quantity of change occurring. Obviously, many intervening variables occur in a school experimental design, so that it is not always possible to utilize the most powerful research designs. Also, the process must be consistently monitored and the history of the project taken into consideration. Not only should evaluation include some of the typical research methods, but school districts should also try to rely heavily on the information gained from tracking individuals through the aptitude-treatment paradigm and case studies. Information about what is most effective for whom under what circumstances cannot usually be obtained through the treatment of group data, but by the tracking of individual cases, and by cumulative inferences obtained from looking at general tendencies deduced from individual data.

Finally, given the complexities of human social interaction, and the need for assessing multiple inputs, a computer program can be of inestimable assistance in the regularization of diagnostic interpretation. The computer can provide the data for recognizing important individual and group differences. With this information in hand, decisions about needed personnel, training procedures, relationships to teacher or counselor education training programs, parental involvement, and district resources can be postulated and evaluated. Above all, budgetary considerations can be worked out and the cost-effectiveness of the procedures per pupil can be ascertained.

Notes

[1] Some details on these studies are relevant to this discussion. Barclay (1967) utilized the instrument as a criterion of change relating to three treatments tried out with some fifth graders. Treatments included teacher modeling and reinforcement for socially approved behaviors, a program for training a teacher to select appropriate behaviors and reinforce them, and a placebo program substituting a teacher intern for a regular teacher for five weeks. The results indicated that the greatest changes in poorly accepted children were evinced in the modeling and social reinforcement group. Considerable changes also took place in the classroom where the teacher intern replaced the regular teacher.

The impact of the social status of parents was examined in relationship to BCCI scores. The scores here were treated as dependent variables with the classification of the father by occupation as the independent variable (Barclay, Stilwell and Barclay, 1972). A multivariate analysis was completed on data from 1386 students indicating that the paternal occupational status of children has a powerful effect on self-report, peer judgments, and teacher expectations.

Using the multi-method multi-trait approach to factor analysis, factors such as sociability, intellectual task-orientation, seclusiveness, aggression, and enterprising activity were obtained (Barclay et al., 1972). Tapp (1972) examined the convergent and discriminant validity of the BCCI by designing another similar multiple-input system tapping the same kinds of self, group, and teacher judgments. He also compared the output of the two systems and found that they generally agree.

References

Barclay, J. R. "Interest Patterns Associated with Measures of Social Desirability: Some Implications for Dropouts and the Culturally Disadvantaged." *Personnel and Guidance Journal* 45 (1966a): 56-60.

Barclay, J. R. "Sociometric Choices and Teacher Ratings as Predictors of School Dropouts." *Journal of School Psychology* 4 (1966b): 40-44.

Barclay, J. R. "Variability in Sociometric Choices and Teacher Ratings as Related to Teacher Age and Sex." *Journal of School Psychology* (1966c): 52-58.

Barclay, J. R. "Sociometry: Rationale and Technique for Effecting Behavior Change in the Elementary School," *Personnel and Guidance Journal.* 44 (1966d): 1067-76.

Barclay, J. R. Effecting Behavior Change in the Elementary Classroom: An Exploratory Study. *Journal of Counseling Psychology* 14 (1967): 240-47.

Barclay, J. R. (with the assistance of L. K. Barclay and W. E. Stilwell). *The Barclay Classroom Climate Inventory, A Research Manual and Studies.* Lexington, Kentucky: Educational Skills Development, 1972.

Barclay, J. R. "System-Wide Analysis of Social Interaction and Affective Problems in Schools." Paper read at 5th Banff International Conference on Behavior Modification, March 1973, Calgary, Alberta, Canada.

Barclay, J. R., Stilwell, W. E., and Barclay, L. K., "The Influence of Paternal Occupation on Social Interaction Variables in Elementary School Children." *Journal of Vocational Behavior* 2 (1972): 443-46.

Cronbach, L. J., and Snow, R. E. *Final Report: Individual Differences in Learning Ability as a Function of Instructional Variables,* Stanford, California: Stanford University Press, 1969.

Holland, J. L. *Psychology of Vocational Choice,* Boston: Ginn & Co., 1966.

Tapp, G. S. "Convergent and Discriminant Validity of the BCCI." Ph.D. dissertation, University of Kentucky, 1972.

5. CLASSROOM CLIMATES
H. Dean Nielsen
Diana H. Kirk

The purpose of this chapter is to present some of the findings in the literature on the kinds of instrumentation available for assessing environments and on the relationship of environment to learning outcomes. Obviously, a learning environment could be everywhere and entail practically everything; so in this chapter we have decided to concentrate on research done on elementary and secondary schoolroom environments, with special attention to research which also investigated learning outcomes. Except for the Walberg and Anderson Learning Environment Inventory, which is considered separately in chapter 6, most of the significant instruments developed to assess classroom climates will be examined.

Theoretical Models

The theoretical models and concepts upon which most of the climate studies are based come from social psychology, and relate individual needs to social structural variables. In the process, these models have provided researchers with operational definitions of "climate" and have helped to generate theories about the relationship of climate to both antecedent and outcome variables. Two models have gained a certain preeminence in this literature: Murray's Need-Press Model (Stern, 1970) and Getzels and Thelen's Classroom as a Social System Model (1960). Under Murray's model, the demands, sanctions, and expectations within an environment (environmental press) give a social system its particular climate. In Getzels and Thelen's model, "climate" develops as a result of the teacher's transactional style, that is, the way in which he or she balances role requirements and personality needs within the classroom. More recently Walberg (1971) has proposed a linear regression model which links the environment with students' aptitudes and instruction in predicting learning outcomes. Since these models help researchers and practitioners to conceptualize the linkages between certain structural variables on one hand and learning outcomes on the other, they have been important in determining the direction of school climate research and in suggesting the kinds of instrumentation needed.

Instrumentation

Measuring environments is no simple problem. Among the many ways of assessing the classroom or school environment, the two most popular are observational systems and questionnaire surveys. In addition to the actual instrumentation, the investigator must consider the degree of inference he wishes to make from the data he collects, which affects the level of inference he demands from his respondents or subjects. Rosenshine (1970) makes the distinction between "low inference" responses and "high inference" responses. Low inference responses or variables tap the directly observable, specific, explicit phenomena of the environment, such as counting the number of teacher statements or asking a student if his teacher ever has them work together in subgroups of the class. High inference responses or variables ask the respondent to make a judgment about the meaning of what is going on around him and of what he thinks or feels about it; for example, asking a student to agree or disagree with the statement, "Your teacher is friendly towards you," or "Your teacher likes you.

Observation Instruments

The observation instruments most employed in school climate research are "category systems," which record and categorize discrete behavioral events in a low inference manner. These instruments concentrate on the classroom behavior of the teacher or the interaction between students and teacher, following the Getzels and Thelen model, in which the teacher's transactional style is critical in determining climate. The pioneering work in instrument development for measuring student-teacher interaction was done by Wright-stone (1934) with the development of his Pupil-Teacher Rapport Scale. Using this instrument, teacher behavior was categorized as either "integrative" or "dominative." Anderson and Brewer (1945), who were concerned with teacher control of pupil behavior in kindergartens, also used the integrative-dominative dichotomy. Withall (1949) introduced the concept of classroom climate, operationally defining it with his Climate Index in terms of the teachers' verbal behavior. His index allows the researcher to categorize teacher statements as either "teacher-centered" or "learner-centered," according to the way they are categorized on the following continuum:

1. *Learner-supportive* statements that have the intent of reassuring or commending the pupil.
2. *Acceptant and clarifying* statements having an intent to convey to the pupil the feeling that he was understood and help him elucidate his ideas and feelings.
3. *Problem-structuring* statements or questions which proffer information or raise questions about the problem in an objective manner with intent to facilitate learner's problem-solving.
4. *Neutral* statements which comprise polite formalities, administrative comments, verbatim repetition of something that has already been said. No intent inferable.
5. *Directive* or hortative statements with intent to have pupil follow a recommended course of action.
6. *Reproving* or deprecating remarks intended to deter pupil from continued indulgence in present "unacceptable" behavior.
7. *Teacher self-supporting* remarks intended to sustain or justify the teacher's position or course of action.

The Climate Index has been widely used in its original form (Perkins, 1951; Mitzel and Rabinowitz, 1953), and has formed the basis for the development of new instruments.

Medley and Mitzel (1958) developed their Observation Schedule and Record (OScAR) as an improvement and expansion of Withall's method. In addition to the teacher's verbal behavior, OScAR classifies nonverbal behavior and classroom social structure according to the following scheme:

1. *Emotional Climate:* The amount of hostility observable in a classroom; a high score indicates a room in which external manifesta-

tions of warmth and friendliness are common and hostile reactions are rare. Sample items:

Positively weighted: Teacher demonstrates affection for pupil.

Negatively weighted: Teacher makes reproving remark.

2. *Verbal Emphasis:* The degree to which verbal activities predominate. Sample item:

Pupil reads or studies at his seat.

3. *Social Organization:* The amount of social grouping and pupil autonomy in a class. A class scoring high was one in which it was relatively common to find the class broken into two or more groups working independently, and in which the teacher talked relatively little.

The most elaborate and widely used observational instrument developed so far is Flanders's (Amidon and Flanders, 1963) Interaction Analysis System (IA). This system, which also records the sequence of behavioral events, focuses on teacher influence, distinguishing between "direct" and "indirect" influence according to the following ten items:

Teacher Talk

Indirect Influence:

1. *Accepts Feeling:* accepts and clarifies the feeling tone of the students in a nonthreatening manner. Feelings may be positive or negative. Predicting or recalling feelings is included.

2. *Praises or Encourages:* praises or encourages student action or behavior. Jokes that release tension, not at the expense of another individual, nodding head or saying, "um hum?" or "go on" are included.

3. *Accepts or Uses Ideas of Student:* clarifying, building, or developing ideas suggested by a student. As teacher brings more of his own ideas into play, shift to Category 5.

4. *Asks Questions:* asking a question about content or procedure with the intent that a student answer.

Direct Influence:

5. *Lecturing:* giving facts or opinions about content or procedure; expressing own ideas, asking rhetorical questions.

6. *Giving Directions:* directions, commands, or orders to which a student is expected to comply.

7. *Criticizing or Justifying Authority:* statements intended to change student behavior from nonacceptable to acceptable pattern; bawling someone out; stating why the teacher is doing what he is doing; extreme self-reference.

Student Talk

8. *Student Talk—Response:* talk by students in response to teacher. Teacher initiates the contact or solicits student statement.
9. *Student Talk—Initiation:* talk by students which they initiate. If "calling on" student is only to indicate who may talk next, observer must decide whether student wanted to talk. If he did, use this category.
10. *Silence or confusion:* pauses, short periods of silence, and periods of confusion in which communication cannot be understood by the observer.

Used by many in its original or slightly modified form (Amidon and Hough, 1967; Wallen, 1966; La Shier, 1967; Furst, 1967; Soar, 1967, 1968), the Interaction Analysis System also became the point of departure for the development of more comprehensive instruments. Honigman (1967) developed his Multidimensional Analysis of Classroom Interaction (MACI) in order to measure not only the affective domain as tapped by Flanders, but also procedural and cognitive dimensions. Cognitive dimensions such as the one included in MACI have become more important in climate research in recent years, beginning with Guilford's (1956, 1959) "structure of intellect" model and moving to Bellack's (1966) categories for analysis, including "pedagogical moves," "teaching cycles," and "categories of meanings." From this model-building has emerged a concern for measuring "cognitive climate" (Furst, 1967) or "intellectual climate" (Siegel and Siegel, 1967), and a promising new observation system, the Topic Classification System (TCS) (Gallagher et al., 1966) which includes the following dimensions:

1. *Level of Instructional Intent*—distinguishes between two different approaches to instruction: the teaching of skills and the teaching of content.
2. *Level of Conceptualization*—distinguishes between three different levels in presenting lessions:
Data—discussion of specifics

Concepts—general ideas and their applications

Generalizations—larger ideas or concepts in relation to one another.

3. *Level of Style*—distinguishes among six different modes of handling discussion in the classroom: description, expansion, explanation, evaluation-justification, evaluation-matching, and activity.

New trends for observation studies point in two directions. First, in an effort to link classroom behaviors to outcome variables according to specific theories, researchers have narrowed their scope to specific teaching acts such as "explaining behavior" (Fortune, Gage, and Shutes, 1966) or specific psychological concepts such as "openness" (Macdonald and Zaret, 1967). (Such studies are summarized in B. Rosenshine's excellent book, *Teaching Behaviors and Student Achievement.*) The second direction is to find ways of recording almost everything of major significance that might go on in a classroom, which requires extremely intricate instruments of limited replicability (Spaulding, 1963; Minuchin, 1969) or the help of videotape (Biddle and Adams, 1967). The time and expense involved in such procedures have prompted researchers to rely more heavily on the self-reports of students and teachers as a means of assessing the environment.

Self-Report Questionnaires

Self-report questionnaires have become more popular in recent years and so will receive extensive treatment here. In contrast to observation instruments, this method of gathering data generally requires high inference treatment and conforms more closely to Murray's Needs-Press Model, which considers the student's perception of his environment, its pressures and demands, as the most crucial aspect of climate.

The High School Characteristics Index (HSCI) is one of four instruments developed by Stern, Stein, and Bloom (1956) to measure environmental press variables. The Index consists of three hundred items describing daily activities, policies, procedures, attitudes, and impressions that might be characteristic of various high schools. The items are statements with which the respondent can agree or disagree, such as, "You need permission to do anything around here." There are thirty independent press scales of ten items each yielding an eleven point range of scores, 0 through 10. The subscales are generally factor analyzed to identify the prominant "press" variables. The thirty subscales are: Abasement, Achievement, Adaptability, Affiliation, Aggression, Change, Conjunctivity, Counteraction, Deference, Dominance, Ego-Achievement, Emotionality, Energy, Exhibitionism, Fantasied Achievement, Harm Avoidance, Humanism, Impulsiveness, Narcissism, Nurturance, Objectivity, Order, Play, Practicalness, Reflectiveness, Scientism, Sensuality, Sexuality, Succorance, and Understanding. Based on a sample of 947 high school students, the Kuder-Richardson 20 coefficients range from .28 to .72 for the thirty subscales.

Sinclair (1969) recently developed the Elementary School Environment Survey (ESES) instrument, consisting of one hundred statements about elementary school conditions, processes, and activities to obtain a measure of student perceptions of the educational environment. The ESES is very similar to Pace's College and University Environment Scale (Pace, 1969). The items indicate five dimensions of environmental press: Practicality, Community, Awareness, Propriety, and Scholarship.

1. *Practicality:* Emphasis on the concrete and realistic more than the speculative or abstract; defines an environment in which personal status and benefits are important.
2. *Community:* Emphasis on cohesiveness, supportiveness, and sympathy of the environment as well as the feeling of group welfare and group loyalty.
3. *Awareness:* Emphasis on concern for self-understanding and identity, a wide range of aesthetic opportunities and appreciations, and a sense of personal involvement in the world's problems and conditions of man.
4. *Propriety:* Emphasis on decorum, politeness, consideration, thoughtfulness, and caution.
5. *Scholarship:* Emphasis on competitively high academic achievement and interest in scholarship.

Trickett and Moos (1971), prompted by the Murray Need-Press conceptualization, developed the Classroom Environment Scale (CES) to identify aspects of the psychosocial environment of the classroom. Nine dimensions of classroom climate were identified, with ten items per dimension. These dimensions are:

1. *Involvement:* Extent to which students pay attention to and show interest in the activities of the class.
2. *Affiliation:* Extent to which students work with and come to know each other within the classroom.
3. *Support:* Extent to which the teacher expresses a personal interest in the students.
4. *Task Orientation:* Extent to which the activities of the class are centered around the accomplishment of specified academic objectives.
5. *Competition:* Amount of emphasis on academic competition within the class.
6. *Order and Organization:* Emphasis within the classroom on maintenance of order and the degree to which the activities of the class are well organized.
7. *Rule Clarity:* Degree to which the rules for conduct in the classroom are explicitly stated and clearly understood.
8. *Teacher Control:* Degree to which student conduct in the classroom is delimited by enforcement of the rules.
9. *Innovation:* Extent to which different modes of teaching and classroom interaction take place in the class.

The questionnaire itself contains ninety statements, to which the respondent answers true or false. Based on a sample of 443 high school students, the alpha internal consistencies for the nine subscales range from .67 to .86.

Ehman (1969), in order to assess the process of political socialization in high school social studies classes, developed a short five-item questionnaire. The items form a Guttman scale (reproducibility of .86), based on a sample of 334 high school students. The high end of this scale represents pupils' reports of teachers who deal with controversial political and social issues quite often, and who maintain a neutral but objective position in a free discussion climate (open climate). The low end represents pupils' reports of teachers who rarely deal with controversial issues; when these topics are treated, the teacher expresses his or her own position, while the students feel reluctant to join in, and rarely express ideas in the closed climate of discussion. The five dimensions of classroom climate in this questionnaire are: Teacher Treatment of Controversial Issues, Teacher Objectivity, Teacher Neutrality, Discussion Climate, and Teacher Discussion of Racial Problems.

Steele, House, and Kerins (1971) developed a Classroom Activities Questionnaire (CAQ) which measures the prevalence of activities in both the affective and cognitive domains of the respondent's class using "low-inference" indicators. Cognitive dimensions of the scale are based upon Bloom's (1956) taxonomy. The questionnaire itself consists of twenty-five statements with a four point Likert scale by which the respondent indicates his degree of agreement with the statements. Based on a sample of 3138 elementary school children, the reliability coefficients for Lower Thought Processes, Higher Thought Processes, Classroom Focus, and Classroom Climate range from .76 to .88; for the first sixteen factors in the table, the coefficients range from .58 to .94. The test-retest reliabilities of a random sample of 79 students for the four dimensions ranged from .59 to .91. The dimensions of the classroom sought by the questionnaire, as well as the factors composing them, are as follows:

Lower Thought Processes
1. *Memory:* Activities calling for recall or recognition of information presented.
2. *Translation:* Activities calling for paraphrasing or expressing information in a different symbolic form.
3. *Interpretation:* Activities calling for recognition of relationships and seeing implications of information.

Higher Thought Processes
4. *Application:* Activities calling for selection of appropriate methods and performance of operations required by problem situations.
5. *Analysis:* Activities calling for recognition of the structure of material, including the conditions that affect the way it fits together.
6. *Synthesis:* Activities calling for the generation of new ideas and solutions.
7. *Evaluation:* Activities calling for development and application of a set of standards for judging worth.

Classroom Focus
8. *Discussion:* Student opportunity for and involvement in class discussion.
9. *Test/Grade Stress:* High pressure to produce teacher-selected answers for a grade.

10. *Lecture:* Teacher role is information-giver with a passive, listening role for students.

Classroom Climate

11. *Enthusiasm:* Student excitement and involvement in class activities.
12. *Independence:* Tolerance for and encouragement of student initiative.
13. *Divergence:* Tolerance for and encouragement of many solutions to problems.
14. *Humor:* Allowance for joking and laughter in the classroom.
15. *Teacher talk:* Proportion of class time consumed by teacher talk.
16. *Homework:* Weekly amount of outside preparation for class.

Halpin and Croft (1963) constructed the Organizational Climate Description Questionnaire (OCDQ) which portrays the organizational climate of the elementary school through the self-reports of its teachers and principal. The OCDQ was used to analyze the climates of seventy-one elementary schools in six different regions of the United States. Analysis of the OCDQ items was based on descriptions of the schools given by 1151 respondents. The OCDQ contains sixty-four six-point Likert items which were assigned to eight subscales delineated by factor analytic methods. A profile of a school's organizational climate was constructed from the scores of the eight subtests. When resulting profiles of the seventy-one schools were factor analyzed, it was determined that they differentiated six types of organizational climate, ranging from "open" to "closed." The six climates and their descriptions, and the eight subscales and their descriptions, are:

Climates

1. *Open:* Energetic, lively organization which is moving toward its goals, and which provides satisfaction for the group members' social needs.
2. *Autonomous:* Organizational members initiate leadership acts as opposed to initiation by leader.
3. *Controlled:* Impersonal or highly task-oriented leadership.
4. *Familiar:* Highly personal and undercontrolled organization in terms of task orientation.
5. *Paternal:* Leader attempts to restrict leadership acts by members and initiates most of these acts himself.

6. *Closed:* High degree of apathy on the part of all members of the organization.

Subscales

Teachers' Behavior

1. *Disengagement:* Teachers do not work well together.
2. *Hindrance:* Teachers feel that the principal burdens them with unnecessary busywork.
3. *Esprit:* Teachers' social needs satisfied; morale high, sense of accomplishment in their job.
4. *Intimacy:* Teachers' social relations with one another are friendly.

Principal's Behavior

5. *Aloofness:* Principal's behavior is formal and impersonal.
6. *Production Emphasis:* Principal's behavior is highly directive and task-oriented through close supervision.
7. *Thrust:* Principal's behavior is highly directive and task-oriented through personal example.
8. *Consideration:* Principal treats teachers "humanly."

Walberg and Thomas (1972) developed an instrument using both a questionnaire and an observation schedule to investigate open education cross-culturally (the validation sample included schools in the United States and Britain). The Teacher Questionnaire and parallel Observation Rating Scale consist of fifty Likert items which tap eight themes thought to be relevant to open education. Reliabilities are based on a sample of sixty-two classrooms in the United States and Great Britain; alpha internal consistencies for the eight themes range from .22 to .97. Reliabilities between teacher self-reports and observer ratings for the themes ranged from .11 to .81, with a median of .47. The eight themes and sample items considered "open" are:

1. *Provision for Learning:* Manipulative materials are supplied in great diversity and range with little replication.
2. *Humaneness, Respect, Openness, and Warmth:* The environment includes materials developed or supplied by the children.
3. *Diagnosis of Learning Events:* Teacher gives children tests to find out what they know.
4. *Instruction, Guidance, and Extension of Learning:* Teacher bases instruction on each individual child and his interaction with materials and equipment.

5. *Evaluation of Diagnostic Information:* Teacher keeps a collection of each child's work for use in evaluating his development.
6. *Seeking Opportunities for Professional Growth:* Teacher uses the assistance of others in a supportive, advisory capacity.
7. *Self-Perception of Teacher:* Teacher tries to keep all children within her sight so that she can make sure they are doing what they are supposed to do. (Traditional item requiring reverse coding.)
8. *Assumptions about Children and Learning Process:* The emotional climate is warm and accepting.

Evaluation of Instruments

An important consideration for users of these methods is the relative implementation cost of each method. Observational techniques are costly in terms of time considerations and reimbursement to observers, severely limiting the size and characteristics of the samples one's resources can cover. Although each study is replicable in principle, most researchers develop new observation schemes for their own research and so only a few studies have been replicated in practice. On the other hand, self-report questionnaires are easily standardized and a good deal less costly. As a consequence, they can be used in studies by other researchers with far greater ease and confidence in the replicability of the critical phenomena. Also, the samples of respondents can be large enough to ensure maximum statistical confidence. However, since these instruments are high inference measures, test validation is of major concern to anyone who uses them. Researchers make a great leap of logic when they assume that their intended meaning and feeling for the items is the same as that of the respondents. One student's "open" environment may be another's "chaotic" one, resulting in different learning consequences, although both may answer items on constraints in the environment in much the same way. As Shaw and Wright (1967, p. 14) have pointed out:

> The attitude toward the object is inferred from the statements endorsed by the subject, based upon the consensual evaluation of the nature of the characteristics attributed to the object by the acceptance of these statements.
> It is clear that our conception of attitude is implicit in the techniques of attitude measurement. The only inferential step involved is the assumption that the evaluations of the persons involved in scale construc-

tion correspond to those of the individuals whose attitudes are being measured. This may or may not be true. . . .

Test validation procedures are of five kinds: face, content, concurrent, predictive, and construct. Since the literature shows that concurrent and predictive are the two validation procedures most commonly used, only those two will be discussed here. Concurrent and predictive validity are conceptually the same in that they entail comparing the results of the questionnaire to criterion measures which are believed to be indicative of the phenomena. These procedures involve making a prediction regarding how the questionnaire compares with the criterion measure before analyzing the data. The difference between the two procedures is primarily one of the relative time which elapses between the questionnaire administration and when the criterion measures are taken. If one intends to emphasize that no time has elapsed between measures, the validation is termed concurrent. "Predictive" indicates that some time has elapsed.

It is important for the potential users of these instruments to note that validating procedures are an effective way of screening out those instruments whose utility is questionable. Unfortunately, few of the studies reviewed discuss in any depth the procedures used in instrument validation. Among the questionnaires for which there were discussions of validation, the tendency was to show that the instrument could differentiate between various instances of a criterion at significant levels.

The Elementary School Environment Survey, ESES (Sinclair, 1969), the Classroom Environment Scale, CES (Trickett and Moos, 1971), and the High School Characteristics Index, HSCI (Mitchell, 1968), discriminated between *schools* at a significance level of at least .05. The CES, the Climate Index (Mitzel and Rabinowitz, 1953) and the Integrative-Dominative Index (Anderson and Brewer, 1945) discriminated between *classrooms* at a significant level. The Organizational Climate Description Questionnaire (OCDQ) has shown an inconsistent capability to discriminate differences. Heller (1968) found that it did not discriminate between the perceptions of faculty in different informal groups; Gentry and Kenney (1965) found that it discriminated between the ways that black and white faculties view their schools; Andrews (1965) found variable results when the OCDQ attempted to discriminate between schools (elementary and secondary) and teachers (by age, years training, percent male teachers, years experience, years in present school).

Another form of criterion-oriented validation found in this literature compares the results of one instrument with those of another. Using this method, Kenney, White, and Gentry (1967) established the concurrent validity of the OCDQ, while Andrews (1965) produced more inconsistent results, establishing predictive validity with one test and rendering questionable the concurrent validity of the instrument with another. Less ambiguous are the findings of Withall (1951) with respect to his Climate Index, which correlated (r tetrachoric) at .68 with the Anderson and Brewer Index. Flanders's Interaction Analysis System has been validated several times on the basis of high correlations with various student achievement tests in math, social studies, and biology, as will be seen in the following section on student outcomes. Finally, the validity of the Teacher Questionnaire (Walberg and Thomas, 1972) was established by the fact that six of its eight themes correlated with an observational rating of the classrooms at a significance level of .001, with correlations ranging from .42 to .86. It is difficult to assess the validity of the other instruments, primarily because of incomplete information regarding their validation procedures and results.

Learning Outcomes

To practitioners in education, the determination of the affective and cognitive climate of a classroom becomes meaningful only when these aspects are related to learning outcomes, either in terms of attitude change or achievement gains. Lamentably, of the dozens of studies examined by the reviewers, only the few presented in Chart 5-1 were designed to relate climate variables to student performance.

What is most striking is the observation that, with the exception of the Ehman research, which used a very restricted definition of classroom climate, none of the studies using self-report questionnaires reviewed in this paper have reported on cognitive or affective outcomes related to characteristics of the learning environment. This reflects in part the authors' preoccupation with instrument development and in part the treatment of classroom climate as a dependent variable.

Those studies which do relate climate to student outcomes have in most cases focused upon affective climate, with Flanders and his

Chart 5-1: Studies Relating Climate to Student Outcomes

Author and Date	Research Instrument	Age Group Studied	Relationship
1. Guggenheim, 1961	Pupil-Teacher Rapport Scale (Wrightstone)	3rd Grade	No significant difference in math achievement between classrooms at different ends of the dominative-integrative scale.
2. Brown, 1960	Climate Index (Withall)	3rd Grade	Positive significant relationship between climate index and arithmetic reasoning.
3. Perkins, 1951	Climate Index (Withall)	Experiment with Elementary Teachers	Group-centered climate less conducive to tensions in classroom and more likely to reduce tensions when they arise.
4. Flanders, 1965, 1970	Interaction Analysis System (Flanders)	Grades 2-8	Clear relationship between "indirectness" and achievement in social studies and math, with "liking teacher more" as intervening variable.
5. La Shier, 1967	Interaction Analysis System (Flanders)	8th Grade	Positive significant relationship between teacher's indirectness and achievement in biology; positive attitudes.
6. Furst, 1967	Interaction Analysis System plus Bellack System	High School	High achieving classes differed from others in "extended" indirect teacher talk, more positive than negative feedback, more extended participation, with some evidence of curvilinearity.
7. Powell, 1968	Interaction Analysis System	3rd & 4th Grades	Positive significant relationship between indirectness and math achievement during years 1-3; no significant relationship in 4-h grade.

Author and Date	Research Instrument	Age Group Studied	Relationship
8. Soar, 1967, 1968	Interaction Analysis System plus Observation Schedule and Record	Grades 3-6	Pupil growth closely related to "extended discourse vs. rapid teacher-pupil interchange"; frequency of verbal hostility and criticism negatively related to pupil gains in arithmetic; indirectness related to creativity score gains and liking for class.
9. Wallen, 1966	Modified Interaction Analysis System	Grades 1-3	Positive correlations between achievement gains and "stimulating teacher," liking school and warm, permissive teacher; negative correlation between increased anxiety and supportive behavior, creativity and controlling behavior.
10. Medley and Mitzel, 1958, 1959	Observation Schedule and Record (OScAR)	Grades 3-5	Emotional climate accounts for difference in teacher rapport with students; not related to teacher's ability to help pupils learn.
11. Spaulding, 1963	Transaction Sample: Classroom (TSC)	4th & 6th Grades	Positive relationship between child's self-concept and socially integrative as well as learner supportive behaviors of teachers; reading and math gains not related to type of teacher nor were originality and flexibility related to creativity in teacher; reading achievement significantly related to "businesslike" lecture method, attention to task, and conformity to rules of procedure.

| 12. Minuchin et al., 1969 | No name (unique instrument) | Elementary School | Modern school philosophy related to more differentiated and imaginative thinking in children, also to more acceptance of negative impulses and more investment in childhood status; traditional school philosophy related to better performance on conventional achievement tests. |
| 13. Ehman, 1969 | Classroom Climate Scale | High School Social Studies Classes | Intellectually open climate has positive intervening effect between exposure to controversial issues and positive political attitude changes. |

students dominating the field. Even these studies have shown no clear-cut relationship between climates and achievement. Of the ten studies where a relationship exists, six indicate a positive relationship between a "good climate" and higher achievement, and four show no significant relationship. Of the six studies showing a positive relationship, four used the Flanders concept of "indirectness." Within the domain of cognitive climate only three studies report student outcomes (Spaulding, 1963; Furst, 1967; Minuchin et al., 1969). Once again, mixed results have been found. Minuchin et al. and Spaulding report a positive relationship between student achievement and more traditional classroom climates, though both also show that "openness" is positively related to affective outcomes such as creativity or improved self-concept. Furst shows a positive relationship between achievement and cognitive climates, although the relationship appears to be curvilinear.

The lack of a clear-cut relationship between climate and student outcomes leads us to the following possible conclusions: 1) some measurements of climate have been of questionable validity; 2) classroom climate, as operationally defined in the studies reviewed, may be too global a concept to have any strong predictive value with respect to outcome variables; 3) the definitions of climate may have been so diverse that comparable results cannot be expected; and 4) even valid measures of climate may not be related to student outcomes in any simple linear fashion.

Conclusions

Most of the literature reviewed here has been descriptive in nature; much work has been done in characterizing the learning environment and in measuring its association with other variables prevalent in the classroom. However, the real benefit of measuring environment comes when we can successfully predict the outcomes of the various kinds of learning environment, as well as explain how environment brings about the various outcomes it is thought to affect. The correlational studies reviewed here are important to this endeavor, but they are merely a start. Even so, there are disappointing discoveries to be made in reviewing this literature.

The weaknesses in validation reporting have already been discussed in a previous section of this paper. And for some reason not evident to these reviewers, the self-report pupil questionnaires were not often correlated with cognitive achievement and attitude development as dependent variables. Presumably, it is these very things that we wish to affect in the classroom, and it would be helpful to know if high inference instruments measure anything which systematically varies with them. Another problematic area has to do with teacher perceptions: most of this research assumes that the teacher is the principle agent of the climate of the classroom; surely her perception of the environment of her classroom has something to do with how she teaches and, therefore, with student outcome. Yet we found no studies that correlated teacher perceptions with student achievement or development.

Much work has already been done with observational techniques and they are in widespread use by educational practitioners. However, self-report questionnaires are potentially more useful in the classroom because they can be standardized, are economical, and can pick up far more data than observers in a much shorter amount of time. Beyond this, the entire educational community, both scholars and practitioners, would benefit if the two main currents of this research could be merged in such a way that the best techniques and conceptualizations of each could be used in the complicated task of validly assessing the school environment. Combining observation and survey techniques would both provide a more complete and detailed picture of the environment and allow for more powerful tests of validity.

As emphasized earlier, the real payoff comes when these instruments can successfully be used as predictors of learning, and that requires explanatory as well as descriptive research. We need theories that specify which aspects of environment are critical to learning and which are not; theories that specify the processes by which environment affects learning; theories that will test our ideas of what constitutes a "good" learning environment. And these theories need systematic testing. Education climate research has achieved a certain maturity over the past forty years. But many why, how, when and where questions still need to be answered in order to make this body of research of lasting value to evaluators of educational performance.

References

Amidon, E. J., and Flanders, N. A. *The Role of the Teacher in the Classroom*. Minneapolis: Paul S. Amidon & Assoc. 1963.

Amidon, E. J., and Hough, J. *Interaction Analysis: Theory, Research, and Application.* Reading, Mass: Addison-Wesley, 1967.

Anderson, H. H., and Brewer, H. M. "Studies of Teachers' Classroom Personalities. I: Dominative and Socially Integrative Behavior of Kindergarten Teachers." *Psychological Monographs* 6 (1945).

Andrews, J. H. M. "School Organizational Climate: Some Validity Studies." *Canadian Education and Research Digest* 5 (1965): 317-34.

Bellack, A. et al. *The Language of the Classroom.* USOE Cooperative Research Project. New York: Teachers College, Columbia University, 1966.

Biddle, B. J., and Adams, R. S. "An Analysis of Classroom Activities." Final Report, USOE Contract No. 3-20-002. Columbia, Mo.: Center for Research in Social Behavior, 1967.

Bloom, B. S., ed. "Taxonomy of Educational Objectives," in *Handbook: Cognitive Domain.* New York: Longmans Green, 1956.

Brown, G. I. "Which Pupil to Which Classroom Climate?" *Elementary School Journal* 60 (1960): 265-69.

Ehman, Lee H. "An Analysis of the Relationships of Selected Educational Variables with the Political Socialization of High School Students." *American Educational Research Journal* 6, no. 4 (1969): 559-80.

Flanders, N. A. "Some Relationships among Teacher Influence, Pupil Attitudes, and Achievement." In *Contemporary Research on Teacher Effectiveness,* edited by Biddle and Ellena. New York: Holt, Rinehart and Winston, 1964.

Flanders, N. A. *Analyzing Teacher Behavior.* Reading, Mass.: Addison-Wesley Co., 1970.

Fortune, J. C., Gage, N. L., and Shutes, R. E. "A Study of the Ability to Explain." Paper at AERA Annual Meeting, 1966.

Furst, N. F. "The Multiple Languages of the Classroom: A Further Analysis and a Synthesis of Meanings Communicated in High School Teaching." Ph.D. dissertation, Temple University, 1967.

Gallagher, J. J., et al. *A System of Topic Classification.* Urbana: Institute for Research on Exceptional Children, University of Illinois, 1966.

Gentry, H. W., and Kenney, J. B. "A Comparison of the Organizational Climates of Negro and White Elementary Schools." *The Journal of Psychology* 60 (1965): 171-79.

Getzels, J. W., and Thelen, H. A. "The Classroom as a Unique Social System." *The 59th Yearbook of the National Society for the Study of Education.* Part II, 1960, 53-82.

Guggenheim, F. "Classroom Climate and the Learning of Mathematics." *Arithmetic Teacher* 8 (1961): 363-67.

Guilford, J. P. "The Structure of Intellect." *Psychological Bulletin* 53 (1956): 267-93.

Guilford, J. P. "The Three Faces of Intellect." *American Psychologist* 14 (1959): 469-79.

Halpin, A. W., and Croft, D. B. "The Organizational Climate of Schools." *Administrators Notebook* 11, no. 7 (1963): 1-4.

Heller, R. W. "Informal Organization and Perceptions of the Organizational Climate of Schools." *Journal of Educational Research* 61 (1968): 405-11.

Herr, E. I. "Differential Perceptions of 'Environmental Press' by High School Students as Related to Their Achievement and Participation in Activities." *Personnel and Guidance Journal* 43, no. 7 (1965): 678-86.

Honigman, F. K. *Multidimensional Analysis of Classroom Interaction.* Villanova, Pa.: Villanova University Press, 1967.

Kenney, J. B., White, W. F., and Gentry, H. W. "Personality Characteristics of Teachers and Their Perception of Organizational Climate." *Journal of Psychology* 66 (1967): 167-74.

La Shier, W. S. "The Use of Interaction Analysis in BSCS Laboratory Block Classrooms." *Journal of Teacher Education* 18 (1967): 439-46.

MacDonald, J. B., and Zaret, E. "A Study of Openness in Classroom Interactions." Paper read at AERA Annual Meeting, 1967.

Medley, D. M., and Mitzel, H. E. "A Technique for Measuring Classroom Behavior." *Journal of Educational Psychology* 49 (1958): 86-92.

Medley, D. M., and Mitzel, H. E. "Some Behavior Correlates of Teacher Effectiveness." *Journal of Educational Psychology* 50 (1959): 239-46.

Minuchin, P. et al. *The Psychological Impact of School Experience: A Comparative Study of Nine-Year-Old Children in Contrasting Schools.* New York: Basic Books, Inc., 1969.

Mitchell, J. V., Jr. "Dimensionality and Differences in the Environmental Press of High Schools." *American Educational Research Journal* 5, no. 4 (1968): 513-30.

Mitzel, H. E., and Rabinowitz, W. "Assessing Social-Emotional Climate in the Classroom by Withall's Technique." *Psychological Monographs: General and Applied* 67, no. 18 (1953): 1-19.

Pace, R. "College and University Environment Scale." *Technical Manual,* 2nd Edition. Princeton, New Jersey: Educational Testing Service, 1969.

Perkins, H. V. "Climate Influences on Group Learning." *Journal of Educational Research* 45 (1951): 115-19.

Powell, E. R. "Teacher Behavior and Pupil Achievement." Paper read at AERA Annual Meeting, 1968.

Rosenshine, B. "Some Criteria for Evaluating Category Systems: An Application to the Topic Classification System." *AERA Monograph Series on Curriculum Evaluation #6: Classroom Observation,* edited by J. J. Gallagher, G. A. Nuthall, and B. Rosenshine. Chicago: Rand McNally and Co., 1970.

_____ . *Teaching Behaviors and Student Achievement.* Sussex, England: King, Thorne and Stace, Ltd., 1971.

Shaw, M. E., and Wright, J. M. *Scales for the Measurement of Attitudes.* New York: McGraw-Hill, 1967.

Siegel, L., and Siegel, L. C. "The Instructional Gestalt." In *Instruction: Some Contemporary Viewpoints,* edited by L. Siegel. San Francisco: Chandler Publishing, 1967.

Sinclair, R. L. "Elementary School Educational Environment: Measurement of Selected Variables of Environmental Press." *Dissertation Abstracts,* University of Massachusetts, 1969.

Soar, R. S. "Pupil Growth over Two Years in Relation to Differences in Classroom Process." Paper read at AERA Annual Meeting, 1967.

Soar, R. S. "Teacher-Pupil Interaction and Pupil Growth." Paper read at AERA Annual Meeting, Chicago, 1968.

Spaulding, R. L. *Achievement, Creativity, and Self-Concept Correlates of Teacher-Pupil Transactions in Elementary Schools.* U.S. Office of Education Cooperative Research Project No. 1352. Urbana: University of Illinois, 1963.

Steele, J. M., House, E. R., and Kerins, T. "An Instrument for Assessing Instructional Climate through Low-Inference Student Judgments." *American Educational Research Journal* 8, no. 3 (1971): 447-66.

Steele, J. M. et al. *Instructional Climate in Illinois Gifted Classes.*

Center for Instructional Research and Curriculum Evaluation. Urbana: University of Illinois, 1970.

Stern, G. G. *People in Context.* New York: Wiley, 1970.

Stern, G. G., Stein, M. I., and Bloom, B. S. *Methods in Personality Assessment.* Glencoe, Illinois: Free Press, 1956.

Trickett, F. J., and Moos, R. H. *Assessment of the Psychosocial Environment of the High School Classroom.* Stanford, California: Stanford University School of Medicine, 1971.

Walberg, H. J. "Models for Optimizing and Individualizing School Learning." *Interchange* 2, no. 3 (1971): 15-27.

Walberg, H. J., and Thomas, S. C. "Open Education: An Operational Definition." *American Educational Research Journal* 9, no. 2 (1972): 197-208.

Wallen, N. E. *Relationships Between Teacher Characteristics and Student Behavior,* Part 3. U.S. Office of Education Cooperative Research Project No. SAE OE5-10-181. Salt Lake City: University of Utah, 1966.

Withall, J. "Development of the Climate Index." *Journal of Educational Research* 45 (1951): 93-99.

Withall, J. "The Development of a Technique for the Measurement of Social-Emotional Climate in Classrooms." *Journal of Experimental Education* 17, (1949): 347-61.

Wrightstone, J. W. "Measuring Teacher Conduct of Class Discussion." *Elementary School Journal* 34 (1934): 454-60.

6. LEARNING ENVIRONMENTS
Gary J. Anderson
Herbert J. Walberg

This chapter is divided into four sections which treat the following questions: What is the social environment of learning as theoretically conceptualized and operationalized by the present authors? What determines the learning environment? How are aspects of the environment related to cognitive, affective, and behavioral learning outcomes? And how can measurements of the environment be used in evaluative research?

The Social Environment of Learning

In the last decade, the study of environments has emerged as an area of strong interest in social science research. This research has focused on the context, ecology, or milieu of behavior, particularly the social-psychological aspects. Originating with Darwin, social science research was applied to the study of society by Herbert Spencer and incorporated into the mainstreams of sociology and psychology by George Herbert Mead and John Dewey, becoming known as "social" or "symbolic interactionism" in sociology and "Chicago functionalism" in psychology during the 1920s. More recently, the psychological study of the context of behavior has had its advocates in Egon Brunswick, Kurt Lewin, and Richard Snow. (See Walberg, 1971, for additional background.)

The authors thank Andrew Ahlgren and Wayne Welch for comments on an earlier draft manuscript.

Bloom (1964) made a strong case for environmental research in education. Reviewing and consolidating work on growth rates and environmental effects, Bloom pointed to the development of measures of environment as crucial for accurate prediction and effective manipulation of learning. The work of Dave (1963) and Wolf (1963) on home environments and of Pace and Stern (1958) and others on college environments has confirmed the powerful effects of contextual variables on learning (see Bloom 1964).

Since 1966, a series of studies has demonstrated that student perceptions of the classroom learning environment can be measured reliably and that environmental measures are valid predictors of learning (Walberg, 1969a). Environmental variables themselves can be manipulated (Anderson, Walberg, and Welch, 1969) and predicted from the class size, the biographical characteristics of its members, the mean ingelligence, prior interests and achievements of pupils, and instructional variables (Walberg and Ahlgren, 1970). Moreover, powerful interactions have been identified between environment and both instructional variables (Walberg, 1969b) and individual differences in aptitudes and personality (Anderson, 1968; Bar-Yam, 1969).

The classroom environment may be conceptualized as one of four components of the learning process (Walberg, 1971), as shown in Table 6-1. The working definitions in the table indicate that environment has the same relation to instruction as ability has to achievement: while environment has to do with the context of learning and ability with the student, both are more general, implicit, and endur-

Table 6-1. Definitions of, and relations between, four domains

Relative characteristics

Locus	Specific, Intended, Temporary	General, Implicit, Enduring
Student	Learning (or Achievement) —a change in (or state of) thought, feeling or behavior	Aptitude (or Ability)—a characteristic of the individual that predicts learning
Context	Instruction—a stimulus intended to bring about learning	Environment—a stimulus, aside from instruction, that predicts learning

ing than their more specific, intended and temporary counterparts, instruction and achievement. Thus, as factor analysts have sought those general abilities that underlie surface academic achievements, we have sought the underlying environmental forces manifested in the context of learning through the content and method of instruction.

The research considered here involves three major instruments that have been developed to assess aspects of the learning environment: the Learning Environment Inventory, the My Class Inventory, and the Class Activities Questionnaire. The fifteen scales on the Learning Environment Inventory (LEI) are intended to be comprehensive and valid for predicting learning outcomes. The first version of the instrument was patterned by Walberg on Hemphill's (1956) Group Dimensions Description Questionnaire, an instrument designed to tap fourteen group characteristics that had been derived from one of the most extensive (in terms of numbers of groups and variables) factor analytic studies of small adult groups ever conducted. While the LEI proved to be valid (Anderson and Walberg, 1968; Walberg and Anderson, 1968a), content, item, and factor analyses suggested a number of improvements that were carried out by Walberg and Anderson. This first revision was again validated (Anderson, 1970; Walberg, 1971), and on the basis of these results Anderson (1971) prepared a final version by rewriting some items and adding a fifteenth scale.

A typical item on the "Satisfaction" scale is, "The students enjoy their class work." In evaluating their own class, the students choose among four responses: Strongly Agree, Agree, Disagree, or Strongly Disagree. Unlike teacher observation and counting schedules that require elaborate hand coding and processing, the LEI may be easily machine-scored by key punching the item responses and adding the appropriately keyed answers on a computer. There are seven items on each of the fifteen scales listed in Table 6-2.

The LEI is convenient and easy to administer. It does not mention the teacher at all and so does not pose the threat of other instruments that explicitly focus on teacher characteristics and behavior. Moreover, in not singling out the teacher, the LEI acts on our assumption that the class members themselves, as well as the teacher, are an important determinant of the learning environment. For research efficiency, the instrument has typically been administered to

Table 6-2. Learning environment inventory scales

| Scales | Sample Items | Reliabilities | | Class |
| | | Individual | | |
		Alpha[1]	Test Re-test[2]	Intraclass
Cohesiveness	Members of the class are personal friends.	.69	.52	.85
Diversity	The class divides its efforts among several purposes.	.53	.43	.31
Formality	Students are asked to follow a complicated set of rules.	.76	.55	.92
Speed	The class has difficulty keeping up with its assigned work.	.70	.51	.81
Environment	The books and equipment students need or want are easily available to them in the classroom.	.56	.64	.81
Friction	Certain students are considered uncooperative.	.72	.73	.83
Goal Direction	The objectives of the class are specific.	.85	.65	.75
Favoritism	Only the good students are given special projects.	.78	.64	.76
Difficulty	Students are constantly challenged.	.64	.46	.78
Apathy	Members of the class don't care what the class does.	.82	.61	.61

Democratic	Class decisions tend to be made by all the students.	.67	.69	.67
Cliqueness	Certain students work only with their close friends.	.65	.68	.71
Satisfaction	Students are well-satisfied with the work of the class.	.79	.71	.84
Disorganization	The class is disorganized.	.82	.72	.92
Competitiveness	Students compete to see who can do the best work.	.78	—	.56

1. Alpha coefficients were obtained from 1048 individual pupils while intraclass correlations for the reliability of class means are based on 64 classes in the Montreal sample, but do not differ substantially from those calculated using the Harvard data. The intraclass reliabilities are for half-classes and would be somewhat higher for the whole class.

2. Test re-test coefficients were calculated using 139 students in three Boston high schools, and were obtained over a four-week interval under extremely poor conditions (see Miller, 1971).

random halves of the class while other class members complete other instruments; however, all class members can complete the LEI if higher reliability is desired. Also, it is possible to omit some scales that are not of interest in a particular evaluation to cut down on the regular testing time of about thirty-five minutes. Over two hundred American, British, Canadian, French, German, Swedish, Indian, Australian, and New Zealand investigators, who have written for the LEI, have been encouraged to tailor the selection and adaption of scales to their specific research or evaluation objectives.

While a full theoretical rationale for the LEI would require a more comprehensive treatment than the publications devoted to it (Anderson, 1967, 1970; Walberg, 1971), a few comments on why the methodology has proven comparatively valid are in order here. First, the student is the intended recipient of instruction and other cues in the classroom, particularly social stimuli; and he may be the best judge of the learning context. Compared with a short-term observer, he weights in his judgment not only the class as it presently is but how it has been since the beginning of the year. He is able to compare from the child-client point of view his class with those in past grades, with others he is presently taking, or even with other small groups of which he is a member. He and his classmates form a group of twenty or thirty sensitive, well-informed judges of the class; an outside observer is a single judge who has far less data and, though highly trained and systematic, may be insensitive to what is important in a particular class.

On the other hand, the LEI scales are "high-inference" measures (Walberg, Sorensen, and Fischbach, 1972) in that they require subjective ratings of perceived behavior, unlike "low-inference" measures which are objective counts of observed behavior. Because they reflect psychology's current behavioristic ethos, low-inference measures of teacher and class behavior are far more prevalent. Low-inference scales have the advantage that, if valid, they directly suggest changes in specific teacher behavior, such as, "increase the number of questions you ask from two to four per minute." However, low-inference measures are generally substantially less valid in predicting learning outcomes than are high-inference measures (Walberg, 1971). Why? Perhaps because counts of praise or questions measure quantity rather than quality, and may have limited relevance to student abilities, interests, and needs. For example, one profound and appropriate question may inspire learning more than ten superficial ones; and one sincere "not bad" from an intellectually demanding teacher or student peer may be more potent than "great, good, right" from one who says it often. Thirty students may be able to judge these things better than an evaluator or researcher who counts them.

Two additional instruments of interest in this review are the My Class Inventory (MCI) (Anderson, 1973; Maguire, Goetz, and Manos, 1972), and the Class Activities Questionnaire (CAQ) (Walberg, House, and Steele, 1973). The MCI is a reworked version of the LEI, consisting of five, nine-item scales in a simple agree-disagree format appropriate for younger children. The MCI, with its scales Friction, Competitiveness, Difficulty, Satisfaction, and Cohesiveness, has proved useful in a variety of studies with six- to twelve-year-olds.

The Class Activities Questionnaire is similar to the LEI except that it was constructed to measure the six levels of Bloom's (1956) taxonomy. It would be interesting to investigate the relations of the LEI socio-psychological variables with CAQ cognitive dimensions. Moreover, both instruments might be used in evaluation research to assess the affective-social and cognitive domains.

Determinants of the Learning Environment

What determines the learning environment? In this section, a number of studies are briefly described under three subheadings: curriculum, class size, and other correlates.

Curriculum

Anderson, Walberg and Welch (1969) reported a study conducted with the LEI on a national sample of 150 high school classes. A national random sample of physics teachers were randomly assigned to teach either Harvard Project Physics (HPP), a new course undergoing evaluation, or the course they ordinarily taught; also, a group teaching HPP for a second year was included in the analysis. Multivariate and univariate statistical tests revealed that, as the course developers had hoped, HPP was seen as less difficult, more diverse, and as providing a more stimulating environment than other courses; cliques and friction among class members were perceived as less frequent among HPP students. The classes of teachers using HPP for the first time were viewed as more democratic and cohesive than those of the other two groups of teachers.

The main evaluation of the HPP course (Welch and Walberg, 1972) compared only the randomly assigned groups for a true experiment. While this comparison confirmed that the HPP classes are perceived as less difficult and the activities as more diverse, the two studies taken together suggest that the environmental differences between courses increase with teachers' increasing experience with a new course.

Anderson (1971), using discriminant function analysis, compared the learning environments of sixty-two science, mathematics, humanities, and French classes in Montreal. Mathematics classes were seen as relatively high on Favoritism, Difficulty, Disorganization, and Cliqueness and low on Formality and Goal Direction; apparently, mathematics classes at the high school level do not reflect the elegant formality and organization of the subject. A second dimension of differences between the courses showed that science classes are more formal, difficult, and fast-moving, while humanities courses are relatively disorganized and easy. The last dimension showed that French classes are comparatively high on Goal Direction and low on Friction and Disorganization.

Walberg, Steele, and House (1974) followed up on this study and compared several subject areas on the CAQ ratings of cognitive emphasis in 121 classes. Three discriminant functions were found. The first, Convergence-Divergence, contrasts mathematics with other subjects; the second, Substance-Syntax, contrasts social studies and science with language arts and mathematics; and the third, Objectivity-Subjectivity, contrasts science with social studies. The pattern of cognitive press on the first two functions was very reminiscent of Anderson's first two functions, despite the instrument differences.

Shaw and MacKinnon (1973) used the LEI to evaluate mathematics classes at Lord Elgin High School in Ontario. The main comparison involved almost 600 students in the experimental mathematics program whose scores were contrasted with those of the 1048 subjects obtained in 1969 by Anderson (1971). Lord Elgin students perceived their classes as more cohesive, goal directed, satisfying, and as containing more Friction, Favouritism, Cliqueness, Disorganization, Difficulty, and Competitiveness.

These four, involving subject matter differences in social environment and cognitive press, suggest that there are important heretofore unanalyzed differences in the various parts of the curriculum. More research is needed to produce a typology of social and cognitive stimulation provided in different courses and subject areas.

Class size

Many studies of class size have failed to produce consistently significant correlates with cognitive and affective qualities. However, two studies of the LEI replicated two significant correlates. Walberg (1969c) using 149 physics classes and Anderson and Walberg (1972) using 61 Montreal classes in several subject areas found smaller classes to be significantly higher on Cohesiveness and Difficulty. While small groups of many kinds are generally perceived as more cohesive (Cartwright and Zander, 1968), we speculate that smaller classes are perceived as more difficult because students are less able to use them to conceal low personal productivity. Smaller classes might be encouraged not only because teachers and students prefer them but because the two significant correlates have been associated with cognitive and affective outcomes in other studies. The LEI may be tapping those aspects of environment that stimulate educational growth that are not well measured by conventional achievement tests.

Other studies

Walberg, House, and Steele (1973) investigated the relation of grade level with cognitive press and affective characteristics measured on the CAQ. A cross-sectional study of 121 classes in grades six through twelve revealed that students in higher grades saw their classes as less stimulating and enjoyable than did students in the lower grades. High school students also viewed their classes as emphasizing factual memorization, while elementary school students saw greatest emphasis on higher-level cognitive processes such as analysis, synthesis and evaluation. The most undesirable classes in the students' perception were at the sophomore and junior levels, the years of highest drop-out rates.

Walberg and Ahlgren (1970) investigated the predictability of the LEI scales from other educational variables in 144 physics classes. Initial class interest and ability in physics were associated with high levels of perceived Difficulty, Disorganization, and Speed and low levels of Formality, Goal Direction, and Democracy. With respect to biographical characteristics of class members, classes with sociable, less bookish members were rated higher on Cohesiveness; classes with more college-bound students, science prize winners, and those with high grade point averages scored higher on Difficulty.

Walberg, Sorensen, and Fischbach (1972) adapted the LEI to measure school environment in the middle grades and administered the scales to all fifth grade students in forty Wisconsin high schools. The analysis revealed that the higher the socioeconomic (SES) levels of the school, the less competitive the high-SES children perceive the school as being, but the more competitive low-SES children see it as being. Thus the LEI is sensitive to the composition of the student body, and it can be used as one set of indicators for the success of social interventions such as bussing for integration and also to measure the effectiveness of the school in providing a good learning environment for different types of children.

Shaw and MacKinnon's (1973) study of mathematics classes included subjects in grades 9-13, enabling a comparison across grade levels. Four significant results were obtained: Formality, Favouritism, and Goal Direction got progressively less at the higher grade levels while Democratic scores got lower. It should be noted that the Goal Direction and Formality differences are no doubt due in part to the extensive use of behavioral objectives in the lower grades.

In addition to these nine studies, several others can be cited to illustrate the range of variables that have been related to perceptions of the learning environment. Walberg (1968) examined the relationship of teacher personality to the environment of their classes; Van Kovering (1969) related the LEI to changing physics enrollments; MCI scores have been compared for Title I children and others (Walberg and Anderson, 1968b); graded schools have been compared to continuous progress schools by Ramayya (1971); and the effects of bussing for integration have been explored using the MCI (Walberg, 1970).

Environments and Learning

The past five years have seen a variety of research on the correlates of classroom social climate and various measures of student learning. These Learning Environment Inventory studies have included a variety of units of analysis, measures of learning outcomes, and statistical techniques. Researchers have examined the relationships between individual and class mean measures of the learning environment on the one hand, and individual and class mean learning outcomes on the other. Thus there are four combinations of individual and group variables to be compared. Note that the various combinations address themselves to different kinds of questions. To answer the question, "How does an individual student's perception of his learning environment affect the amount of learning which he himself can demonstrate over the course of the year," one would compare individual classroom climate scores with measures of individual learning. The bulk of research done to date, however, suggests that measures of the learning environment are essentially group characteristics and that the most meaningful way of analyzing the effects of the learning environment on outcomes is to use climate measures as class variables by calculating the class mean score or the mean for some fraction of class members. We can, moreover, examine the effects of group climate both on the learning of the group as a whole and on the learning of individual members within it. It must be stressed that measures of learning for the class mean are not readily transferable to individual students. In many cases the effects are similar, but this is not necessarily so.

The first major question to be answered is, "Is the Learning Environment Inventory a useful predictor of student learning?" To answer this question adequately we should examine the results of other well-known predictors of student learning and determine whether or not such instruments as the LEI predict substantially more variance in learning than do better-established predictors. Several research studies have attempted to do this by using the most successful predictor of learning yet devised, the intelligence quotient, to determine both whether the LEI predicts more variance in learning than does IQ, and whether it predicts different variance from that predicted by IQ.

Table 6-3 lists a number of studies in which this question was considered. As demonstrated by the studies in this table, IQ generally accounts for no more than 16 percent of the variance in learning, when the effect of present scores has been removed. The combination of all the LEI scales accounts for between 13 and 46 percent, and a substantial percentage of this variance in learning outcomes is predicted uniquely by the LEI. The studies in Table 6-3 consider cognitive, affective, and behavioral learning outcomes. While the

Table 6-3. General predictability of learning outcomes
from LEI scales.

Percent Learning Variance Predictable[1]

	IQ Alone	LEI Scales Alone	LEI Scales with IQ Partialled out
Anderson & Walberg (1968)			
Cognitive$_1$	0	33	—
Cognitive$_2$	7	46	—
Affective$_1$	0	34	—
Walberg & Anderson (1972)			
Cognitive$_1$	7	43	38
Cognitive$_2$	12	46	36
Walberg (1971)			
Cognitive$_1$	16	30	—
Cognitive$_2$	12	21	—
Cognitive$_3$	13	18	—
Affective$_1$	3	19	—
Affective$_2$	1	17	—
Behavioral	0	13	—

1. In these studies learning criteria have been adjusted for pre-tests, reducing considerably the amount of variance predictable from measures of IQ alone.

methods of assessing the latter have not always been optimal, they have generally been predictable from LEI scales.

What are the effects of individual measures of classroom social climate on student learning? To consider this question, let us consider three studies, selected because they represent three different samples of subjects and because they are fairly comprehensive in scope. Their findings supplement previous studies using earlier forms of the Learning Environment Inventory.

Anderson (1970) related class means on the LEI to individual cognitive, affective, and behavioral measures of student gains in learning. Subjects included those participating in the Harvard Project Physics Evaluation, and specific students who had fulfilled certain criteria were randomly selected. Thus the analysis incorporated the effects of students' IQ, interactions between LEI class scores and individual student IQ, as well as nonlinear LEI effects on the various measures of learning. In overall terms, individual scales on the LEI were significantly related to cognitive and affective measures of student learning, but there were fewer relationships with paper-and-pencil measures of behavioral outcomes. Positive effects on learning were reported for the Cohesiveness and Difficulty scales. Friction bore a negative relationship to learning but in one instance, with the female sample, was positively related to a measure of "science understanding." For the two cognitive measures, class mean IQ accounted for 5 percent to 25 percent of variance in learning, while the best LEI scales practically doubled these figures to a maximum of 36 percent. This study illustrates that some environments are best for students at high IQ levels while other environments are more appropriate for other types of students.

Walberg (1971) examined the relationships of a large number of student and class characteristics to six learning criteria. His sample included over 150 classes in the Harvard Project Physics Evaluation, and the analysis revealed positive correlations between class difficulty and cognitive learning, and between satisfaction and measures of interest. Negative correlations were reported between class friction and perceived apathy and the various measures of learning, and apathy and cliqueness were negatively related to measures of behavioral learning which included science activities.

The Walberg and Anderson (1972) study had the advantage of incorporating a sample which included sixty-four classes in eight different subject areas: mathematics, physics, chemistry, biology, English, history, geography, and French. As reported in the other two studies, the scales Cohesiveness, Environment, and Satisfaction bore positive relationships to cognitive learning, while Friction, Cliqueness, and Apathy were negatively related to learning measures. Speed, Favoritism, and Disorganization were also negatively related to learning. This was the only one of the three studies incorporating the Competitiveness scale that bore both positive and negative relationships to learning in the various subject areas. For example, Competitiveness was positively correlated with learning in mathematics classes and bore an equally high negative correlation with achievement in physics classes. In this study, the learning criteria included such measures as course achievement, with the effect of class IQ statistically removed. With the effect of IQ removed in this way, the correlations were reduced by about 10 percent, again indicating the power of the LEI to predict learning outcomes.

In summary, these studies imply that about half the LEI scales— Cohesiveness, Environment, Friction, Cliqueness, Satisfaction, Disorganization, and Apathy—account for substantial variance in measures of student learning. While the directions of relationship are generally what one would expect, the studies have served to document these relationships.

The data reported so far have involved overall effects on samples. In many cases these studies have been subdivided and analyses have included different subject matters, sex differences, levels of initial ability, and other such important variables. It is beyond the scope of this chapter to include all the findings incorporating these combinations of variables, but a few will be reported to indicate the types of effects that have been uncovered.

Anderson (1970) found that classroom climate scores were positively related to scores on the Science Process Inventory for females but that the relationship was negative for male subjects. Scales such as Cohesiveness, Apathy, and Environment have been differentially related to student learning in the various subject areas. Strong relationships were found between these scales and the learning of history, physics, and mathematics, but the relationships were much less strong in such subject areas as chemistry, biology, and English. Clearly, these types of differential findings indicate a need for more intensive, in-depth study of the relationships between classroom social climate and student learning.

Evaluation and Research

How can measures of the learning environment best be used in evaluative research? A major concern of researchers is the use of appropriate measures for comparing various educational methods, treatments, curricula, student groups, and teaching strategies, to name just a few of the hundreds of research questions of this type.

The high-inference measures described in this chapter have proven to be extremely sensitive in tapping differences among groups—indeed, these measures of the learning environment have often been the only source of statistically significant comparisons. Researchers are learning increasingly that valid and useful differences among educational treatments are often reflected first and most strongly in changes in students perceptions of their learning environment. Later, and in moderated form, these changes also show up in terms of student learning and other such indicators of outcome. Thus, dimensions of the MCI, LEI, and CAQ are useful additions to the types of instruments typically used in evaluative research.

The sensitivity of LEI-type instruments in post hoc analysis should not be an excuse for weak experimental designs. Indeed, the instruments are probably most useful when administered both "prc" and "post" experimental treatment. Although little work has been conducted to date on changes in environmental perceptions as a result of intervention, such a line of inquiry should become a preoccupation in the future. The usefulness of documenting how children's feelings about their classes change as a result of curricular, organizational, or even behavior modification methods can hardly be denied by researchers or practitioners.

In conclusion, educators interested in affective areas of school evaluation must include in their studies measures of the learning environment itself. Cognitive and even affective measures do not in themselves go far enough. Evaluation must take into account the group characteristics and social climate properties of groups of learners, however they may be organized in schools and beyond. Evaluators should explore the use of measures of the social climate of learning as a means of assessing the product of their educational efforts; in this case a desirable classroom climate would be a primary process goal of the school rather than a means to increase measurable learning outcomes.

References

Anderson, G. J. "The Reliability and Validity of a Measure of Classroom Climate." Qualifying paper, Harvard University, 1967.

_____ . "Effects of Classroom Social Climate on Individual Learning." Ph.D. dissertation, Harvard University, 1968.

_____. "Effects of Classroom Social Climate on Individual Learning." *American Educational Research Journal* 7, no. 2 (1970): 135-52.

_____. "Effects of Course Content and Teacher Sex on the Social Climate of Learning." *American Educational Research Journal* 8, no. 4 (1971) 649-63.

_____. *The Assessment of Learning Environments: A Manual for the Learning Environment Inventory and the My Class Inventory* (2nd ed.). Halifax, Nova Scotia: Atlantic Institute of Education, 1973.

Anderson, G. J., and Walberg, H. J. "Classroom Climate and Group Learning." *International Journal of the Educational Sciences* 2 (1968): 175-80.

Anderson, G. J., and Walberg, H. J. "Class Size and the Social Environment of Learning: A Mixed Replication and Extension." *Alberta Journal of Educational Research* 18, no. 4 (1972): 227-86.

Anderson, G. J., Walberg, H. J., and Welch, W. W. "Curriculum Effects on the Social Climate of Learning: A New Representation of Discriminant Functions." *American Educational Research Journal* 6, no. 3 (1969): 315-28.

Bar-Yam, M. "The Interaction of Student Characteristics with Instructional Strategies." Ph.D. dissertation, Harvard University, 1969.

Bloom, B. S., ed. *Taxonomy of Educational Objectives: Cognitive Domain.* New York: Longmans, Green, 1956.

_____. *Stability and Change in Human Characteristics.* New York: Wiley, 1964.

Cartwright, D., and Zander, A. *Group Dynamics: Research and Theory.* 3rd ed. Evanston, Illinois: Row, Peterson, 1968.

Dave, R. "The Identification and Measurement of Environmental Process Variables that are Related to Educational Achievement." Ph.D. dissertation, University of Chicago, 1963.

Hemphill, J. K. *Group Dimensions: A Manual for Their Measurement.* Columbus: Ohio State University Press, 1956.

Maguire, T. O., Goetz, E., and Manos, J. "Evaluation Activities of the IPI Project Year 2: The Evaluation of Two Instruments for Assessing Classroom Climate for Primary Grades." Alberta, Canada: Alberta Human Resources Research Council, 1972.

Miller, E. "Report on a Preliminary Study to Ascertain the Test-Retest Reliability of the Learning Environment Inventory." Mimeographed. Harvard Graduate School of Education, 1971.

Pace, C. R., and Stern, G. G. "An Approach to the Measurement of Psychological Characteristics of College Environments." *Journal of Educational Psychology* 49 (1958): 269-77.

Ramayya, D. P. "A Comparative Study of Achievement Skills, Personality Variables and Classroom Climate in Graded and Nongraded Programs." Ph.D. dissertation, University of Utah, 1971.

Shaw, A. R. and Mackinnon, P. *Evaluation of the Learning Environment.* Burlington, Ontario: Mathematics Department, Lord Elgin High School, 1973.

VonKovering, T. E. "The Distinguishing Characteristics of High Schools with High and Low Enrollments in Physics." Ph.D. dissertation, Michigan State University, 1969.

Walberg, H. J. "Teacher Personality and Classroom Climate." *Psychology in The Schools,* 5 (1968): 163-69.

————. "Predicting Class Learning. A Multivariate Approach to the Class as a Social System." *American Educational Research Journal* 4 (1969a): 529-42.

————. "The Social Environment as a Mediator of Classroom Learning." *Journal of Educational Psychology* 60 (1969b): 443-48.

————. "Class Size and the Social Environment of Learning." *Human Relations* 22, no. 5 (1969b): 465-75.

————. "An Evaluation of an Urban-Suburban Bussing Program: Student Achievement and Perception of Class Learning Environments." Boston, Mass: Metropolitan Council on Educational Opportunity, 1970.

————. "Models for Optimizing and Individualizing School Learning." *Interchange* 3, (1971): 15-27.

Walberg, H. J., and Ahlgren, A. "Predictors of the Social Environment of Learning." *American Educational Research Journal,* 7 (1970): 153-68.

Walberg, H. J., and Anderson, G. J. "Classroom Climate and Individual Learning." *Journal of Educational Psychology* 59 (1968a): 414-19.

Walberg, H. J., and Anderson, G. J. "The Evaluation of a Title I

Project Using the My Class Inventory." Harvard University, unpublished paper, (1968b).

Walberg, H. J., and Anderson, G. J. "Properties of the Achieving Urban Classes." *Journal of Educational Psychology* 63, no. 4 (1972): 381-85.

Walberg, H. J., House, E. R., and Steele, J. M. "Grade Level, Cognition and Affect: A Cross-Section of Classroom Perceptions. *Journal of Educational Psychology,* 1973, in press.

Walberg, H. J., Steele, J. M., and House, E. R. "Subject Matter Areas and Cognitive Press." *Journal of Educational Psychology*, 1974, in press.

Walberg, H. J., Sorenson, J., and Fischbach, T. "Ecological Correlates of Ambience in the Learning Environment." *American Educational Research Journal* 9, no. 1 (1972): 139-48.

Welch, W. W., and Walberg, H. J. "A National Experiment in Curriculum Evaluation." *American Educational Research Journal* 9 (1972): 373-83.

Wolf, R. M. "The Identification and Measurement of Environmental Process Variables that Are Related to Intelligence." Ph.D. dissertation, University of Chicago, 1963.

7. AFFECTIVE OUTCOMES
David W. Johnson

All learning has affective components. No matter what knowledge or skills a student masters, he will have feelings about the process and results of instruction. In mastering the skills of reading or in
learning about history a student develops feelings about reading and
about history, as well as about education and instruction, that will
influence his behavior in the future. Because students' affective responses to school experiences influence future behavior, the development of positive affective reactions may be more important than the
mastery of specific knowledge and skills. It does little good to teach
a student to read if he ends up disliking reading and avoids it whenever possible.

Since the overall purpose of the schools is to develop each
student to maximum capacity as a productive and happy member of
society, the real measure of success is not the degree to which students master material and skills, but whether the students voluntarily
use such knowledge and skills in their daily life outside of school. If
the school is to be successful in influencing a person's behavior after
he has completed his formal education, then the development of
positive affective responses toward learning and school-related skills
is of major importance.

The rapid technological and cultural change experienced by our
society over the past thirty years or so has greatly increased the
importance of affective outcomes of education, as has the increasing

99

emphasis on self-actualization and interpersonal skills. Bennis (1970), Slater (1970), Michael (1968), and Johnson (1972a, 1972b, 1973a) have all emphasized the need for persons who are skilled at being human within the organized complexity and constant change of our society.

Finally, in order to manage a school or a classroom productively it is important to specify affective objectives and to evaluate their accomplishment. In addition to knowing school and classroom procedures and regulations, the student should value and support them. Developing positive attitudes toward school can significantly improve the quality of school life and decrease problems in classroom and school management.

Definition of Affective Outcomes

There seems to be some confusion regarding the definition of affective outcomes of education. "Affective" is most often contrasted with "cognitive" in a way that implies that the two are quite separate aspects of learning. In this sense "affective" refers to the feeling or emotional aspects of experience and learning, while "cognitive" refers to the conceptual activity of the mind knowing an object, or to intellectual functioning. This separation of affect and cognition has been promoted by the traditional focus of schools on verbal-conceptual priorities. By and large, our schools are organized to produce people who can deal with the words, concepts, and mathematical or scientific symbols so necessary for success in our technological society, while the attitudes and values developed in students by those schools are generally ignored. Yet it should be emphasized that a person's affect and cognitions cannot be separated. Each affective behavior has a cognitive counterpart, and for every cognitive outcome there are changes in affect. To teach any concept, principle, or theory is to teach not only for its comprehension but also for an attitude toward it. For example, a school not only wants to teach the student to read, but to enjoy, appreciate, and value reading. Correspondingly, in order for a person to be aware of his feelings he has to conceptualize them and place them in the context of the situation he is experiencing. At the very least this calls for cognitions about his feelings; generally, it means that there is a cognitive component in experiencing a feeling.

Affective outcomes of education may be defined, without presenting a false dichotomy between feelings and cognitions, through the concepts of *attitude* and *value* (Watson and Johnson, 1972). Both attitudes and values are a combination of cognitions and feelings. An *attitude* may be defined as a predisposition to respond to a particular person, object, or situation in a favorable or unfavorable manner; an attitude is usually defined as having cognitive, affective, and behavioral components. A *value* exists whenever an emotion implying like or dislike attaches to a cognition; values express a relationship between a person's feelings and his particular cognitive categories. When a person states, "stealing is wrong," he is expressing a value by attaching feeling (wrongness) to the category "stealing." Anything that a person approaches, desires, or espouses reflects a positive value, while anything he avoids, dislikes, or deplores reflects a negative value. Both attitudes and values have properties that define what behavior is expected and desired; they can both, therefore, be thought of as motivational-perceptual states that direct action. That is, both attitudes and values serve as perceptual sets that motivate an individual to take certain actions when confronted with certain situations. Despite these common qualities, attitudes and values are usually differentiated. For one thing, individuals hold many more attitudes than values. An adult has hundreds of attitudes, but only dozens of values. A cluster of attitudes surrounds a value; a number of attitudes may express any given value. The affective outcomes of education may be defined, therefore, as the feelings, attitudes and values promoted by the school as a part of the instructional and socialization program.

It is important that the school emphasize certain attitudes and values. Positive self-attitudes, for example, have been shown to influence achievement as well as personal adjustment and acceptance of other individuals (Johnson, 1970, 1972a). Positive attitudes toward subject areas such as science and social studies are important in motivating learning, and positive attitudes toward skills such as reading and writing are essential for the educational programs of the school. Certainly being "role responsible" (having the capacity to live up to general expectations of appropriate role behavior, such as promptness, cleanliness, etc.) and having "role readiness" (the ability to meet the demands of many organizational settings with the proper cooperation) are important outcomes of schools. The commitment to an occupational role or to further education in preparation for an occupational role is an important affective outcome. Commitment to the development of personal resources and abilities, and to the experiencing of positive emotions and a sense of fulfillment, is an increasingly important educational outcome. Valuing a pluralistic, democratic society, freedom of choice, equality of opportunity, self-reliance, differences among individuals, and a lack of ethnic prejudice are important outcomes of schooling. Values relating to the importance and utility of education and to free and open inquiry into all problems are essential to the effective function of a school.

There is one final point that should be made about attitudes and values, and that is their relation to behavior. There is little consistent evidence to support the hypothesis that knowledge of an individual's attitudes will allow one to predict how he will behave. A learning theorist would argue that the learning of behavior occurs independently, so that there may be little relation between a person's attitudes and his behavior. For example, a student may learn to have positive attitudes toward teachers, but whether he engages in friendly behavior toward a particular teacher depends on the reinforcement he receives for doing so. Another problem in trying to predict a person's behavior from a knowledge of his attitudes is that most situations are so complex that several attitudes may be relevant to any action taken. Predicting whether a student who has favorable attitudes toward teachers will engage in friendly behavior toward a specific teacher at a specific time, for example, may depend on knowing such things as how the student feels physically (he may be sick and want to avoid other people) and what behaviors are competing with the predicted behavior (he may want to study for an exam or he may want to talk with his friends more than he wants to be friendly toward the teacher).

Improving School Functioning

Since education is a process that helps the learner to change in many ways, three of the principal tasks of students and school personnel are to decide, as far as possible: what changes should take place in learners; what part instructional programs (teachers, curriculum materials, etc.) can play in assisting learner change; and whether or not learners have changed in the desired ways. Students and school personnel may also be interested in determining whether any unanticipated changes have taken place in students. In the past, affective changes in learners have not been specified, planned for, or evaluated in many schools, although lip service is usually paid to the importance of affective outcomes. There are at least two reasons for this. The first is the lack of procedures and methods for obtaining evidence concerning the accomplishment of affective objectives in order to modify and improve instructional programs. A specific instrument for measuring students' affective responses to their school experience is discussed in a later section of this chapter.

A second reason for the lack of focus on affective variables is related to a narrow view of the concept of evaluation and the misperception that evaluation takes place only to help assign a grade to a student or to judge the effectiveness of teachers and other school personnel. Evaluation is a much broader process, employing a multitude of evidence-gathering techniques to help in decisions about the quality of an individual's or a group's performance, or the success of an instructional program in relation to stated objectives, or the impact of the school upon the student. It is important to emphasize that the results of any evaluation of the success of an instructional program in influencing student affective reactions are for the school personnel to use to modify and improve instruction, not to evaluate individual students or individual teachers. Students should not be graded on whether or not they have positive attitudes toward education, and teachers should not be evaluated on the basis of whether their students have positive attitudes. The instructional program consists of far more than the behavior of an individual teacher. Measurement of students' affective reactions can be used to improve the instructional program of the school and to evaluate the success of innovations and interventions aimed at this improvement.

Improving the functioning of a school or a school system includes several broad components:

1. *Specifying a normative model indicating the variables upon which school functioning should be evaluated.* This model should include both affective and verbal-conceptual variables. Traditionally, one of the major problems in improving school functioning has been ambiguity concerning the goals of the school. The normative model provides a sense of direction in building a productive educational program by specifying the desired changes in learners and the goals and objectives of the schooling experience.

2. *Measuring the current functioning of the school on the variables specified in the normative model.* The second major problem

traditionally handicapping efforts at improving school functioning has been the lack of valid and accurate information concerning the present functioning of the school. Information is gathered to examine what discrepancies, if any, exist between the current functioning and the desired functioning of the school in order to set goals and to motivate efforts for improvement. From awareness of the gap between the actual and desired states of affairs grow the commitment and motivation to improve the functioning of the school.

3. *Specifying the variables to be changed (the needs and problems of the school).* The third major problem in improving school functioning is the possibility of specifying an inappropriate target for change or of making a faulty definition of the problems of the school. Based on the information gathered in the diagnosis of present school functioning, a decision has to be made about which aspects of school experience need to be changed. In this chapter, affective variables are emphasized as targets for change efforts. The attitudes and values students develop as a result of their school experiences are important educational outcomes, for which schools need to be held accountable.

4. *Deciding upon, and applying, intervention procedures aimed at the variables to be changed.* It is important to use intervention procedures appropriate for the variables to be changed. One of the most effective interventions, "survey feedback" (Johnson, 1970), involves gathering information concerning the present functioning of the school, analyzing the information, summarizing it in a way that is clear and useful to the particular audience, and then feeding back the information to the appropriate individuals or work teams in the school. After examining the information, action planning is implemented in response to problems made salient by the information and the problem-solving activities. The goal of survey feedback is the improvement of school functioning through an objective assessment of problems by the school personnel. This approach gives objective, factual bases to the problems of the school, with the emphasis on open discussion of facts and figures in a task-oriented atmosphere where people seek to analyze the problem, identify possible causes, and agree on possible solutions.

An example of an intervention focusing on the structure of educational experiences is the structuring of cooperative learning situations. Cooperative learning structures, as compared with traditional competitive learning structures, will increase student achievement in problem solving tasks, increase positive interactions among students, increase positive attitudes toward learning and school, increase values of egalitarianism and appreciation for differences among individuals, and decrease anxiety about learning (Johnson, 1970, 1973a; Watson and Johnson, 1972). The direct teaching of interpersonal skills as part of the educational experiences of the school is an example of an intervention focusing on innovations in the curriculum (see Johnson, 1972a, for an example of such a curriculum).

5. *Building normative and structural supports for the new behaviors and new procedures generated by the intervention procedures.* Once the specified variables have been changed, the problem remains of maintaining the changes over time. Without supports, new behaviors, attitudes, values, and skills fade and disappear. Cues to elicit the new behaviors, skills, attitudes, and values must be planned for, and reinforcement for their expression must be structured into school life.

6. *Evaluating the success of the intervention procedures and measuring the current functioning of the school on the variables originally specified in the normative model.* Information gained from this evaluation provides feedback indicating the extent to which the change program has been successful, whether the problems have been successfully solved, and whether any new discrepancies exist between current and desired school functioning.

Instrumentation for Diagnosis and Evaluation

The key to improving the functioning of schools or school systems is the quality of the information collected concerning the present functioning of the schools and the effectiveness of interventions (such as curriculum innovations or in-service teacher training projects) in affecting the specified targets of change. To date, few prepared questionnaires have sufficiently well-established validity and reliability to be used by a teacher or by a school district in measuring the affective outcomes of schooling. Teachers can build their own questionnaires and use observational systems to evaluate the impact of the instructional program on students' attitudes and values (Johnson, 1973b); but to evaluate the impact of the educational programs of schools and school districts on the affective reactions of students, an instrument with established validity and reliability is needed.

A new instrument, the Minnesota School Affect Assessment (MSAA), is now being developed by three faculty members of the University of Minnesota, Andrew Ahlgren, David W. Johnson, and Paul Johnson, and by the Director of Curriculum and Instruction of Minnesota Public School District 196, Donald J. Christensen. This three-year project, now in its second year, is funded by Title III. The principal goals of the project are to develop a reliable and valid instrument to assess the affective domain, gather data about the affective reactions of students in Minnesota Public School District 196, feed results back into the curriculum-and-instruction machinery of the school district, and monitor what kinds of uses are made of what kinds of information.

In developing the MSAA, the project investigators first held a series of meetings to define the set of attitude and value targets to be assessed. Several schemes to generate targets systematically were considered, and eventually five categories were established which, it was hoped, would suggest the full range of possible targets. The categories were: People (teachers, students), Things (books, school building), Activities (writing stories, listening to music), Concepts (feelings, ideas), and States or Skills (knowing how things work, being liked by the teachers, reading). Groups of teachers were contacted and asked to list targets appropriate to their own fields under these five categories. Based on theoretical concepts in educational psychology and on their personal interests, the project investigators specified a list of possible targets. A word association task was given to a small sample of students to derive additional targets; it consisted of having students write the first three words that came to mind for each of thirty-two single words specifying possible targets. A list of all targets was then presented to all the teachers in the school district, who were asked to express for each target (1) interest in information about student responses to the target, (2) flat disapproval, (3) editorial changes, or (4) additional target suggestions. On the basis of the teachers' response and theoretical considerations raised by the project investigators, 187 questions were derived. Two forms of the MSAA were constructed, a main form to be used for grades four through twelve and a brief form to be used for grades K through three.

Two basic formats were used for the items in the MSAA. The first was a semantic differential type of question (Osgood, Suci, and Tannenbaum, 1957), in which a series of five-point rating scales of bipolar adjective pairs were listed underneath the attitude or value target. The second type of item provided a statement with which the student could express four degrees of agreement. In deciding which bipolar adjective pairs to use in the semantic differential questions, the following procedure was employed. First, the project investigators made a list of possible word pairs. Additional word pairs were gathered from teacher groups. A trial set of word pairs was given to a small sample of students, who were asked to perform a word association task to generate other possible word pairs. The results of this pilot study were factor analyzed and three dimensions were chosen on the bases of comprehensibility by young children and low intercorrelation with each other. On these bases the dimension labelled "worth" was represented by the word pair "important-unimportant," the dimension labelled "fun" was represented by the word pair "play-work," and the dimension labelled "threat" was represented by the word pair "dangerous-safe." One hundred and five semantic differential type questions were included in the original version of the MSAA.

The procedures used for obtaining the eighty-two statements to which students could express four degrees of agreement had two parts. First, the project investigators gathered, from the research literature in educational psychology, a series of scales to measure such factors as "cooperation," "competition," "importance of school," "attitudes toward teacher," and "locus of control"; and second, selected items from the Learning Environment Inventory (Walberg and Anderson, 1968) were included.

The first version of the MSAA was administered to the entire student population of Minnesota Public School District 196 near the beginning of the 1971 school year, and the results were factor analyzed. Within two months of that time the instrument was given again to a subsample of the student population in order to establish test-retest correlations for reliability, and a series of validation procedures were conducted. The validation procedures consisted of interviews with students to assess their interpretation of and reaction to the questions and response alternatives; a second instrument that measured some of the same factors with different scales; observations of student behavior in selected areas of the schools, such as libraries and hallways; and a series of sorting tasks to determine whether students grouped questions in categories similar to those formed by the factor analysis of the data. In addition, the entire Learning Environment Inventory was given to selected subsamples of students. And during the spring of 1972 the first version of the MSAA was readministered to the entire student population of the school district.

During the summer of 1972 the data from the factor analysis of the instrument, the test-retest reliability data, and the validation data were used to revise the instrument and to prepare a second version of the MSAA. Teacher interest in the information provided by the questions was also used as a criterion for revising the MSAA. The number of semantic differential items was reduced to seventy-seven, and the number of agree-disagree statements was raised to eighty-four. Only two bipolar scales, "important-unimportant" and "pleasant-unpleasant," were retained in the semantic differential questions on the revised form. These bipolar adjective pairs were selected on the basis of the validation and factor analysis data and a second word association task given to a sample of students during the summer of 1972. The constructs selected to be measured by scales of agree-disagree statements were: academic press, academic support, acceptance, behavioral constraint, communication, competition, cooperation, extrinsic motivation, independence, intrinsic motivation, locus of control, marking basis, marking fairness, marking relevance, mastery, need for direction, tracking, personal support, perseverence, personal worth as a student, curriculum perspective, objectives, social inclusion, understanding, and vocational relevance. The revised form of the MSAA was administered to all students in the school district during the fall of 1972, and will be readministered during the winter and spring of 1973. Further factor analyses, validation procedures, and test-retest procedures are being conducted in order to revise the MSAA again and put it in final form during the summer of 1973.

Feedback of Results

Several aspects of presenting the results of questionnaires such as the MSAA to various groups of school personnel and students should be noted. Results of data collection are presented within the framework of action planning to improve the instructional program of a school or school district. On the basis of the data there is an evaluation of the present instructional program and a discussion of what modifications should be made in order to improve it.

The first issue in presenting results is to make the data clear, meaningful, and easy to understand. This is often difficult because of the amount and complexity of the data, and because of the variety of ways in which the data can be presented. The second issue involves deciding what data to present to what group of school personnel or students. Different groups of teachers, for example, will be interested in different data, depending on their interests and expertise. Finally, school personnel and possibly the students need adequate time and opportunity to study the data, discuss its implications with the individuals who gathered and analyzed it, and decide what impact it should have on the instructional program. It should be kept in mind that the data provides helpful information for problem solving, not definitive facts.

The investigators are currently presenting the results from the first year of the MSAA Project to teachers and students. During the summer of 1972, three one-day sessions were held for all elementary and secondary staff. At the end of these sessions, the teachers submitted requests for copies of data displays that they thought would be particularly appropriate to share within subject area or grade level teacher groups. Funding for the project included purchasing release time for teachers to study and discuss the findings. The investigators cannot at this point state what impact this data feedback is having on the instructional program of the school district, but wide variability in teacher interest in seeing and discussing the data has been noted. The investigators have developed a computer program to print out response summaries and profiles in order to efficiently and reliably handle the data obtained from the first year. Some examples of how the data have been presented are given in Figure 7-1.

Adapting the MSAA

The MSAA can be used to evaluate the effectiveness of schools in accomplishing objectives in the affective domain, as a diagnostic instrument to illuminate problem areas, and as an evaluation instrument to assess the results of innovations and interventions. Schools interested in using the MSAA, however, may have individual needs or interests not fully represented on the instrument. They can, if they

Figure 7-1

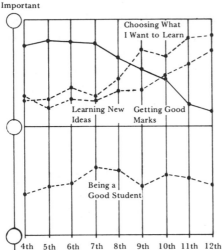

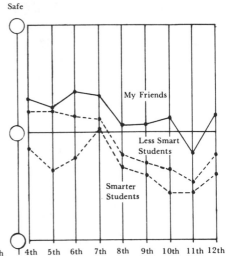

The solid line shows that older boys and girls thought *getting good marks* was not so important; but the dashed line shows that the importance of *being a good student* was about the same from the 4th to the 12th grade; and the dotted lines show that the importance of *learning new ideas* and *choosing what I want to learn* was higher in the upper grades.

These graphs show that students in all grades from 4th to 12th saw *my friends* as safer than other students. That isn't surprising. But the graphs also show that *students not as smart as me* were seen as distinctly safer than *students smarter than me* in the 4th, 5th, and 6th grades —and that the gap was much less from 7th grade on.

Importance of Learning About "Animals and Plants."

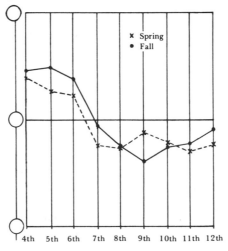

wish, build their own instrument, following a procedure similar to that used in building the MSAA. Or they may wish only to add questions.

Several points should be kept in mind when using any instrument such as the MSAA in schools.

1. The instrument should be given near the beginning and end of the school year for several years in order to determine attitude and value changes during the year and to establish norms concerning how students have responded in past years.

2. It is best to use more than one question in measuring student affective reactions to any important target.

3. A rapid feedback system should be established so that students and school personnel receive test results in a way they can understand clearly and use easily. The data gathered are only as good as the motivation of faculty and students to give accurate information. It is vitally important for students and faculty to have positive attitudes toward the testing program and view the information being collected as interesting and useful. This can best be accomplished by presenting the results of the testing in interesting and useful ways to both students and faculty. Sharing the results of the testing indicates that their cooperation is appreciated. Failure to provide feedback concerning results and uses of the information is the major flaw with most large testing programs, and is a major source of decreasing motivation to provide accurate and valid information. Much care and attention must be given to the delivery of testing results within the school district.

4. It should be made clear that the information gathered by the testing program will be used to improve instructional programs, not to evaluate specific teachers and students. The anonymity of students should be protected. The affective reactions of students to their schooling experiences and the instructional programs of the school do not depend only on teacher behavior; curriculum materials, time of day, classroom setting, community norms, and other factors may all affect how students respond. If teachers and students are worried about how the information may be used, the validity and accuracy of the information may decrease.

References

Bennis, W. A. "A Conversation." *Psychology Today* 3 (1970): 48.

Johnson, D. W. *The Social Psychology of Education.* New York: Holt, Rinehart, and Winston, 1970.

————. *Reaching Out: Interpersonal Effectiveness and Self-Actualization.* Englewood Cliffs, N.J.: Prentice Hall, 1972a.

————. "The Social Psychology of Humanizing Social science education." In *Social Studies: The Humanizing Process,* edited by M. Kleg and J. Litcher. Winter Haven, Florida: Florida Council for the Social Studies, 1972b.

————. *Contemporary Social Psychology.* Philadelphia: J. B. Lippincott, 1973a.

————. "The Affective Side of the Schooling Experience." *Elementary School Journal* 73 (1973) 306-13(b).

Michael, D. N. *The Unprepared Society: Planning for a Precarious Future.* New York: Basic Books, 1968.

Osgood, C. E., Suci, G. J., and Tannenbaum, P. H. *The Measurement of Meaning.* Urbana: University of Illinois Press, 1957.

Slater, P. E. "Cultures in Collision." *Psychology Today* 4 (1970): 31.

Walberg, H. J. and Anderson, G. J. "Classroom Climate and Individual Learning." *Journal of Educational Psychology* 59 (1968): 414-19.

Watson, G. and Johnson, D. W. *Social Psychology: Issues And Insights.* Philadelphia: J. B. Lippincott, 1972.

8. A COURSE EVALUATION
Wayne W. Welch
Herbert J. Walberg

Although the need for true experiments on broadly defined populations has long been recognized, there are very few local experiments and no national experiments in curriculum research. For example, among 46 government-sponsored course development projects in science and mathematics, a few relied on teacher reports and classroom visits for evaluation, but only four used true experiments in their evaluation strategies (Welch, 1969). The purpose of the present chapter is to report the feasibility of a national educational experiment and to present the summative findings regarding Project Physics, a physics course for high school students.

The Course

The developers of Project Physics were originally concerned about the continuing drop in the proportion of students who take physics in high school. To attract students who are not bound for mathematical, scientific, or technical careers, and without compromising on the physics content, they attempted to develop an interest-awakening, module system of course components using a variety of media and methods for learning: a basic text, film loops, programmed instruction booklets, transparencies, laboratory apparatus, special cameras, a student handbook, and other materials. The structure of the course allows students to emphasize aspects which interest them most; for example, rigorous mathematics, laboratory

113

experiments, or historical readings. Perhaps the most distinctive aspect of Project Physics is its humanistic orientation—an attempt to show the place of physics in the history of ideas, and its relation to technology and social development. At the present time (1971-72), the course is being used by approximately 80,000 students in all 50 states. The research reported below was conducted during the final year of the course development. While some 60 other evaluation and research papers are based on Project Physics data (Welch, 1971), the present study concerns only the experimental part of the evaluation.

Method

A list of the names and addresses of 16,911 physics teachers was purchased from the National Science Teachers Association (NSTA), which maintains the U.S. Registry of Junior and Senior High School Science and Mathematics Teaching Personnel. The NSTA reported that the list is compiled from responses received from 81 per cent of all secondary schools in the United States. Because of travel costs for teacher training, we limited our population to the 16,702 physics teachers listed for the continental United States. Numbers were assigned to each of the teachers according to his ordinal position on the list, and a table of random numbers was used to select a total of 136 names.

Each of the 136 teachers was sent a registered letter describing the curriculum project and inviting him to participate in an experimental evaluation of the course. Each was informed that a teacher agreeing to participate would be randomly assigned to either an experimental group or a control group. The responsibilities of both groups were described in the letter: the experimental group would attend a six-week Briefing Session, take a series of tests, teach the course during the academic year 1967-68, and administer pre, mid, and posttests to their physics students. The control group would attend a two-day briefing session, take a series of tests, and administer the same pre, mid, and posttests to their students: but they would continue to teach their regular physics courses. Travel expenses, summer school stipends, and course materials were to be provided by Project Physics.

A total of 136 letters of invitation were mailed, but only 124 teachers were actually contacted. Nine letters were "returned to sender," and three others could not be reached by telephone follow-up. Of those contacted, 72 agreed to participate according to the conditions specified, while 52 were unable to accept because of prior commitments or lack of interest. The nature and frequency of non-acceptors are listed below:

Continuation of work on Master's degree in summer school	12
No longer teaching physics	11
Summer job commitment	10
Not interested	6
Physics no longer offered at their school	5
Health reasons prevent extended travel	3
Miscellaneous (changing jobs, expecting baby, etc.)	5
	52

Questionnaires were returned by 124 teachers—72 acceptors and 52 nonacceptors. T-tests revealed that teachers who accepted the invitation, when compared to the nonacceptors, are more likely to teach in larger schools and to be currently teaching the Physical Science Study Committee (PSSC) physics course. (PSSC is a recently developed physics course—one of the first of the national curriculum projects.) It seems reasonable to interpret these differences as a greater receptiveness to innovation in larger schools where previous innovations have been accepted. The findings must be interpreted in the light of the sampling limitations: refusals, listing by NSTA, etc. However, the target group for generalization would be the kinds of teachers in the sample, i.e., those willing to try new courses.

A table of random numbers was used to assign 46 of the teachers to the experimental group and 26 to the control group. Because of transfers and illnesses, the final sample consisted of 53 physics teachers. As shown in Table 8-1, 34 of these attended the six-week summer Briefing Session and taught the course. Because of the possibility of the so-called (and as yet unreplicated) "Hawthorne

Table 8-1. Cell sizes for analysis of variance

IQ Group	HPP	Other	Total
Low (112.1 or less)	11	6	17
Middle (112.2 - 119.3)	11	8	19
High (119.4 or over)	12	5	17
Total	34	19	53

effect," the 19 control group teachers were brought to Harvard University for two days, entertained by university physicists, and impressed with the importance of their participation in the experiment. They were asked to teach their regular physics courses during the coming academic year.

Instruments

Nearly 40 instruments were suggested or proposed for construction. Independently, three judges assigned priorities to these tests based on perceptions of the goals of the course, availability and usability of instruments, conversations with other Project personnel, and the experience of the evaluators. From the long list of instruments suggested, those described in Table 8-2 were selected because they were believed to represent the goals of the course, the purposes of the evaluation, sample a broad range of anticipated student outcomes, and fit within the restriction of time and problems of testing on a national basis.

Procedure

The system of randomized data collection employed in the testing plan increases the number of testing instruments that can be used in any given class period (Walberg and Welch, 1967). Briefly, a random half of a class takes one test while the other half is taking a different test. Tests for a given administration were arranged randomly before the tests were sent to the teachers. The teachers were asked to hand the first test to the first student in the first row, the second test to the second student, and so on. By this procedure, the assignment of test to student is random within the room. Thus, in a two-period testing program, mean scores were obtained on four different tests, and individual scores on each test were obtained from one-half the total number of students.

The IQ test (Henmon and Nelson, 1960) and Learning Environment Inventory were given in December of the academic year of the experiment using randomized data collection. The Student Questionnaire was administered in March to all students, and all other criterion instruments were administered using the randomized technique in May.

The unit of analysis used was the posttest teacher-mean, that is, the average score on a test of all physics students taught by a single teacher. The groups were assigned to three levels of mean IQ: Low—less than 112.1; Middle—from 112.2 to 119.3; and High—more than 119.4. Treating IQ as a factor in the design permitted testing for course and IQ interactions. This was particularly of interest in the current evaluation because of the Project's goal of appealing to a broader spectrum of student abilities. Leveling on IQ, of course, also increased the precision of the experiment by reducing the within-cell variance.

Because the cell sizes for corresponding levels are unequal as indicated in Table 8-1, a nonorthogonal analysis of variance solution was used (Bock and Haggard, 1968). Because main effects are confounded in the statistical analysis of nonorthogonal designs, the order is important when examining the main effects. In this study, the effect of IQ was examined first, followed by the course effect, and then the interaction. This provides an unconfounded test of the course effect which was of major interest in this evaluation study.

The null hypotheses tested were that the mean differences between treatment groups (Project Physics versus Other Physics) equal zero for all variables simultaneously within each cluster. An F-ratio was computed for the multivariate test of the equality of the mean vectors. If the F-value exceeded the two-tailed .10 level of probability, which suggested an overall difference between the two groups, then the univariate F-tests of differences in means for each variable were examined to determine the direction and relative sizes of the course effects on each of the dependent variables. The two-tailed level of significance for the univariate F-tests was also set at the .10 level. The two-tailed .10 level was adopted for three reasons: multivariate and univariate tests were employed; a two-tailed .10 is equivalent to a one-tailed .05 test which could validly be used because the directions were hypothesized; and because the results were to be used for applied decision making.

Results and Discussion

Table 8-3 reveals that of the six clusters of criteria, three were significant for the IQ factor, four were significant for the course effect, and one interaction was significant. The results for each significant cluster are discussed successively.

The lack of significant differences in the cognitive criteria may be disappointing to some because of the Project Physics goal to

Table 8-2. Test information and reliabilities

Instrument	Reliability
Cognitive	
Test on Understanding Science. Assesses students' understanding of the scientific enterprise, scientists, and the methods and aims of science (Cooley & Klopfer, 1961).	.76[a]
Physics Achievement Test. Locally-developed test of general topics in physics. Derived from the six unit achievement tests developed for Project Physics (Winter & Welch, 1967).	.77[a]
Science Process Inventory. Assesses students' knowledge of the activities, assumptions, products, and ethics of science (Welch & Pella, 1967-68).	.86[a]
Course Grade. Final grade received by students.[d]	
Affective	
Physical Science Interest Measure. One of six subject matter interest measures (Halpern, 1965).	.93[a]
Pupil Activity Inventory. An operational measure of science interests (Walberg, 1967). Derived from Reed Science Activity Inventory (Cooley & Reed, 1961).	.90[b]
Course Satisfaction. Assesses students' satisfaction in course. Derived from cluster analysis of twenty items from Student Questionnaire (Welch, 1969).	.80[c]

Learning Environment

Fourteen cluster scores from the Learning Environment Inventory. Used as a substitute for direct classroom observation in determining the social climate of the classroom (Walberg and Anderson, 1968).   .58-.86[b]

Course Reaction

Twenty item scores from Student Questionnaire. Score obtained by computing percentage of students agreeing with each of twenty statements about physics courses in general.[d]

Semantic Differential

Fourteen cluster scores from the Semantic Differential Test. Assesses students' attitudes relating to physics (Geis, 1969).   .60-.86[c]

Physics Perception

Fifteen item scores from Special Semantic Differential. Forced choice semantic differential instrument. Assesses students' perceptions of physics.[d]

[a] Kuder-Richardson Formula 20 reliability

[b] Cronbach Alpha reliability

[c] Stepped-up mean item intercorrelation (equivalent to Cronbach Alpha reliability)

[d] Reliability not computable (single item scores used)

Table 8-3. Multivariate F-values for analysis of variance

(df) and Multivariate F-Value

Cluster	IQ	Course	Interaction
Cognitive	(8/88) 4.32***	(4/44) .82	(8/88) .48
Affective	(6/90) 1.18	(3/45) 3.36**	(6/90) 1.54
Learning Environment	(28/68) 1.13	(14/34) 1.74*	(28/68) .65
Course Reaction	(40/56) 2.06***	(20/28) 7.15***	(40/56) .79
Semantic Differential	(28/68) 2.50***	(14/34) .69	(28/68) 1.77**
Physics Perception	(30/66) 1.40	(15/33) 4.74***	(30/66) 1.52

Note: F-values significant at the .10, .05, and .01 levels are indicated, respectively, with one, two, and three asterisks.

increase science-process understanding. Perhaps the course developers can find some solace in the fact that other objectives were achieved (see below) without a resulting loss in student physics achievement and understanding.

Because the multivariate test of the affective criteria was significant, the univariate F-tests were examined. Only the Course Satisfaction scale was found to be significant on this test (see Figure 1 for all significant univariate F-tests for the course effects). The standardized course contrast (obtained by dividing the least-square estimates of course differences by the within-group standard deviation) is shown in Figure 1. Project Physics students scored nearly one standard deviation higher than the other students on this criterion, and the contrast is highly significant.

The Learning Environment scales were significant on the multivariate test, and three scales were significant on the univariate tests. Project Physics students scored higher on (perceived their classes as having more) Diversity, while students in other courses saw their classes as having more Favoritism and Difficulty.

On the Course Reaction items, Project Physics students found a historical approach interesting, thought physics could be understood without an extensive mathematics background, found their text enjoyable to read, hoped the course would not change, and finished the course during the year in contrast to students in other courses. Students in other courses more often found physics to be one of the

Figure 8-1. Significant standardized course contrasts and f-ratios

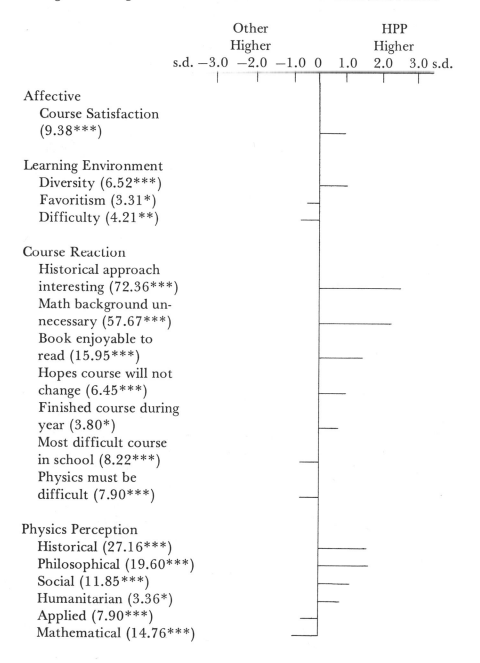

most difficult courses they had taken in high school, and concluded that physics has to be difficult.

The course effect on the Semantic Differential scales was not significant on the multivariate test; however, it interacted significantly with IQ on the multivariate test and on nine univariate tests: Doing Laboratory Work as Valuable and Interesting; Learning about Science as Interesting; Physics as Interesting, Valuable, Safe, Orderly, and Understandable; and Universe as Interesting. Plots of the significant interactions revealed that, for the low IQ group (teacher-mean IQ less than 112.3; see Table 8-1), students in other courses responded significantly more favorably to these scales. For the middle IQ group, the reverse holds: Project Physics students responded more favorably. There were no significant differences between the two groups in the high IQ classification.

For the Physics Perception scales, the multivariate and six univariate tests were significant. Project Physics students rated the concept Physics as more Historical, Philosophical, Social, and Humanitarian and less Mathematical and Applied than did students in other courses.

Conclusions

From the experimental part of the evaluation, it appears that Project Physics has reached several main goals which were established for it. Students exposed to the course perform as well as students in other courses on cognitive measures. In keeping with the humanistic, affective, and multimedia elements of the course, they perceived their classroom environments as more diverse and egalitarian and less difficult. They found their textbook more enjoyable, a historical approach more interesting, and physics less difficult. Reflecting the way the subject was to be portrayed in the course, they saw physics as more historical, philosophical, and humanitarian and less mathematical. Finally, the course does seem to have a special appeal to the middle-range IQ group, 112 to 119, which has increasingly tended to elect not to take physics in high school in the last decade.

With respect to national curriculum experiments, we concluded that they are feasible and necessary. Not only do they meet canons of broader inference, but they also are more convincing to evaluation consumers. Our liberally-estimated extra costs of a national, over a regional experiment, are $1,000 for random sampling, long distance calls, and mailing and $8,500 in transportation expenses for bringing the 57 teachers to Cambridge, Massachusetts from various parts of the country. Compared to the developmental costs of a government-sponsored high school science course, which often runs into the millions of dollars, the benefits of national experiments (and other evaluation activities) seem worthwhile.

References

Bock, R. Darrell and Haggard, Ernest A. The Use of Multivariate Analysis of Variance in Behavioral Research. In Dean Kay Whitla (Ed.) *Handbook of Measurement and Assessment in Behavioral Sciences.* Boston: Addison-Wesley Publishing Co., 1968.

Cooley, William W. and Klopfer, Leo E. *Test on Understanding Science.* Princeton, N. J.: Educational Testing Service, 1961.

Cooley, William W. and Reed, H. B. The Measurement of Science Interests: An Operational and Multidimensional Approach. *Science Education,* 1961, 45, 320-326.

Geis, Fred, Jr. *The Semantic Differential Technique as a Means of Evaluating Changes in "Affect."* Doctor's thesis. Cambridge, Mass.: Graduate School of Education, Harvard Univ., 1968.

Halpern, Gerald. *Scale Properties of the Interest Index.* Princeton, N. J.: Educational Testing Service, 1965.

Henmon, V. A. C. and Nelson, M. J. *The Henmon-Nelson Tests of Mental Ability Manual.* Boston: Houghton Mifflin Company, 1960.

Walberg, Herbert J. Dimensions of Scientific Interests in Boys and Girls Studying Physics. *Science Education,* 1967, 51, 111-116.

Walberg, Herbert J. and Anderson, Gary J. The Achievement-Creativity Dimension and Classroom Climate. *Journal of Creative Behavior,* 1968, 2, 281-291.

Walberg, Herbert J. and Welch, Wayne W. A New Use of Randomization in Experimental Curriculum Evaluation. *School Review,* 1967, 75, 369-377.

Welch, Wayne W. Curriculum Evaluation. *Review of Educational Research,* 1969, 39, No. 4, 429-443.

Welch, Wayne W. A Review of the Research and Evaluation Program of Harvard Project Physics. ERIC Center for Science and Mathematics, Ohio State University, Columbus, Ohio (mimeo), 1971.

Welch, Wayne W. Some Characteristics of High School Physics Students: Circa 1968. *Journal of Research in Science Teaching,* September, 1969.

Welch, Wayne W. and Pella, Milton O. The Development of an Instrument for Inventorying Knowledge of the Processes of Science. *Journal of Research in Science Teaching,* 1967-68, 5, 64-68.

Winter, Stephen S. and Welch, Wayne W. Achievement Testing Program of Project Physics. *The Physics Teacher,* 1967, 5, 229-231.

9. INSTRUCTIONAL MATERIALS
Maurice J. Eash

This chapter reports the findings of a field test of an instrument developed for assessing instructional materials and offers some general formative observations gathered from the use of the instrument in a number of field trials. Before launching into the presentation of the findings, a brief description of the instrument reproduced in the following section seems in order.

The instrument grew out of an attempt to deal with the embarrassment of riches in instructional materials available to schools. It is necessary to make selections from this cornucopia of materials and to implement them effectively in the classroom, for not only has the range of materials increased in this decade, but also the sophistication of the instructional design has advanced to the stage where change of instructional materials frequently entails extensive retraining of teachers. Moreover, failure to implement instructional materials in the classroom in keeping with the instructional design requirements of the originator and producer is a frequent cause of failure in instructional innovations once the materials are outside the developmental or experimental setting.

The instrument was developed to provide data on two broad questions: (1) What materials shall we select for use in the classroom? and (2) What are the characteristics of the instructional design of the materials, and what will it take to implement them effectively, given the demands of a particular program?

It is important to make clear at this point that the instrument does not make the judgment; but it does systematize the gathering of data, focuses the analysis, and provides a data base for a critical judgment that has the further advantage of being grounded in the literature and research on instruction. Thus, it is to be hoped, the decision-making process in choosing instructional materials will be removed from the realm of vague intuitions to one where the selected materials will have a degree of predictive validity for student learning outcomes. Progress toward rational decision making in choice of instructional materials is the subject of the remainder of this chapter.

By eliciting data on constructs central to micro and macro designs of curriculum, the instrument illuminates the instructional design potentials of a range of instructional materials. The constructs are labeled (I) objectives; (II) organization of the material (its scope and sequence); (III) methodology; and (IV) evaluation. Under each construct are listed as many of the customary approaches to instructional materials as feasible without making the instrument too long. An open-ended response is permitted in case of an exception to the listed approaches. In developing a summary statement on the material, the rater is encouraged to note examples of how the construct is being satisfied. This format permits the extraction and selection of data on how the instructional materials satisfy the four constructs of an instructional design. Also included are items of information on the development of the materials, and particularly on whether the materials were field tested or researched with prospective consumers.

At the end of the section on each construct, and at the end of the instrument proper, the rater is asked to use a seven-point scale to render a judgment on each of the four constructs and a comprehensive judgment on the overall worth of the instructional materials. These scales are defined through descriptions of the characteristics of the materials that would fall at each of three points; materials having a mix of these characteristics fall somewhere in between the defined points. The rater progresses through an atomistic analysis of the material, then moves to a summary rating of the construct (a process devised after bitter experience with wildly inconsistent ratings, which resulted when only the summary qualitative ratings were used to judge the constructs). On completion of this assessment, the rater is asked to prepare a short summary statement, presumably arrived at through a competent understanding of the materials and of their potential in an instructional setting.

Procedures

The subjects for this study were twenty-five graduate students in an advanced class in curriculum design. Of the twenty-five subjects, eleven were elementary teachers, fourteen were secondary teachers, and all had over five years of teaching experience. Two types of materials were used with the instrument. In the first trial, a sixth-grade reading package from a widely used reading series, composed of a teacher's guide and student's reader and workbook (Robinson, 1965) was assessed individually by the twenty-five subjects. In the second trial, the twenty-five subjects were grouped into seven teams that rendered collective ratings on the reading package. The third trial was conducted on a curriculum bulletin in seventh grade science developed by a major city system (Board of Education of the City of New York, 1963). One of a series designed to assist the classroom teacher in science by providing a comprehensive micro design for twenty-four classroom and laboratory lessons, the bulletin featured the chemistry of matter (elements, compounds and mixtures, and atomic theory). Only judgments by the seven teams were gathered on the science bulletin.

In the first trial, the subjects were asked to fill out the forms individually and maintain a record of the time they spent in assessing the reading package. The range of time spent was from two to four hours, with a mean of three hours. The collective team judgments in the other two trials were gathered in a two-hour period. After becoming familiar with the instrument, subjects could assess material quite rapidly, and the time in the team sessions was mainly devoted to reconciling differing judgments. While the reading package was longer and more complex than the other unit, the subjects, except for four science teachers, were not as familiar with the content of the other unit. Thus the elements of length of reading package and unfamiliarity with science content balanced out in terms of assessment time. Two hours appeared sufficient time for the groups to complete their collective assessments of both learning packages.

An Instrument for the Assessment of
Instructional Materials (Form IV)

I. Objectives	Yes	No

A. Are there objectives stated for the use of the material?   _____ _____
  1. General objectives?   _____ _____
  2. Instructional objectives?   _____ _____
  3. Are the objectives stated in behavioral terms?[1]   _____ _____
  4. If stated in behavioral terms, do the objectives specify:
      a) The type of behavior?   _____ _____
      b) Conditions under which it will appear?   _____ _____
      c) Level of performance expected?   _____ _____
  5. List examples of objectives.

B. If there are no objectives stated for the use of the material, are the objectives instead implicit[2] or readily obvious?   _____ _____
  1. If yes, please outline below what objectives *you* believe govern the purpose of the material.

C. What appears to be the source of the objectives (both stated and implicit objectives)?
  1. Are the objectives related to a larger frame of instruction?   _____ _____
  2. Are the objectives specific to a subject skill?   _____ _____
  3. Are the objectives related to a broader behavioral pattern[3] that is to be developed over a period of time?   _____ _____
  4. What seems to be the emphasis of the objectives:
      (Check as many as are appropriate.)
      a) Attitudinal[4] _____   b) Motor skills _____
      c) Cognitive development skills[5] _____   d) Subject skills _____
  5. Are the objectives drawn from:
      (Check as many as are appropriate.)
      a) A learning approach[6] _____
      b) Society needs (citizenship) _____
      c) Demands of subject _____
      d) Demands and needs of child[7] _____

D. Quantitative rating: objectives

Directions: Please make an X on the rating scale below at the point that represents your best judgment on the following criteria. Please place the X ON a specific point.

```
|———————|———————|———————|———————|———————|———————|
1       2       3       4       5       6       7
```

Objectives vague, unclear, or missing. Those included not useful. Fails to distinguish between general and instructional objectives, mixes various types of objectives, confusing to the teacher.

Average, some of the criteria for objectives met, some missing, at times inconsistent, objectives only partially operational for the classroom teacher.

The objectives are stated clearly and in behavioral terms. Both general and instructional objectives are stated in a consistent conceptual framework. Excellent, one of the best, useful for a teacher.

II. Organization of the Material (Scope and Sequence)   Yes   No

A. Has a task analysis[8] been made of the material and some relationship specified between the tasks?   ____   ____

B. If a task analysis has been made, what basis was used to organize the materials:
(Check as many as are appropriate.)
1. Errorless discrimination[9] ____   2. Simple to complex ____
2. Figure-ground[10] ____   4. General to specific ____
5. Logical order ____   6. Chronology ____

C. If no indication of a task analysis has been made, what assumptions do you believe the authors have made concerning the organization of the instructional sequence of the material?

D. Is there a basis for the scope of the material included in the instructional package?   ____   ____
1. If there is a basis, is it:
a) Related to a subject area   ____   ____
b) To a motor skill development   ____   ____
c) To a cognitive skill area   ____   ____
d) To an affective response system[11]   ____   ____
e) Other (specify)_____

2. Has the scope been subjected to analysis for:
   a) Appropriateness to students   _____ _____
   b) Relationship to other material   _____ _____
E. Is there a recommended sequence?   _____ _____
   1. What is the basis of the recommended se-
      quence?
      (Check as many as appropriate)
      a) Interrelationships of a subject[12] _____
      b) Positive reinforcement and programmed sequence[13] _____
      c) Open ended development of a generalization[14] _____
      d) Advanced organizer (cognitive)[15] _____
      e) Other (please specify) _____
F. Briefly outline the scope and sequence.
G. Quantitative rating: organization of the materials
   (scope and sequence).
   Directions: Please make an X on the rating scale below at the
   point that represents your best judgment on the following criteria.
   Please place the X ON a specific point.

```
|-------+-------+-------+-------+-------+-------|
1       2       3       4       5       6       7
```

Sequence illogical or unstated, teacher is left to puzzle it out. Does not appear to have subjected material to any analysis to build an instructional design. Scope is uncertain, seems to contradict sequence. Little help unintentionally to teacher or children in organizing material.	Average in organization. Some help but teacher must supply much of organizational sequence. Scope somewhat limited, may be too narrow (or broad). Sequence is not detailed enough and may not have been tested with a range of children.	Excellent organization of scope and sequence. Conceptually developed based on a consistent theory; task analysis or other appropriate investigation has been done. Tested for appropriateness of recommended sequence.

III. Methodology   Yes   No

A. Does the author(s) and/or material suggest any
   methodological approach?   _____ _____

B. Is the methodological approach, if suggested, specific to the mode of transaction? ____ ____
   1. Does the mode of transaction:[16]
      (Check as many as appropriate)
      a) Rely upon teacher-centric method[17] (largely teacher directing?) ____ ____
      b) Rely upon pupil-centric method[18] (largely self-directing?) ____ ____
      c) Require active participation by the students? ____ ____
      d) Passive participation by the students? ____ ____
      e) Combination of active and passive participation by the students? ____ ____
      f) Direct students' attention to method of learning as well as the learning product? ____ ____
      g) Provide for variation among students—uses several approaches to method? ____ ____
C. Does the methodology suggested require extensive preparation by the teacher? ____ ____
   1. How much deviation is permitted in methodology?
      Much ____ Some ____ Little ____
   2. Does the methodology require unusual skills obtained through specific training? ____ ____
   3. Is there any statement on how methodology was tested—any experimental evidence? ____ ____
   4. If you have tried the recommended methodology, how successful did it seem for your students?
      Most succeeded ____ Approx. half succeeded ____
      Few succeeded ____
      a) Please provide a brief description of the students who *were* successful and those who *were not* successful.
      b) What variations on recommended methodology have you used?
D. In a brief statement describe the recommended methodology.
E. Quantitative rating: methodology.
   Directions: Please make an X on the rating scale below at the

point that represents your best judgment on the following criteria. Please place the X ON a specific point.

| | | | | | | |
|1|2|3|4|5|6|7|

Very little help is given on methodology, or methodology is too abstract and complex for most students and teachers. Methodology appears to be unrelated to content and an afterthought in the learning package. Too active or passive for most students. Teacher required to participate fully with too many students at every step. Doesn't have appropriate methodology for variety of learning ability among students.

Gives help to the teacher, but would like more. Some students would be able to cope with suggested methodology, but others not. Doesn't appear to have been widely field tested. Teacher has to work out variety for students with special learning difficulties.

Uses a variety of modes in the transactions. Does not chain a teacher to a mode without reason, but provides assistance for different abilities. Describes the field test of the methodology. Teachers will find methodology easy to use and believe students will respond. Methodology is part of goals of instruction and not just vehicle for content.

IV. Evaluation

                Yes   No

A. Are there recommended evaluation procedures for teachers and students in the instructional package? ____ ____

  1. What do the evaluation procedures emphasize? (Check as many as appropriate)
     a) Cognitive skills ____   b) Subject skills ____
     c) Psychomotor skills[19] ____
     d) Affective responses[20] ____

  2. Are the evaluation procedures compatible with the objectives? ____ ____

  3. Are evaluation procedures developed for several different levels: (Check as many as appropriate)

a) Immediate feedback evaluation for the pupil
_____

b) Evaluation for a variety of the areas in #1 above, and over a period of time _____

c) Immediate feedback evaluation for the teacher _____

d) Evaluation on a norm referent[21] _____

e) Evaluation on a criterion referent[22] _____

B. Are the evaluation procedures contained in the package? _____ _____

C. Does the evaluation give attention to both product and process learning? _____ _____

D. Is there information on how evaluation procedures were tested and developed? _____ _____

E. Briefly state what evaluation procedures are included. If possible, give examples.

F. Quantitative rating: evaluation.
Directions: Please make an X on the rating scale below at the point that represents your best judgment on the following criteria. Place the X ON a specific point.

```
|-------+-------+-------+-------+-------+-------+-------|
1       2       3       4       5       6       7
```

Haphazard in approach. Product and process learning either entirely neglected or confused. Lists items, but poorly constructed, no evidence of testing of evaluation approach. Students receive no assistance through feedback. Fails to recognize and examine different types of learning where appropriate.	Some examples given, range of evaluation limited. Samples given but limited and sketchy. Teacher finds useful that which is given, but needs more examples. Evaluation is limited to product or process. Unsure on whether evaluation has ever been tested, but seems logical though limited in types of learning examples.	Many suggestions and helps in evaluation for the teacher. Has criterion reference procedures where appropriate. Student obtains assistance in learning through feedback evaluation. Gives attention to several kinds of learning, consistent with objectives of learning package.

V. Comment

A. Draw up an overall statement of the strengths and weaknesses of the material as an instructional package. Prepare your statement as if it were to be addressed to your fellow classroom teachers who are going to use it to make a decision on these instructional materials.

B. Quantitative rating: overall assessment of material.
   Directions: Please place an X on the point in the rating scale which best represents your overall judgment of these materials. Place the X ON the specific point.

1	2	3	4	5	6	7

Poorly designed, conceptually weak and inconsistent or haphazard design. Does not appear to have been field tested: inaccurate assumptions about children who will be using material. Overpriced, underdeveloped, a bad bargain.

Has strengths and weaknesses, but most teachers would find satisfactory. On the balance comes out about average, would need considerable supplementary effort by teacher. A compromise of price and availability.

Excellent, one of the best by comparison with other available material. Theoretically strong and carefully field tested. Shows consistent instructional design. Would recommend highly; well worth the price.

A Glossary of Terms Used in This Instrument

1. *Objectives stated in behavioral terms*—a work picture of the type of behavior product which one might expect when the objective is achieved. Objectives stated in behavioral terms will usually name the behavior, state the conditions under which it will appear, and the level of performance expected, e.g. the child will be able to spell (type of behavior), in formal and informal writing (condition under which it will appear), 98 percent of the words in his written work (level of performance).

2. *Implicit objectives*—an examination of the content will permit the reader to readily identify the objectives that the student

should accomplish, even if the producer has not stated them. If a filmstrip gives the sequential steps in solving arithmetic problems using long division, one would assume the implicit objective to be to teach the student the process of long division.

3. *Broader behavioral pattern*—instructional materials frequently are geared to goals that include complex behavior which is to be developed over time. Example: voting behavior as a function of citizenship involves a broader behavioral pattern which chains together a complex of behaviors ranging from knowing the candidates and the issues, to being registered, and knowing how to operate a voting machine. The instructional material may be designed to contribute to a broader behavioral pattern rather than a simpler, more specific behavior. Even if the objective is geared to a single specific behavior there should be some relationship to a broader behavioral pattern.

4. *Attitudinal objectives*—objectives that are designed to develop feelings and predispositions to act in accordance with internalized values and beliefs. These may be listed as attitudes, values, interests, and appreciations. They may be fairly direct as to develop in each student an interest in listening to a newscast at least once a day, or more complex as to form an attitude of critically evaluating the news by investigating the source of reports.

5. *Cognitive development skills*—objectives which have cognitive development skills (thinking) as a basis will usually emphasize thinking processes as their focus, such as understanding, discriminating, utilizing, chaining, and evaluating as opposed to emphasizing specific subject products.

6. *Objectives drawn from a learning approach*—objectives may be drawn utilizing approaches to learning, in some cases emphasizing wholeness of learnings prior to fragmenting into specifics for instruction. Example: the student will become familiar with the background of the 12th and 13th century European interest in colonies and trade, prior to studying the specific explorations. The extreme of the above approach would be a small step by step sequencing of the material on Europe in the 12th and 13th centuries in which concepts on European interests in trade and colonies were fed to the student on a programmed basis eventually leading the students through the various explorations. These objectives are based on different approaches to learning.

7. *Objectives based on demand and needs of child objectives*—

using this emphasis usually have as their focus some developmental sequence (physical, emotional or social) as their central organizer. Example: the student will express affection as well as receive affection. The behavior of expressing affection is developmentally more advanced than simply receiving affection. Example: the student will cooperate with another student on taking turns in using a game. If this objective is to be taught, it is usually sequenced with other objectives according to the way most children develop.

8. *Task analysis*—the materials have been developed into specific tasks for the learner which have behavioral requirements that suggest a sequence for presentation and which allow an observer to determine if the learner accomplishes the task.

9. *Errorless discrimination*—the tasks are sequenced in such a manner that the student should move from step to step without making errors. This technique is used in some types of programmed instruction.

10. *Figure-ground*—the organization of materials, frequently perceptual in nature, in a field so that one stands out in a distinct way (figure) and the rest remains in the background (ground). Figure-ground organization can be used with other characteristics such as sounds, where one sound is heard over and above a background of others.

11. *To an affective response system*—where recognition is given to different levels of attitudes, from the simplest of merely attending to an object, to the building up of complex attitudes which predispose one's behavior toward a wide range of stimuli, e.g. enjoying a variety of forms of music.

12. *Interrelationships of a subject*—where the subject matter contains a logical relationship of concepts and processes. Example: adding must be mastered prior to multiplying. The local community is studied prior to more distant entities of state or federal government.

13. *Positive reinforcement and programmed sequence*—where the material has been developed into small steps that lead the learner toward a larger concept through a sequence that permits the learner to receive reinforcement through knowledge of right answers.

14. *Open-ended development of generalization*—the instructional sequence is purposely quite open, e.g., letting the learner try out many possibilities and alternatives before arriving at a generalization.

15. *Advanced organizers (cognitive)*—a framework of key concepts, crucial to understanding and relating concepts of the larger body of material, are strategically placed in the sequence, forming an ideational ladder to which other material can readily be related. In some materials a short summary preceding the main body of instructional material delineates the key concepts or stresses their relationships to other concepts known by the learner, thus serving as advance organizers through the ideational anchors it gives to the learner for organizing, relating, and remembering the new material.

16. *Modes of transaction*—a transaction is the interaction of a learner and stimuli in this context consisting of instructional materials. A mode is the channel that is used. Is the student asked to passively view, manipulate, verbally organize? Is the teacher an important part of the mode through exercising control over the learner's channels of transaction (methodological) to be used with instructional materials?

17. *Teacher-centric method*—the teacher is largely responsible for choosing and directing the mode of transaction for the learner. Teacher-centric modes of transaction prescribe that the "teacher will . . ." and are predicated on obtaining specific learner responses.

18. *Pupil-centric method*—the learner is responsible for choosing the modes of transaction with the instructional material and is frequently left to evaluate and revise his behavior toward materials without teacher supervision.

19. *Psychomotor skills*—muscular or motor skills which require manipulation of material or objects. The ability to stack blocks is a psychomotor skill.

20. *Affective response*—responses which emphasize feelings, emotion or degree of acceptance or rejection stemming from internal attitudinal sets. Such responses may be labeled attitudes, biases, interests, etc.

21. *Norm-referent evaluation*—judging a learner's performance by what other known groups of learners do on the same tasks. Achievement test scores, aptitude tests and mental test scores report their results in norm referent terms. The statement, "This particular learner scored at 4th grade level," is using a norm referent evaluation of the learner's performance.

22. *Criterion-referent evaluation*—the learner is judged on his ability to do a specified task or demonstrate the behavior appropriate to the task. The learner is judged on whether he can or cannot

demonstrate the appropriate behavior that signifies task accomplishment and is not judged by comparison of his performance with another group of learners.

Results

The Data

Following completion of the three trials, the data were compiled by item. Since the purposes of this study were primarily formative, the data presented in the following pages are confined to the numeration of each item on assessment of the reading learning package in the interests of brevity.

Table 9-1 presents the proportionate distribution of the individual's responses and the frequency distribution of the teams' responses on the "yes-no" items in the instrument.

Table 9-1. Item tabulation of responses by individuals
and teams on the learning package in reading

Question Category	Proportions (25 individuals)					Frequencies (7 teams)		
	Yes	No	No reply	Mean	S.D.	Yes	No	No reply
I. OBJECTIVES								
A.	.92	0	.08	1.00	0	7	0	0
1.	1.00	0	0	1.00	0	6	0	1
2.	.96	0	0	1.00	0	6	0	1
3.	.92	.08	0	.92	.27	6	0	1
4. Instructions								
a)	.92	.04	.04	.96	.20	6	0	1
b)	.68	.28	.04	.71	.45	4	2	1
c)	.20	.76	.04	.21	.41	1	5	1
5. (Anecdotal)								
B.	.12	.12	.76	.50	.50	0	0	7
1. (Anecdotal)								
C. Instruction								
1.	1.00	0	0	1.00	0	6	0	1
2.	.96	.04	0	.96	.20	6	0	1
3.	.92	.08	0	.92	.27	6	0	1
4. Instructions								
a)	.92	0	.08	1.00	0	7	0	0
b)	.32	0	.68	1.00	0	1	0	6
c)	1.00	0	0	1.00	0	7	0	0
d)	.96	0	.04	1.00	0	7	0	0

	Yes	No	No reply	Mean	S.D.	Yes	No	No reply
5. Instruction								
a)	.84	0	.16	1.00	0	5	0	2
b)	.92	0	.08	1.00	0	7	0	0
c)	1.00	0	0	1.00	0	7	0	0
d)	.84	0	.16	1.00	0	6	0	1

D. (See Tables 9-2 and 9-3.)

II. ORGANIZATION OF THE MATERIAL

	Yes	No	No reply	Mean	S.D.	Yes	No	No reply
A.	.84	.16	0	.84	.37	6	1	0
B. Instructions								
1.	.04	0	.96	1.00	0	0	0	7
2.	.88	0	.12	1.00	0	5	0	2
3.	.20	0	.80	1.00	0	1	0	6
4.	.68	0	.32	1.00	0	5	0	2
5.	.64	0	.36	1.00	0	4	0	3
6.	.16	0	.84	1.00	0	0	0	7
C. (Anecdotal)								
D.	.84	0	.16	1.00	0	7	0	0
1. Instructions								
a)	.92	.04	.04	.96	.20	6	1	0
b)	.28	.52	.20	.35	.48	2	4	1
c)	1.00	0	0	1.00	0	7	0	0
d)	.92	0	.08	1.00	0	7	0	0
e) (Anecdotal)								
2. Instructions								
a)	.64	.12	.24	.84	.36	4	3	0
b)	.56	.16	.28	.78	.42	3	3	1
E.								
1. Instructions								
a)	.80	0	.20	1.00	0	5	0	2
b)	.28	0	.72	1.00	0	0	0	7
c)	.52	0	.48	1.00	0	2	0	5
d)	.80	0	.20	1.00	0	5	0	2
e) (Anecdotal)								

F. (Anecdotal)

G. (See Tables 9-2 and 9-3.)

III. METHODOLOGY

	Yes	No	No reply	Mean	S.D.	Yes	No	No reply
A.	1.00	0	0	1.00	0	7	0	0
B.	.96	0	.04	1.00	0	7	0	0
1. Instructions								
a)	.88	.12	0	.88	.32	7	0	0
b)	.20	.68	.12	.23	.42	0	5	2
c)	.60	.20	.20	.75	.43	3	2	2
d)	.60	.20	.20	.75	.43	5	0	2

	Yes	No	No reply	Mean	S.D.	Yes	No	No reply
e)	.76	.12	.12	.86	.34	6	1	0
f)	.84	.16	0	.86	.34	6	1	0
g)	.52	.44	.04	.54	.50	4	2	1
C.	.72	.20	.08	.22	.41	0	6	1
1. (See Tables 9-2 and 9-3.)								
2.	.04	.96	0	.04	.20	1	6	0
3.	0	.96	.04	0	.00	0	7	0
4.[a]								
a) (Anecdotal)								
b) (Anecdotal)								
D. (Anecdotal)								
E. (See Tables 9-2 and 9-3.)								

IV. EVALUATION

	Yes	No	No reply	Mean	S.D.	Yes	No	No reply
A.	.88	.08	.04	.92	.28	6	0	1
1. Instructions								
a)	.92	0	.08	1.00	0	7	0	0
b)	.96	0	.04	1.00	0	7	0	0
c)	.04	0	.96	1.00	0	0	0	7
d)	.52	0	.48	1.00	0	3	0	4
2.	.92	0	.08	1.00	0	7	0	0
3. Instructions								
a)	.76	0	.24	1.00	0	5	0	2
b)	.72	0	.28	1.00	0	5	0	2
c)	.84	0	.16	1.00	0	6	0	1
d)	.76	0	.24	1.00	0	5	0	2
e)	.70	0	.24	1.00	0	5	0	2
B.	.96	.4	0	.96	.20	7	0	0
C.	.56	.32	.12	.64	.48	3	3	1
D.	0	.96	.04	0	0	0	7	0
E. (Anecdotal)								
F. (See Tables 9-2 and 9-3.)								

V. COMMENT

A. (Anecdotal)
B. (See Tables 9-2 and 9-3.)

[a]Responses were: most succeeded, 0; approximately half succeeded, 20%; few succeeded, 4%; omitted, 76%.

Tables 9-2 and 9-3 present the individuals' and teams' ratings of the reading materials on the seven-point scale for each of the four constructs and give their overall assessment under section V (Comment).

Table 9-2. Summary ratings by individuals of constructs
on seven-point scale (reading)

Constructs	Frequencies (25 individuals)								
	1	2	3	4	5	6	7	MEAN	S.D.
Objectives (I)	0	0	1	6	12	4	2	5.00	0.95
Organization (II)	0	1	1	11	8	3	1	4.56	1.04
Methodology (III)	0	0	3	12	5	4	1	4.52	1.04
Evaluation (IV)	0	3	2	14	5		1	4.00	1.07
Comment (overall assessment) (V)	0	0	2	8	12	3	0	4.64	0.80

Table 9-3. Summary ratings by teams of constructs
on seven-point scale (reading)

Constructs	Frequencies (7 teams)								
	1	2	3	4	5	6	7	MEAN	S.D.
Objectives (I)	0	0	0	2	4	0	1	5.00	1.00
Organization (II)	0	0	1	2	3	1	0	4.57	0.97
Methodology (III)	1	0	1	3	2	0	0	3.71	1.37
Evaluation (IV)	0	1	0	5	1	0	0	3.85	0.90
Comment (overall assessment) (V)	0	0	1	3	3	0	0	4.28	0.75

Table 9-4 presents the team's ratings of the science materials in terms of each of the four constructs and gives their overall assessment under section V.

Table 9-4. Summary ratings by teams of constructs
on seven-point scale (science)

Constructs	1	2	3	4	5	6	7	MEAN	S.D.
Objectives (I)	0	1	4	1	1	0	0	3.28	0.94
Organization (II)	0	0	1	4	1	1	0	4.28	0.94
Methodology (III)	0	0	1	3	2	1	0	4.42	0.97
Evaluation (IV)	0	3	2	1	0	1	0	3.14	1.46
Comment (overall assessment) (V)	0	0	2	3	2	0	0	4.00	0.81

The large amounts of anecdotal data elicited by the instrument are not reported in this paper except for those from the final section, where the raters summed up the strengths and weaknesses of the materials. Table 9-5 presents summaries of their individual comments in section V on the strengths and weaknesses of the learning package on reading. For purposes of analysis, these comments have been subdivided according to whether the respondents taught at the elementary or the secondary level. Tables 9-6 and 9-7 present summaries of the teams' comments on the strengths and weaknesses of the learning packages on both reading and science.

Table 9-5. Summary comments by individuals on overall assessment of learning package (reading)

Elementary Teachers

Strengths:

1. Topics are very diverse and appeal to the children.
2. Pictures are colorful: print is large.
3. Tests in workbook after each unit.
4. Exercises on skills to be developed appear in teacher's guide.
5. Suggestions on approaches to each story.
6. Basic reading test is available.
7. Workbook is good for independent activities.
8. Stories selected have high interest level.
9. Teacher's guide presents a variety of methodologies.
10. Good supplementary reading list presented, keeps kinds in mind.
11. Variety of subject matter geared to this age group (grade 6).
12. Objectives good, varied, and clearly stated.
13. Provides for evaluation, feedback, and reinforcement.
14. Will adapt easily to higher ability levels (workbook).
15. Has criterion reference procedures for evaluation.
16. Provides norm references.
17. Good objectives (behavioral).

Weaknesses:

1. No level of performance in behavioral objectives.
2. No immediate evaluative feedback for student.
3. No indication that material has been field tested.

Table 9-5 (continued)

4. Psychomotor skills are not clearly indicated.
5. Strongly teacher-centric.
6. Evaluation poor; methodology poor; no allowance for individual differences.
7. Book itself does not provide materials for the below or above average.
8. I question the interest level of the selections.
9. Criteria for evaluation not clearly stated.
10. No objectives for children set forth in workbook exercises: why they are doing the exercises.
11. Not enough reinforcement of skills in a logical sequence.
12. No enough variety of activities in workbook.
13. Additional material for evaluation of concepts is needed.

Secondary Teachers

Strengths:

1. Strength lies in its objectives and somewhat in scope and sequence.
2. Topics selected have a high interest level and are timely.
3. Graphic presentations are excellent.
4. Lessons help develop cognitive and subject skills.
5. Includes many aids for the teacher.
6. A thoroughly linguistic base.
7. Stimulates extensive reading.
8. Has workbook.
9. Survey test and basic reading test available.
10. Good modes of transaction and evaluation in reading skills area.
11. Valuable for the new teacher who needs a well-structured package.
12. Local organization.
13. Multi-ethnic appeal.
14. Remedial exercises to strengthen reading abilities.
15. Reading level appropriate for grade and preadolescent.
16. Allows teacher lots of variety in approach.

Table 9-5 (continued)

Weaknesses:

1. Range of evaluation limited to behavior product as criterion measure.
2. Provisions for measure of learner behavior should be included.
3. Evaluation limited to product with little process attention.
4. No immediate student feedback.
5. Does not appear to have been widely field tested.
6. Objectives do not specify level of performance. (Sometimes implied.)
7. Psychomotor skills not enumerated in specific terms.
8. Perhaps the objectives could have been more clearly developed.
9. Very structured and does not permit for a variety of modes of transaction.
10. Weak in methodology and evaluation.
11. Overemphasized facts and knowledge in modes of transaction.
12. Overly teacher-centric.
13. Lacks reinforcement throughout.
14. Makes no provision for variations in individual ability.
15. Selection of content lacks imagination.
16. Teacher would need some training before using the reading materials.

Table 9-6. Summary comments by teams on overall assessment of learning package (reading)

Strengths:

1. It is structurally designed.
2. Scope and sequence well organized.
3. Variety of modes of transaction (especially in follow-up activities).
4. Criterion reference for evaluation—workbook. Norm reference for evaluation—test kit.
5. Materials highly structured.
6. Cognitive skills and objectives state the type of expected behavior and have structured formal and informal evaluation.

Table 9-6 (continued)

7. Objectives frequently behaviorally stated.
8. Multi-ethnic wide story appeal.
9. Could be useful to new teachers who need a structured program.
10. Availability of tests.
11. Suggested methodology as well as organization of material.
12. Stories selected for high interest level.
13. Various aids for the teacher in manual and workbook.
14. Methodology is spelled out for those who need it.
15. Good independent activities in workbook.
16. Tests in workbook for each unit; also, survey and inventory tests available.

Weaknesses:

1. Not enough variety in evaluation and reinforcement exercises for weaknesses.
2. More pupil-centered activities needed.
3. Makes only limited provision for individual variations in ability and skills.
4. Teachers need some training to use overall program.
5. Graphic presentations poor.
6. Very teacher-centric.
7. Overemphasis on facts, especially in the dominant modes of transaction.
8. Overly concerned with product.
9. Overly teacher-centric approach.
10. Teacher-centric to an extreme.
11. Little allowance for variety of modes of transaction—limited provision for individual differences.
12. Has not been evaluated as an effective teaching method.
13. Has a traditional subject-logic, teacher-centric mode of transaction.
14. Levels of performance for objectives on a day-to-day basis not stated.
15. Lacks immediate feedback for pupils.
16. Modes of transaction and evaluation of attitudes are weak.
17. Psychomotor skills not enumerated in specific terms.

Table 9-6 (continued)

18. No evidence of field testing.
19. Lack of immediate feedback for students to get assistance.
20. No indication of field evaluation.

Table 9-7. Summary statements by teams on overall assessment of learning package (science)

Strengths:

1. Operational for the teacher without science background.
2. General objectives are stated.
3. Scope and sequence are set forth.
4. Scope and sequence are logical; organization is orderly and clear.
5. Part of a sequential K-12 program, clear on how it fits in.
6. Good format, understandable.
7. Some strengths on teacher orientation to the area.

Weaknesses:

1. No behavioral objectives.
2. Limited interrelationships between units.
3. Gap between goals and design; for example, little or no emphasis on process or discovery.
4. Few evaluation tools; no field testing.
5. Organization rigid and subject demand-oriented.
6. Objectives not stated in behavioral terms; instructional objectives weak and difficult to operationalize.
7. Methodology does not provide for individual differences—but average in this respect.
8. Too factual in its orientation.
9. Teacher-centric modes of transaction.
10. Poor evaluation tools in the package.
11. Scope and sequence lack any behavioral statements.
12. Subject-centered; product rather than process oriented.

Discussion

Examination of the individual responses in Table 9-1 shows considerable agreement in fifty-six of the sixty-four responses. Including the data from Tables 9-2 and 9-3, the greatest disagreement occurred on the following items:

I.A.4(b)   If the objectives are stated in behavioral terms, do they specify the conditions under which the type of behavior will appear?

II.B.5.   Was logical order used as a basis to organize the materials?

II.D.1(b)   If there is a basis for the scope of the material, is it related to a motor skill development?

II.D.2(a)   Has the scope been analyzed for its appropriateness to students?

II.D.2(b)   Has the scope been analyzed for its relationship to other material?

II.G.   Quantitative rating: organization of the materials.

III.B.1(c)   Does the mode of transaction require active participation by the students?

III.B.1(g)   Does the mode of transaction provide for variation among students—use several approaches to method?

IV.A.1(d)   Do evaluation procedures emphasize affective responses?

IV.C.   Does the evaluation plan give attention to both product and process?

IV.F.   Quantitative rating: evaluation.

In a few instances, disagreements among individuals were compressed and disappeared in the team judgments, as in the responses to question I.B, "If there are no objectives stated for the use of the material, are the objectives instead implicit or readily obvious?" The weight of opinion among individuals—about three-quarters did not reply—tipped the scales in the team responses. In a triumph of group pressure over the individual, every one of the teams failed to answer the item.

A somewhat comparable situation occurred in responses to question 1.A.4(c), "If stated in behavioral terms, do the objectives specify level of performance expected?" In response to this question, five individuals said yes, nineteen said no, and one did not reply. Similarly, one team said yes, five teams said no, and one team did not reply. In this section, respondents were asked to list examples of objectives, and inspection of their comments lends weight to the correctness of the majority's interpretation, since none of the objectives listed specify performance criteria. Examples of objectives listed are: "Teaches pupils to listen, speak, and write effectively and well," "Increases competence in reading skills and encourages personal reading," "Children use guide words to locate entries," "Children generalize about a main idea." This problem appears to be centered around the application of a definition to specific cases; in the case of the team that responded affirmatively to the item it is probable that three respondents were randomly teamed together who incorrectly assessed the question in their individual ratings.

Some disagreements apparently resulted from differing interpretations of some questions. For example, in question II.D.2(b), "Has the scope (of the material in the instructional package) been subjected to analysis for relationship to other material?" three teams answered yes, three answered no. Evidently a question that seemed straightforward to the author was ambiguous to the raters. Considering the attention given to instructional design in reading packages, lack of unanimity on this question is troubling, and one suspects that "scope and sequence" was not seen as a unitary concept by the teams and served as a dual stimulus in the assessment; that is, different teams may have been answering two different questions.

Other problems resulting from differing subjective interpretations arose in responses to questions II.D.1(b), III.B.1(c), and III.B.1 (g). Since there were a multitude of stimuli and literally hundreds of pupil activities to judge in the reading package, individuals and teams may very well have been using different samples of data as a basis for their judgments.

Some additional paradoxes emerge when the individuals' statements on strengths and weaknesses of the reading package are compared (see Table 9-5). The same item was occasionally listed as a strength by one and as a weakness by another. Again, a source of difficulty may have been the range of the stimuli to which the respondents were reacting, as well as real differences in their subjective judgments of whether the stories in the reading package would be of interest to students. It is worth noting that a number of these paradoxes do not appear in the teams' listing of strengths and weaknesses in Table 9-6. The hypothesis that resolution of the differences of individual assessments comes through agreement on what stimuli to judge is confirmed in the teams' assessment of the science bulletin (see Table 9-7). As in the teams' assessment of the reading package, the teams' listings of the science bulletin's strengths and weaknesses tend to be mutually exclusive, greatly increasing the value of their overall summary judgment of the potential of the learning package for classroom use.

Inter-rater reliability was estimated by using the odd-even technique of comparing the scores of every other respondent. The results indicate that on each of the ratings of the constructs and on the overall score the reliability estimates were greater than .9. On the other hand, inter-item reliability estimates calculated for each subscore and for the overall score were as follows: objectives .38; organization of material .37; methodology .77; evaluation .99 (although this last statistic is suspect since four responses were inadvertently omitted from the calculation); and overall .55. In this latter analysis, certain of the reliability estimates on the subscores suggest some internal consistency, but the general conclusion can be drawn that the instrument had low reliability for this administration.

There are only small differences in the mean ratings assigned to the constructs by the individuals and the teams; results show considerable consistency in the average ratings assigned in the three trials; and the means cluster around the midpoint of the scale. However, the distribution of the ratings becomes slightly more compressed in the team, as shown by a comparison of estimates of the standard deviation in Tables 9-2, 9-3, and 9-4. This can also be seen by comparing the frequency distributions of the ratings for points 6 and 7 with that for points 1 through 5.

Some Persistent Issues

While some experts have agreed that the categories of the instrument contain a high degree of content validity, no criterion-related validity studies have been made. A follow-up study on the use of instructional packages by teachers after they have assessed the materials with the instrument would provide useful data on the instrument's effectiveness in improving implementation, as well as on the value of its a priori assessment of the learning packages.

Criticism has been voiced that the seven-point scale at the end of each construct and the overall assessment require judgments on a variety of stimuli and hence are confusing to the rater. Granted, a rater must weigh several factors in his mind as he makes a general judgment on the construct and the overall worth of the material; but few decisions we make in life are simple. Seldom are variables discrete and free of ambiguity, and instructional packages, being the organized complexities they are, pose problems resulting in selections based upon compromise. Should we accept weak evaluation techniques and limited teacher aids on methodology for material that has carefully delineated objectives and a well-prepared scope and sequence? Do we put up with poorly stated objectives for the sake of a well-developed methodology of proven interest to students? Such questions are not atypical of the ones decision makers must face in selecting materials. The instrument encourages an examination of the trade-offs that must be made, by helping the rater to establish specifically what the options are in the designs of different materials.

Another criticism that has been raised and dealt with concerns the feasibility of an instrument that stresses instructional design and ignores content. As the form is now constructed, instructional materials that lean toward a programmed approach and stress instructional design over content would be favored in assessment. Repeated field trials with the instrument have shown that instructional materials that stress design, such as reading packages, and materials that have a tight internal logic, such as arithmetic materials, lend themselves to easier assessment within the framework of the instrument. Nevertheless, they do not receive exceptionally high ratings, since raters judge them against similar materials and not against materials in other subject fields where design has not been as prominent a concern. In early forms of the instrument an attempt was made to allow for the assessment of content, but the present instrument does not address this problem directly, except in the items on the organization (scope and sequence) of the materials. Even so, section II does reflect the knottiness of the problem in the somewhat lower internal consistency estimates.

So far I have concluded that the judgment of content is better handled as an issue separate from instructional design, although I have encountered well-designed materials that are strong on quality of content, indicating that the design-content relationship is a synergistic one. The problem is not an unfamiliar one, and is similar to the issue of whether one stresses process or content. In the past, unfortunately, the process-content debate was framed with process and content occupying polar positions that were seen as irreconcilable. Now they are seen more comprehensively, as interactive variates of a successful educational program directed toward the production of specific competencies and behavioral patterns.

For optimum results in use of the instrument it is necessary to have a training period. Teachers are not used to looking at materials analytically, and in the training period I have found that old and cherished instructional packages are often seen in a new light after assessment. "I used to think this was a great series," is a frequent comment. But disillusionment is not the goal. Rather, critical awareness of the constraints and potential of the learning package should be the objective. With several administrations of the instrument, teachers become quite adept in assessment; however, the first time through it is time-consuming.

Are we at a stage where we can insist that instructional packages take explicit cognizance of some principles of instructional design and reflect some consistency in the application of these principles? I have always thought that judging a book by its cover had limitations —but I am inclined to believe that most of our assessment of instructional materials has not moved much beyond that. The influence of instructional materials on curriculum and instruction has been noted by Jovanovich (1964, p. 56): "The schools inscribed a pattern, the publishers issued books to fit it, and in that gradual transmutation that became usual over the past half-century, the books made the course as often as the course made the books." It is my hope that the instrument presented in this paper encourages criticism in producing, assessing, and utilizing instructional materials, and assists in focusing the search for a more scientific and rational approach in these three areas.

References

Board of Education of the City of New York. *Science Grade 7: The Chemistry of Matter*. Curriculum Bulletin 9a, 1962-63 Series (Experimental Edition). New York: Board of Education, 1963.

Jovanovich, William. *Now Barabbas*. New York: Harper, 1964.

Robinson, Helen, et al. *Calvalcades,* Book 6 (Teachers Edition); *Cavalcades,* Book 6 (Student Edition); *Think and Do* (Student Edition). Chicago: Scott, Foresman & Co., 1965.

Smock, Richard, and Kelly, Edward. "A Preliminary Instrument for Assessing Curriculum Materials: A Field Report and Discussion." Report #110. Urbana, Ill.: Course Development Division, Office of Instructional Resources, University of Illinois, 1969. Mimeographed.

10. URBAN SYSTEM PERFORMANCE

Erik Van Hove
James S. Coleman
Kenneth Rabben
Nancy Karweit

Recent practice in a number of cities has begun to make possible somewhat more precise and systematic comparisons of educational development than has been possible until now. This practice is the publication of test score data in two or more grades on a school-by-school basis for widely-used standard tests, and publication of the single best student-background predictor of performance, racial composition of schools.

It is likely that the practice of making such information public to everyone interested in school performance will become more widespread in the future in response to continued public pressure. In order for this publication to be of aid to education rather than harm, it is important that the data be subject to some analysis, rather than merely "consumed," with implicit comparisons suggested by the form in which data are presented. This chapter initiates a kind of examination that we anticipate will be extensively developed in the future: intercity comparisons of the performance of schools in inducing student achievement.

In this study, data from six cities which used some of the same national tests in approximately the same grades are compared, in ways which we feel allow for valid inferences about educational growth in these cities. Some analysts will object that valid inferences about educational growth are impossible unless the *same* children are compared at two different times. However, in ongoing institutions like schools, the statistical problems of such a design are perhaps even greater than those of a cross-sectional study. For example, the mobility of students among schools makes the students present in a given school at two times a very nonrepresentative sample of the total student population in that school. Although inferences about an individual's academic growth from test scores in two different grades during the same calendar year are necessarily not ironclad, the sources of error in this method may in fact be smaller than those of other procedures which measure the same students at two points in time.

The cities and grades for which school-by-school test data and racial composition of the schools are available for comparison are:

City	Grades	Testing Date	Test Scores Reported Iowa Test of Basic Skills
New York	4, 6	Spring, 1969	Arithmetic, language total
Philadelphia	4, 6	Spring, 1968	Arithmetic, reading
Detroit	4, 6	Fall, 1968	Arithmetic, reading, language total
Baltimore	4, 6	Spring, 1969	Arithmetic, reading, language total

Another comparison is possible between New York and Chicago, since in the spring of 1969 both administered the reading section of the Metropolitan Achievement Test, New York for grades 4 and 6, and Chicago for grades 3 and 6. In addition, comparison may be made with Los Angeles, which administered the reading section of the Stanford Achievement Test in grade 3 in Spring 1969, and in grade 6 in Fall 1968. However, this comparison must be tentative because of the different test used in Los Angeles.

In this chapter, the cities are compared in three ways: according to achievement *level* at a given grade; according to inferred *growth* in achievement from grade 4 (or 3) to 6; and according to degree of racial segregation of schools. In addition to these three types of comparisons of cities, the same data are used to examine achievement in racially integrated schools compared to achievement in racially segregated schools. This examination, as will be evident, is subject to several methodological pitfalls, if inferences about effects of integrated education are attempted. Nevertheless, the examination provides descriptive data about such performance in these different-ly-composed schools.

Comparisons of Achievement Levels and Growth in Six Cities

Individual test scores are often reported in two ways. First, the grade equivalent score is reported, indicating the grade level of the average student obtaining such a score. That is, at each actual grade level, the absolute score obtained by the "average student" is recorded. (This "average student" is intended, in the norms used here, to be an average over the country as a whole, although the norming is carried out on samples that may not be truly representative.) Then any student who obtains this same absolute score is assigned this "grade equivalent." A student who obtains a different absolute score is assigned as his "grade equivalent" the actual grade level for which the average student obtained that same score. Second, the percentile score of the individual is reported, indicating the percent of students in a representative sample of students at the same actual grade level whose scores fall below that score.

Neither of these standardizations is correct for our purposes; the correct standardization would be a transformation to standard scores (i.e., the number of standard deviations below or above the national average for that grade and month in school). However, we will use the standardizations that exist, the only available procedure.

Summary reports for the school are ordinarily obtained by averaging the grade equivalent score; however, sometimes the median grade equivalent score is reported. Although averaging of individual percentiles would not be a correct procedure, averaging of individual standard scores would be.

The scores reported here are obtained as follows: by averaging over a subset of the schools for a city (using an unweighted average, since most schools covering a given grade level in a city are about the same in size) the average grade equivalent in that subset of schools at the particular grade tested is obtained. This can be thought of as the grade equivalent score of the average student in the given subset of schools in that city. Then the percentile position of that score is found. This can be thought of as the percentile position of that hypothetical average student.

Tables 10-1, 10-2, and 10-3 give the mean scores in Arithmetic

Table 10-1. Average test scores in arithmetic by grade and racial composition of school

	Baltimore			Detroit			New York			Philadelphia		
	4	6	D	4	6	D	4	6	D	4	6	D
Grade Equivalent Scores												
National Norm	4.7	6.6	1.9	4.1	6.1	2.0	4.7	6.6	1.9	4.7	6.6	1.9
Percent Minority												
0-19	4.4	6.5	2.1	3.7	5.6	1.9	4.7	6.7	2.0	4.5	6.3	1.8
20-39	4.4	6.4	2.0	3.4	5.1	1.7	4.5	6.2	1.7	4.1	6.1	2.0
40-59	4.1	6.0	1.9	3.3	5.1	1.8	4.2	5.8	1.6	3.9	5.8	1.9
60-79	3.9	5.8	1.9	3.0	4.6	1.4	3.9	5.4	1.5	3.8	5.5	1.7
80-100	3.7	5.6	1.9	3.0	4.5	1.5	3.6	4.8	1.2	3.6	5.1	1.5
Percent Scores												
National Norm	50	50		50	50		50	50		50	50	
Percent Minority												
0-19	40	46	+6	36	37	+1	50	52	+2	44	41	−3
20-39	40	44	+4	26	25	−1	44	39	−5	31	36	+5
40-59	31	33	+2	22	25	+3	34	29	−5	25	29	+4
69-79	25	29	+4	13	13	0	28	19	−9	22	21	−1
80-100	19	24	+5	13	11	−2	17	8	−9	17	13	−4

Table 10-2. Average test scores in reading by grade and racial composition of school

	Baltimore			Detroit			New York			Philadelphia		
	4	6	D	4	6	D	4	6	D	4	6	D
Grade Equivalent Scores												
National Norm	4.7	6.7	2.0	4.1	6.1	2.0				4.7	6.7	2.0
Percent Minority												
0-19	3.9	6.2	2.3	3.7	5.8	2.1				4.2	6.3	2.1
20-39	4.1	6.1	2.0	3.3	5.3	2.0				3.8	6.0	2.2
40-59	3.6	5.9	2.3	3.2	5.3	2.1				3.6	5.8	2.2
60-79	3.6	5.8	2.2	3.0	4.8	1.8				3.5	5.4	1.9
80-100	3.2	5.4	2.2	3.0	4.7	1.7				3.3	4.9	1.6
Percent Scores												
National Norm	50	50		50	50					50	50	
Percent Minority												
0-19	29	39	+10	39	43	+4				36	41	+5
20-39	34	37	+3	29	31	+2				27	34	+7
40-59	23	32	+9	27	31	+4				23	30	+6
60-79	23	30	+7	22	20	−2				21	22	+1
80-100	16	22	+6	22	19	3				17	14	−3

Table 10-3. Average test scores in language total by grade and racial composition of school

	Baltimore			Detroit			New York			Philadelphia		
	4	6	D	4	6	D	4	6	D	4	6	D
Grade Equivalent Scores												
National Norm	4.7	6.7	2.0	4.1	6.1	2.0	4.7	6.7	2.0			
Percent Minority												
0-19	4.2	6.2	2.0	3.9	5.4	1.5	5.0	6.8	1.8			
20-39	4.4	6.3	1.9	3.6	5.2	1.6	4.7	6.4	1.7			
40-59	4.0	5.8	1.8	3.5	5.0	1.5	4.4	5.9	1.5			
60-79	3.7	5.7	2.0	3.3	4.8	1.5	4.1	5.4	1.3			
80-100	3.5	5.4	1.9	3.3	4.7	1.4	3.7	4.8	1.1			
Percent Scores												
National Norm	50	50		50	50		50	50				
Percent Minority												
0-19	37	40	+3	44	35	−9	56	52	−4			
20-39	41	42	+1	36	31	−5	49	44	−5			
40-59	32	33	+1	33	27	−6	41	35	−6			
60-79	25	31	+6	28	24	−4	34	26	−8			
80-100	20	26	+6	28	22	−6	25	16	−9			

Total, Reading, and Language Total for the four cities using the ITBS at grades 4 and 6, for schools with differing racial composition.

In New York, the large number of students with Puerto Rican backgrounds complicates the comparisons. In the tables, the percent Negro and percent Puerto Rican have been combined, so that the reported school populations are "percent Negro and Puerto Rican." (Scores were also calculated for schools that are predominantly Negro, and for schools that are predominantly Puerto Rican, and the results are nearly the same as for the combined category for Negro and Puerto Rican. Other studies have also shown that Puerto Rican and Negro students in American schools perform at about the same levels.)

Table 10-1 shows that for the nearly all-white schools at grade 4, performance is highest in New York schools, in fact above the national norm. Performance is lower in Philadelphia and Baltimore and lowest in Detroit. For the nearly all-Negro or all-Negro and Puerto Rican schools, the average in all four cities is considerably below the national norm, and all four cities are nearly the same, at a grade level of 1.0 or 1.1 years behind the national norm, and at the 13th, 17th, and 19th percentiles.

The scores at grade 6, however, differ sharply. In Baltimore schools, the difference between grade 4 and grade 6 in grade-equivalents is approximately the same for schools of all racial composition, about 2.0 grade equivalents. In Philadelphia and Detroit there is somewhat less difference between grades 4 and 6 in the schools with highest proportions of Negroes than in the schools with the lowest proportions. In New York, this reduced grade 4 to grade 6 increment for minority schools is even more pronounced. The increment is progressively less for schools with higher proportions of Negroes and Puerto Ricans. In the nearly all-Negro and Puerto Rican schools, the grade-equivalent difference is only 1.2 grade equivalents for an actual grade difference of two years.

In percentile scores, this difference between the three cities can be seen even more clearly. In Baltimore, the 6th grade percentile scores are from 2 to 6 points higher than the 4th grade scores. In Philadelphia, the percentile scores are slightly higher at grade 6 for the racially mixed schools, but 3 and 4 percentile points lower at grade 6 for the nearly all-white and nearly all-Negro ones. In New York, the nearly all-white schools at grade 6 are 2 percentile points higher than the grade 4 scores; but the nearly all-Negro and Puerto Rican schools are 9 percentile points lower at grade 6 than at grade 4. In Detroit nearly all-white schools are 1 percentile point higher, while nearly all-black schools are 2 percentile points lower.

In reading scores, no direct comparison of Baltimore, Detroit, and Philadelphia with New York is possible. As Table 10-4 shows, however, Philadelphia, Detroit, and Baltimore show a pattern similar to that of the arithmetic test. The difference in reading performance between grades 4 and 6 is, for Baltimore schools, greater than the national norm, exceeding 2.0 years for schools of every population group. There is a percentile increment of +3 to +10, showing that the performance at grade 6 is distinctly better than that at grade 4 for schools of each racial mix.

In Philadelphia, the predominantly white schools show a positive percentile increment; but for the nearly all-Negro schools, the percentile score at grade 6 is 3 points lower than at grade 4.

Altogether, the Baltimore and Philadelphia patterns in reading are much like their patterns in arithmetic, except that in Philadelphia, the reading percentile for nearly all-white schools is higher at grade 6 than at grade 4, while the arithmetic score is lower.

A comparison between Baltimore, Detroit, and New York is possible for the language totals test, which was not reported in Philadelphia. This test measures language skills related to reading (spelling, capitalization, punctuation, and word usage). Table 10-3 shows the Baltimore-Detroit-New York comparison in language totals. For Baltimore and New York, the pattern is similar to the results of the arithmetic test. The average student in New York's nearly all-white schools is above the national norm at both grades. In all other types of schools, for each city, the scores are below the national norm. Comparison of grade 6 with grade 4 in the three cities shows that, once again, there is a positive increment in Baltimore schools of all racial compositions, ranging from +1 to +6. In New York, there is a lower percentile at grade 6 than at grade 4, for schools of all compositions, ranging from −4 to −9. Detroit shows a general slow progress in language skills for schools of all racial compositions, leading to a loss in percentile points most pronounced for nearly all-white schools.

Although New York did not administer the Iowa Reading Test at these grade levels, it did give another standardized test, also reported in grade-equivalents and percentiles measured against national norms. This is the Metropolitan Achievement Test, another of the widely-used tests of reading skills. The test results in New York of schools with differing racial compositions are shown in Table 10-4. These results show the same pattern as for the previous tests: the nearly all-white schools above the national norm at grade 4 and at

Table 10-4. Reading section of metropolitan achievement test

	New York			Chicago (Averages of School Median)		
	4	6	D	3	6	D*
Grade Equivalent Scores						
National Norm	4.7	6.7	2.0	3.5	6.7	2.2
Percent Minority						
0-19	5.4	7.3	1.9	3.9	6.8	1.9
20-39	4.9	6.8	1.9	3.4	5.7	1.5
40-59	4.5	6.2	1.7	3.5	5.7	1.5
60-79	4.2	5.8	1.6	3.3	5.4	1.4
80-100	3.7	4.9	1.2	3.1	4.9	1.2
Percent Scores						
National Norm	50	50		50	50	
Percent Minority						
0-19	63	58	−5	60	51	−6
20-39	55	51	−4	44	36	−5
40-59	45	44	−1	50	36	−9
60-79	35	38	+3	38	31	−5
80-100	23	22	−1	32	22	−7

*For comparability, two thirds of difference is used here, since tests were given in the 3d and 7th grades in Chicago, and the 4th and 6th in all other cities.

grade 6; and the nearly all-Negro or Puerto Rican schools sharply lower at grade 4, and lower still at grade 6. Chicago administered the same reading test as New York, but at grades 3 and 6. These results are also given in Table 10-6. Chicago shows a pattern very similar to that of New York, with an even more dramatic differential. The fact that the percentile and grade-equivalent scores are generally higher on the Metropolitan Achievement Test than on the Iowa test of language and arithmetic skills suggests that one of the two test publishers has a defective normalization procedure; but even though the levels are displaced on the Metropolitan test compared to the Iowa test, the general trends are the same: there is a lower percentile position at grade 6 than at grade 4, for all types of schools.

Los Angeles is another large city for which standardized tests in reading by school are available. While the New York, Philadelphia, and Baltimore scores have not previously been published, the Los Angeles scores were reported on a school-by-school basis in the *Los Angeles Times* of September 30, 1969 for grade 6, and December 16, 1969 for grades 1, 2, and 3. In addition, the combined percent of Negro or Spanish-surname students (in Los Angeles, Negro or Mexican American) was reported school-by-school, allowing a comparison with the other five cities. Unfortunately, a different test is used in Los Angeles: the reading section of the Stanford Achievement Test, mandated for all California schools by the California legislature. Again, however, national norms allow an indirect comparison with the other cities.[1]

The test results for Los Angeles are shown in Table 10-5. The

Table 10-5. Average test scores on reading section of
Stanford Achievement Test in Los Angeles,
for schools with differing population compositions

	3rd	6th	Difference
Grade Equivalent Scores			
National Norm	3.8	6.2	2.4
Percent Negro and Mexican American			
0-19	3.8	5.8	2.0
20-39	3.3	5.1	1.8
40-59	3.2	4.9	1.7
60-79	3.0	4.6	1.6
80-100	2.5	4.1	1.6
Percent Scores			
0-19	50	43	−7
20-39	32	27	−5
40-59	28	23	−5
60-79	22	16	−4
80-100	10	8	−2

6th grade test was given in the fall, with a national norm of 6.2, while the test for grade 3 was given in the spring, with a national norm of 3.8.

At both grade levels, the difference in grade equivalents or percentiles between the schools at the extremes of racial composition is very large, even larger than in New York. Comparing grades 3 and 6, the positions in Los Angeles are from 2 to 7 percentile points lower for all racial compositions at grade 6 than at grade 3. In a direct comparison of percentiles with those of the other cities, the Los Angeles schools show a generally lower performance at grade 6 than do any of the other cities, except for the nearly all-white schools. Since there is no published breakdown of Negro and Mexican American by school, it is not possible to determine whether the low reading scores are due to the special language problems of the Mexican American students.

An important caution must be introduced in comparing Los Angeles with the other cities. Since none of the tests in these cities is the same as that used in Los Angeles, differences could arise from erroneous norming of the tests by one of the test publishers. The norms are intended to be "national norms," and are based on samples that the test publisher believes are representative of the nation. But there exists no National Bureau of Standards for educational tests to insure that these test norming procedures adequately reflect the nation. Therefore the comparisons between Los Angeles and the other cities have an added degree of uncertainty. It appears unlikely, however, that the lower performance of Los Angeles schools at grade 6 than at grade 3 is due solely to differences between test publishers, and in the absence of directly comparable tests, these comparisons provide the best evidence at hand on the performance of Los Angeles schools relatively to those of the other cities.

In comparing the scores of the average student in schools of varying racial composition in the six cities, several patterns emerge. These patterns can be expressed by first stating the relative positions at the earlier grade (grade 4 or grade 3), and then stating grade 6 scores as higher or lower than the scores at earlier grades. Since the cities showed similar patterns in all the different tests, general patterns can be stated, covering both arithmetic and reading skills.

Table 10-6 gives for the nearly all-white and nearly all-minority students the average percentile scores for each city. Because of the

Table 10-6. Average percentile rank over parts of the same
test battery for nearly all-white and nearly all-minority schools
at earlier and later grade

| | Nearly All-White Schools | | |
	Earlier Grade (3 or 4)	Later Grade (6)	Difference
Baltimore (Iowa)	35	42	+7
Detroit (Iowa)	40	38	−2
Philadelphia (Iowa)	40	41	+1
New York (Iowa)	53	52	−1
New York (Metropolitan)	63	58	−5
Chicago (Metropolitan)	60	51	−9
Los Angeles (Stanford)	50	43	−7
	Nearly All-Minority Schools		
Baltimore (Iowa)	18	24	+6
Detroit (Iowa)	21	17	−4
Philadelphia (Iowa)	17	13	−4
New York (Iowa)	21	12	−9
New York (Metropolitan)	23	22	−1
Chicago (Metropolitan)	32	22	−10
Los Angeles (Stanford)	10	8	−2

different standardizations, tests from different companies are shown
separately.

In the nearly all-white schools at the earlier grade, grade 3 or
grade 4, the Iowa tests show Baltimore to be low and New York
high, with Detroit and Philadelphia in between. The Metropolitan
test shows New York also to be above Chicago. At the later grade,
grade 6, Baltimore is the one city in which the nearly all-white
schools show a substantial percentile gain; Chicago shows the greatest
percentile loss, with Los Angeles and New York also showing some
loss, and Detroit and Philadelphia remaining about constant.

In the nearly all-minority (Negro, Puerto Rican, Mexican American) schools, the pattern is somewhat different. In the earlier grade, Baltimore, Detroit, Philadelphia, and New York are all around the 20th percentile. The New York-Chicago comparison on the Metropolitan test shows Chicago to be considerably above New York; and although there is no direct comparison with Los Angeles because the test is different, the very low percentile suggests that its minority students are probably lowest. In summary, the minority students appear to be highest in Chicago and lowest in Los Angeles, with the other cities in between. At the later grade, the minority students in Baltimore show a substantial gain, but in every other city there is a decline, which is quite substantial in several cities. The decline seems to be greatest in Chicago, and although the differences between the Metropolitan and Iowa tests in New York make any inferences inconclusive, the decline appears large there as well.

Considering the already low percentile rank at the earlier grade, a drop in percentile rank at that level constitutes a serious drop in performance.

Racial Composition of Schools in the Six Cities

Schools in the six cities show rather great differences in racial composition. Table 10-7 shows the proportion of schools at 10 percent intervals, ranging from 0-9 percent minority (Negro or Negro-Puerto Rican or Negro-Mexican American) to 90-100 percent minority. The final column of the table shows the proportion of schools in each city that fall into the two extreme categories: 0-9 percent minority, and 90-100 percent minority. This gives a rough measure of the racial segregation of education in each city at the indicated grades. The Baltimore schools are the most racially segregated, with the Chicago schools almost as segregated. The New York schools are the least segregated, with Detroit, Philadelphia, and Los Angeles schools between the two extremes, but closer to New York than to Baltimore and Chicago.

It should be pointed out that most of the analysis above is focussed on the racially segregated schools in all cities, the schools with 0-19 percent or 80-100 percent minority students. The performance of racially mixed schools generally falls between these extremes, and further analysis is necessary to learn whether, in each city,

Table 10-7. Racial composition of schools by grade

	Percent Minority											Percent
	0-9	10-19	20-29	30-39	40-49	50-59	60-69	70-79	80-89	90-100	(N)	Segregated
Third Grade												
Chicago	.39	.07	.03	.04	.02	.02	.02	.02	.02	.38	(444)	.77
Los Angeles	.28	.12	.08	.06	.04	.03	.03	.03	.05	.27	(435)	.55
Fourth Grade												
Baltimore	.26	.02	.02	.02	.03	.03	.01	.01	.04	.57	(142)	.83
Detroit	.22	.09	.07	.03	.03	.04	.03	.02	.03	.43	(205)	.65
New York	.16	.13	.08	.05	.06	.05	.05	.03	.05	.34	(595)	.50
Philadelphia	.21	.07	.06	.07	.05	.07	.03	.04	.05	.36	(198)	.57
Sixth Grade												
Baltimore	.26	.02	.02	.02	.03	.02	.01	.01	.05	.54	(137)	.80
Chicago	.38	.07	.03	.04	.02	.02	.02	.02	.02	.38	(416)	.76
Detroit	.23	.09	.07	.03	.03	.04	.03	.03	.03	.43	(199)	.66
New York	.17	.13	.09	.06	.06	.05	.05	.03	.07	.30	(479)	.47
Philadelphia	.21	.07	.06	.06	.04	.06	.03	.03	.06	.38	(188)	.59
Los Angeles	.28	.12	.08	.06	.04	.03	.03	.03	.05	.27	(435)	.55

students in the racially mixed schools are performing at higher levels than their racial or ethnic counterparts in racially segregated schools.

Performance in Integrated Schools

Much of the analysis of achievement carried out in the preceding pages is based on schools that are nearly all-white or nearly all-minority. While this procedure is justified in part by the fact that most schools fall into one of these two types in all the cities studied, it does not provide any information about the performance of minority and white students in integrated schools. The large number of elementary schools in each of these cities makes such an examination possible despite the small proportion of schools that are racially mixed to any substantial degree.

let y_i = achievement of school i
  p_i = proportion white in school i

then $y_i = a + bp_i + e_i$ (10.1)

where

  a = the estimated achievement level of the average minority student
  b = the estimated additional achievement of the average white student beyond that of the average minority student (so that $a + b$ is the estimated achievement of the average white student)
  e_i = random deviation of school i.

The model used in these regressions assumes that the expected achievement level of the school is simply a weighted average of the expected achievement of the white students and of the minority students in the school. If the achievement of integrated schools is generally above this regression line (that is, if the error e_i for integrated schools is generally positive), it means that students in them (white students, or minority students, or both) are performing better than would be expected on the basis of the performance of their counterparts in segregated schools. If the achievement is generally below the regression line, it means the opposite.

The data show no general overwhelming tendency in either direction. In all cities, schools near the center in racial composition may be found both above and below the regression line. There do seem to be differences among the different cities, and they will be examined below. At this point, however, it is useful to examine the parameters of the univariate regression equations, because they provide more accurate estimates of the performance of the average white student and the average minority student in each city at the two grade levels than are provided by the tabulations in Tables 10-1 through 10-5.

It should be noted that the regressions were carried out only for grade-equivalent scores, not for percentiles. Because these two scores are not linearly related, the results need not be the same for the two, though they would give rise to the same qualitative inferences. Better than either of these would have been to use standard scores at the individual level, and carry out all operations on these. The testing companies' reports, however, were not done in this way, and thus it was only possible to use grade equivalents or percentiles for the regressions.

The performance of students in integrated schools can be compared to that of students in segregated schools; but it is important to indicate first just what is and is not possible with these data. It is possible, using the data from Table 10-7, to predict the performance of students in a school of any racial composition. If the proportion of white students in the school is p_i, as denoted above, then the predicted score in the school would be a weighted average of the white and minority scores: $(1 - p_i)a + p_i(a + b)$, where a is the estimated minority score, and $a + b$ is the estimated white score.

If the score in a school is above that (that is, if e_i is positive), and if the school contains both minority and white students, it is not possible to tell where the higher than expected performance comes from. It is possible to know only that the minority students or the white students or both in the school are performing above their overall expected averages. Similarly, if the deviation e_i is negative, it is not possible to tell from which group the deficient performance comes.

The deviation of integrated schools from predicted values can be estimated by extending the simple linear regression above. Suppose that there is a positive additive effect on the performance of minority students, which is a linear function of the proportion of whites in the school. Then the performance of the average minority student in a school with a proportion p_i of white students is not a as in the previous model, but $a + b_2 p_i$, where b_2 is an integration effect. Similarly, if there is a positive additive effect on the performance of white students which is also linearly dependent on the number of white students in the school, the performance of the average white student is not $a + b$ as in the previous model, but $a + b_1 + b_3 p_i$, where $a + b_1$ is the individual effect, and b_3 is the effect of other whites in the school. If b_3 were negative, this would mean that the performance of white students in all-white schools is *less* than their performance in integrated schools.

The overall expected performance in a school with p_i white students is thus again a weighted average:

$$y_i = (1 - p_i)(a + b_2 p_i) + p_i(a + b_1 + b_3 p_i) + e_i \qquad (10.2)$$

which can be put in a form in which the independent variables are proportion white, p_i, and the product of the proportion white and the proportion minority, $p_i(1 - p_i)$:

$$y_i = a + (b_1 + b_3)p_i + (b_2 - b_3)p_i(1 - p_i) \qquad (10.2')$$

This is a two-variable regression equation, where one variable is the proportion white students in the school p_i, and the second is the product of the proportion white and the proportion minority. This second variable is proportional to the number of white-minority pairs there are in the school, and thus is a variable expressing the potential white-minority interaction in the school.

The constant term, a, is as before the estimated minority score (in the absence of any whites), while the coefficient of the "interaction" or "integration" term, $b_2 - b_3$, is the *difference* between the increment in performance of a minority student in the presence of whites and a white student in the presence of other whites. If this coefficient is positive it means that minority students' scores are increased more in an integrated school than the white students' scores are reduced. (In that case, the regression line is convex upward.) If the coefficient is negative, it means the whites' scores are reduced more in an integrated school than the minority students' scores are raised. (In that case, the regression line is concave upward.)

The coefficient of p_i, the proportion white, is $b_1 + b_3$, the increment of white individual scores (b_1) plus the increment to white students of being in the presence of other whites (b_3). It is not possible to distinguish these parameters—to distinguish between higher scores of white students per se and higher scores due solely to being in the presence of other whites. For example, suppose there were no individual effect of being white, i.e., $b_1 = 0$, and that the increment to white and to minority student performance due to being in school with whites is positive and equal, i.e., $b_2 = b_3 > 0$. Then equation (10.2′) reduces to $y_i = a + b_3 p_i + e_i$, which is a single-variable regression indistinguishable from the case in which there was no effect except b_1, and the equation reduces to equation (10.1).

Thus from these data it is not possible to distinguish the individual white effect from the contextual white effect; but it is possible to determine whether the contextual effect of whites is greater for whites or for minority students, i.e., whether $b_2 - b_3$ is positive or negative. In effect, this means it is possible to determine whether students in integrated schools are performing higher or lower than would be expected from the performance of minority students in all-minority schools and white students in all-white schools.

Using data from the six cities for arithmetic and reading (except in New York, where language total substitutes for reading, and Chicago and Los Angeles, which have reading only), the coefficients a, $b_1 + b_3$, and $b_2 - b_3$ can be estimated in a bivariate regression equation. This analysis has been carried out, and the results are shown in Table 10-8.

The first two columns of either side of Table 10-9, a and $b_1 + b_3$, give much the same information as shown in the comparable columns of Table 10-8. Here, however, the interpretation is different; in this more complex model, which allows contextual effects, it is not possible to distinguish the individual and contextual contribution of whites to the school average. The next column, showing $b_2 - b_3$, gives the excess or deficiency in achievement in integrated schools. To give an idea of the magnitude of the effect, something about the scale of these numbers should be indicated. The greatest effect in this model is calculated to occur at the point where $p_i = 0.5$. Thus $p_i(1 - p_i)$ at this point is 0.25. The greatest magnitude of the "integration effect," then, at the 50 percent point, is one-fourth of the value of $b_2 - b_3$. In New York in the sixth grade arithmetic score, for example, where $b_2 - b_3 = 0.9$, the greatest magnitude of the integration effect for a student would be 0.9/4, or 0.2 years.

The data in Table 10-9 show no consistent integration effect over all the cities, but they do show certain patterns:

Table 10-8. Estimates of grade equivalent achievement of average white and average minority student in six cities by use of regression equation

	Earlier Grade (3 or 4)				Later Grade (6)			
	Norm	Minority (a)	Slope (b)	White (a+b)	Norm	Minority (a)	Slope (b)	White (a+b)
Arithmetic								
Iowa Test								
New York	4.7	3.52	1.43	4.95	6.6	4.73	2.42	7.15
Philadelphia	4.7	3.53	1.03	4.56	6.6	5.11	1.34	6.45
Baltimore	4.7	3.70	0.70	4.40	6.6	5.56	0.91	6.47
Detroit	4.1	2.97	0.71	3.68	6.1	4.44	1.18	5.62
Language Total								
Iowa Test								
New York	4.7	3.62	1.48	5.10	6.7	4.69	2.39	7.08
Baltimore	4.7	3.51	0.73	4.24	6.7	5.41	0.79	6.20
Detroit	4.1	3.22	0.66	3.88	6.1	4.61	0.83	5.44
Reading								
Iowa Test								
Philadelphia	4.7	3.20	1.13	4.33	6.7	4.93	1.54	6.47
Baltimore	4.7	3.22	0.74	3.96	6.7	5.38	0.84	6.22
Detroit	4.1	2.83	0.85	3.68	6.1	4.62	1.16	5.78
Metropolitan								
New York	4.7	3.81	1.62	5.43	6.7	5.13	2.37	7.50
Chicago	3.5	3.05	0.85	3.90	6.7	4.88	1.99	6.87
Stanford								
Los Angeles	3.8	2.55	1.24	3.79	6.2	4.18	1.63	5.81

Table 10-9. Estimates of grade equivalent achievement with two-variables model, estimated white individual and contextual effect, and integration effect

| | Minority | Earlier Grade (3 or 4) | | Minority | Later Grade (6) | |
| | | White Individual and Contextual Effect | Integration Effect | | White Individual and Contextual Effect | Integration Effect |
	a	b_1+b_3	b_2-b_3	a	b_1+b_3	b_2-b_3
Arithmetic						
Iowa Test						
New York	3.55	1.37	0.2	4.63	2.40	0.9
Philadelphia	3.48	1.08	0.0	5.09	1.26	0.8
Baltimore	3.72	0.65	0.3	5.57	0.89	0.1
Detroit	3.03	0.75	−0.9	4.51	1.19	−0.8
Language Total						
Iowa Test						
New York	3.64	1.43	0.2	4.58	2.39	0.8
Baltimore	3.48	0.73	0.6	5.36	0.82	0.3
Detroit	3.22	0.72	−0.6	4.65	0.84	−0.5
Reading						
Iowa Test						
Philadelphia	3.23	1.10	0.0	4.89	1.42	1.3
Baltimore	3.17	.75	0.6	5.37	0.82	0.4
Detroit	2.85	.93	−0.9	4.68	1.17	−0.7
Metropolitan						
New York	3.60	1.89	0.9	4.83	2.70	1.3
Chicago	3.15	.82	−1.1	5.04	2.01	−2.8
Stanford						
Los Angeles	2.68	1.16	−0.7	4.15	1.63	0.4

New York: a positive integration effect, greater at grade 6 than at grade 4.

Philadelphia: a zero integration effect at grade 4, positive at grade 6.

Baltimore: a positive integration effect, slightly less at grade 6 than at grade 4.

Detroit: a negative integration effect, slightly less at grade 6 than at grade 4.

Chicago: a negative integration effect, greater at grade 6 than at grade 4.

Los Angeles: a negative integration effect at grade 4, positive at grade 6.

Thus three cities, New York, Baltimore, and Philadelphia, show positive integration effects, while two, Detroit and Chicago, show negative effects, and one, Los Angeles, shows a negative effect at grade 4 and a positive effect at grade 6. No overall statement for all these cities can be made about performance of students in integrated schools compared to segregated ones, nor can the higher or lower performance where it is found be identified as white or minority higher or lower performance. But there is consistency by city, and consistency in trends from grade 4 to 6 by city.

A further important caution is necessary. The increment or decrement in performance found does not imply a positive or negative *effect* of integration on performance. It would be fortunate if one could make such inferences from these aggregate data; but nothing is known about the backgrounds of students in integrated and segregated schools. Neither the minority students nor the white students in integrated schools are random samples of minority and white students in the city as a whole. It may well be that the negative effects shown in Detroit and Chicago and the positive effects shown in New York, Philadelphia, and Baltimore differ only because the patterns of residential succession by race differ in those cities. This analysis only shows descriptively the degree to which students in integrated schools perform above or below their counterparts in segregated schools, and cannot attribute that difference in performance to selection or effect.

Note

1. The "reading" score on the Stanford test battery is a combined score from the "Paragraph Meaning" and "Word Meaning"

tests. Grade equivalents are reported by the school system in the published newspaper report; but percentiles shown in Table 10-7 have been obtained by establishing a new grade-equivalent-percentile conversion table, combining the two tables given for the two subtests in the scoring manual.

11. EQUALITY FOR MINORITIES
Arthur R. Jensen

Americans' faith in education is tangibly substantiated in the fact that the American people now invest in educational institutions annually almost as much as all other nations combined. In the past two decades educational spending nationwide has increased fivefold while personal consumption merely doubled. Since World War II school enrollments have increased 88 per cent, while school expenditures (in constant dollars) increased 350 per cent. While employment in private industry increased 38 per cent, it increased 203 per cent in public education. With such an abundant outlay for education, the question naturally arises whether the benefits are equitably distributed to all segments of our population. A keystone of public education is the promise that no child should be denied the opportunity to fulfill his educational potential, regardless of his national, ethnic, or socioeconomic background. When substantial inequalities in educational achievement are evident between large segments of the population nominally sharing the same educational system, serious questions are raised, and rightly so. Numerous attempts have been and are being made to find the answers to the inequities in the benefits of education. In California the chief sub-population differences in scholastic attainments involve majority-minority differences, the minorities in this case being Negroes and Mexican-Americans.

The causes of educational inequalities, in terms both of input and output, cannot be discussed very fruitfully in general terms.

There are considerable regional and local differences in educational expenditures and facilities and in their distribution within local districts. In assessing the existence and degree of educational inequities, we must get down to specific cases. That is what is intended in this article. We shall take a rather close look at some of the questions and answers involved in assessing inequalities within a single school system which serves three sub-populations: a majority group, which we shall refer to as Anglos, and two sizeable minorities, Negroes and Mexican-Americans. Before going into the details of this study, however, a few more general points should be reviewed.

School Comparisons of Academic Achievement

The now famous Coleman Report (Coleman et al., 1966), which surveyed 645,000 pupils in more than 3,000 schools in all regions of the United States, found relatively minor differences in the measured characteristics of schools attended by different racial and ethnic groups, but very great differences in their achievement levels. The Report also argued that when the social background and attitudes of students are held constant, per pupil expenditures, pupil-teacher ratio, school facilities and curricula show very little relation to achievement. The Report concluded ". . . that schools bring little influence to bear on a child's achievement that is independent of his background and general social context" (p. 325). A critical examination of this study by Bowles and Levin (1968) led them to the conclusion that Coleman's methodology could have resulted in an underestimation to some unknown degree of the extent of the relationship between school differences and pupil achievement. They also criticize the conclusion of the Coleman Report that "There is a small positive effect of school integration on the reading and mathematics achievement of Negro pupils after differences in the socio-economic background of the students are accounted for" (pp. 29-30). Bowles and Levin claim that ". . . the small residual statistical correlation between proportion white in the schools and Negro achievement is likely to be due, at least in part, to the fact that the proportion white in a school is a measure of otherwise inadequately controlled social background of the Negro student. Thus, we find that the conclusion that Negro achievement is positively associated with the proportion of fellow students who are white, once other influences are taken into account, is not supported by the evidence presented in the Report." Here then is one critique of the Coleman Report which suggests just the opposite of the most popularly held conceptions of what was proved by the Report. Bowles and Levin argue that school effects are probably larger than suggested by the study, and racial composition of the school per se is probably a more negligible factor than suggested in the Report's conclusions. A smaller-scale but statistically more thoroughly controlled study by Wilson (1967) found that after controlling for other factors, the racial composition of the school had no significant direct association with Negro achievement, thus supporting the conclusion of Bowles and Levin, at least in the one California school district studied by Wilson.

But probably the most compelling argument for requiring racial balance in schools is not the direct effect of a school's racial composition per se, but the fact that it could lead to a greater equalization of school facilities for majority and minority groups so that disadvantaged minorities would not be largely confined to schools with inferior resources. This may be a valid argument in some parts of the country, but one may justifiably question whether it is a cogent factor in California schools.

Consider the following evidence. A rather coarse-grained analysis of the relationship between the proportion of minority enrollment and certain school characteristics in California is made possible by the State Department of Education's recent publication of statistics on several scholastic variables for all school districts in the State. The present analysis, carried out by the writer, is based on only the total of 191 school districts in the ten counties of the greater Bay Area.[1]

The variables on which all school districts were ranked were: Grade 6 Reading Achievement (age 11), Grade 10 Reading (age 15), Grade 6 median IQ, Grade 10 median IQ, Proportion of Minority Enrollment, Per Pupil Expenditure, Teacher Salary, Teacher-Pupil Ratio (Grades 4-8), Number of Administrators per 100 Pupils, and General Purpose Tax Rate in the school district. The rank order correlations[2] among these variables for the 191 school districts are shown in Table 11-1. We see that minority enrollment has quite negligible correlations with all the school facility variables except number of administrators per 100 pupils (Variable 10), and this correlation is positive. On the other hand, there is a strong negative

Table 11-1. Correlations (Spearman's ρ) among ten educational variables in 191 California school districts (decimals omitted)

Variable	2	3	4	5	6	7	8	9	10
1. Grade 6 Reading (age 11)	81	94	87	−73	23	21	18	19	−09
2. Grade 10 Reading (age 15)		75	90	−70	08	06	02	−03	−06
3. Grade 6 IQ			85	−67	25	21	17	19	−08
4. Grade 10 IQ				−67	05	05	09	−13	00
5. Minority Enrollment					02	05	08	−10	17
6. Per Pupil Expenditure						35	53	42	47
7. Tax Rate							54	−06	24
8. Teacher Salary								18	45
9. Teacher/Pupil Ratio									01
10. Number of Administrators/100									

correlation between minority enrollment and the 6th and 10th grade reading and IQ scores. This correlation matrix can be elucidated by factor analysing it, thereby reducing it to three independent components which account for most of the variance (78 per cent). This was accomplished by a varimax rotation of the first three principal components. The rotated factors are shown in Table 11-2. Factor I is

Table 11-2. Rotated factor loadings for ten educational variables in 191 California school districts

Variable	Factors		
	I	II	III
1. Grade 6 Reading (age 11)	.95	.12	.15
2. Grade 10 Reading (age 15)	.92	.00	−.08
3. Grade 6 IQ	.92	.13	.17
4. Grade 10 IQ	.95	.06	−.17
5. Minority Enrollment	−.82	.19	−.09
6. Per Pupil Expenditure	.10	.67	.55
7. Tax Rate	.11	.75	−.15
8. Teacher Salary	.06	.83	.17
9. Teacher/Pupil Ratio	.03	.01	.96
10. No. of Administrators	−.13	.71	.01
Per Cent of Variance	42.0	22.8	13.6

scholastic aptitude (IQ), reading achievement and minority enrollment. Factor II represents the financial resources of the schools, with the highest loading on teacher salary. Factor III is teacher/pupil ratio and that part of per pupil expenditure not associated with Factor II. What this analysis shows most clearly is the absence of any appreciable correlation between the aptitude-achievement variables and the school district's financial outlay. If there were a substantial relationship between the financial resources and the reading achievement of the various school districts, the factors shown in Table 11-2 could not be so clearly separated. Note also that while minority enrollment has a negative correlation (−.82) with Factor I (IQ-Reading), it has a small positive correlation (+.19) with Factor II (expenditures). The negative correlation (−.09) between minority enrollment and Factor III indicates a slight disadvantage to districts with a high proportion of minorities in terms of average class size. Overall, these data suggest that there is no appreciable relationship between those particular school resources and minority enrollment, and if anything the correlation is in just the opposite direction to the popular belief that educational facilities are relatively inadequate in districts with a higher percentage of minority students.

Since this analysis is based on data in which the smallest unit for analysis is the school district, it permits no inference concerning the allocation of educational resources to the various schools, which probably differ in minority enrollments, within the districts. A similar analysis could be performed within a district, using the individual schools as the unit of analysis, but different indices of a school's resources would have to be used, since there would be relatively little variance on such variables as teacher salary and per pupil expenditure *within* any given school district. More fine-grained indices of the school's specific educational facilities should be included. In any case, the first and most obvious step in assessing the equality of educational facilities is to make a direct examination of the facilities, per pupil expenditures, etc. The recreational, hygienic, safety, and aesthetic aspects of the school plant should be considered no less than those facilities deemed to have more direct educational consequences, such as pupil/teacher ratio and special services.

The Misuse of National and State Norms

School boards, the public, and the press commonly misuse the published and state norms on standardized achievement tests. Schools and districts are compared against "norms," which are intended to represent national or state averages, as if achieving a close approximation to the norms, if not exceeding them, should be the primary goal of every school system. Deviation from the norm, above or below, is commonly regarded as a credit or a discredit to the particular school system. The fallacy in this, of course, is the fact that the average level of scholastic achievement in a community is highly predictable from a number of the community's characteristics over which the local schools have no control whatsoever. Thorndike (1951), for example, correlated average IQ and an average scholastic achievement index (based on half a million children) with twenty-four census variables for a wide range of communities, large and small, urban and rural. Eleven of the correlations were significant at the one per cent level. Census variables with the highest correlation with IQ and achievement were educational level of the adult population (.43), home ownership (.39), quality and cost of housing (.33), proportion of native-born whites (.28), rate of female employment (.26), and proportion of professional workers (.28). In a multiple correlation these census variables predicted IQ and achievement between .55 and .60. Essentially the same picture is revealed in many other similar studies (Wiseman, 1964, Chapter IV). A school's or district's deviation from the mean achievement predicted from a multiple regression equation based on a host of community characteristics would, therefore, make much more sense than a mere comparison of the school's average with national or state norms.

Majority-Minority Comparisons within a School District

Even when a school district has equalized the educational facilities in all of its schools in terms of physical plant amenities, teacher salaries and qualifications, per pupil expenditures, teacher/pupil ratios, special services, curriculum, and the like, the question may still be asked whether majority-minority differences in scholastic achievement are a product of more subtle and less tangible factors operating in the school situation. We have in mind, for example, such factors as racial and socioeconomic composition of the school, and different teacher attitudes and expectancies in relation to majority and minority pupils. Is there any way we can assess the degree to which schools afford unequal educational advantages to majority and minority pupils over and above what can easily be reckoned in terms of pupil expenditures and the like?

I have tried to answer this question as best as I believe it can be answered with the psychometric and statistical methodology now available and with the rather modest resources within the financial means of most school systems. Although it would be impossible to present all the technical details and results of this study within the limits of this paper, it is possible to indicate some of the methods and the most relevant results they have yielded.

The study was conducted in 1970 in a fairly large (thirty-five schools) elementary school district of California. This school district was ideal for this kind of study for four main reasons: (1) the district's school population has substantial proportions of Negro (13 per cent) and Mexican-American (20 per cent) students; (2) the majority (Anglo) population is very close to state and national norms for

Anglos in IQ, for both mean and standard deviation, and the same is true for the two minority groups in relation to norms for their respective populations in the US; (3) the schools are largely de facto segregated due to rather widely spaced residential clustering of the three ethnic groups, and (4) the district had made a thorough effort to provide equal educational facilities in all of its schools, if anything favouring those schools with the largest minority enrollments to whom additional federal and state funds were allocated for special compensatory programs.

Large representative samples totalling 28 per cent of the school population from kindergarten to the eighth grade (age thirteen) were selected for study. A total of 6,619 children were tested; more or less equal numbers were tested at each grade. The three main ethnic classifications were Anglo (N = 2,453), Mexican-American (N = 2,263), and Negro (N = 1,853). Approximately half the sample (selected randomly with the classroom as the unit of selection) were tested by a small staff of specially trained testers, and half were tested by their regular classroom teachers. Because of the large sample sizes the tester and teacher results often differ significantly but do not differ appreciably or systematically except that the results of teacher-administered tests consistently have somewhat greater variance and lower reliability which would tend to attenuate intercorrelations among measures and lessen the statistical significance of group differences. Parallel analyses for testers and teachers were run on all the data, which were combined when there were no significant or systematic differences between the two forms of testing. For the sake of simplicity in the present summary only the tester results are reported here when the two sets of data were not combined.

Rationale of the Study

In terms of this study one can think of the educational process as being analogous to an industrial production process in which raw materials (input) are converted to a specified product (output). The output will be a function both of the input and of the effectiveness of the process by means of which the input is converted into output. In the case of schooling, the input is what the child brings with him to school by way of his abilities, attitudes, prior learning, cultural background, and personality characteristics relevant to learning in the classroom. The school itself has relatively little, if any, control over these input variables. The school, however, can have considerable influence on one variable—prior learning—for children who are already somewhere along the educational path, and if the school's instructional program is deficient for some children, the deficiencies in prior learning in earlier grades should show up increasingly in later grades as a cumulating deficit in scholastic achievement.

Whatever else one may say about it, schooling is essentially a process whereby children are helped to acquire certain skills, which are the output of the system. The effectiveness of the process can be judged, among other ways, in terms of the relationship between input and output. Meaningful comparisons cannot be made between the output (scholastic achievement) of different pupils, classes, schools, or school districts without reference to the input variables. The main purpose of the present study is the comparison of the outputs, i.e., educational achievements, of three categories of pupils —Anglo, Negro, and Mexican-American—when these groups are statistically equated on the input variables. In this way we can make some judgment concerning the relative efficiency of the educational process for each of the three groups. The adequacy of the statistical equating of the groups in terms of input depends upon a judicious selection of instruments for measuring the input variables. The chief aims in selecting the input control variables are (1) to represent the domain of educationally relevant abilities, personality, and home background factors as broadly as feasible, and (2) to include only those ability and background variables which are not explicitly taught by the schools or are not under direct control of the schools. That is to say, they should represent the raw materials that the schools have to work with. The output, on the other hand, should represent objective measures of those skills which it is the school's specific purpose to teach. These are best measured by standardized tests of scholastic achievement.

The input variables can be classified into three categories: (1) ability or general aptitude tests, (2) motivation, personality, and school-related attitudes, and (3) environmental background variables reflecting socioeconomic status, parental education, and general cultural advantages.

Input Variables

Ability Tests

Lorge-Thorndike Intelligence Test. This is a nationally standardized group-administered test of general intelligence. In the normative sample, which was intended to be representative of the nation's school population, the test has a mean IQ of 100 and a standard deviation of 16. It is generally acknowledged to be one of the best paper-and-pencil tests of general intelligence.

The Manual of the Lorge-Thorndike Test states that the test was designed to measure reasoning ability. It does not test proficiency in specific skills taught in school, although the verbal tests, from grade 4 (age nine) and above, depend upon reading ability. The reading level required, however, is intentionally kept considerably below the level of reasoning required for correctly answering the test questions. Thus the test is essentially a test of reasoning and not of reading ability, which is to say that it should have more of its variance in common with nonverbal tests of reasoning ability than with tests of reading per se.

The tests for grade K-3 do not depend at all upon reading ability but make use exclusively of pictorial items. The tests for grades 4-8 consist of two parts, Verbal (V) and Non-verbal (NV). They are scored separately and the raw score on each is converted to an IQ, with a normative mean of 100 and SD of 16. The chief advantage of keeping the two scores separate is that the Non-verbal IQ does not overestimate or underestimate the child's general level of intellectual ability because of specific skills or disabilities in reading. The Non-verbal IQ, however, correlates almost as highly with a test of reading comprehension as does the Verbal IQ, because all three tests depend primarily upon reasoning ability and not upon reading per se. For example, in the fourth grade sample, the correlation between the Lorge-Thorndike Verbal and Non-verbal IQs is .70. The correlation between Verbal IQ and the Paragraph Meaning Sub-test of the Standard Achievement Test is .52. The correlation between the Non-verbal IQ and Paragraph Meaning is .47. Now we can ask: what is the correlation of Verbal IQ and Paragraph Meaning when the effects of Non-verbal IQ are partialled out, that is, are held constant? The partial correlation between Verbal IQ and Paragraph Meaning (holding Non-verbal IQ constant) is only .29.

The following forms of the Lorge-Thorndike Intelligence Tests were used:

Level 1, Form B	Grades K-1
Level 2, Form B	Grades 2-3
Level 3, Form B Verbal and Non-verbal	Grades 4-6
Level 4, Form B Verbal and Non-verbal	Grades 7-8

Figure Copying Test. The Figure Copying Test was given in grades K-6. Beyond grade 6 (age eleven) too large a proportion of children obtain the maximum possible score (30) for the test to be useful in making group comparisons. In fact, by grades 5 and 6 group differences are very probably underestimated by this test, since a larger proportion of the higher-scoring group will obtain the maximum score and this "ceiling" effect will prevent the group's full range of ability from being represented. The ceiling effect consequently spuriously depresses the group's mean and reduces the variance (or standard deviation). Nevertheless, this test is extremely valuable for group comparisons because it is one of the least culture-loaded tests available, and successful performance on the test is known to be significantly related to readiness for the scholastic tasks of the primary grades, especially reading readiness.

The Figure Copying Test was developed at the Gesell Institute of Child Study at Yale University as a means of measuring developmental readiness for the traditional school learning tasks of the primary grades. The test consists of the ten geometric forms shown in Figure 11-1, arranged in order of difficulty, which the child must simply copy, each on a separate sheet of paper. The test involves no memory factor, since the figure to be copied is before the child at all times. The test is administered without time limit, although most children finish in ten to fifteen minutes. The test is best regarded as a developmental scale of mental ability. It correlates substantially with other IQ tests, but it is considerably less culture-loaded than most usual IQ tests. It is primarily a measure of general cognitive development and not just of perceptual-motor ability. Children taking the test are urged to attempt to copy every figure.

Each of the ten figures is scored on a three-point scale going from one (low) to three (high). (A score of zero is given in the rare instance when no attempt has been made to copy a particular figure.) A score of one is given if an attempt is made but the child's drawing

Figure 11-1. The ten simple geometric forms used in the Figure Copying Test. In the actual test booklet each figure is present singly in the top half of a 5½" x 8½" sheet. The circle is 1¾" in diameter.

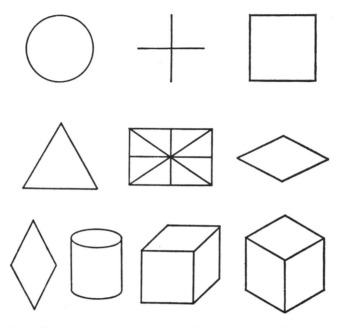

completely fails to resemble the model. A score of two is given if there is fair resemblance to the model—the figure need not be perfect but it must be easily recognizable as the model which the child has attempted to copy. A score of three is given for an attempt which duplicates the figure in all its essential characteristics—this is an essentially adult level of performance. Since there are ten figures in all, the possible range of scores goes from 10 to 30 (or 0 to 30 if zeros are counted, but this is rare, since virtually all subjects attempt all ten figures).

The high level of motivation maintained by this test is indicated by the fact that the minimum score obtained in each group at each grade level increases systematically with grade level. This suggests that all children were making an attempt to perform in accordance with the instructions. Another indication that can be seen from the test booklets is that virtually 100 per cent of the children in every ethnic group at every grade level attempted to copy every figure. The attempts, even when unsuccessful, usually show considerable effort, as indicated by redrawing the figure, erasures and drawing over the figure repeatedly in order to improve its likeness to the model. It is also noteworthy about this test that normal children are generally not successful in drawing figures beyond their mental age level and that special instructions and coaching on the drawing of these figures hardly improves the child's performance. This test, in other words, is not very susceptible to training, but measures some fundamental aspects of mental development. The diagnostic significance of this test has been explicated extensively in *School Readiness* (Harper and Row, 1967, pp. 63-129) by Drs. Frances L. Ilg and Louise Bates Awes of the Gesell Institute of Child Development at Yale University.

Raven's Progressive Matrices. This non-verbal reasoning test, devised in England, is intended to be a pure measure of *g*, the general factor common to all intelligence tests. It is a highly reliable measure of reasoning ability, quite free of the influence of special abilities, such as verbal or numerical facility. It is probably the most culture-free test of general intelligence yet devised by psychologists. The test mainly gets at the ability to grasp relationships; it does not depend upon specific acquired information as do tests of vocabulary, general information, etc. The test, which is group-administered, begins with problems that are so easy that all children by third grade can catch on and solve the problems even without instructions.

Two forms of the test were used. The Coloured Progressive Matrices, which is the children's form, was used in grades 3 to 6. This test is appropriate even for kindergarten children, but to ensure that all children tested could go through the first few problems without difficulty, giving them a chance to catch on easily and experience success in the early part of the test, we used this test only from the third grade and above. The Coloured Matrices consist of thirty-six matrix problems which are administered without time limit. Children are encouraged to attempt all problems. There is no penalty for guessing.

The Standard Progressive Matrices were used in grades 7 and 8. These begin as easily as the coloured matrices but advance in difficulty more rapidly and go up to a level appropriate for average adults. There are sixty matrix problems in all, and the subjects are encouraged to attempt all of them, without penalty for guessing.

Listening-Attention Test. In the Listening-Attention Test the child is presented with an answer sheet containing one hundred pairs of digits in sets of ten. The child listens to a tape recording which speaks one digit every two seconds. The child is required to put an X over the one digit in each pair which has been heard on the tape recorder. The purpose of this test is to determine the extent to which the child is able to pay attention to numbers spoken on a tape recorder, to keep his place in the test, and to make the appropriate responses to what he hears from moment to moment. Low scores on this test indicate that the subject is not yet ready to take the Memory for Numbers test which immediately follows it. High scores on the Listening-Attention Test indicate that the subject has the prerequisite skills for taking the digit span (Memory for Numbers) test. The Listening-Attention Test thus is intended as a means for detecting students who, for whatever reason, are unable to hear and to respond to numbers read over a tape recorder. The test itself makes no demands on the child's memory, but only on his ability for listening, paying attention, and responding appropriately—all prerequisites for the digit memory test that follows.

It has been found in previous studies using the Listening-Attention Test that the vast majority of subjects from grade 2 and above obtain perfect scores; the median score is one hundred, and the lower quartile rarely goes below ninety-five. This means that nearly all subjects have the prerequisite skills for the Memory for Numbers test to yield a valid measure of the subjects' short-term memory ability.

Memory for Numbers Test. The Memory for Numbers test is a measure of digit span, or more generally, short-term memory. It consists of three parts. Each part consists of six series of digits going from four digits in a series up to nine digits in a series. The digit series are presented on a tape recording on which the digits are spoken clearly by a male voice at the rate of precisely one digit per second. The subjects write down as many digits as they can recall at the conclusion of each series, which is signalled by a "bong." Each part of the test is preceded by a short practice test of three-digit series in order to permit the tester to determine whether the child has understood the instructions, etc. The practice test also serves to familiarize the subject with the procedure of each of the sub-tests. The first sub-test is labelled Immediate Recall (I). Here the subject is instructed to recall the series *immediately* after the last digit has been spoken on the tape recorder. The second sub-test consists of Delayed Recall (D). Here the subject is instructed not to write down his response until after ten seconds have elapsed after the last digit has been spoken. The ten-second interval is marked by audible clicks of a metronome and is terminated by the sound of a "bong" which signals the child to write his response. The Delayed Recall condition invariably results in some retention loss. The third sub-test is the repeated series test, in which the digit series is repeated three times prior to recall; the subject then recalls the series immediately after the last digit in the series has been presented. Again, recall is signalled by a "bong." Each repetition of the series is separated by a tone with a duration of one second. The repeated series almost invariably results in greater recall than the single series. This test is very culture-fair for children in second grade and beyond and who know their numerals and are capable of listening and paying attention, as indicated by the Listening-Attention Test. The maximum score on any one of the sub-tests is 39, that is the sum of the digit series from four through nine.

Motivational and Personality Tests

Speed and Persistence Test (Making X's). The Making X's Test is intended as an assessment of test-making motivation. It gives an indication of the subject's willingness to comply with instructions in a group testing situation and to mobilize effort in following those instructions for a brief period of time. The test involves no intellectual component, although for young children it probably involves some perceptual-motor skills component, as reflected by increasing mean scores as a function of age between grades 1 to 5. The wide range of individual differences among children at any one grade level would seem to reflect mainly general motivation and test-making attitudes in a group situation. The test also serves partly as an index of classroom morale, and it can be entered as a moderator variable into correlational analyses with other ability and achievement tests. Children who do very poorly on this test, it can be suspected, are likely not to put out their maximum effort on ability tests given in a group situation and therefore their scores are not likely to reflect their "true" level of ability.

The Making X's Test consists of two parts. On Part I the subject is asked simply to make X's in a series of squares for a period of 90 seconds. In this part the instructions say nothing about speed. They merely instruct the child to make X's. The maximum possible score on Part I is 150, since there are 150 squares provided in which the child can make X's. After a two-minute rest period the child turns the page of the test booklet to Part II. Here the child is instructed to show how much better he can perform than he did on Part I and to work as rapidly as possible. The child is again given 90 seconds to make as many X's as he can in the 150 boxes provided. The gain in score from Part I to Part II reflects both a practice effect and an increase in motivation or effort as a result of the motivating instructions, i.e. instructions to work as rapidly as possible.

Ethnic and social-class group differences on this test are generally smaller than on any other test, with the exception of the Listening-Attention Test (on which there are almost no group *or* individual differences).

Eysenck Personality Inventory-Junior. The EPI-Junior is the children's form of the EPI for adults. It is a questionnaire designed to measure the two factors of personality which have been found to account for most of the variance in the personality domain—Extraversion and Neuroticism. The Extraversion (E) scale represents the continuum of social extraversion-introversion. High scores reflect sociability, outgoingness and carefreeness. The Neuroticism (N) scale reflects emotional instability, anxiety proneness, and the tendency to develop neurotic symptoms under stress. The Lie (L) scale is merely a validity detector consisting of a number of items which are very rarely answered in the keyed direction by the vast majority of subjects. A high score on L indicates that the subject is "faking good" or is answering the questionnaire items more or less at random, either intentionally or as a result of insufficient comprehension of the items. Naivity is also reflected in elevated L scores, and it is probably mainly this factor which causes a decrease in L scores as children mature.

The EPI scales were included in the present study as a control variable because previous studies had shown the E and N scales to predict a small but significant part of the variance in scholastic performance. Because of the reading level required by the EPI, it was not given below the fourth grade.

Student Self-Report. This twenty-one-item self-report inventory was composed mainly of items in the self concept inventory used by James Coleman in his study, *Equality of Educational Opportunity*. It reveals the student's attitudes towards school, towards himself as a student, and other attitudes affecting motivation and self-esteem. The questionnaire was administered by the classroom teachers to grades 4 to 8. Because of the reading level required, it was not administered below grade 4.

Background Information

The Home Index. This is a 24-item questionnaire about the home environment, devised by Harrison Gough (1949). It is a sensitive composite index of the socioeconomic level of the child's family. Factor analysis of past data by Gough has shown that the 24 items fall into four categories, each of which can be scored as a separate scale. Part I (Items 6, 7, 8, 9, 10, 15, 16, 23) reflects primarily the educational level of the parents. Part II (Items 1, 2, 3, 4, 5, 13, 20, 24) reflects material possessions in the home. Part III (Items 17, 18, 21, 22) reflects degree of parental participation in middle or upper-middle class social and civic activities. Part IV (Items 11 and 19) relates to formal exposure to music and other arts.

Output Variables: Scholastic Achievement

Stanford Achievement Tests. Scholastic achievement was assessed by means of the so-called "partial battery" of the Stanford Achievement Tests, consisting of the following sub-tests: Word Meaning, Paragraph Meaning, Spelling, Word Study Skills, Language (grammar), Arithmetic Computation, Arithmetic Concepts, and Arithmetic Applications. The Stanford Achievement battery was administered to grades 1 to 8.

Distinction between Aptitude and Achievement

Can we justify the separation of our tests into two categories, ability or aptitude tests versus scholastic achievement tests, and then regard the former as *input* and the latter as *output*? Do not intelligence or aptitude tests also measure learning or achievement? The answer to this question is far from simple, but I believe there are at least six kinds of evidence which justify a psychological distinction between intelligence tests and achievement tests.

(1) Breadth of learning sampled. The most obvious difference between tests of intelligence and of achievement is the breadth of the domains sampled by the tests. Achievement tests sample very narrowly from the most specifically taught skills in the traditional

curriculum, emphasizing particularly the three R's. Achievement test items are samples of the particular skills that children are specifically taught in school. Since these skills are quite explicitly defined and the criteria of their attainment are fairly clear to teachers and parents, children can be taught and can be given practice on these skills to shape their performance up to the desired criterion. Because of the circumscribed nature of many of the basic scholastic skills, the pupil's specific weaknesses can be identified and remedied. The skills or learning sampled by an intelligence test, on the other hand, represent achievements of a much broader nature. Intelligence test items are sampled from such a very wide range of potential experiences that the idea of teaching intelligence, as compared with teaching, say, reading or arithmetic, is practically nonsensical. Even direct coaching and practice on a particular intelligence test raises individual's scores on the average by only five to ten points; and some tests, especially those referred to as "culture fair," seem to be hardly amenable to the effects of coaching and practice. The average five year old, for example, can copy a circle or a square without any trouble, but try to teach him to copy a diamond and see how far he gets! Wait until he is seven years old and he will have no trouble copying the diamond without any need for instruction. Even vocabulary is very unsusceptible to enlargement by direct practice aimed at increasing vocabulary. This is part of the reason why vocabulary tests are regarded as such good measures of general intelligence and always have a high g loading in factor analyses of various types of intelligence tests. The items in a vocabulary test are sampled from such an enormously large pool of potential items that the number that can be acquired by specific study and practice is only a small proportion of the total, so that few if any are likely to appear in any given vocabulary test. Furthermore, persons seem to retain only those words which fill some conceptual "slot" or need in their own mental structures. A new word encountered for the first time which fills such a conceptual "slot" is picked up and retained seemingly without conscious effort, and will "pop" into mind again when the conceptual need for it arises, even though in the meantime the word may not have been encountered for many months or even years. If there is no conceptual slot needing to be filled, that is to say, no meaning for the individual which the word serves to symbolize, it is very difficult to make the definition of the word stick in the individual's memory, and even after repeated drill, it will quickly fade beyond retrieval, as when a student memorizes a long list of foreign words in order to pass his foreign language exam for the PhD. Since intelligence tests assess the learning that occurs in the total life experiences of the individual, they are more general and more valid measures of his learning potential than are scholastic achievement tests. It should come as no surprise that there is a substantial correlation between the two classes of tests, since both measure learning or achievement, one in a broad sphere, the other in a much narrower sphere. In a culturally more or less homogeneous population the broader-based measure called "intelligence" is more generally representative of the individual's learning capacities and is more stable over time than the more specific acquisitions of knowledge and skill classed as scholastic achievement.

(2) Equivalence of Diverse Tests. One of the most impressive characteristics of intelligence tests is the great diversity of means by which essentially the same ability (or abilities) can be measured. Tests having very diverse forms, such as vocabulary, block designs, matrices, number series, "odd-man out," figure copying, verbal analogies, and other kinds of problems can all serve as intelligence tests yielding more or less equivalent results because of their high intercorrelations. All these types of tests have high loadings on the g factor, which, as Wechsler (1958, p. 121) has said, ". . . involves broad mental organization; it is independent of the modality or contextual structure from which it is elicited; g cannot be exclusively identified with any single intellectual ability and for this reason cannot be described in concrete operational terms." We can accurately define g only in terms of certain mathematical operations; in Wechsler's words "g is a measure of a collective communality which necessarily emerges from the intercorrelation of any broad sample of mental abilities" (p. 123).

Assessment of scholastic achievement, on the other hand, depends upon tests of narrowly specific acquired skills—reading, spelling, arithmetic operations, and the like. The forms by means of which one can test any one of these scholastic skills are very limited indeed. This is not to say that there is not a general factor common to all tests of scholastic achievement, but this general factor common to all the tests seems to be quite indistinguishable from the g factor of intelligence tests. Achievement tests, however, usually do not have as high g loadings as intelligence tests but have higher loadings on group factors such as verbal and numerical ability factors and they also contain more task-specific variance. It is always possible to make achievement tests correlate more highly with intelligence tests by requiring students to reason, to use data provided, and to apply their factual knowledge to the solution of new problems. More than just the mastery of factual information, intelligence is the ability to apply this information in new and different ways. With increasing grade level, achievement tests have more and more variance in common with tests of g. For example, once the basic skills in reading have been acquired, reading achievement tests must increasingly measure the student's comprehension of more and more complex selections rather than the simpler processes of word recognition, decoding, etc. And thus at higher grades, tests of reading comprehension, for those children who have already mastered the basic skills, become more or less indistinguishable in factorial composition from the so-called tests of verbal intelligence. Similarly, tests of mechanical arithmetic (arithmetic computation) have less correlation with g than tests of arithmetic thought problems, such as the Arithmetic Concepts and Arithmetic Applications sub-tests of the Stanford Achievement battery. Accordingly, most indices of scholastic performance increasingly reflect general intelligence as children progress in school. We found in our study, for example, that up to grade 6, verbal and non-verbal intelligence tests could be factorially separated, with the scholastic achievement tests lining up on the same factor with verbal intelligence. But beyond grade 6 both the verbal and non-verbal tests, along with all the scholastic achievement tests, amalgamated into a single large general factor which no form of factor rotation could separate into smaller components distinguishable as verbal intelligence versus non-verbal intelligence versus scholastic achievement. By grades 7 and 8 the Lorge-Thorndike Non-verbal IQ and Raven's Progressive Matrices are hardly distinguishable in their factor composition from the tests of scholastic achievement. At the same time it is important to recognize that the Lorge-Thorndike Non-verbal IQ and Raven's Matrices are not measuring scholastic attainment per se, as demonstrated by the fact that totally illiterate and unschooled persons can obtain high scores on these tests. Burt (1961), for example, reported the case of separated identical twins with widely differing educational attainments (elementary school education versus a university degree), who differed by only one IQ point on the Progressive Matrices (127 versus 128).

(3) Heritability of Intelligence and Scholastic Achievement. Another characteristic which distinguishes intelligence tests from achievement tests is the difference between the heritability values generally found for intelligence and achievement measures. Heritability is a technical term in quantitative genetics referring to the proportion of test score variance (or any phenotypic variance) attributable to genetic factors. Determinations of the heritability of intelligence test scores range from about .60 to .90, with average values around .70 to .80 (Jensen, 1969a). This means that some 70 to 80 percent of the variance in IQs in the European and North American Caucasian population in which these studies have been made is attributable to genetic variance, and only 20 to 30 per cent is attributable to non-genetic or environmental variability. The best evidence now available shows a somewhat different picture for measures of scholastic achievement, which on the average have much lower heritability. A review of all twin studies in which heritability was determined by the same methods for intelligence tests and for achievement tests shows an average heritability of .80 for the former and of only .40 for the latter (Jensen, 1967). It is likely that scholastic measures increase in heritability with increasing grade level and that the simpler skills such as reading, spelling, and mechanical arithmetic have lower heritability than the more complex processes such as reading comprehension and arithmetic applications. The reason is quite easy to understand. Simple circumscribed skills can be more easily taught, drilled, and assessed and the degree of their mastery for any individual will be largely a function of the amount of time he spends in being taught and in practising the skill. Thus children with quite different learning abilities can be shaped up to perform more or less equally in these elemental skills. If Johnny has trouble with his reading or arithmetic or spelling his parents may give him extra tutoring so that he can more nearly approximate the performance of his brighter brother. Siblings in the same family differ considerably less in scholastic achievement than in intelligence. Conversely, identical twins reared apart differ much more in scholastic achievement than in intelligence. From these facts we conclude that environmental factors make a larger contribution to individual differences in achievement than in intelligence as measured by standard tests.

(4) Maturational Aspects of Intelligence. An important characteristic of the best intelligence test items is that they clearly fall along an age scale. Items are thus "naturally" ordered in difficulty.

The Figure Copying Test (see Figure 11-1) is a good example. Ability to succeed on a more difficult item in the age scale is not functionally dependent upon success on previous items in the sense that the easier item is a prerequisite component of the more difficult item. By contrast, skill in short division is a component of skill in long division. The age differential for some tasks such as figure copying and the Piagetian conservation tests is so marked as to suggest that they depend upon the sequential maturation of hierarchical neural processes (Jensen, 1970b). Teaching of the skills before the necessary maturation has occurred is often practically impossible, but after the child has reached a certain age successful performance of the skill occurs without any specific training or practice. The items in scholastic achievement tests do not show this characteristic. For successful performance, the subject must have received explicit instruction in the specific subject matter of the test. The teachability of scholastic subjects is much more obvious than of the kinds of materials that constitute most intelligence tests and especially non-verbal tests.

Cumulative Deficit and the Progressive Achievement Gap

The concept of "cumulative deficit" is fundamental in the assessment of majority-minority differences in educational progress. Cumulative deficit is actually an hypothetical concept intended to explain an observable phenomenon which can be called the "progressive achievement gap" or PAG for short. When two groups show an increasing divergence between their mean scores on tests, there is potential evidence of a PAG. The notion of cumulative deficit attributes the increasing difference between the groups' means to the cumulative effects of scholastic learning such that deficiencies at earlier stages make for greater deficiencies at later stages. If Johnny fails to master addition by the second grade he will be worse off in multiplication in the third grade, and still worse off in division in the fourth grade, and so on. Thus the progressive achievement gap between Johnny and those children who adequately learn each prerequisite for the next educational step is seen as a cumulative deficit. There may be other reasons as well for the PAG, such as differential rates of mental maturation, the changing factorial composition of scholastic tasks which means that somewhat different mental abilities are called for at different ages, disillusionment and waning motivation for school work, and so on. Therefore I prefer the term "progressive achievement gap" because it refers to an observable effect and is neutral with respect to its causes.

Absolute and Relative PAG. When the achievement gap is measured in raw score units or in grade scale or age scale units, it is called *absolute*. For example, we read in the Coleman Report (1966, p. 273) that in the metropolitan areas of the northwest region of the US ". . . the lag of Negro scores (in Verbal ability) in terms of years behind grade level is progressively greater. At grade 6, the average Negro is approximately 1 1/2 years behind the average white. At grade 9, he is approximately 2 1/4 years behind that of the average white. At grade 12, he is approximately 3 1/4 years behind the average white."

When the achievement difference between groups is expressed in standard deviation units, it is called *relative*. That is to say, the difference is relative to the variation within the criterion group. The Coleman Report, referring to the findings quoted above, goes on to state: "A similar result holds for Negroes in all regions, despite the constant difference in number of standard deviations." Although the absolute white-Negro difference increases with grade in school, the relative difference does not. The Coleman Report states: "Thus in one sense it is meaningful to say the Negroes in the metropolitan Northeast are the same distance below the whites at these three grades—that is, relative to the dispersion of the whites themselves." The Report illustrates this in pointing out that at grade 6 about 15 per cent of whites are one standard deviation, or 1 1/2 years, behind the white average; at grade 12, 15 per cent of the whites are one standard deviation, or 3 1/4 years, behind the white average.

It is of course the absolute progressive achievement gap which is observed by teachers and parents, and it becomes increasingly obvious at each higher grade level. But statistically the proper basis for comparing the achievement differences between various sub-groups of the school population is in terms of the relative difference, that is, in standard deviation units, called sigma (σ) units for short.

Except in the southern regions of the US, the Coleman study found a more or less constant difference of approximately one sigma (based on whites in the metropolitan north-east) between whites and Negroes in Verbal Ability, Reading Comprehension, and Maths Achievement. In other words, there was no progressive achievement gap in regions outside the south. In the southern regions, there is evidence for a PAG from grade 6 to 12 when the sigma unit is based on the metropolitan north-east. For example, in the non-metropolitan south, the mean Negro-white differences (Verbal Ability) in sigma units are 1.5, 1.7, and 1.9 for grades 6, 9, and 12, respectively. The corresponding number of grade levels that the southern Negroes lag behind at grades 6, 9, and 12 are 2.5, 3.9, and 5.2 (Coleman, 1966, p. 274). The causes of this progressive achievement gap in the south are not definitely known. Contributing factors could be an actual cumulative deficit in educational skills, true sub-population differences in the developmental growth rates of the mental abilities relevant to school learning, and selective migration of families of abler students out of the rural south, causing an increasing cumulation of poor students in the higher grades.

Cross-Sectional versus Longitudinal PAG. Selective migration, student turnover related to adult employment trends, and other factors contributing to changes in the characteristics of the school population may produce a spurious PAG when this is measured by comparisons between grade levels at a single cross-section in time. The Coleman Report's grade comparisons are cross-sectional. But where there is no reason to suspect systematic regional population changes, cross-sectional data should yield approximately the same picture as longitudinal data, which are obtained by repeated testing of the same children at different grades. Longitudinal data provide the least questionable basis for measuring the PAG. Cross-sectional achievement data can be made less questionable if there are also socioeconomic ratings on the groups being compared. The lack of any grade-to-grade decrement on the socioeconomic index adds weight to the conclusion that the PAG is not an artifact of the population's characteristics differing across grade levels. (This type of control was used in the present study reported in the following section.)

Another way of looking at the PAG is in terms of the percentage of variance in individual achievement scores accounted for by the mean achievement level of schools or districts. If there is an achievement decrement for, say, a minority group across grade levels, and if the decrement is a result of school influences, then we should expect an increasing correlation between individual students' achievement scores and the school averages. In the data of the Coleman Report, this correlation (expressed as the percentage of variance in individual scores accounted for by the school average) for "verbal achievement" does not change appreciably from the beginning of the first school year up to the 12th grade. The school average for verbal achievement is as highly correlated with individual verbal achievement at the beginning of grade 1 as at grade 12. If the schools themselves contributed to the deficit, one would expect an increasing percentage of the total individual variance to be accounted for by the school average with increasing grade level. But no evidence was found that this state of affairs exists. The percentage of total variance in individual verbal achievement accounted for by the mean score of the school, at grades 12 and 1 is as follows (Coleman, et al., 1966, p. 296):

	Grade	
Group	12	1
Negro, South	22.54	23.21
Negro, North	10.92	10.63
White, South	10.11	18.64
White, North	7.84	11.07

Progressive Achievement Gap in a California School District

We searched for evidence of a PAG in our data in several ways, which can be only briefly summarized here. Separate analyses for each of the achievement tests did not reveal any striking differences in PAG, so the results can be combined without distortion of the essential results.

Mean Sigma Differences. The mean difference in sigma (standard deviation) units, based on the white group, by which Negro and Mexican-American pupils fall below the white group at each grade from 1 to 8 is shown in Table 11-3. The first three columns show the sample sizes on which the sigma differences are based. The sigma differences (i.e., σ below white mean) for Negroes and Mexican-Americans shown in columns 4 and 5 is the average of all the Stanford Achievement Tests given in each grade. Note that there is a reliable and systematic increase in the sigma difference from grade 1 to grade 3, for both Negro and Mexican groups, after which there is no further systematic change in achievement gap. The mean gap over all grades is .66 sigma for the Negroes and .55 sigma for the Mexicans. By comparison, look at columns 6 and 7, which show the mean sigma differences for those non-verbal ability tests in our battery which do not depend in any way upon reading skill and the content of which is not taught in school; this is the average sigma difference for the Lorge-Thorndike Non-verbal IQ, Figure Copying, and Raven's Progressive Matrices. We see that the sigma differences show a slight

Table 11-3. Number of white sigma units by which minority group means fall below the white mean

Grade	Sample Size (N)			Stanford Achievement Tests		Non-verbal Intelligence		Home Index (SES)		Adjusted Achievement Means	
	White	Negro	Mexican	Negro	Mexican	Negro	Mexican	Negro	Mexican	Negro	Mexican
1	285	218	258	.25	.34	1.07	.53	—	—	-.09	.15
2	229	162	250	.57	.37	1.03	.70	—	—	.15	.06
3	281	207	241	.83	.68	0.98	.53	.58	1.13	.11	.05
4	237	189	239	.69	.59	0.95	.48	.38	1.18	.17	.15
5	242	198	211	.75	.54	1.05	.62	.70	1.18	.21	.10
6	219	169	218	.84	.69	1.23	.67	.47	1.36	.09	.02
7	388	262	305	.71	.57	1.13	.72	.71	1.36	.07	.08
8	356	289	303	.64	.62	1.18	.79	.77	1.34	.06	.08
Mean				.66	.55	1.08	.63	.60	1.26	.10	.09

upward trend from the lower to the higher grades. Furthermore, the sigma differences are very significantly larger for the non-verbal intelligence tests than for the scholastic achievement tests in the case of Negroes (1.08 sigma for non-verbal intelligence versus 0.66 for achievement). The Mexicans show only a slight difference between their sigma decrement in non-verbal ability and in scholastic achievement (0.63 versus 0.55). If we can regard these non-verbal tests as indices of extra-scholastic learning ability, it appears then that these Negro children do relatively better in scholastic learning as measured by the Stanford Achievement Tests than in the extra-scholastic learning assessed by the non-verbal battery. In this sense, the Negro pupils, as compared with the Mexican pupils, are "over-achievers," although the Negroes' absolute level of scholastic performance is 0.11 sigma below the Mexicans'. For the Negro group especially, the school can be regarded as an equalizing influence: Negro pupils are closer to white pupils in scholastic achievement than in non-scholastic non-verbal abilities. The mean Negro-white scholastic achievement difference is only 61 per cent as great as the non-verbal IQ difference. This finding is exactly the opposite of popular belief. The white versus Mexican achievement difference is 87 percent as great as the non-verbal IQ difference.

Is there any systematic grade trend in our indices of socioeconomic status and home environment? Columns 8 and 9 show the sigma differences below the white group on the composite score of Gough's Home Index, which assesses parental educational and occupational level, physical amenities, cultural advantages, and community involvement. (The Home Index was not used below grade 3.) There is a slight, but not highly regular, upward trend in these sigma differences for both Negro and Mexican groups, as if the students in the higher grades come from somewhat poorer backgrounds. Despite this, the sigmas for scholastic achievement (unlike the non-verbal ability tests) do not show any systematic increase from grade 3 to 8. Note also that on the Home Index the Mexicans, on the average, are further below the Negroes than the Negroes are below the whites. Moreover, the percentage of the Mexican children whose parents speak only English at home is 19.7 per cent as compared with 96.5 per cent for whites and 98.2 per cent for Negroes. In 14.2 per cent of the Mexican homes Spanish or other foreign language is spoken exclusively, as compared with 1.1 per cent for whites and 0.5 per cent for Negroes.

Covariance Adjustments of Achievement Scores. The next step of our analysis consists of obtaining covariance adjusted means on all the achievement tests, using all the ability tests,[3] along with sex and age in months, as the covariance controls. What this procedure shows, in effect, is the mean score on the achievement tests ("output") that would be obtained by the three ethnic groups if they were equated on the ability tests ("input"). Although it is beyond the scope of this paper to explain in mathematical detail just how this kind of covariance adjustment is accomplished, a few words of explanation are in order to remove any mystery that may seem to exist for those who have not studied or used this statistical technique. A simplified illustration will give the reader some notion of what is involved.

The simplest possible illustration consists of two groups, say, Negro and white, who are given two tests, say, an IQ test and an achievement test. What we wish to find out is: what would be the mean achievement scores of the Negro and white groups if they were equated on IQ? What we must determine, in statistical terminology, is the "covariance adjusted mean" achievement for each group. It is defined mathematically as

$$\hat{Y} = \overline{Y}_G - b(\overline{X}_G - \overline{X}..)$$

In terms of our example,

$\hat{Y}_N$ = adjusted mean achievement score of Negro group
$\overline{Y}_N$ = raw mean achievement score of Negro group
$\overline{X}_N$ = mean IQ of Negro group
$\overline{X}..$ = mean IQ of Negro and white groups combined, i.e., total mean IQ
b = the regression coefficient of Y on X, i.e., of achievement on IQ for both groups combined. The regression coefficient is the slope of the regression line. It is $r_{xy}\dfrac{\sigma_y}{\sigma_x}$, where, r_{xy} is the correlation between the two variables, X and Y (or IQ and achievement) and σ_x and σ_y are the standard deviations of these variables.

The situation can be pictured as follows.

Figure 11-2. Simplified correlation scatter diagram illustrating the regression of achievement on IQ and the covariance adjustment of hypothetical white and Negro achievement means

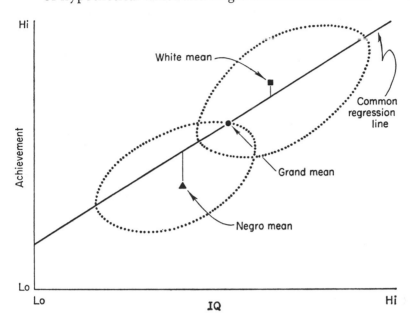

For the sake of graphic clarity, this is a greatly exaggerated picture. The so-called regression line is the one straight line about which the squared deviations of all scores are a minimum. Thus, every individual score plays a part in determining the position and slope of the regression line. It is the one best-fitting line to the data of *all* the subjects in both groups. Although the mean raw achievement scores differ markedly for Negroes and whites in this illustration, we see that each group falls only slightly off the common regression line; in this example, the white mean is above the line and the Negro mean is below. The *adjusted* means for the two groups consist of the grand mean plus (or minus) the deviation of the particular group's mean from the regression line. If the means of both groups fall exactly on the common regression line, the adjusted means will be exactly the same and are equal to the grand mean. If there is zero correlation between the input (IQ) and output (achievement) variables, then the regression line will be perfectly horizontal and parallel to the base line, and the adjusted means will consequently be exactly the same as the raw (or unadjusted) means. In the above example, the white adjusted mean would be slightly higher than the Negro adjusted mean, because the white mean is above the regression line and the Negro below. The regression line can be thought of as predicting the most probable achievement score for any given IQ. If the correlation between IQ and achievement were perfect, one could predict achievement from IQ exactly, and vice versa.

The situation is essentially the same for adjusting the means of three or more groups, and one can easily picture another group placed in the above illustration. It is much more difficult to picture the situation when more than two variables are involved. In this illustration, we have one output variable (achievement) and only one input variable (IQ). It is possible to have two or three or more input variables. If there are two, then the situation would have to be pictured in three dimensions. The common regression line would no longer be a line on a two-dimensional surface but would become a plane in a three-dimensional cube, and we would be adjusting our means in terms of their deviations from the surface of this two-dimensional plane. If we go to three input variables the situation can no longer be pictured, since we would have to deal with a "hyper plane" in four-dimensional space. Four input variables require a five-dimensional space, and so on. Although the problem can no longer be pictured graphically beyond two input variables, it can be solved mathematically for any number of input variables (although the point of diminishing returns is rapidly reached). For the sample sizes and the number of input variables used in the present study, the mathematical computations would be virtually impossible without the aid of a high speed computer.

Columns 10 and 11 of Table 11-3 show the sigma difference by which the Negro and Mexican covariance adjusted mean falls below that of the white group. These differences are quite small for both Negroes and Mexicans (averaging 0.10 and 0.09, respectively), and they show no systematic trend with grade level. In other words, when the minority groups are statistically equated with the majority (white) group on the ability test variables, their achievement, on the average, is less than 0.1 sigma below that of the white group. On an IQ scale that would be equivalent to 1.5 points, a very small difference indeed. The adjusted decrement is statistically significant, however, which raises the question of why it should differ significantly from zero at all. The reason could be actual differences between minority and majority schools in the effectiveness of instruction, or incomplete measurement of all the input variables relevant to scholastic learning, or some lack of what is called homogeneity of regression for the three ethnic groups, which works against the covariance adjustment. We know the latter factor is involved to some extent, and some combination of all of them are most likely involved. But taken all together, the fact that the majority-minority difference in mean adjusted achievement scores is still less than 0.1 sigma means the direct contribution of the schools to the difference must be even smaller than this, if existent at all. Surely it is of practically negligible magnitude.

When the personality variables (the Junior Eysenck Personality Inventory) and the four scales of the Home Index are also included with the ability variables in obtaining covariance adjusted means, the ethnic differences in scholastic achievement are wiped out almost entirely. Two-thirds of the majority-minority differences (for various achievement sub-tests at various grades) are not significant at the five per cent level and are less than 0.1 sigma. The adjusted mean differences *between* ethnic groups are smaller than the grade-to-grade sigma differences *within* ethnic groups. From this analysis, then, the school's contribution to ethnic achievement differences must be regarded as nil. If the input variables themselves are strongly influenced by the school to the disadvantage of the minority children, we should expect to find a greater sigma difference for non-verbal IQ at grade 8 (age thirteen) than at kindergarten. In the present study Negroes are 1.11 sigma below whites in non-verbal IQ in kindergarten as compared with 1.17σ in grades 7 and 8—a trivial difference. Mexican children are 0.98 sigma below whites in non-verbal IQ at kindergarten and .88 sigma below at grades 7 and 8. Thus the minority children begin school at least as far below the majority children in non-verbal ability as they are by grades 7 and 8. The schools have not depressed the ability level of minority children relative to the majority, but neither have they done anything to raise it. Differences in verbal IQ are slightly more likely to reflect the effects of schooling, and we note that in grades 7 and 8 Negroes are 1.00 sigma below the white mean and Mexicans are 0.90 sigma below.

Paired Ethnic Group Differences. The maximum discrimination

that we can make between the three ethnic groups in terms of all of our "input" variables (ability tests, personality inventories, and socio-economic indexes) is achieved by means of the multiple point-biserial correlation coefficient. The product-moment correlation obtained between a continuous variable (e.g., IQ) and a quantized (dichotomous) variable (e.g., male versus female, where male = 1 and female = 0) is called a point-biserial correlation (r_{pbs}). Mathematically it is defined as:

$$r_{pbs} = \frac{\overline{X}_1 - \overline{X}_2}{\sigma_t} \sqrt{pq}$$

where $\overline{X}_2$ and $\overline{X}_1$ = means of groups 1 and 2

σ_t = standard deviation of total (i.e., groups 1 and 2 combined)

p and q = proportions of total sample in groups 1 and 2, respectively (p + q = 1.00)

It is also possible to compute r_{pbs} in the same manner that one computes the Pearson product-moment correlation between any two continuous variables, except that the dichotomous variable is quantized by assigning 0 and 1 to its two categories. It is also possible to obtain a multiple point-biserial correlation, which gives the maximum possible correlation between the quantized variable and the best weighted combination of a number of "predictor" variables. The multiple correlation thus represents the maximum degree of discrimination that can be achieved between the two categories of the quantized variable by means of the particular set of predictor variables. Since the multiple correlation capitalizes upon sampling error (chance deviations from population values) to achieve the maximum value of the correlation, it is spuriously inflated by a degree that is inversely proportional to the sample size and the number of variables correlated. For this reason, the obtained multiple correlation should be "shrunk" down to its estimated population value (i.e., its value if there were no sampling error). The method for doing this is given in most statistics textbooks (e.g., Guilford, 1956, pp. 398-399). All the multiple correlations reported here have thus been "shrunk" and therefore represent a conservative estimate of the amount of discrimination achieved between the ethnic groups by our battery of "input" tests. . . .

Table 11-4 gives the multiple point-biserial correlations between each ethnic dichotomy and all the "input" variables—first just the ability tests and second the ability tests plus the personality inventory and socioeconomic index. Note that the three groups are almost equally discriminable from one another in terms of the multiple correlation, especially after the personality and social background variables are added to the predictors. This is interesting, because it means that the two minority groups, though both are regarded as educationally and socioeconomically disadvantaged, actually differ from one another on this composite of all input variables almost as much as each one differs from the majority group. The Negro and Mexican groups each differ from the majority group in a somewhat different way in terms of total pattern of scores, and they differ from one another almost as much. A factor analysis, shown in the next section, helps to reveal the ways in which the three groups differ from one another.

The last three columns in Table 11-4 show the correlation between each ethnic dichotomy and the Stanford Achievement Tests, with all the "input" variables partialled out, i.e., statistically held constant. These correlations represent the average contribution made to the ethnic discrimination by the Stanford Achievement Tests regarded independently of the "input" variables. It can be seen that these correlations are very small indeed. For the sample sizes used here, correlations of less than 0.10 can be regarded as statistically non-significant at the five per cent level. The proportion of the total variance between the ethnic groups that is accounted for by the achievement tests is represented by the square of the correlation coefficient. Applied to the partial correlations for the Achievement Tests in Table 11-4, this shows how trifling are the ethnic group achievement differences after the ethnic group differences on the input variables have been controlled.

Factor Analysis of All Variables. A factor analysis (varimax rotation of the principal components having Eigenvalues greater than 1) was carried out at each grade level on all test variables obtained at that grade level plus three others: sex, chronological age in months, and welfare status of the parent (whether receiving welfare aid to dependent children). The latter variable was added to supplement the indices of socioeconomic status (the four scales of Gough's Home Index). Since grades 4, 5, and 6 had all the measures (twenty-seven

Table 11-4. Point-biserial multiple correlations for "input" variables and partial correlation for "output" with "input" held constant

Grade	"Input" All Ability Tests			"Input" Ability + Personality + Home Index			"Output" Stanford Achievement Minus All "Input" Variables		
	W-N	W-M	M-N	W-N	W-M	M-N	W-N*	W-M	M-N
1	.49	.28	.29	—	—	—	—	—	—
2	.54	.47	.37	—	—	—	—	—	—
3	.54	.45	.35	.62	.59	.46	.06	.02	.07
4	.48	.38	.41	.55	.60	.55	.15	.07	.09
5	.47	.38	.27	.60	.59	.36	.13	.05	.11
6	.53	.47	.42	.69	.67	.59	.14	.11	.04
7	.52	.42	.26	.68	.70	.45	.09	−.04	.11
8	.57	.42	.43	.65	.66	.46	.06	−.02	−.07
Mean	.52	.41	.36	.63	.64	.48	.11	.05	.07

Note: Partial correlations of less than 0.10 are not significant at the five per cent level.

*The quantized ethnic groups are White = 3, Mexican = 2, Negro = 1, so that for W-N and W-M positive correlations indicate higher achievement scores for the white group, and a positive correlation for M-N indicates higher scores for the Mexican group.

variables) and the same tests were used at each of these grades, they are the most suitable part of our total sample for factor analytic comparisons. The results are essentially the same at all grade levels, although because the personality inventory and the Home Index were not used in the primary grades, and the Figure Copying Test was not used beyond grade 6, not all of the factors that emerged at grades 4, 5, and 6 come out at one or another of the other grades. Moreover, because of the large number of variables entering into the analysis at grades 4-6, more small factors come out which, in a sense, 'purify' the main factors by partialling out other irrelevant and minor sources of variance.

Factor analyses were performed first on the three ethnic groups separately to determine if essentially the same varimax factors emerged in each group. They did. All three groups yield the same factors, with only small differences in the loadings of various tests. This finding justifies combining all three groups for an overall factor analysis of the total student sample at each grade level. This was done. Eight factors with Eigenvalues greater than 1 emerged at grades 4, 5, and 6, accounting respectively for 67 per cent, 66 per cent and 70 per cent of the total variance.

The first principal component can be regarded as the general or g factor for this set of twenty-seven variables. Table 11-5 shows the loadings of each of the twenty-seven (or twenty-five in grades 7 and

Table 11-5. Loadings of variables on first principal component
for grades 4 to 8 (decimals omitted)

Variable	Grade				
	4	5	6	7	8
1. Sex (M = 0, F = 1)	14	14	03	08	12
2. Extraversion	25	28	46	33	24
3. Neuroticism	00	−06	−21	−12	01
4. Lie Scale	−17	−11	−19	−27	−39
5. Home Index−1	31	45	41	49	48
6. Home Index−2	29	30	34	41	45
7. Home Index−3	36	41	27	50	44
8. Home Index−4	29	43	28	47	40
9. Aid to Dependent Children	−21	−43	−32	−31	−26
10. Age in Months	−05	−09	−04	−04	−12
11. Lorge-Thorndike Verbal IQ	85	88	85	88	87
12. Lorge-Thorndike Non-verbal IQ	73	75	76	79	83

Table 11-5 (continued)

			Grade		
Variable	4	5	6	7	8
13. Raven's Progressive Matrices	54	55	54	54	63
14. Figure Copying	45	51	57	—	—
15. Listening-Attention	11	19	21	06	12
16. Memory—Immediate	45	40	36	27	32
17. Memory—Repeat	44	33	24	25	27
18. Memory—Delayed	43	41	41	25	27
19. Making X's 1st Try	14	02	31	53	10
20. Making X's 2nd Try	19	14	29	48	19
21. SAT: Word Meaning	83	81	81	—	—
22. SAT: Paragraph Meaning	80	79	89	86	83
23. SAT: Spelling	75	76	78	73	73
24. SAT: Language	83	84	87	78	75
25. SAT: Arithmetic Computation	57	45	63	73	73
26. SAT: Arithmetic Concepts	72	62	80	76	83
27. SAT: Arithmetic Applications	77	71	82	72	71
Percent of Variance	22	26	29	28	27

8) variables on the first principal component in grades 4 to 6. The first principal component is the single most general factor accounting for more of the variance than any other factor. It is most heavily loaded in the Stanford Achievement Tests and Verbal IQ. Inspection of the loadings of the other variables gives an indication of their correlation with this most general achievement factor.

The eight principal components were rotated to approximate simple structure by the varimax criterion. In grades 4, 5, and 6 four substantial and clear-cut factors emerged. The remaining factors serve mainly to pull out irrelevant variance from the main factors. The four main factors that emerge are:

Factor I. Scholastic Achievement and Verbal Intelligence

	Factor Loading		
Variables	Grade 4	Grade 5	Grade 6
Lorge-Thorndike Verbal IQ	.75	.75	.85
Word Meaning	.83	.69	.82
Paragraph Meaning	.83	.77	.89
Spelling	.82	.77	.81
Language	.82	.79	.86

Arithmetic Computation	.64	.58	.65
Arithmetic Concepts	.73	.69	.83
Arithmetic Applications	.77	.71	.85

Factor II. Non-verbal Intelligence

	Factor Loading		
Variables	Grade 4	Grade 5	Grade 6
Lorge-Thorndike Non-verbal IQ	.61	.57	.32
Raven's Progressive Matrices	.75	.75	.55
Figure Copying	.69	.68	.41

Factor III. Rote Memory Ability

	Factor Loading		
Variables	Grade 4	Grade 5	Grade 6
Memory Span—Immediate Recall	.85	.81	.77
Memory Span—Repeated Series	.85	.81	.86
Memory Span—Delayed Recall	.83	.79	.74

Factor IV. Socioeconomic Status

Variables (Home Index)	Factor Loading		
	Grade 4	Grade 5	Grade 6
1. Parental Education and Occupation	.75	.74	.77
2. Physical Amenities	.69	.77	.72
3. Community Participation	.66	.76	.75
4. Cultural Advantages	.66	.59	.66
Receives Welfare Aid to Dependent Children	−.40	−.34	−.46

The remaining four minor factors are: (1) Speed, motivation, persistence as defined principally by the Making X's Test, (2) Neuroticism, (3) Extraversion, (4) Age in months. These variables, having their largest loadings on separate factors, are in effect partialled out of the major factors. The four major factors listed above are orthogonal, i.e., uncorrelated with one another, and each one is thus viewed as a "pure" measure of the particular factor in the sense that the effects of all the other factors are held constant.

Ethnic Group Comparisons of Factor Scores. The final step was to obtain factor scores for every student on each of these four main factors. For the total sample, within each grade, these factor scores

Table 11-6. Mean varimax factor scores for three ethnic groups in grades 4, 5 and 6

Mean Factor Scores

Grade	Group	N	I Verbal IQ and Achievement		II Non-verbal IQ		III Memory		IV Socioeconomic Status	
			Mean	SD	Mean	SD	Mean	SD	Mean	SD
4	White	113	55.2	10.7	51.6	8.1	51.6	9.4	53.8	10.3
	Negro	129	47.1	6.5	44.6	8.9	51.0	11.2	51.7	7.9
	Mexican	145	49.5	8.5	51.0	9.3	48.1	7.7	43.6	7.8
5	White	144	54.7	8.7	52.3	8.2	50.4	9.1	54.1	9.2
	Negro	132	45.5	8.4	47.0	11.1	51.1	9.9	49.7	9.5
	Mexican	135	49.6	8.5	50.1	8.5	48.2	9.5	44.6	8.1
6	White	131	55.0	8.8	50.9	7.2	50.7	8.8	53.8	9.4
	Negro	124	47.1	8.3	44.1	10.5	50.5	9.9	51.5	8.0
	Mexican	126	49.1	9.3	51.0	8.7	48.0	10.2	42.5	7.5

are represented on a T-score scale, i.e., they have an overall mean of 50 and a standard deviation of 10. Table 11-6 shows the mean and standard deviation of the factor scores for each of the ethnic groups.

Note that the ethnic group differences in Factor I do not show any systematic increase from grade 4 to 6, thus lending no support to the existence of a cumulative deficit in the minority groups. Analysis of variance was performed on the factor scores and Scheffé's method of contrasts was used for testing the statistical significance of the differences between the means of the various ethnic groups at each grade level. The results of these significance tests are shown in Table 11-7. We see that in Factor I (Verbal IQ and Scholastic Achievement) both minority groups are significantly below the majority group, and Negroes are significantly below the Mexican group except in grade 6, where the difference is in the same direction but falls short of significance.

Table 11-7. The significance of ethnic group differences in mean factor scores, by Scheffé's method of contrasts

Contrasts (Means)	Grade	I Verbal IQ and Achievement	II Non-verbal Intelligence	III Memory	IV Socio-economic Status
				Factors	
Negro-White	4	—**	—**	—NS	—NS
	5	—**	—**	+NS	—**
	6	—**	—**	—NS	—NS
Mexican-White	4	—**	—NS	—*	—**
	5	—**	—NS	—NS	—**
	6	—**	+NS	—NS	—**
Mexican-Negro	4	+*	+**	—*	—**
	5	+**	+*	—*	—**
	6	+NS	+**	—NS	—**

*p < 0.05
**p < 0.01
NS = not significant

On Factor II (Non-verbal Intelligence) Negroes fall significantly below whites and Mexicans at all grades, and the differences between Mexicans and whites are non-significant at all grades. It should be remembered that this non-verbal intelligence factor represents that part of the variance in the non-verbal tests which is not common to the verbal IQ and achievement tests or to the memory tests. The Mexican-white difference is significant on the part of the ability tests variance which has most in common with scholastic achievement and is represented in Factor I.

Factor III (Rote Memory) shows no significant differences between the Negro and white groups; the Mexican group is significantly below the white at grade 4 and below the Negro at grades 4 and 5. This finding is consistent with the findings of other studies that mean differences between groups of lower and middle socioeconomic status are smallest on tests of short-term memory and rote learning (Jensen, 1968b).

Factor IV (Socioeconomic Status) shows relatively small differences between the Negro and white groups, while the Mexican group is significantly below the other two. Again, it should be realized that we are dealing here with "pure" factor scores which are independent of all the other variables. Thus Factor IV shows us the relative standing of the three ethnic groups in socioeconomic status when all the other variables are held constant. What these results indicate is that Negro and white children statistically equated for intelligence, achievement, and memory ability differ very little in socioeconomic status as measured by our indices, but that Mexican children, when equated on all other variables with white children or with Negro children, show a comparatively much poorer background than either the white or Negro groups. On the present measures, at least, the Mexicans must be regarded as much more environmentally disadvantaged than the Negroes, and this takes no account of the Mexican's bilingual problem. In view of this it is quite interesting that Mexican pupils on the average significantly exceed the Negro pupils in both verbal and non-verbal intelligence measures and in scholastic achievement.

Equality of Educational Opportunity:
Uniformity or Diversity of Instruction?

The results of our analysis thus far fail to support the hypothesis that the schools have discriminated unfavorably against minority pupils. When minority pupils are statistically equated with majority children for background and ability factors over which the schools have little or no control, the minority children perform scholastically about as well as the majority children. The notion that poor scholastic achievement is partly a result of the pupil's ethnic minority status per se, implying discriminatory schooling, is thus thoroughly falsified by the present study. This does not imply that the same results would be obtained in every other school system in the country. Where true educational inequalities between majority and minority pupils exist, we should expect the present type of analyses to reveal these inequalities, and it would be surprising if they were not found in some school systems which provide markedly inferior educational facilities for minority pupils. It should be noted, on the other hand, that the present study was conducted in a school district which had taken pains to equalize educational facilities in schools that serve predominantly majority or predominantly minority populations. The success of this equalization is evinced in the results of the present analyses.

But we can take a bold step further and ask: Is equalization of educational facilities enough? Is the real meaning of equality of educational opportunity simply uniformity of facilities and instructional programs? Is it possible that true equality of opportunity could mean doing whatever is necessary to maximize the scholastic achievement of children, even if it might mean doing quite different things for different children in terms of their differing patterns of ability? Note that I did not say in terms of their ethnic or social class status, but in terms of their individual patterns of ability. The fact that different social classes and ethnic groups show different modal patterns of ability, of course, means that different proportions of various subpopulations will have different patterns of strength and weakness in various mental abilities. Is such a fact to be deplored and swept out of sight, or should it be examined with a view to utilizing the differences in the design of instructional programs that might maximize each individual's benefits from schooling? A couple of years ago I wrote: "If we fail to take account either of innate or acquired differences in abilities and traits, the ideal of equality of educational opportunity can too easily be interpreted so literally as to be actually harmful, just as it would be harmful for a physician to give all his patients the same medicine. One child's opportunity can be another's defeat" (Jensen, 1968a, p. 3). At that time I suggested that we look for differential ability patterns that might interact with different instructional methods in such a way as to maximize school learning for all individuals and at the same time minimize individual and group differences in scholastic achievement and any other benefits derived from schooling.

In our laboratory research we have discovered two broad classes of abilities which show marked differences in their relation to social class and race (Jensen, 1968b, 1969b, 1970a; Jensen and Rohwer, 1968, 1970). Briefly, what we have found is that children of low socioeconomic status, especially minority children, with low measured IQs (60 to 80) are generally superior to middle-class children with similar IQs in tests of associative learning ability—free recall, serial rote learning, paired-associates learning, and digit span memory. This finding has been interpreted theoretically in terms of a hierarchical model of mental abilities, going from associative learning to conceptual thinking, in which the development of lower levels in the hierarchy is necessary but not sufficient for the development of higher levels. Our hypothesis states that the continuum of tests going from associative to conceptual is the phenotypic expression of two functionally dependent but genotypically independent types of mental processes, which we call Level I and Level II. Level I processes are perhaps best measured by tests such as digit span and serial rote learning; Level II processes are represented in tests such as the Progressive Matrices. Level I and Level II abilities are distributed differently in upper and lower social classes and in different ethnic groups. Level I is distributed fairly evenly in all sub-populations. Level II, however, is distributed about a higher mean in upper than in lower social classes. The majority of children now called "culturally disadvantaged" show little or no deficiency in Level I ability but are about one standard deviation below the general population mean on tests of Level II ability. Children who are above average on Level I but below average on Level II ability usually appear to be bright and capable of normal learning and achievement in many life situations, although they have unusual difficulties in school work under the traditional methods of classroom instruction. Many of these children, who may be classed as retarded in school, suddenly become socially adequate persons when they leave the academic situation. But children who are below average on both Level I and Level II seem to be much more handicapped. Not only is their scholastic performance poor, but their social and vocational potential also seem to be much less than those of children with normal Level I functions. Yet both types of children look much alike in overall measures of IQ and scholastic achievement.

These findings are important because they help to localize the nature of the intellectual deficit of many children called "culturally disadvantaged." We must ask whether we can discover or invent instructional methods that engage Level I more fully and thereby provide a means of improving the educational attainments of many of the children now called "culturally disadvantaged." In our current instructional procedure are we utilizing so exclusively those mental abilities we identify as IQ (Level II) that children who are relatively low in IQ but have strength in other abilities are unduly disadvantaged in the traditional classroom? The whole complex process of classroom instruction as we know it has evolved in relation to a relatively small upper-class segment of Anglo-European stock. The modal pattern of development in learning abilities of this group has probably shaped to a considerable degree the particular educational procedures public education has long regarded as standard for everyone, regardless of differences in cultural background or inherited patterns of ability. But so far we have not successfully met the challenge presented by our ideal of a rewarding education for all segments of the population, with their diverse patterns of ability.

Looking, for example, at the factor scores shown in Table 11-6 we note that the minority groups are not significantly below the majority group on Factor III (Memory), which we would identify with Level I ability. Lest anyone try to argue that these "pure" factor scores do not correspond to any "impure" scores that could be obtained with actual tests, we can look at Figures 11-3 and 11-4, showing the grade-to-grade growth curves of a good Level II test (Raven's Progressive Matrices) and a good Level I test (a composite of the three digit memory tests).

The results of both tests have been put on the same scale of T scores, with an overall mean of 50 and a standard deviation of 10 (based on the standard deviation of raw scores in the white group at grade 5). The differences between the growth curves shown in Figures 11-3 and 11-4 are striking. The approximately one standard deviation difference between the Negro and white groups on the Level II test (Matrices) can be seen to have rather drastic implications in terms of grade level comparisons. By drawing a horizontal line from the Negro or Mexican mean at any grade to the point where it

Figure 11-3. Mean T scores ($\overline{X}$=50, SD=10) on Raven's
Progressive Matrices in grades 3 to 8

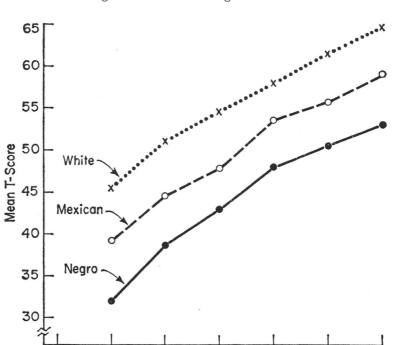

crosses the curve for the white group and dropping a perpendicular
to the baseline, we can read off the grade equivalent of the minority
group mean. The average Negro eighth-grader in this school system,
for example, performs on the matrices at a level equivalent to white
children at grade 4.5. Mexican children at grade 8 perform at grade
6.3. The grade 6 performance of Negroes and Mexicans is equivalent
to the white's performance in grades 3.4 and 4.5, respectively.

On the other hand, note the small differences between the
groups on the Level I test (Memory Span) in Figure 11-4. It is interesting to conjecture whether instruction in scholastic skills specifically aimed at Level I ability in children who are low in Level II would
significantly reduce majority-minority differences in scholastic
achievement. We do not know and can find out only through further

Figure 11-4. Mean T scores ($\overline{X}$ = 50, SD = 10) on
composite memory score in grades 2 to 8

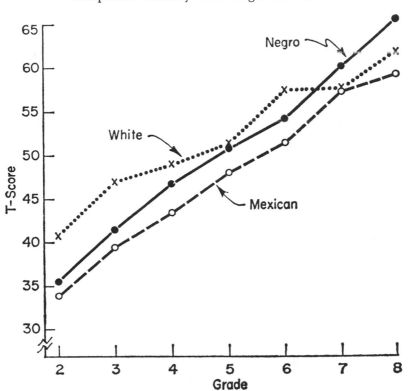

research. If instruction is aimed only at Level II ability for all children, we should expect sizeable majority-minority differences in
achievement. If instruction could somehow be aimed at Level I ability for all those children (regardless of ethnic identification) who are
significantly stronger in Level I than in Level II, would their achievement be brought appreciably closer to that of the majority? Or is
scholastic learning so intrinsically dependent on Level II ability that
no form of instruction attempting to capitalize on Level I ability
could possibly succeed beyond the most elementary aspects of any
academic subject matter? Again, we do not know. But until these
possibilities are explored, schools may be accused of cheating many
children, especially large numbers of minority children, by providing

uniform facilities but not sufficiently diversified instructional programmes to minimize differences in achievement and also maximize the overall level of achievement.

Some scholastic subjects would seem to lend themselves more to Level I processes and instructional methods than other subjects. For instance, the learning of spelling and arithmetic computation would seem to be less dependent upon Level II ability than, say, reading comprehension, arithmetic concepts or arithmetic applications. If this is true, we should expect majority-minority differences to be smaller on the Level I types of subject matter than on the Level II types. Let us make the relevant comparisons in the data of the present study. Table 11-8 shows these comparisons in sigma units.

Table 11-8. Mean sigmas (based on white group) below white mean of Negro and Mexican pupils in grades 4-8 on level I-like and level II-like tests of scholastic achievement

Tests	Negro (N=1, 107)	Mexican (N=1, 276)
Level I-Like Tests:		
Spelling	.62	.52
Arithmetic Computation	.56	.36
Level II-Like Tests:		
Paragraph Meaning	.90	.75
Arithmetic Concepts	.71	.60
Arithmetic Applications	.72	.55

They bear out our hypothesis; the pupils of both minority groups fall below the majority mean about one-fifth of a sigma more on Level II-like scholastic achievement than on Level I-like subjects. Clearly, school subjects which by their nature seem to permit greater utilization of Level I ability show smaller majority-minority differences than those subjects which involve more Level II ability. This raises the interesting question whether all scholastic subjects can be taught in ways that *maximize* their dependence on Level I and *minimize* their dependence on Level II. If this can be done for children who are low in Level II ability—and we will never know without trying—it should reduce not only the scholastic achievement gap between majority and minority children but the achievement differences among all children of every group. If it succeeds, it would do so, not by pulling anyone down toward the common average, but by capitalizing on each child's particular strengths and minimizing the role of his particular weaknesses in learning any given kind of subject matter. This would seem to be an avenue worth exploring in our efforts to achieve not only equality of educational opportunity but greater equality of scholastic performance as well.

References

Bowles, S. and Levin, H. M. (1968). 'The determinants of scholastic achievement—an appraisal of some recent evidence', *J. Hum. Resources*, Winter.

Burt, C. (1961). 'The gifted child', *Brit. J. Statist. Psychol.*, 14, 123-39.

Coleman, J. S. et al. (1966). *Equality of Educational Opportunity*. Washington, DC: US Office of Education.

Gough, H. G. (1949). 'A short social status inventory', *J. Educ. Psychol.*, 40, 52-6.

Guilford, J. P. (1956). *Fundamental Statistics in Psychology and Education* (3rd ed.). New York: McGraw-Hill.

Ilg, F. L. and Ames, L. B. (1964). *School Readiness: Behaviour Tests Used at the Gesell Institute*. New York: Harper & Row.

Jensen, A. R. (1967). 'Estimation of the limits of heritability of traits by comparison of monozygotic and dizygotic twins', *Proceedings of the National Academy of Sciences*, 58, 149-57.

Jensen, A. R. (1968a). 'Social class, race, and genetics: implications for education', *Amer. Educ. Res. J.*, 5, 1-42, (a).

Jensen, A. R. (1968b). 'Patterns of mental ability and socioeconomic status', *Proceedings of the National Academy of Sciences*, 60, 1330-7, (b).

Jensen, A. R. (1969a). 'How much can we boost IQ and scholastic achievement?', *Harv. Educ. Rev.*, 39, 1-123, (a).

Jensen, A. R. (1969b). 'Intelligence, learning ability, and socioeconomic status', *J. Special Educ.*, 3, 23-35, (b).

Jensen, A. R. (1970a). 'A theory of primary and secondary mental retardation'. In: Ellis, N. R. ed. *International Review of Research in Mental Retardation*, Vol. IV. New York: Academic Press.

Jensen, A. R. (1970b). 'Hierarchial theories of mental ability'. In: Dockrell, B. ed. *On Intelligence*. London: Methuen.

Jensen, A. R. and Rohwer, W. D., jr. (1970a). 'Mental retardation, mental age, and learning rate', *J. Educ. Psychol.* 59, 402-403.

Jensen, A. R. and Rohwer, W. D., jr. (1970b). *An Experimental Analysis of Learning Abilities in Culturally Disadvantaged Children.* Final Report, Office of Economic Opportunity. Contract No. OEO2404.

Thorndike, R. L. (1951). 'Community variables as predictors of intelligence and academic achievement', *J. Educ. Psychol.*, 42, 321-38.

Wechsler, D. (1958). *The Measurement and Appraisal of Adult Intelligence.* (4th ed.). Baltimore: Williams & Wilkins.

Wilson, A. B. (1967). 'Educational consequences of segregation in a California community'. *Racial isolation in the public schools,* Appendices, Vol. II, p. 185. US Commission on Civil Rights, Washington, DC.

Wiseman, S. (1964). *Education and Environment.* Manchester: Manchester University Press.

Notes

1. Alameda, Contra Costa, Marin, Napa, San Francisco, San Joaquin, San Mateo, Santa Clara, Solano, Sonoma.

2. A smaller rank order (e.g. 1) indicates: high reading scores, high median IQ, high proportion of minorities, high expenditure per child, high teacher salaries, high tax rate, high teacher/pupil ratio (i.e., smaller classes), and a larger number of administrators per 100 pupils.

3. Lorge-Thorndike Verbal and Non-verbal IQ, Figure Copying, Raven's Matrices, Making X's, Listening-Attention, and three memory tests.

12. SCHOOL EQUALITY
Herbert J. Walberg
Mark Bargen

Since *The Republic,* men have argued over the definition and provision of quality education in a good society. Plato, it will be recalled, devoted much of his dialectic to specifying the conditions of education that produce excellent individuals for a just state. But he was also concerned with a second ideal—equality of opportunity; and he pointed out that children of gold are sometimes produced by parents of brass and that educators should identify and nurture them to join the ranks of philosopher kings. As shown by deToqueville's *Democracy in America* and Myrdal's *An American Dilemma,* no country has taken the second ideal more seriously, continuously, or with greater anguish than our own. Yet we still have far to go in providing quality and equality in American education.

The empirical researcher, faced with a host of philosophical, legal, polemical, and romantic concepts of educational equality, must attempt to develop measures of the concepts to evaluate school equality. Like the astronomer who cannot clearly observe all he wishes, let alone manipulate the heavens, the educational research worker must work cautiously with measures of schools that are imperfect operational representations of abstract concepts. The main intent of this chapter is to analyze such measures and show their spatial distribution in the Chicago Public Schools. Before doing so, however, the underlying concepts are set forth and critically examined.

Table 12-1. Concepts of educational equality*

Definition	Problems
1. *Negative:* quality of education does not depend on individual, social, ethnic, or other characteristics of the student or where he happens to receive his education.	What is "educational quality?" What should be equalized: individual, class, school, district, city, or state education?
2. *Political:* appointed or elected individuals representative of all majorities and minorities have equal control over resources and quality.	A definition of decision making rather than concept. What groups should be represented: social, ethnic, or geographical? What unit should they control: school, district, city, or state?
3. *Racial:* integrate racial or ethnic groups in unit of geographical area.	Little consistent evidence of racial inequalities in resources within certain geographical areas. Little consistent evidence that racial segregation in schools is harmful by itself. May discourage cultural pluralism. Expense and public resistance to bussing. How define groups and areas?
4. *Socioeconomic:* integrate socioeconomic groups within unit of geographical area.	Same problems as racial definition except that there is some moderately creditable evidence that socioeconomic integration can help lower socioeconomic groups.
5. *Economic:*	Assumes expenditures determine educational quality.
a. Utopian: continue to allocate additional funds to each student until additional increments produce no gains.	Economic limitations of society or higher priorities for other social and individual goals.
b. Minimum: establish minimum expenditure level; state supplies funds to localities that cannot supply minimum; willing districts can spend more than minimum.	Amount spent still depends on place of residence.
c. Egalitarian: spend more on lower ability students so that all students leave school with an equal chance for success.	How measure ability? May be relatively poor social investment. Is the purpose of the school to compensate for inequalities? Can it? May discourage excellence.

d. Elite: spend more on higher ability students since they may benefit more from scarce resources and later contribute more to social quality and equality.	How measure ability? May further enrich the advantaged.
e. Financial: spend equal funds on each student.	Costs may vary for different children and in different parts of the state.
f. Maximum Variance: set limit on ratio of expenditures for education in high and low districts, e.g. 1½ to 1.	May curb local initiative.
g. Classification: equal treatment of equals; expenditures assigned to students on the basis of statewide classifications, such as "creative" and "blind."	How classify students?
6. *Resource:* use any of the economic variants except school resources such as physical plant, teacher qualifications, and library books as the units of allocation or equalization rather than expenditures.	Measureable resources may not determine quality of education.

*Adapted and synthesized from: A. E. Wise, *Rich Schools, Poor Schools: The Promise of Equal Educational Opportunity* (Chicago: University of Chicago Press, 1968); and M. T. Katzman, *The Political Economy of Urban Schools* (Cambridge, Mass.: Harvard University Press, 1971).

Apparently only two writers, Wise (1968) and Katzman (1971) have tried to draw up comprehensive lists of definitions of educational equality. Their lists do not overlap completely, and we have synthesized their definitions in Table 12-1. Among the six definitions and twelve variants, the first one, the negative, raises the least dissent because it is the most abstract; however, it is nearly useless for generating a measure of equality. The second column of Table 12-1 lists the problems encountered with each of the definitions. The political, racial, and socioeconomic definitions force us to categorize people in ways that are not only unacceptable to many but also impractical to carry out in attaining equality. Would we equate a Negro or white immigrant from rural Mississippi or Appalachia with a member of an established Negro or white Chicago family in composing the Chicago school board? Should Latins and Orientals be integrated with whites or Negroes? Or, indeed, is the term "Oriental" adequate in view of the cultural differences among Chinese, Japanese, and Koreans? Difficulties are also encountered with the economic and resource definitions, as shown in Table 12-1. Moreover, problems and costs in obtaining measurements would still exist even if the definitions were entirely acceptable.

Perhaps the only way to obtain indubitable equality is to provide no education at all, or to devise a programmed machine that would completely control each child's environment from birth. Because these alternatives are unacceptable, and because imperfect concepts and limited information are generally better than none at all in reaching a conclusion, we turn to an analysis of some national, state, and large city data on educational equality.

Table 12-2 shows "coefficients of variation," indices calculated by dividing the standard deviation by the mean, that measure the variation in expenditure or resource distribution from the arithmetic average. If there is no variation, the coefficient will be zero; if there is large variation, the index will approach unity. This index is superior to the range or ratio of highest to lowest unit that has been used in popular accounts of expenditure inequalities because it takes into account the entire distribution of all units rather than the two most extreme.

The first row of coefficients shows that inequalities in total expenditures per student are far larger in schools across the nation, across states, and within states than they are within the three large

Table 12-2. Coefficients of variation (inequalities) for providing education at several levels

	Total	Interstate	Intrastate	Intracity			
				1967 Atlanta	1971 Boston	1967 Chicago	1971 Chicago
Expenditures per student	.72	.25	.24	.14	.13	.15	.08
Teacher Education	.48	—	.21	—	.23	.26	.15
Teacher Experience	.40	—	.60	.25	.24	.69	.27
Class Size	.26	—	.18	.11	.24	.05	.06

Note. The figures in the first six columns are adapted from those compiled from several sources by M. T. Katzman in *The Political Economy of the Urban Schools* (Cambridge, Mass.: Harvard University Press, 1971), pp. 120 and 136.

cities sampled. These figures suggest that the largest inequalities in student expenditures are among states and among school districts within states rather than within large cities. This hypothesis is further supported by scattered evidence (Katzman, 1971) that student expenditures are generally highest in wealthy, highly industrialized states and in affluent suburban districts.

Consider the large city inequalities in expenditures per student. Three major studies have been conducted. Sexton (1961) reported large inequalities in the Detroit public schools, but did not present figures that can be comprehensively analyzed. Studies by Burkhead, Fox, and Holland (1967) of Atlanta and Chicago and by Katzman (1971) of Boston revealed relatively small inequalities in total expenditures per student as shown in Table 12-2. Moreover, our analysis of Chicago high school data in the last column shows that total expenditures were more equal in 1971 than in 1967 and that inequalities in teacher education and experience were reduced while variations in class size remained at about the same low level.

Table 12-3 shows some additional measures of inequality for 389 elementary and 46 secondary public schools in Chicago. If racial integration provides equality, the Chicago schools, like those in the rest of the nation (Coleman et al, 1966), are highly unequal. While the mean percent Negro of elementary schools is 46, 41 percent of the schools are more than 95 percent Negro and 40 percent are more than 95 percent white; and the corresponding coefficient of variation is very high, .99. The same coefficient for high schools is smaller, .89, because these schools have larger attendance boundaries and are therefore more likely to include mixed populations.

The variation coefficients for other indexes of equality in Table 12-3, however, present a different picture. (See Table 13-2 for further definitions of the variables.) Inequalities in total expenditures, expenditures for regular teachers, mean class size, and mean coded teacher education are relatively small in the elementary and secondary schools. Expenditures for materials are unequal but they are a small component of total operating expenditures per student. However, mean teacher experience and expenditures for extra personnel (principals, counselors) are unequally distributed in both elementary and secondary schools. Since total expenditures are equal but their components and what they purchase are not, we now turn to the spatial distribution of separate variables throughout the city (Figures 12-1—12-3).

Table 12-3. Statistics on the Chicago Public Schools

	Elementary (N = 389)				Secondary (N = 46)			
	Mean	Standard Deviation	Variation Coefficient	Achievement Correlation	Mean	Standard Deviation	Variation Coefficient	Achievement Correlation
Percent Negro	.46	.46	.99	−.60	.47	.42	.89	−.81
Total expenditures	$472.94	63.10	.13	.30	636.02	51.37	.08	.17
Regular teachers	$367.80	45.00	.12	.41	518.26	40.78	.08	.30
Extra personnel	$91.68	26.96	.29	.02	100.57	19.75	.20	−.16
Materials	$13.46	4.28	.32	.00	17.20	2.42	.14	−.07
Class size	33.48	2.71	.08	.18	23.02	1.47	.06	.51
Teacher education	1.29	.16	.13	.64	1.53	.23	.15	.88
Teacher experience	7.67	2.63	.34	.75	6.77	1.85	.27	.82

Figure 12-1 shows the distribution of mean coded teacher education and experience, and mean class size of 389 elementary schools throughout the city. For all computer maps in this chapter, the darker the area, the higher it is (in ten equal intervals) on the variable mapped. The darkness at any particular point depicts the mean value of schools in the immediate area. Figure 12-1 is particularly important because the three resources mapped account for about 80 percent of the operating expenditures of the Chicago Public Schools and other large school systems in the United States. Teacher education and experience and class size show definite spatial patterns. Schools with highly educated, experienced teachers are concentrated in the outlying areas of the city, particularly in the north, northwest, and southwest. Schools with smaller mean class sizes, however, are concentrated in the remaining areas, especially in the inner city and in two sectors extending west and south from the center city. Thus, total operating expenditures per student tend to be equal throughout the city because their two main components, teacher salaries (based on degree and graduate credits attained and years of experience) and class size are traded off in the school system: the inner city, western and southern sectors get smaller classes; the remaining areas get higher "teacher quality," that is, more experienced, more highly educated teachers. And now, one wonders, which are the areas of higher achievement?

Figure 12-2 shows the distribution of first-grade reading readiness, sixth-grade reading achievement, and the extent to which sixth-grade students outperform or underperform a regression prediction from first-grade readiness scores on students in the same schools. (See Chapter 13 for information on these tests.) Comparing Figures 12-1 and 12-2 reveals that both higher readiness and achievement and, to a lesser extent, performance are found in areas of higher teacher quality rather than in areas with smaller classes. The achievement correlations in Table 12-3 bear out this pattern: sixth grade achievement is correlated .64 with teacher education, .75 with experience, and .18 with class size; and the corresponding correlations are even higher in the secondary schools. For example, class size is correlated .51 with eleventh grade achievement (of course, no causal relations can be safely assumed). From the high negative correlations in Table 12-1 between achievement and percent Negro in the school (−.60 and −.81 for elementary and secondary schools respectively),

Class Size　　　　　　　Teacher Education　　　　　　　Teacher Experience

Figure 12-1. Distribution of major educational resources in the Chicago Public Schools

Percent Ready for School (Grade 1)   Achievement (Grade 6)   Achievement (Grade 6) Adjusted for Achievement (Grade 4)

Figure 12-2. Distribution of readiness, achievement, and achievement gains

Percent Negro Enrollment (1970-1971)   Change in Percent Negro Enrollment (1969-1971)

Figure 12-3. Distribution of Negro enrollment and change in Negro enrollment

one might infer that racial percentages are spatially linked to the chain of teacher quality, class size, and achievement.

Figure 12-3 reveals that this is indeed the case. The areas of lower teacher quality, smaller class sizes, and lower achievement in the inner city and southern and western sectors tend to contain schools with more than 95 percent Negro students. The figure also shows the pattern of segregation very clearly: most schools are nearly all Negro or all white. Moreover, the part of the figure showing change in percent Negro from the 1969-1970 to 1970-1971 school years shows not a random dispersion of Negroes throughout white areas of the city, as some have hoped, but an obvious growth in school percent Negro around the perimeters of the Negro areas. The in-migration of rural southern Negroes to Chicago and the out-migration of middle class whites to the suburbs, noted for several decades (Tauber, 1972), is apparently continuing, while the city's population has remained fairly constant.

To examine the pattern of expenditures and resources allocated to the main racial-ethnic groups in the city, the 389 schools were divided into five groups, as shown in Table 12-4: 147 schools, in which more than 95 percent of the students were white, were classified as white; 36 predominantly white, 50 to 95 percent; 30 predominantly Negro, 50 to 95 percent; 147 Negro, above 95 percent; and 29 Latin, where this was the largest ethnic group in the school. A multivariate analysis of variance showed that the patterns of allocation are significantly different (probability less than .001) in the five groups of schools, and Table 12-4 shows the group means. As suggested by the spatial patterns on the maps, white schools have higher teacher expenditures and hence more experienced and better-educated staffs, but larger classes. Negro and Latin schools have lower teacher expenditures but smaller class sizes, and slightly higher expenditures on extra personnel.

Finally, let us consider the achievement levels of the five groups of schools on first-grade reading readiness, and fourth- and sixth-grade reading achievement. Table 12-5 shows a pattern of differences that are highly significant (probability less than .001) in a multivariate analysis of variance. In the white schools, an average of about 77 percent of the first graders are "ready" for the school reading program, while in the Negro and Latin schools the corresponding average percentages are 45 and 40, respectively. The large differences

Table 12-4. Expenditures and resources for the five groups

School	Expenditures Per Student				Resources		
	Regular Teachers	Extra Personnel	Materials	Class Size	Teacher Education	Teacher Experience	
White	379.40	90.48	13.03	34.43	1.39	9.55
Predominately White	381.14	93.42	14.61	33.32	1.34	8.28
Predominately Negro	368.50	94.07	14.37	33.95	1.26	7.33
Negro	356.26	90.63	13.56	32.45	1.19	6.02
Latin	350.33	96.15	12.59	33.80	1.20	5.89
F-ratios	6.99***	.041	1.69	11.28***	45.00***	59.52***

Note. F-ratios with three asterisks are significant at the .001 level; those with no asterisks are not significant at the .10 level.

Table 12-5. Mean achievement at three grade levels
for five groups of schools

School	First-Grade Reading Readiness Percent Ready	Fourth-Grade Reading Achievement National T-scores	Sixth-Grade Reading Achievement National T-scores
White	76.59	51.54	50.15
Predominately White	71.33	49.40	48.21
Predominately Negro	64.53	48.34	46.48
Negro	45.31	44.95	42.53
Latin	39.52	44.28	43.57
F-ratios	66.98	70.22	75.59

Note. All F-ratios are significant beyond the .001 level.

among the groups persist on reading tests in the fourth and sixth grades, except that Latin schools outperform Negro schools slightly at the sixth-grade level. Even at these grade levels, however, Latin and Negro schools are about .6 of a standard deviation below white schools in Chicago.

Do the Chicago schools provide educational equality? The answers are complex and depend on one's concept of equality. If equality means racial integration, the answer is no. If it means equal expenditures, the answer is yes. If it means equal resources and reading achievement, the answer is no. As we have shown, white schools in the outlying areas of the city have high achievement levels, large classes, and more experienced, well educated teachers. In minority schools in the central area and the western and southern sectors, the achievement and school resource pattern is reversed: large percentages of students enter first grade unready for school and, confirming reanalysis of the Coleman data (Mosteller and Moynahan, 1972), remain behind in the later grades. Thus the Chicago schools, like others in the nation, do not appear to overcome family origins.

These major findings must be considered with caution. Political and socioeconomic concepts of educational equality are neglected here; gathering data on these concepts would be a major undertaking and perhaps worthwhile despite our reservations about their definitions in Table 12-1. Moreover, data on only three major racial-ethnic groups—Negroes, Latins, and whites—have been examined; surely there are large differences in social class, cultural, and other characteristics within these groups that might profitably be investigated with respect to educational equality. Limiting the analysis to only one output measure—reading achievement—is unfortunate given the many goals of education, but perhaps inevitable given the limited number of correlated output measures available. Moreover, it should be remembered that inequalities in expenditures and resources in Chicago and other large cities surveyed are small compared to differences between cities and their suburbs and among states.

Even with these cautions in mind, however, the findings may have some substantive and practical implications. It is disturbing that minority groups get lower "teacher quality," even though they are compensated with smaller class sizes, because minority children, particularly Negroes, appear to benefit more than whites from better teachers (Mosteller and Moynihan, 1972). No one has defined "good teaching" with scientific rigor, but advanced degrees, recency of education, teaching experience, and verbal aptitude have been fairly consistently associated with student achievement gains in a number of large-scale surveys (Katzman, 1971). Class size, on the other hand, is usually found to be uncorrelated with achievement goals. Like the cancer—smoking correlation, the scientific case for teacher qualities cannot be made without experiments. Yet, even in the face of noncausal evidence, the prudent man reconsiders smoking, and the just society reconsiders the distribution of effective educational resources.

On moral, if not scientific, grounds, then, efforts should be made to equalize teacher quality in Chicago. At least as far back as 1950, ill-prepared novice teachers in Chicago have typically started their careers in the most difficult minority schools (Becker, 1950). About half, disillusioned and traumatized by the experience (Walberg, 1968), abandon their teaching careers within two years. (Some, of course, leave for other reasons, such as child rearing.) Those who remain are allowed to transfer to higher achieving schools after several years. These two factors make for very high rates of staff inexperience and mobility in these minority schools, which are also encumbered by many other problems. More seasoned and specially prepared teachers should be brought in to help solve the educational problems of these schools.

In conclusion, three points are worth repeating. The schools as they are presently organized, or as they might be organized with the best research and wisdom we have, cannot compenstate for individual, family, and institutional inequalities in the community beyond their control. The Chicago schools provide relatively equal educational opportunity as far as determined here, but the quality of teaching staffs should be more fairly distributed. The large identifiable educational inequalities in our society extend beyond the metropolitan area and are between the city and rural areas of poverty on one hand and the affluent suburbs on the other.

References

Becker, H. S. "The Career of the Chicago Public School Teacher." *American Journal of Sociology* 57 (1950): 570-77.

Burkhead, J., Fox, T. G., and Holland, J. W. *Input and Output in Large-City High Schools.* Syracuse, N.Y.: Syracuse University Press, 1967.

Coleman, J. S. et al. *Equality of Educational Opportunity.* Washington, D.C.: U.S. Government Printing Office, 1966.

Katzman, M. T. *The Political Economy of Urban Schools.* Cambridge, Mass.: Harvard University Press, 1971.

Mosteller, F. W. and Moynihan, D. P. *On Equality of Educational Opportunity.* New York: Random House, 1972.

Tauber, K. E. "The Demographic Context of Metropolitan Education," in *Human Intelligence,* edited by J. McV. Hunt. New Brunswick, N.J.: Transaction Books, 1972, 77-97.

Sexton, P. C. *Education and Income: The Inequalities of Opportunity in our Public Schools.* New York: Viking Press, 1961.

Walberg, H. J. et al. "Effects of Tutoring and Practice Teaching on Self-Concept and Attitudes in Education Students." *Journal of Teacher Education* 19 (1968): 283-91.

Wise, A. E. *Rich Schools, Poor Schools: The Promise of Equal Educational Opportunity.* Chicago: University of Chicago Press, 1968.

13. SCHOOL PERFORMANCE
Mark Bargen
Herbert J. Walberg

This chapter reports the input-output performance of the general elementary and secondary public schools of Chicago. It examines the possible effects of "teacher quality" (professional experience and extent of graduate education, upon which salaries are based) and class size on student achievement as measured with nationally-standardized tests. The two school inputs determine about 80 percent of the operating expenditures of the schools, and the per-student cost for regular teachers was about $368 for elementary and $518 for high schools in Chicago in 1970-71. With an enrollment of more than 500,000 students in Chicago, the total cost of these expenditures runs to more than $200 million per year, an amount of tax money large enough to make it worthwhile to estimate the quality and impact of the educational services purchased. As indicated in other chapters, standardized achievement is not the only criterion for school output; nor are the school inputs mentioned the only ones. Nevertheless, these are important measures, available for analysis, and of interest in an era of financial stringency in education.

Prior studies of school input-output performance are summarized in Table 13-1 from a synthesis of the reviews by Averch et al. (1972), Guthrie (1970), and Katzman (1971). Of the twenty-three studies (seven of which analyzed parts of the Coleman data (1966), twenty-one used socioeconomic status or background to control for the quality of student input, four employed prior student

Table 13-1. Major studies of teacher quality and class size

Investigator	Grades	Sample	Control Variables	Significant Correlates with Student Achievement
Armor (1972)	6	U.S. schools	SES, background	Teacher salary, verbal ability
Averch and Kiesling (1970)	9	U.S. schools and individuals	SES	Teacher salary, class size
Benson (1965)	5	California schools	SES (district)	Teacher salary
Bowles (1969)	12	U.S. Negro individuals	Background	Teacher verbal ability, education; class size
Bowles and Levin (1968)	12	U.S. individuals	Background	Teacher verbal ability, experience
Burkhead, Fox, and Holland (1967)	12	Chicago and Atlanta schools	Median family income (census), lower-grade achievement	Teacher salary, experience; class size nonsignificant
Cohn (1968)	12	Iowa districts	Prior achievement	Teacher salary; class size nonsignificant
Coleman et al. (1966)	3,6,9,12	U.S. individuals	Background	Teacher verbal ability; teacher experience, education, and class size nonsignificant, but these findings are disputed
Goodman (1959)	7,11	New York State individuals	SES	Teacher experience, observer rating of ability to relate subject matter to student ability and interest, instruction expenditures per student
Guthrie, Kleindorfer, Levin, and Stout (1971)	6	Michigan individuals	SES	Teacher experience, attitude toward teaching, school, and other teachers; verbal ability

Study	Grade	Sample	Control	Findings
Hanushek (1970)	3	California individuals	SES, prior achievement	Teacher experience and education nonsignificant
Hanushek (1968)	6	Northern urban individuals	SES, background	Teacher experience, verbal ability
Katzman (1971)	6	Boston districts	SES (by census tracts)	Teacher experience, education, accreditation; lack of teacher turnover in school; class size
Kiesling (1969)	6	New York State districts	SES, prior achievement	Expenditures per student
Kiesling (1970)	8	New York State districts	SES	Teacher experience, education—mixed; salary—negative; class size—mixed
Levin (1970)	6	Eastern city individuals	SES, student attitudes, grade aspirations, parents' attitudes	Teacher experience, satisfaction, and attendance at university rather than college; teacher verbal ability nonsignificant; only teacher experience significant when all control variables included in model
Michaelson (1970)	6	Eastern city individuals	SES	Teacher experience, tenure, verbal ability, academic rather than education major in college
Mollenkopf and Melville (1956)	9,12	U.S. schools	SES	Teacher experience and education nonsignificant; class size
Plowden (1967) (Central Advisory Council for Education)	Kindergarten, elementary	British individuals	SES, background	Teacher experience, education; observer rating of teacher quality; class size nonsignificant
Raymond (1968)	College freshmen	Virginia districts	SES	High school teacher salary; class size

Table 13-1 (continued)

Investigator	Grades	Sample	Control Variables	Significant Correlates with Student Achievement
Ribich (1968)	High school	U.S. individuals	SES	Expenditures per student
Smith (1972)	6,9,12	U.S. northern individuals	SES, background	Teacher experience, attitude, and verbal ability nonsignificant
Thomas (1962)	10,12	U.S. schools	SES characteristics of home and community	Teacher salary; expenditures per student; class size

*SES refers to socioeconomic status measured by parental or average community education and/or income. Background refers to number of books in the home, appliances, and other factors thought to be related to student achievement.

achievement, and three employed both kinds of control variables. Nearly all the studies show that per-student expenditures for teachers and teacher experience or education are significantly associated with student achievement as measured in most cases by student verbal or reading achievement. The consistency of these results is especially striking since verbal skills are importantly conditioned by the stimulation of the home environment and by heredity. The relation of teacher quality input to other areas of achievement such as mathematics, social studies, and science is likely to be even more impressive. Six studies revealed class size positively related to achievement; three showed nonsignificant relationships; and one showed mixed results. Thus average class size in the school is not consistently related to achievement; but the degree of inconsistency should be interpreted cautiously since class size is related to how much students (and teachers) like their classes (see chapter 6). Now let us consider some input-output relations in the Chicago Public Schools.

Method

Input-outcome regression studies are subject to measurement and specification error and colinearity. Measurement error concerns inaccuracy or unreliability of the measures employed. Specification error concerns the form (e.g., raw, logrithmic, quadratic) and comprehensiveness of the set of input variables. Colinearity refers to correlated input variables and the difficulty of estimating the separate, unique effect of a given variable when it is confounded with another or, in most cases, others.

Research has repeatedly shown that school inputs are confounded with student socioeconomic status (SES), family background, and ethnicity. Schools in Chicago attended by low SES or minority group children are characterized by small classes and a staff of inexperienced teachers who have completed little or no graduate study. It is necessary to control as best one can for these confounding and other types of error. In this study, control is provided indirectly: for each school the "prior" achievement of students in a lower grade in the school at the same point in time is used as a proxy for student input in assessing the effect of school input on achievement in a later grade. This procedure is open to question on two counts: the degree to which students in the lower grade of a school are representative of those in the upper grade in the same school, and the extent to which earlier-grade achievement adequately represents or controls student input. The procedure chosen, while subject to these uncertainties, permits an examination of the possible interaction of school and student inputs and thus asks if school resources are differentially effective for schools of different earlier-grade achievement levels.

A second issue relating to the elimination of confounding effects is the choice of the method of statistical analysis. The three most commonly used methods are sample stratification, ordinary multiple regression, and ordered stepwise multiple regression. In stratification analysis, the sample is subdivided into several strata with respect to the variable or combination of variables to be controlled, and separate analyses are performed in each sample. Such stratification is effective only to the degree to which homogeneity (with respect to the controlled variables) is achieved within the subsamples. In order to obtain accurate control, the sample must be divided into many levels and cells, resulting in a loss of degrees of freedom and power of the statistical tests.

In the case of ordinary multiple regression, the control variable remains unstratified, and the test of any input variable is based on the size of the raw weight the variable receives in the regression equation, relative to the size of its standard error. On the other hand, ordered stepwise regression concerns the amount of variation in the dependent variable explained by an independent variable (such as a school input) after partialling out variance attributable to control variables (such as student input). In general, ordered regression provides a more committal and stringent test than ordinary regression of the contribution of an input to determining the variance of an output. Since both kinds of regression are useful in answering different questions, both are employed in the present study.

Another problem associated with education input-output studies is the choice of unit for statistical analysis. This point is critical in that the units used must be independent units in order to meet the assumptions of statistical inference. Obviously, individual students cannot be used as the unit of analysis, since the traits of one student can be expected to influence other students in the same class, and perhaps even in the same school. In the past the most common units of analysis for such studies have been the school or the district (see Table 13-1), with scores averaged across all students in the school or district. However, aggregation of schools within districts mixes effects of different schools, and the best choice of unit appears to be the school.

For the present study, data were obtained on all Chicago public general elementary and general high schools for the academic year 1970-71. The variables selected for analysis (see Table 13-2) included median reading achievement scores for the first, fourth, sixth, eighth, ninth, and eleventh grades; a measure of teacher quality; average class size; and the percentage of the enrollment consisting of Negro students.

Table 13-2. Definition of variables

Achievement

First grade—Percent of entering first grade students judged ready for school on Metropolitan Readiness Test.
Fourth, sixth, and eighth grades—Median percentile rank (converted to T-score) of fourth, sixth, and eighth grade students on reading subtest of Metropolitan Achievement Test (Elementary, Intermediate, and Advanced batteries, respectively).
Ninth grade—Median percentile rank (converted to T-score) of ninth grade students on Metropolitan Reading Test.
Eleventh grade—Median percentile rank (converted to T-score) of eleventh grade students on Davis Reading Test.

Percent Negro enrollment

Negro enrollment as percentage of total enrollment

Teacher quality

Sum of
Teacher experience—Mean number of years teaching experience of faculty (converted to T-score).
and
Teacher education—Mean number of degrees of faculty: Bachelor's=1, Master's=2, 36 hours past Master's=3 (converted to T-score).

Class size

Number of students enrolled in subject classes divided by the number of subject teaching positions.

The availability of achievement data spanning the full range of students' schooling made it possible to assess the impact of school inputs at several grade levels. Four parallel analyses were performed, using fourth, sixth, eighth, and eleventh grade achievement as dependent variables and first, fourth, sixth, and ninth grade achievement, respectively, as measures of student input. It should be noted that, although the fourth, sixth, and eighth grade analyses were all conducted using elementary school data, some variation existed in the sample sizes for these analyses, since some Chicago elementary schools do not include the full range of grades from first through eighth grade. A total of 407, 389, 260, and 46 schools were included, respectively, in the fourth, sixth, eighth, and eleventh grade samples.

An initial ordered stepwise regression analysis was performed to assess the impact of the two school inputs at the four grade levels. The top part of Table 13-3 shows the additional variation in achievement accounted for by earlier-grade achievement, teacher quality, and class size, in that order. As expected, earlier-grade achievement accounted for a sizable, highly significant fraction of the variation in

Table 13-3. Variance accounted for and regression weights for three inputs

Variance Accounted For

Grades	Achievement	Teacher Quality	Class Size	R^2
1-4	57.58***	9.25***	0.03	.67***
4-6	69.23***	3.56***	0.36*	.73***
6-8	74.64***	3.30***	0.75**	.79***
9-11	91.93***	2.13***	0.06	.94***

Regression Weights and Standard Errors

Grades		Achievement	Teacher Quality	Class Size
1-4	B	0.09	0.13	0.03
	σ_B	0.01	0.01	0.05
4-6	B	0.69	0.08	0.12
	σ_B	0.04	0.01	0.05
6-8	B	0.65	0.08	0.17
	σ_B	0.04	0.01	0.06
9-11	B	0.70	0.06	0.11
	σ_B	0.06	0.02	0.17

Note—Increments in variance and overall R^2's significant at the .05, .01, and .001 levels are indicated respectively by 1, 2, and 3 asterisks.

achievement outcomes. The additional variation predictable from teacher quality was sizable and highly significant at all grade levels, but the incremental variance accounted for by class size was small, though significant for fourth and sixth grades. As shown in the bottom part of Table 13-3, both teacher quality and class size received positive regression weights; that is, higher achievement is associated with higher teacher quality and (weakly) with larger classes.

Thus a ten-unit increase in teacher quality (for example, an additional degree and 2.5 years experience for one-fifth of the faculty) is associated with an estimated 1.3 T-score points higher achievement at the fourth-grade level; a unit increase in class size (one student per teacher) is associated with only .17 T-score points higher achievement at the eighth-grade level. We believe higher student achievement is partially determined by teacher quality, as measured by training and experience; however, because larger classes are found in middle-class areas of Chicago where student achievement progresses more rapidly, we believe the relation between achievement and class size is not causal but that both are probably determined in part by third causes, such as community status and school attractiveness.

Two striking trends across grade levels should be noted in Table 13-3: an increase in the strength of the relationship between earlier-grade achievement and subsequent achievement at the higher grade levels, and a corresponding drop in the contribution of teacher quality to achievement outcomes. High dropout rates of lower-achieving schools would diminish the eleventh-grade variance in achievement among schools and thus lower the grade-to-grade predictability at these levels. Thus, the fact that predictability is actually higher is all the more striking. Does adolescence stabilize the progress of school achievement? Is reading no longer emphasized in the later grades? Are children more responsive than adolescents to teacher quality? If so, should more resources and expenditures be allocated to elementary grades, instead of the present situation in which children are discriminated against relative to adolescents in the allocation of school resources?

In order to examine the interactions between student achievement and school inputs, the products of earlier-grade achievement with teacher quality and class size were added to the regression equation described above. At the fourth-grade level, a positive achievement-teacher quality interaction accounted for an additional 1.30

percent of the variance in the criterion (p less than .001), beyond which the achievement-class size interaction accounted for .35 percent (p less than .05). The regression weights and their standard errors (in parentheses) for this equation were as follows:

Achievement (4th Grade)$_{est}$ =

.075 Achievement (1st Grade) + .010 Teacher Quality +
(.086)   (.035)

.289 Class Size + .002 Ach X Teacher Quality —
(.128)   (.000)

.005 Achievement X Class Size
(.002)

Thus, in schools where first-grade students are high achievers, teacher quality has greater and class size has less importance, than in schools where first-grade students are low achievers. No interactions between student achievement and school inputs were significant for the other grade levels.

A further analysis was performed to relate ethnic composition of the school to student achievement and to differential impacts of school inputs for schools of differing ethnic composition. The set of predictors consisted of earlier-grade achievement, percent Negro enrollment, teacher quality, class size, and two interaction terms—percent Negro enrollment by teacher quality and percent Negro enrollment by class size. As shown in Table 13-4, the size of the Negro enrollment in the school is inversely related to student achievement, although the strength of the relationship diminshes at later grade levels, and by eleventh grade the relationship is not statistically significant. In addition, significant interactions between the percent Negro enrollment and teacher quality were found at fourth and eleventh grades. Again, a trend can be seen across grade levels, progressing from a significant negative interaction at fourth grade, through nonsignificant near-zero interactions at sixth and eighth grades, to a significant, positive interaction at eleventh grade. The slopes of the regression lines for achievement against teacher quality show that teacher quality is most strongly related to achievement outcomes at the early grades in predominantly white schools, and at the later grades in predominantly Negro schools. The interactions

Table 13-4. Ethnic regression variance and equations

Variance accounted for

Grade	Achievement	Percent Negro	Teacher Quality	Class Size	Percent Negro Interactions		R^2
					Teacher Quality	Class Size	
1-4	57.61***	4.20***	6.40***	0.02	0.37*	0.10	.69***
4-6	69.23***	2.13***	2.51***	0.10	0.06	0.17	.74***
6-8	74.64***	1.68***	2.40***	0.52*	0.02	0.14	.79***
9-11	91.93***	0.47	1.67**	0.07	0.61*	0.02	.95***

Regression weights and standard errors

Grade		Achievement	Percent Negro	Teacher Quality	Class Size	Percent Negro Interactions	
						Teacher Quality	Class Size
1-4	B	0.08	-1.62	0.13	-0.09	-0.04	0.13
	σ_B	0.01	4.56	0.02	0.08	0.02	0.11
4-6	B	0.63	-6.15	0.08	-0.03	-0.02	0.19
	σ_B	0.05	4.58	0.01	0.08	0.02	0.12
6-8	B	0.62	-8.50	0.06	0.07	0.01	0.18
	σ_B	0.05	5.29	0.01	0.08	0.02	0.14
9-11	B	0.72	-4.71	0.05	0.16	0.10	-0.16
	σ_B	0.06	8.79	0.02	0.32	0.05	0.42

Note—Increments in variance and overall R^2's significant at the .05, .01, and .001 levels are indicated respectively by 1, 2, and 3 asterisks.

between Negro enrollment and class size did not account for a significant portion of the variance in student achievement at any of the four grade levels.

As can be seen by comparing the top parts of Tables 13-3 and 13-4, the inclusion of both earlier-grade achievement and percent Negro enrollment in the equations provides a more stringent test of the impact of teacher quality on achievement outcomes than that provided in the earlier regression analysis, which used only earlier-grade achievement as a control variable. It is worth noting that although teacher quality accounts for a smaller increment in the variance of the criterion when that attributable to Negro enrollment is partialled out, the relationship is still highly significant; that is, teacher quality is still associated with higher levels of student achievement.

In order to test for curvilinear relationships with student achievement, the squares of Negro enrollment, teacher quality, and class size were computed and used in two final analyses. In the first case, squared Negro enrollment accounted for .99 percent of eleventh grade achievement variance (p less than .01) beyond that accounted for by ninth grade achievement, Negro enrollment, the school inputs, and the percent Negro enrollment by school input interactions, and for a negligible (nonsignificant) fraction of variance at the other grade levels. The fitted regression shows that there is a more rapid decline in student achievement associated with percent Negro enrollment in predominantly black schools than in predominantly white schools.

In a step-wise regression analysis using earlier-grade achievement, teacher quality, class size, squared teacher quality, and squared class size as predictors, curvilinear school input-student outcome relations were found for the fourth, sixth, and eighth grades. As shown in Table 13-5, the quadratic class size term accounted for 1.31 percent and .27 percent additional variance in achievement at fourth and sixth grades, respectively, while the squared teacher quality term accounted for .63 percent variance in eighth grade achievement beyond that predicted by the linear terms. The regression shows that the optimum class size at fourth grade is thirty-four students, and at sixth grade a positive relationship between class size and student achievement can be seen, with the relationship growing stronger as class size increases. A positive relationship between teacher quality and achievement is also apparent, but in this case the gains resulting

Table 13-5. Curvilinear regression variance and equations

Variance Accounted For

Grade	Achievement	Teacher Quality	Class Size	Quadratic Terms Teacher Quality	Quadratic Terms Class Size	R^2
1-4	57.61***	9.24***	0.03	0.05	1.31***	.68***
4-6	69.23***	3.56***	0.36*	0.02	0.27*	.74***
6-8	74.64***	3.30***	0.75**	0.63**	0.29	.80***
9-11	91.93***	2.13***	0.06	0.07	0.00	.94***

Regression Weights and Standard Errors

Grade		Achievement	Teacher Quality	Class Size	Quadratic Terms Teacher Quality	Quadratic Terms Class Size
1-4	B	0.09	0.06	2.26	0.00	−0.03
	σ_B	0.01	0.09	0.55	0.00	0.01
4-6	B	0.70	0.05	−1.03	0.00	0.02
	σ_B	0.05	0.07	0.59	0.00	0.01
6-8	B	0.64	0.30	−1.07	−0.00	0.02
	σ_B	0.04	0.07	0.66	0.00	0.01
9-11	B	0.69	0.15	−0.01	−0.00	0.00
	σ_B	0.06	0.13	2.30	0.00	0.05

Note—Increments in variance and overall R^2's significant at the .05, .01, and .001 levels are indicated respectively by 1, 2, and 3 asterisks.

from increasing teacher quality in a school with low-quality teachers are substantially greater than those resulting from a similar increase in a school with well-trained or highly experienced teachers.

We cannot be certain of the causal directions suggested by the relations of teacher quality to student achievement described above. Nevertheless, the descriptive relations confirm prior school-effects research and support the educational policy of rewarding more experienced, well educated teachers with higher salaries. The results also suggest how school systems might use routinely-collected data to analyze and monitor the aspects of school effects and equality throughout the system. Finally, as shown in the next three chapters, such findings can serve as useful starting points for more detailed evaluation research and school troubleshooting.

References

Armor, D. J. "School and Family Effects on Black and White Achievement: A Reexamination of the USOE Data." In *On Equality of Educational Opportunity,* edited by Frederick Mosteller and Daniel P. Moynihan. New York: Vintage Books, 1972.

Averch, H. A. et al. *How Effective is Schooling? A Critical Review and Synthesis of Research Findings.* Santa Monica, Calif.: The Rand Corporation, 1972.

Averch, H. A. and Kiesling, H. J. *The Relationship of School and Environment to Student Performance: Some Simultaneous Models for the Project TALENT High Schools.* Unpublished paper. Santa Monica, Calif.: The Rand Corporation, 1970.

Bowles, S. S. *Educational Production Functions,* Final Report, U. S. Office of Education, ED 037 590, Cambridge, Mass.: Harvard University, 1969.

Bowles, S. S. and Levin, H. M. "The Determinants of Scholastic Achievement: An Appraisal of Some Recent Findings." *Journal of Human Resources* 3 (1968): 3-24.

Burkhead, J., Fox, T. G. and Holland, J. W. *Input and Output in Large City High Schools.* Syracuse, New York: Syracuse University Press, 1967.

Central Advisory Council for Education. *Children and their Primary Schools.* London: Her Majesty's Stationery Office, 1967.

Cohn, E. "Economies of Scale in Iowa High School Operations." *Journal of Human Resources* 3 (1968): 422-34.

Coleman, J. S. et al. "Pupil Achievement and Motivation." In *Equality of Educational Opportunity*. Washington, D.C.: U. S. Office of Education, 1966, 218-333.

Goodman, S. M. *The Assessment of School Quality*. Albany: State Education Department of New York, 1959.

Guthrie, James W. "A Survey of School Effectiveness Studies." In *Do Teachers Make a Difference?* Washington, D.C.: U. S. Office of Education, 1970, 25-54.

Guthrie, J. W. et al. *Schools and Inequality*. Cambridge, Mass.: M.I.T. Press, 1971.

Hanushek, E. *The Value of Teachers in Teaching*. Santa Monica, Calif.: The Rand Corporation, 1970.

————. *The Education of Negroes and Whites*. Ph.D. dissertation, Massachusetts Institute of Technology, 1968.

Katzman, M. T. *The Political Economy of Urban Schools*. Cambridge, Mass.: Harvard University Press, 1971.

Kiesling, H. J. *The Relation of School Inputs to Public School Performance in New York State*. Santa Monica, Calif.: The Rand Corporation, 1969.

Kiesling, H. J. *A Study of Cost and Quality of New York School Districts*. Washington, D.C.: U. S. Office of Education, 1970.

Levin, H. M. "A New Model of School Effectiveness." *Do Teachers Make A Difference?* Washington, D.C.: U. S. Office of Education, 1970, 55-75.

Michaelson, S. "The Association of Teacher Resourcefulness with Children's Characteristics." In *Do Teachers Make a Difference?* Washington, D.C.: U. S. Office of Education, 1970, 120-68.

Mollenkopf, W. G. and Melville, S. D. *A Study of Secondary School Characteristics as Related to Test Scores*. Princeton, N.J.: Educational Testing Service, 1956.

Raymond, R. "Determinants of the Quality of Primary and Secondary Public Education in West Virginia." *Journal of Human Resources* 3 (1968): 450-69.

Ribich, T. I. *Education and Poverty*. Washington, D.C.: Brookings Institution, 1968.

Smith, M. S. "Equality of Educational Opportunity: The Basic Findings Reconsidered." In *On Equality of Educational Opportunity*, edited by F. Mosteller and D. P. Moynihan. New York: Vintage Books, 1972.

Thomas, J. A. *Efficiency in Education: A Study of the Relationship Between Selected Inputs and Mean Test Scores in a Sample of Senior High Schools*. Ph.D. dissertation, Stanford University, 1962.

14. ELEMENTARY SCHOOL CASES
Harriet Talmage
Robert M. Rippey

The data examined in this chapter are upsetting to the biases of the authors, showing that appearances are deceiving and that attempts to predict performance of students on the basis of available resources to the schools are difficult. Further, the data demonstrate the uniqueness of each school and the difficulty of generalizing the attributes of an "excellent program" across different schools and communities.

The methodology employed was simple enough. The study began as a search for schools which produced great achievement and schools which produced minimal achievement between grades 4 and 6. Our criteria for achievement had the advantage of being readily accessible. Each year the Chicago Board of Education has published test results for all its schools. From this publication the following variables were selected. The dependent variable was sixth grade achievement. The independent variables were school means on: 1. fourth grade reading scores; 2. teachers' education (B.A., M.A., or M.A. plus 18); 3. number of years in teaching; and 4. class size.

A regression analysis was performed for all the schools in Chicago. Regression analysis predicted the sixth-grade achievement scores on the basis of the other four variables. After the development of this regression equation, residuals were computed. Schools with high residual scores had high sixth-grade achievement, after adjustment for the four independent variables. By adjusting the sixth grade scores for fourth grade scores, high residuals schools are identified as those with substantial gains in these scores over the period of time from fourth grade to sixth grade. By adjusting for such variables as teachers' education, number of years of teaching, and size of class, the sixth-grade reading scores were equalized for the most costly variables. Thus, with the combination of the four variables, high residuals schools would be schools with high achievement gains at low costs. Many other variables could have been included in such an analysis; but the questionable nature of the criterion, which we will discuss presently, made it seem that the addition of further variables would amount to a case of misplaced precision.

Once the ten top residuals schools and ten bottom residuals schools were ascertained, two schools were selected at random from the high residuals group and two from the low residuals group. The authors each took two of these schools, again at random, not knowing which of the schools were high scoring and which of the schools were low scoring. Arrangements were made with the principals to visit the schools and to ask some questions about school operations. After visiting the schools, the authors tried to interpret the findings in some meaningful way. Much to the authors' surprise, however, the schools which they thought were obviously the high scoring schools were not. Review of the research literature, familiarity with current rhetoric, and intuition about good educational practices proved of little predictive value.

In order that the reader may participate in the same kind of surprise, we initial the schools A, B, C, and D. Two of these schools apparently showed high gains in achievement at low costs and two of them showed low achievement at perhaps greater costs. We describe the schools in some detail, and then ask you to identify the two high achieving and the two low achieving schools. After you have made your predictions, the computer-derived answers will be revealed, and you will have the joy of either outguessing the authors or of sharing the same kind of surprise we experienced.

At this point, certain bothersome issues that always affect research in a large city should be discussed. It is proper to ask, why use the fourth and the sixth grade scores in the same school at a single point in time? Why not look at the fourth grade scores in one year and then look at the sixth grade scores two years later, thereby examining the same group of pupils. The answer is that the rate of turnover, as well as the rate of redistricting, bussing, and various other machinations that take place on a yearly basis make it highly unlikely that the sixth-grade scores in a particular school would be scores of the same pupils whose fourth grade scores had been reported two years earlier. An occasional school may have a rate of turnover of 300 percent in a single school year. Through interviews with each principal and assistant principal, we did attempt to rule out schools whose student populations might be changing drastically. The principal reported a stable population from year to year in each of the schools we studied. If this had not been the case, we would have selected other schools for observation.

Methodologically, one might hold out for an ideal situation where students remained in school for over a long period of time. A longitudinal study might not be subject to some of the sources of invalidity that plague the present study. On the other hand, to study achievement effectiveness only in schools of that sort would be to bias the sample unduly. Therefore, we proceeded boldly and bluntly with the task. And although we had our surprises, we also agreed that this method for selecting schools for observation did have one interesting characteristic: we were astonished at the uniqueness of the schools we visited. So, although the residual analysis might not have detected both the most effective and the most ineffective schools in the city, it did detect some of the most interesting.

The Four Schools

Why are some schools high achieving and some low achieving after controlling for class size, teaching experience, and extent of teachers' education? Our investigation focused on the school resources and how these resources were utilized. School resources are used to denote a wide range of variables that have an impact on the school: attitudes and characteristics of the staff, parents, and pupils; the physical and instructional facilities; and the immediate neighborhood. Data were collected by interviewing principals and assistant principals; observing classrooms; inspecting other school facilities (library, lunchroom, washrooms, teachers' lounge); noting the conditions and use of the playground area, hallways, and the movement of pupils in these areas; talking informally with teachers, school clerks, pupils and teacher aides; and recording the general condition and facilities in the immediate neighborhood served by the schools. Observation categories, interview forms, and data sheets are shown in Figures 14-1, 2, 3, and 4.

School A

School A is housed in a slick-looking building, bordered on all sides by parks and located close to a famous library. Happy, well-scrubbed children were playing in the playground. The surrounding community is obviously affluent. The children are a cosmopolitan and ethnically mixed group including somewhat higher than the usual percentage of Oriental children. Signs of vandalism are entirely absent: no spray paint, no broken windows, nothing carved on the desk, and nothing out of place.

The principal, a bright charming woman Ph.D. who had been at the school for fourteen years, was obviously on top of things. A teacher waiting list for assignment attested to the desirability of teaching at School A. The principal felt that the relationship of the teachers with the children was very important, in addition to a strong academic background. She reported that she always observes prospective teachers in action before asking that they be assigned to her school. She also felt that it was important for her teachers to assume responsibility and to have good relationships with parents. She described her present faculty as very good, competent, bright, and hard working. She described the school program as basic skills oriented and highly structured. There was one class in English as a second language for the approximately 15 percent of the students of Latin origin. The school also participated in the Follow Through program from kindergarten through third grade. Decisions were made jointly by the staff, the parents, and the principal. The principal was quite concerned about the objective test scores as well as the reactions of parents and teachers in judging the effectiveness of present and proposed programs.

Students in the school ran the complete range of ability. The principal felt there was no attendance problem, that the children were eager to come to school, and that most of them were adequately prepared for high school.

In describing the community, the principal reported that the parents were extremely cooperative and positively oriented toward the school. They raised thousands of dollars which they turned over to the school. Parent attendance at assemblies was good. Six parents volunteered as classroom aides. Many activities such as art fairs and special programs were sponsored by the PTA and local school council. The PTA and the local council, the Follow Through council, the Kiwanis Club, and the Lions participated actively in school affairs.

The classes were generally standard size, approaching a maximum of thirty-two. The classroom climate was businesslike and persuasive. The educational program seemed excellent, with an emphasis on academic and cultural matters. The students were practicing a Gilbert and Sullivan operetta during the visit. Resources were rich. The principal pointed out that there were no losses of equipment once purchased and therefore supplies and equipment lasted a long time. Presentation of subject matter seemed intellectually challenging and there was strong affective support for the students. A wide variety of schemes for grouping students was apparent, and several parent-tutors were present.

Maintenance of the building was excellent, there was no vandalism, and supervision seemed low-keyed and friendly. The teachers' lounge was quite a surprise. The principal said that it had been panelled by the parents, who had also provided many paintings and rugs. Lunchroom maintenance was fine, people movement orderly in the cafeteria, and supervision was good. Student attitudes were positive and the noise level was low. Additional facilities included a library, a learning center, and plentiful audiovisual materials housed in large rooms. The school had a part-time nurse and only modest counseling facilities. Special education was available. Parent volunteers assisted with the office work. The school had a program to teach four years olds to read. This program was financed by the Board of Education and was a prerequisite which enabled the school to obtain funds from the federally financed Follow Through program.

School B

School B was an older building located on the edge of a gaudy tourist-trap section of the city. Again the students, this time predominantly black, seemed happy and well behaved. The principal was again very businesslike. One's first impression of the school was that the student population might be fairly transient. As it turned out, the student population was quite stable and many of the students had mothers and fathers who had graduated from the school. In addition, about 90 percent of the teachers had been in the school for several years. Most of the teachers were certified, and the principal said that in general they were superior teachers with an average of seven to nine years of experience. The principal was concerned about the attitude of the teachers toward the children, the grades they had received in college, and their cooperativeness, enthusiasm and willingness to take independent responsibilities.

School B had several unique characteristics. The school had been identified as one needing special resources, so that class size was smaller than usual. A nearby building was designated for special education students. Because of the proximity of this center, and its close relationship to the school, the principal assured me that his students were specially screened so that there were no mentally handicapped students in the school. The school was not congested; it had been built for about fifteen hundred students and there were only six hundred in attendance. The school had a library, many audiovisual materials, a school nurse, counselling facilities, an auditorium, a gymnasium, an unofficial program for teaching English as a second language, a special education center, sufficient office help, and lots of teacher aides as well as other instructional support.

The principal stated that most of the new programs generated at the district or area level were based on student needs. He was very anxious to achieve the Board directives emphasizing the teaching of reading. The principal stated that he personally evaluated new programs to see whether or not they were succeeding, and that he was particularly concerned with standardized test scores, as well as with teacher feedback. One of the innovations he looked forward to was the participation of science classes in the new downtown educational facilities center. The school was currently upgrading its own science program.

The principal reported that the students were much like the students elsewhere and that they seemed to be well behaved and that the discipline problems were of no consequence. Vandalism again seemed absent. The principal reported that his school had a 98 percent average daily attendance. He was not satisfied with the adequacy of student preparation for high school, and was concerned about making many improvements in the years ahead. The school's previous principal had recently been advanced to an extremely responsible administrative post in the city.

The principal reported that the parents were very supportive of the school, that they had a high respect for schooling, and that many of the parents had attended the school themselves. A number of community and parent organizations worked with the school. These included the local school council, which he felt was very effective, the local mental health center, the Urban League, the Illinois Community Center, and the Fourth Presbyterian Church. The relationship between the school and the community seemed very close, and this was underscored by the interview with the assistant principal. The assistant principal had been with the school for about fifteen years and had been a coach before becoming assistant principal. When he first came to the school he started policies with the children which seemed still to be paying off. He had gone to the school on weekends to mount basketball hoops on the side of the building and to paint games on the asphalt of the playground. He permitted the children to use the school grounds and spent quite a bit of time playing there with them on his own time. He was dedicated and had a deep affection for the school, the community, and the children. He also let the students take the athletic equipment home with them after school. He said he hardly ever lost any bats and balls because children would take them home and then bring them back the next day so they could be used in school. He was especially proud of the fact that one of the teachers in the school was a former pupil of his.

Visits to classrooms showed that the class size was small. Leadership was strong, the classroom and school building climate were excellent, and educational facilities were quite accessible. The school was connected to the closed circuit system of the Board of Education, and some television instruction was going on while I visited. There were many rooms which were vacant or used for small groups or for tutoring. Building maintenance was good, pupil movement was quiet and orderly. There were practically no signs of vandalism and although supervision was close, it was gentle. The teachers' lunchroom was roomy but somewhat austere and was empty at the time of the visit. Lunchroom supervision was evident without being obtrusive. Some Neighborhood Youth Corps students were working in the lunchroom.

School C

Built over a hundred years ago, School C served the children in what was once the Gold Coast residential area. The rosters of the eighth grade graduating classes over the next forty years included the names of many of the most prominent families in the city. Today School C is distinguished by its small enrollment, high poverty level, and housing pattern. There are no single-family dwellings in the school district. The children live in store fronts or in rundown furnished hotel rooms. The family structure is matriarchal, with the majority of mothers receiving Aid to Dependent Children. All the children participate in the school's free breakfast and hot lunch program. The school is surrounded by light industry, jobbing establishments, and service-type businesses. It borders the central downtown area on the north and the infamous X Street on the south, where the street gangs take over as arbiters of social propriety. There are no clubs, recreational facilities, or social welfare organizations in the school district. There is nothing to give the residents a sense of community. By 6:00 P.M. the business establishments close for the day, leaving the area deserted. Although the children are free of gang harassment as long as they stay clear of the X Street area, their immediate locale offers them no escape from a drab existence, except for television and school. The school is so isolated from the mainstream of the commercial life of the street and from the larger educational establishment that the principal wanted to know how the authors heard about his school.

The big old school building now houses approximately a hundred pupils. There are many empty rooms, including a vacant third floor. Despite loose plaster and some peeling paint, the building is well maintained. The halls and washrooms are clean, there are no signs of vandalism, and the custodian takes a personal interest in the care of the school. The lunchroom is a cheerful place with accommodating lunchroom workers.

The staff reflects the racial composition of the student body. Approximately 85 percent of the pupils are black; the remainder is an ethnic mix of whites, Orientals, and Spanish-surnamed. While the principal, a newly-appointed white male, epitomizes middle class values, the assistant principal sets the tone for the school. He is the father figure, the arbiter of quarrels, the black male model, the confidant and mentor of the pupils, teachers, and parents. He has great empathy for the desperate empty lives of the pupils and their families. Life in his classroom is an experience in social living which he tries to extend to the school as a whole. Over the past eleven years he has tried to build a school climate reminiscent of the one-room school house. The rest of the staff are older women who entered teaching within the past six or seven years. None has a master's degree and most acquired their bachelors degrees during the past few years. As a group they subscribe to the Protestant work ethic of promptness, hard work, and perserverance. There is a little staff turnover.

The school has an Educational Advisory Council, which was described as ineffective. Only three or four parents attend meetings, whether scheduled during the day or evening hours. The mothers leave educational decisions up to the school personnel. They are cooperative but lethargic. This attitude was ascribed to the financial and cultural poverty of their lives. Lack of mobility keeps the school population stable. Only one eighth-grader had not been with the class since the third grade.

The educational program is traditional. It is organized by subjects, and instruction is highly structured. In the middle and upper grades the original forty-eight desks are still fixed to the floor, although each class has between twelve and seventeen pupils. The teachers have not felt it necessary to alter the seating arrangement. There are adequate supplies, books, and audiovisual equipment. The middle-grade teacher was pleased with the room library, which contained a wide variety of reading materials. Ethnicity is recognized and incorporated in the curriculum. A black ethnic picture alphabet decorates the primary room. Black and Asian heroes are on display, and the textbooks tend to employ a pluralistic approach. The school is eligible for outside funded programs. The principal has selected reading programs: DISTAR, the Sullivan Reading Program, and the Special Assistance in Reading program. The atmosphere in the classroom is warm and accepting, although the pupils are held to the work ethic of their teachers. The teachers relate to the children in a highly personal way. Since this is a closed campus school, each teacher and her pupils have lunch together, so that schooling is a total living program.

Life changes dramatically following graduation, which heralds the end of a protected childhood. The graduates enter a very large, overcrowded high school which takes them across X Street into gang-conflict territory. As outsiders, they are likely gang targets. Last year, for the first time in twenty years, School C had one of its pupils graduate from the high school. Usually by Thanksgiving of the first year in high school, over half of the graduates will have dropped from school.

School D

An initial glimpse of School D and surroundings gives the impression of a comfortable 1920 vintage school on a tree-lined street nestled among well-maintained single dwellings and two-flats with green lawns fronting the homes. On closer inspection, one finds traces of glass and paper on the grass between the sidewalk and the street, iron mesh around the windows of the neighborhood grocery store, and makeshift repairs on the BB gun holes in many of the windows of the school building. School D is the focus of racial tension in this old established white neighborhood. Overt militant efforts are being exerted politically and through teen-age gang activities to retain the present ethnic dominance. To date only a few black families have moved into the school district. These black children have been absorbed into the life of the school without confrontation. Over the past decade, as the neighborhood grew older, the school age population decreased, leaving School D with a number of vacant classrooms. To relieve the overcrowding in an all black school to the south of School D, the equivalent of six eighth-grade classrooms was shifted to School D. The black pupils coming into the neighborhood found themselves entering "enemy territory." They were subjected to physical abuse going to and from school at the hands of the neighborhood toughs. It wasn't long before the black children were accompanied by their own gangs. To prevent violence, the school hours for the upper grades were changed to avoid encounters with white teenagers. Before and after school the principal and assistant principal roam the streets to head off trouble and a police guard is stationed outside the school during the lunch hour.

Over a thousand students attend School D, and the school population has begun to grow by three classrooms a year as the older families move out and less affluent white families with more children move into the school district. The school building appears to be well maintained, although signs of pupil disrespect for school authority are evident in some writing on the walls, removal by school authorities of toilet paper and paper hand towels from the washrooms, and some malicious knife carvings in the plaster. Tardiness is a definite problem and absenteeism, especially in the middle and upper grades, is flagrant. While the middle-grade classrooms appear calm, observation of the upper-grade classes reinforces the sense of suppressed tensions, which spills over into the halls, lunchroom, and play ground area.

The principal, who has been at School D for many years, reported his concern for all the children, and said he is determined to create a climate in which integrated education will be possible. He is supported by an equally concerned assistant principal who views his role as that of a social worker first and educator second. Their day is spent dealing personally with a myriad of social, emotional, and educational problems. Both the principal and assistant principal know each child by name and do not hesitate to visit the families or to call in a parent when it is deemed necessary. They view their task as holding the school together and relieving the teachers of disruptive behavior problems so that the teachers are free to work with their classes undisturbed. In most of the classrooms instruction goes on in an orderly manner. There are several very weak upper-grade teachers, and chaos reigns in those classrooms. The principal reported that teaching in the middle grade is competent. He is satisfied with the academic progress, but is concerned that the tensions in the upper grades could affect the performance of the middle-grade pupils. The classes have been getting larger each year; this year they exceeded the school system's desired maximum, averaging around forty pupils in a class.

Although 90 percent of the upper-grade pupils are black, only 15 percent are black, Spanish-surnamed, or Jordanian from kindergarten through sixth grade. One-third of the teachers are black. The staff is stable with little turnover from year to year. Only two or three teachers will leave this year, and those are leaving at the request of the principal. The majority of the teachers are certified; thirty percent hold master's degrees.

The instructional program is traditional. There is no evidence of individualization of instruction or innovative approaches. The classes are teacher-directed. Recitation rather than discussion is the main type of verbal exchange. There are adequate supplies, sufficient updated textbooks, and abundant audiovisual equipment.

An Educational Advisory Council, dominated by active P.T.A. members from the mainline families in the school district, is concerned with maintaining the former quality of School D and with containing the problems that seem to stem from the integrated situation. Seventy-five percent of the eighth graders formerly graduated from the high school, and the Council intends to continue this record. The principal has the support of both the black and white parents.

Discipline is the central concern. The fact that there have been no break-ins has been attributed to the high regard of the residents for their school and to the custodian, who resides in the community. The principal's office is bombarded daily by students involved in fist fights, stealing from each other, and rough talk. Most disruptive behavior takes place outside of the school. Proportionally as many white students as black students are involved in these activities. The principal works closely with at least 5 percent of the pupils who currently have police reports pending. These involve stealing, auto theft, knifing, drug usage, and vandalism. The parents are cooperative in these instances but are ineffective in dealing with their children. Learning is still going on in the school through the Gargantuan efforts of the principal and assistant principal and with the support of the concerned Educational Advisory Council.

Similarities and Contrasts

The four schools vary widely on the independent variables. Class size ranges from small groups to overcrowded. The number of years in teaching ranges as much within three of the schools as between schools. Three schools have faculty with master's degrees, while one had no graduate degree holders except for the principal. Fourth grade reading achievement ranges from the 15th percentile to the 56th percentile.

Figure 14-5 points up the similarities and differences in the school/community resources available among the four schools. Contrary to the usual stereotypes about urban schools, there is no dearth of instructional materials and the school administration is dedicated and responsive to the major problems within the school and problems impinging on the school from the community. In the main, the instructional staff is competent, although School D has several teachers who are considered inadequate. Some of the administrators utilize the community resources better than others. The schools differ most on the extent of interest and participation in school affairs shown by parents and other community members. This interest ranges from active participation to apathy. The attitudes of the pupils in three of the four schools are positive and responsive to the instructional program. All four schools are considered desirable assignments by the faculties, despite problems in several of the schools.

Given the four mini case studies and the summary table, which two schools would you select as the high achieving schools and which two would you select as the low achieving schools? Before you read on, record your selections and give your reasons. Then compare your selections and reasons with those of the authors. Remember, we have controlled for the effects of the four independent variables: fourth grade achievement, teacher education, teaching experience, and class size. Both authors, after reviewing their notes, comparing impressions, and calling upon research studies in school achievement, independently selected the two high and two low achieving schools. Based on the evidence, both authors concurred in their selection. The evidence pointed to Schools A and B as the high achieving schools and Schools C and D as the low achieving schools. Such resources as parent/community interest and positive participation, the experienced, well trained staff, and the utilization of the available community resources accounted for our choosing Schools A and B as high achieving schools. On the other hand, the major factor explaining our choice of School C as a low achieving school was the extent of the poverty. Who could rise above such odds? The overwhelming press of racial antagonism was the most telling evidence for our selecting School D as the other low achieving school.

Much to our consternation, the computer printout selected Schools A and C as the high achieving schools and Schools B and D as the low achieving schools. We batted only .500. Table 14-1 shows the fourth- and sixth-grade achievements in percentile.

Quickly the authors reordered their previous biases. In our zeal to reinforce previous research findings we may have overlooked some telling data. School A has all the resources going for it in the right combinations. Although School A has a larger student body, an able established administrator and a dedicated staff have created a sense of community in the school. It functions as an effective social system. School B is a high cost school. The class size is small, the teachers are experienced, and a number hold graduate degrees.

Table 14-1. Fourth- and sixth-grade achievement

Schools	4th Grade Achievement	6th Grade Achievement	Gain or Loss
A	56th percentile	82nd percentile	+26
B	18th percentile	7th percentile	−11
C	15th percentile	28th percentile	+13
D	49th percentile	19th percentile	−30

Adjusting statistically for these advantages would affect these gain scores in relation to gain scores of low cost schools. School C presents a unique situation. With a total school population of a hundred pupils and an assistant principal who sees these elementary years as the single most important opportunity for the pupils to learn in a warm accepting environment, School C is home for most of its pupils. The shocking high school record does not give an accurate picture of the academic achievement of School C. Possibly, the calm, ordered, nonthreatening learning environment of School C does not prepare the pupils for the hostility, overcrowding, and overt gang activities in the high school. Learning in School D is apparently being affected by the racial antagonism, despite the efforts of a committed administration and concerned parent group.

Conclusion

What made the difference? It was not a racial issue; and, as could be expected from previous research, class size was certainly no predictor. Community participation and good parent/school relationships did not hold up as relevant dimensions. Educational aspiration, stability of staff, a business-like atmosphere, or the number of outside funded programs were not pertinent in explaining school achievement. Nor did any of the instructional variables described in Rosenshine and Furst (1971) seem to make the difference. Nothing that we started out looking for seemed to tell the tale.

Was there anything we felt we should have looked at? Yes, possibly a learning environment that permitted the learner to be himself without the threat of failure, or a school climate that provided the degree of socializing experiences the children could tolerate.

Emerging from the analysis of school resources related to school achievement is the uniqueness of each school and a call for new ways of looking at achievement relative to school resources.

Figure 14-1. School/community observation

Classrooms (4-6)
1. Class size
2. Leadership in the classroom
3. Classroom climate
4. Educational program generally
5. Availability of resources
6. Presentation intellectually challenging
7. Type of affective support
8. General organization
9. Grouping

Halls and Washrooms
1. Maintenance
2. Pupil movement
3. Signs of vandalism
4. Type of supervision

Teachers' Lounge
1. Description
2. Use

Lunchrooms
1. Maintenance
2. Pupil movement
3. Supervision

Students
1. General attitude
2. Dress
3. Noise level

Other Facilities
1. Library—Learning Center
2. Audiovisuals, other hardware and software
3. Other physical facilities: gym, playground, conference rooms
4. Nurse

Figure 14-1 (continued)

5. Counseling services
6. Special resources: TESL
Special Education
Office help
Teacher aides
Adult programs

Surrounding Community
1. Type of homes
2. Community resources (recreational, welfare, medical)
3. Other characteristics

Figure 14-2. Conversation with principal

General Impressions
1. What are the characteristics you look for when hiring a new teacher?
2. In evaluating your experienced teachers each year, what qualities do you emphasize? (new ideas, discipline, pupil achievement)
3. How would you describe your present faculty? (strong, resourceful, weak, unimaginative, agreeable, discontented) (What do you feel are the major faculty strengths and weaknesses?)
4. How can a principal help a weak teacher?

School Program
5. What are the outstanding characteristics of the educational program of the elementary school? (any federally funded programs)
6. Who decides on the new programs needed? How do you get the teachers interested in new programs?
7. What are the new programs responding to: community pressures? pupil needs? district or area office?
8. How do you judge whether a new program is succeeding?

Students
9. Describe the pupils in your school (behaviorally, scholastically)

Figure 14-2 (continued)

10. Is there an attendance problem? tardiness problem? problem with hostile attitudes toward school? How is this handled?
11. Are the students adequately prepared for high school?

Parents

12. Describe the parents and the community. (interest in school problems? supportive?)
13. Do the parents cooperate with you?
14. What community or parent organization is working in the school? Is it effective? In what ways?

Administration

15. Of all the things you have to do as principal, what gives you the most satisfaction?
16. What improvements are you working on this year?
17. To what degree do you feel directly responsible for curriculum improvement?

Figure 14-3. Conversation with assistant principal

1. How would you describe the present faculty? (strong, resourceful, imaginative, contented)

2. How would you describe the pupils?

3. What do you see as the major discipline problems? (Whose responsibility is the classroom discipline?)

4. Do the parents cooperate with you? How do you handle conflict?

5. What do you see as the greatest strengths of the student body?

6. Is vandalism a problem? How is this handled?

7. What type of innovations have been introduced? team teaching? open education? peer teaching? individualization?

8. Who makes the educational decisions?

9. Who makes the personnel decisions?

10. How would a new teacher best get along with the present administration?

Figure 14-4. Description of faculty and school population

Directions: In the items below, give an approximation
that best describes your school.

1. What percent of your faculty have their degrees from a teachers'
   college in contrast to a degree from a university?
   _____ % Teachers College

2. What percent of your faculty hold degrees *beyond* the B.A.?
   _____ %

3. What percent of your faculty is certificated?
   _____ %

4. What proportion of your faculty has taken a university course in
   the past two years? (check one)
   _____ most faculty
   _____ about half
   _____ few

5. What was the faculty turnover in 1970 and 1971?
   _____ % 1970
   _____ % 1971

6. What is the average number of substitutes you need each day?
   _____

7. Do the teachers make home visits as part of their professional
   responsibilities
   _____ yes/no

8. Does your school have any federally or state funded program?
   _____ yes/no
   How many? _____

9. Have the teachers initiated any new projects this year?
   _____ many
   _____ some
   _____ none

Figure 14-4 (continued)

10. Do the teachers *volunteer* for special tasks (such as committee assignments, PTA arrangements, early morning tutoring) that is not covered by release time?

_____ many

_____ some

_____ very few

11. Are the teachers of the same socioeconomic level as the pupil population?

_____ many

_____ some

_____ none

12. Are the teachers of the same ethnic background as the pupils?

_____ many

_____ some

_____ few

_____ none

13. What percent of the teachers live in the community?

_____ %

14. What percent of the faculty is presently experimenting with individualized instruction?

_____ %

15. How many students have been suspended during the school year?

_____

16. Has the school building been vandalized this year?

_____ yes/no

17. What percent of your students graduate from high school?

_____ %

Figure 14-5. Similarities and contrasts of school/community resources

	A	B	C	D
External Resources	Affluent community with available recreational and social resources. Attractive school plant	Older building. Resources of surrounding neighborhood made available to the school.	Commercial area whose resources have not been brought into the school. Residents represent highest incidence of poverty level in the city.	Blue-collar community intent on holding the racial line.
School Administration	Ph.D. who is concerned with the educational program and academic performance of the pupils.	Principal newly appointed. Concerned about quality of education with reading as the main emphasis. Strong assistant principal with close ties to families.	Principal newly appointed. Values conflict with school constituency. Assistant principal is the prime mover with warm relations with pupils.	Committed first to integrated education and welfare of pupils and families, second to educational concerns.
Teaching Staff	Competent faculty, make decisions jointly with principal. Stable faculty.	Experienced, stable faculty. Variety of ancillary staff.	Concerned, hard working, traditional.	Integrated faculty. Ability varies widely—from excellent to incompetent.
Pupils	Congenial. Ethnic mix, enthusiastic about attending school. Orderly, with focus on learning. No vandalism. Stable student body.	Stable student body with little or no behavior problems. Friendly.	Some fighting among themselves but not disruptive. Intent on pleasing the teachers. Want to come to school. Stable student body.	Fairly stable student body. Delinquent behavior outside of school reaching into the middle grades.
Program and Materials	Follow Through and TESL Program. Rich in resources.	Many special resources, closed circuit TV, tutoring.	Special programs available; adequate supplies and equipment.	No special programs. Supplies and equipment are available.

Parents and Community Members	Extremely cooperative, active in school affairs. Raise money for school extras.	Community group active in school affairs.	Apathetic.	White parents concerned about maintaining standards of the school. Black parents concerned for the safety of their children.
Controlled Independent Variables				
Class Size	32 Maximum	Small (well below maximum class size of 23)	12-17 pupils	40+
Teaching Experience	Experienced	7-9 years	3-4 years	Two-thirds are certified with experience, many 20 and 30 years. Staff recently integrated.
Teacher Education	Several with M.A. Many with B.A.+	Several with M.A. Many with B.A.+	Little or no graduate work.	30 percent with M.A.s
4th grade Reading Achievement	56th percentile	18th percentile	15th percentile	49th percentile
6th grade Achievement	?	?	?	?

References

Chicago Public Schools Department of Operational Analysis. *Selected Schools Characteristics*. Chicago: Chicago Board of Education, 1970.

Rosenshine, B. and Furst, N. "Research on Teacher Performance Criteria." In *Research in Teacher Education,* edited by B. O. Smith. Englewood Cliffs, N.J.: Prentice Hall, 1971.

15. SECONDARY SCHOOL CASES
Daniel Powell
Maurice J. Eash

Following the lead suggested in the input-output study of Chicago schools (see chapter 9), four high schools were selected for further investigation of those qualitative data that escape statistical analysis. Two of the schools were selected because they evidenced higher than expected reading achievement in grade 11 relative to grade 9 achievement, teacher quality, and class size. Similarly, two high schools were selected from the bottom ten schools whose grade 11 achievement was far lower than expected. While one can study the limited statistical data available and conjecture about the causal relationships, it was thought that experienced observers might recognize the subtle interactions that make up the educational climate, the total of which fosters a press for or against achievement. Therefore the two authors, using a general conceptual framework, spent a full day gathering data at each of the four high schools. In these visits they interviewed the principal at length, toured the building, examined available resources, and observed a sample of classes.

Each of the four schools is first presented as a case study, providing the reader with descriptive data on its administration, faculty, racial and socioeconomic make-up of the student body, and school setting. Following the description, an analysis is made of the aspects of school press that may explain achievement differences shown in the more generalized input-output study.

In every case the data gathering followed the same procedure. The observers met with the principal and conducted an extensive interview. This interview was followed by a tour of the school to examine the facilities and obtain a feel for the atmosphere in the halls, shops, cafeterias, and classrooms, and to observe the physical condition of the restrooms. Then six English and social studies classes were visited to obtain a flavor of the teaching in the required program of the school.

The authors brought to these observations more than forty years of experience with urban high schools as teachers, supervisors, and consultants. The urban high school is frequently the target of writers whose criticisms often create more confusion than light, thus placing secondary school people on the defensive. But we found most of the high school staffs and administrators to be concerned with providing education to a population with disparate interests and motivations. They welcomed us and willingly discussed their schools. Without this assistance, the four case studies could not have been collected. Presented below are basic data on the schools, with which the reader will want to familiarize himself before reading the case studies:

Table 15-1. Achievement trends, racial composition and social economic status of student population of four high schools which had differential trends in achievement

School	Achievement in Percentiles		Racial Composition %			Social Class*
	9th	11th	White	Black	Latin	
Shadyside	35	48	59	31	0	LMC
Rider	50	42	88	12	0	MC and LMC
Ironton	20	25	60	20	20	LC and LMC
Franklin	15	9	0	100	0	LC

*MC = Middle Class, LMC = Lower Middle Class, LC = Lower Working Class

Shadyside High School

Shadyside High is in a residential section of modest well-kept homes, evidence of a life of diligent savings from steady but low paying jobs. Architecturally the high school is one of a number of plants based on a standard design of the 1920s, an era which saw little distinction between industrial structures that produced material goods and those that turned out human goods on an educational assembly line. Factorylike in appearance, it stands on clean well-kept school grounds with a parking lot for teachers located discreetly in the rear. One is struck by the unruffled character of the school; there is no movement in or out, no coming or going, no students on the grounds or sitting on the steps. This placid exterior, so unusual in a large city high school, is maintained by the local police, who patrol the outside grounds. The officers stand on call to enter the school at the principal's request. During our visit a police car was always parked on one of the streets adjacent to the school, and a patrol car from the local precinct checked hourly with the pair of on-site patrolmen manning the stationary car.

Shadyside had been a center of racial tensions. Its original student population of working class whites of southern and central European derivation had been "invaded," as they say it, by blacks. Through a process of street boundary changes by the school board and changing housing patterns, Shadyside was now 31 percent black. Previous experience with changing neighborhoods and threats to property values and physical safety made the home owners of Shadyside uneasy and resistant to the changing nature of the school population and the school board's efforts to integrate the school through boundary changes. The local racial tensions are often aggravated by black power advocates who have exploited the situation for their own political gain. Despite these tensions, Shadyside High appeared somber, restrained, and the quietest of the four high schools visited. Earlier battles over attendance lines and the racial makeup of the student body were not apparent except for the continuous presence of the police.

Black parents want their children to attend Shadyside High despite the fact that they are not welcome by whites. Neighboring schools with predominantly black student populations have sufficient space to accommodate all black students at Shadyside High, but black parents and pupils alike feel them to be unsafe and academically undesirable.

From the standpoint of financial support, Shadyside High is disadvantaged. It receives very little aid from the many federal programs for inner-city schools. With a traditional curriculum oriented to general education and college preparation, it resembles with few exceptions an academic high school of thirty or forty years ago. Even with racial tensions, the school does not qualify for a community coordinator who would work with the various factions that exist in the community.

Why do parents want their children to attend Shadyside High? We were not able to investigate this question directly, and doubt that the answer would be forthcoming even if pursued directly through questioning of parents. Our interviews and classroom observations, however, lead us to project some hypotheses in answer to this question.

First, the principal and his approach to administration figure strongly in parental preference. Mr. Long (not his real name) has been at the school several years and has roots in the community. As an administrator, he runs a well organized, tight school, as evidenced in the quiet halls monitored by adults, in the orderly lunch room, and in teacher behavior in classes. If there is any dominant theme at Shadyside, it is the situation of strict social control that protects students and faculty from the outbreaks of violence which are a common ingredient of many urban high schools. Mr. Long works at keeping street gang influence minimal and under control in the school. He is especially supportive of teachers, but insists that they document their complaints. In times of tension, he goes into the streets outside the school to mingle with students, ". . . to show them I am unafraid." In his office he showed the interviewers an extensive collection of knives, bludgeons, and other concealable paraphernalia which he had collected from students during the year. While most discipline is handled within the school, he does not hesitate to have the officer on duty at the school arrest and remove students if necessary. An administrator who cares about his school as an educational institution, he believes that school climate must reflect order and purpose. There is follow-up on attendance, which runs approximately 85 percent, and he is concerned that black students have poorer attendance than whites.

Traditional in architecture and administration, Shadyside's classes are textbook oriented, teacher dominated, and inclined to be dreary. Despite these negative aspects, classes do have focus. Teachers ask questions, students study routine lessons, and are usually prepared to respond. Though one might question the direction and worth of much of the learning, demands were being made upon students and teachers in every classroom visited had prepared plans. Students are docile and not overly enthusiastic, but they have a sense of seriousness. At only one point did student response border on the spontaneous, when a teacher remarked that whites are dominant in the power structure of this country. Low, quiet hooting was heard from a majority of the class. Ignoring this response, the teacher moved on to another part of the lesson.

Shadyside High is a school with an external and internal appearance of social control. There is discipline and order. Teachers and pupils are task oriented; 66 percent of its entering freshmen graduate, and 35 percent of its students attend some institution of higher education. Analysis shows that Shadyside High obtains more gains in achievement from grade 9 to grade 11 than any other school in the city. Though it is probable that parents are unaware of the specifics, since knowledge of regression equations is not widely distributed, conventional wisdom tells them that this is a good school for their children to attend. Shadyside High is changing with the influx of black students, but at the time of this study tradition still reigned. Since this study, more recent boundary changes have brought increased racial tension, a white boycott, and further trouble to Shadyside High. The principal has been caught between the school board, which might charitably be considered to have been evasive in its attitude, and militants in both racial groups. Whether Shadyside High can continue to be a school where achievement increases among a student body that is racially different than in the past, using a traditional approach in learning and discipline, is a question for the future. Evidently black parents see the standards maintained in the past as desirable; whether these standards can be sustained if whites flee is a major question.

Rider High School

Rider High is much like Shadyside in physical appearance and in its traditions. However, it differs greatly in its population makeup, and has experienced a major population change in the last few years. At one time Rider had a large Jewish population and the reputation of being an outstanding academic school. In recent years, Rider has changed with the influx of recent immigrants of Spanish and European origin and the corresponding flight to the suburbs of the older population. With the advent of permissive transfers, Rider has attracted a 12 percent black population, all of whom live out of the district. The principal, Mr. Parody (not his real name), told the interviewers that he constantly received calls from black parents who wish to have their children transferred to Rider for academic as well as safety reasons.

Although similar in appearance, Rider is quite different in tone and deportment from Shadyside. Walking up to the building, the interviewers met several students smoking on the steps who continued without so much as a self-conscious glance. However, no large collections of students loitered outside the school. We found that it was not unusual for students to step outside for a smoke or to sneak a cigarette in the washroom. During the lunch hour students dragged the adjoining streets in their cars—the local gendarmes were conspicuously absent during this extralegal activity. Lighting in Rider halls is scandalously poor, creating a gloomy atmosphere. Students were far more boisterous and noisy than at Shadyside, with a number of students running and bouncing off other students in the halls between classes. Washrooms were in worse condition than in any of the other schools visited. Lack of toilet paper and vandalism of plumbing and windows was evident.

Hall monitors and police were not as obviously present in Rider as they were in Shadyside. It was, in short, a far more relaxed and less "tight ship." Where Shadyside regularly used suspensions to deal with infractions, Mr. Parody preferred to exclude students informally and to bring their parents in for a talk before allowing them back in class. Rider had been spared the massive student strikes of 1969-70, and there was little vocal student action. Even athletic contests were relatively quiet. The principal trouble reported was an occasional flare-up between the blacks who attend Rider and blacks from rival schools. A relatively small and inactive parent body makes up a rather lethargic PTA, one of whose few activities is to raise money for the school through the sale of paperbacks in a hall stand manned by parents. Interests of parents are expressed individually through students' concerns. Few overriding group issues seem to motivate parents to take action.

Mr. Parody runs a rather relaxed administration. He believes that his teachers vary considerably in ability but he is confident that they are generally capable and have student interests at heart. The staff is very stable; many of them have been at Rider High from twenty to thirty years. Teacher absence is lower than average. Some black teachers have been assigned to the school under the recent federal order to desegregate faculties. They seem to get along well with Rider students and white faculty. During our day at the school, the principal was free, unharrassed, and receptive to all questions as he visited with the interviewers. As did all of the principals, he seemed pleased that fellow educators had singled him out for attention and were interested in hearing about his school. His assistant principals seemed to assume many of the day-to-day tasks of running the school. Student attendance runs about 85 percent, following a national trend of decline. Parents, in Mr. Parody's opinion, also seem less able to influence their children's conduct. Few resources from federal programs are available for the school.

The investigators visited a number of classrooms. On the surface, one might have judged that the curriculum at Rider was more exciting than that at Shadyside. At least there was not as much reliance on the textbook, and a wider variety of learning experiences was evident. But superficial appearances were misleading as one began to study the patterns of interaction and to chart student interest. One honors class in English was reading *The Godfather,* which had just appeared as a movie. As students sat in informal groups, draped in various postures over the chairs, the teacher attempted to lead a discussion of the book. Students were very relaxed, one sat in his undershirt, others kept up a running conversation with a friend or two. To even the most inexperienced observer it soon became obvious that there was little focus to the activity and that the teacher had a limited purpose in mind—if indeed he had any at all. There were many false starts as a result of top-of-the-head questions to which students did not respond. The teacher obviously had done little thinking about the class other than reading the book, and failed to use the few leads given him to keep the discussion moving. He did 90 percent of the talking, ending up the lifeless session by alternating with students in reading passages from the book. A similar class in humanities, a combination of social studies and English, seemed equally mismanaged.

Classroom activities seemed more directionless and less focused than at Shadyside. This observation was further validated in a class which was using outside "resource people" to stir up interest in English. Two members of a local group calling themselves "Rising Up Angry" were talking with an eleventh grade English class about Viet Nam. The teacher simply mentioned their organizational affiliation and said they were going to make a presentation on Viet Nam. It was not possible to ascertain how their interests were tied in with the on-going curriculum. The students, for the most part, sat silent during the presentation which included ideas such as: the CIA is running the country, drug usage is encouraged by the establishment to keep the underprivileged passive, the military-industrial complex is the government, and revolution is the only answer for social improvement. The two young activists were difficult to follow, as they interlarded unfinished points with a continually repetitious "You know," and used a barnyard expression for certain animal excrement as an explanation for complex events. One was further introduced to several new uses of the word *heavy*—heavy man (meaning intelligent), heavy drug (meaning effect on a person), heavy thing (meaning uncertain). Students sat impassively through this melange of muddled social philosophy and assorted facts communicated through a limited vocabulary and tenuous command of English. One girl timidly raised her hand and asked an innocuous question, but it was given short shrift by the ideologues, as they poured out more conclusions. The teacher sat aside and said nothing throughout the period.

Another class had a new teacher who failed to get any semblance of a lesson going during the period. Following a lecture on "being on time," the group of slow readers was asked to read aloud from a book which was far above them. One was treated to the painful exhibition of blocks, mispronunciations, and inarticulateness that is the lot of poor readers as they struggle with materials too difficult for them. Mercifully, the period extended only forty minutes for this class. The other new teacher observed was in an internship program and was being supervised by a college faculty member from a local university. Although she had prepared a lesson on vocabulary, it fell short of engaging more than a single student at a time in the learning activity. This investigator failed to share the supervisor's enthusiasm for the lesson as a well-planned learning activity, an opinion seconded by the students in their reactions during the hour.

From these observations, one might conclude that the teaching at Rider, while attempting to move away from traditional textbook approaches, was being planned with another student body in mind, one that was much more academically minded, caught up in social issues, and more familiar with popular literature than the one that the teachers were facing. Could this have been the student body of Rider High of the past? We think so. Moreover, Rider has one of the poorest records for boosting achievement from grade 9 to grade 11. In fact, achievement has fallen in these grades. This may be due to population changes but it also may be due to another factor. We would propose as an alternative hypothesis that students at Rider High attend classes where there is a lack of focus and purpose, a brand of teaching that is open-ended and better suited to students from homes where the rich cultural resources make them more independent learners, such as the former student body of Rider High. Thus the traditions of Rider High do not serve the new consumers and a drop in achievement is inevitable.

Ironton High School

In contrast with the two previous schools, Ironton High is a school lacking traditions. Starting out as a branch high school, it took on a life of its own only six years ago. The building is a nondescript mixture of new and old, and still includes an elementary school within the main building. There is very little interaction between the elementary and high school, although they share the same principal. Elementary teachers were observed escorting children to the bathroom, and seemed to hover protectively over their charges. Parent interest is high in the elementary school. What is most unusual about Ironton High is its racial makeup and geographic setting. Its student population is 60 percent black, 20 percent Latin, and 20 percent white. The elementary school student population, drawn exclusively from the immediate area, is mainly of white working class families with central European origins. Ironton High sits in the middle of this white neighborhood, and its black and Latin students traverse this area on their way to and from school. While the residents apparently accept these students if they maintain their decorum, the tight ethnic neighborhood remains suspicious of outsiders and readily reports them to the police. Thus Ironton High reflects a fairly placid environment, devoid of troublesome hangers-on who collect near urban high schools and traffic in drugs, floating crap games, and extortion.

On security and internal tone, Ironton stands between Rider and Shadyside. Students seem to come and go, but hall monitors at the main traffic points check on students and restrict movements at lunch hours. Students' hours are staggered because of split shifts. But movement was orderly, and when asked directions the students were genuinely friendly and helpful to strangers. Washrooms were in good condition with a noticeable absence of vandalism. The library was well run with an active program; the librarian worked with the students and went out of her way to help them. Student conduct in the library and assembly halls was exemplary. In only one area did we see deviation from responsible citizenship and that was in the cafeteria, where students refused to bus their trays, causing an unsightly accumulation. Ironton students are poor, and the majority (60 percent) receive free lunches. The principal feels that this may account for their failure to accept responsibility for returning trays.

The faculty is integrated with a number of new teachers who left the South as a result of loss of positions because of forced integration of schools. Overall, the staff is younger than that of the two previous schools, contains more blacks (about a third), and is less well trained (fewer M.A.s). In investigators' visit it was noted that the faculty sit segregated in the crowded faculty lunchroom, although no tension is apparent among racial groups.

Ironton High students are low achievers; as shown in Table 15-1, they fall into the twentieth percentile. However, there is a small core of able students to whom the principal feels a deep responsibility for providing an academic, college-prep curriculum. Except for a small number of honors classes, which are under pressure from the central office because of their low pupil-teacher load, the curriculum is a standard, essential curriculum common to large city high schools. Ironton High needs to keep these classes, the principal believes, in order to retain its clientele. A core of able students aids in raising the tone of the school and provides more stimulating classes. Like Franklin High, which will be discussed later, Ironton High feels the effects of the vocational and trade schools, which attract the more motivated students and leave Ironton with the least motivated and able students.

In administrative style, Ironton High is well organized and well run. One assistant principal is assigned to work with new teachers, and pursues an active program for upgrading instruction. The principal is quite concerned about teachers who lack technical skills to teach low ability students, and supports the assistant principal's instructional improvement efforts. He also feels that teachers are not well enough trained to cope with discipline problems in low ability classes, and need a better understanding of the psychology of these students. Teachers are expected to have prepared units and to be responsible for providing substitute teachers with plans that will maintain the continuity of instruction during absence. Reading, as one would expect, is a major problem, and much of the instructional effort in the classroom is devoted to coping with the "reading problem." Our visits to social studies and English classrooms turned up some interesting observations that reveal the administrative style reflected in the classroom.

Classroom visits were unannounced in all cases, and were assumed to be representative of usual instruction. Two English classes were visited. In one, a lesson on phonics was being presented to low or nonreaders. The students reacted with enthusiasm and readily engaged in the written assignment which examined their understanding of the lesson at the end of the class session. The teacher was young but skilled, had excellent rapport with this group, and presented a lesson that was of interest, involving a reading skill in which these students were deficient. Classroom activity was directed, involved sufficient practice, used a variety of methods, and evaluated student performance.

In the second English class, the teacher had prepared a lesson that involved the members of the class in a game. The subject matter was the autobiography of Claude Brown, *Manchild in a Promised Land,* which the teacher said they were reading "as a novel." Although the teacher was well prepared, nothing went right. The students were eager to participate, but obviously did not know the rules of the game. Arguments on the scoring occurred which the teacher was unable to resolve. A boy who sat near the investigator volunteered the information that most of the class had not read the book, which may have explained the diversionary arguments. Two students who approached the observer inquired whether he was evaluating the teacher. They both stated they had not read the book. As one commented, "That's an awful big book." Given the reading level of the school, the task was probably too difficult for 80 percent of the student body, and this was a low-average class. Students were not hostile; the lesson was simply inappropriate and degenerated into chaos as student confusion grew. Here was a teacher over her head in instructional problems; and although she tried valiantly she did not succeed in making appropriate responses to the demands of the situation.

In the social studies classes instruction reflected planning, although some misteaching of data was observed in one class. Classroom atmosphere was good, most students were interested in what they were doing, and the teachers were trying to adapt instruction to the students' ability level. Instruction did proceed on a total class basis and, except for one English class, individualization was very limited. The most important factor was that teachers were prepared, and that in teaching low ability students they did not engage in ridicule or employ sarcasm. The observers felt that students like Ironton High and that, despite the cultural inadequacy of many of the students, the steady attention to directed instruction does pay off in a general increase of achievement. Attendance is about 80 percent, high for an inner-city high school. This may be a further indicator of student satisfaction with the school. In general, student-teacher relationships were good—there was a noticeable lack of screaming by teachers.

Franklin High School

Franklin High is a sparkling new palace of glass that sits in sharp contrast to its surrounding deteriorating neighborhood of abandoned, partially burned houses and apartment buildings. Given the external and internal vandalism from which most inner-city schools suffer, one wonders what protects the huge investment in glass—and it *is* glass, not plastic. With an all-black student body, about 35 percent of whom come from outside its attendance zone, Franklin, like Ironton, suffers from the raids of vocational and technical schools, so that the overall academic level of the student population is lowered.

Mr. Noyes, the principal, is a young, articulate, recently promoted black. In his conversation he stresses the citizenship program that is conducted with the students and community. Within the school, there are numerous signs such as "Enter Franklin with pride, dignity, and respect," "Pigs like dirt, Don't be a pig." Upon entering the building, which is in a closed campus, one encounters a large foyer used as a lounge by students. During our visit it was a bustling gathering place for students, but it remained immaculately clean. In the area was a uniformed policeman. When the school was opened, the principal had an agreement with the local police watch commander to have a patrol come through the foyer every hour. In this part of the city, where gangs have a strong impact, it is necessary to provide security for youth from recruiting intimidation. In addition to the patrolman on duty, the school has a full-time city youth officer who is a college graduate. With an office in the school, the youth officer works full time on community problems that relate to the students' activity. The overriding police presence helps Franklin to remain a quiet, restrained school. From all evidence, community support is strong for this approach to social control and respect for property. Restrooms, classrooms, lunchrooms, and hallways were in excellent shape and showed few signs of vandalism.

Two-thirds of the faculty is black, and a broader spectrum of colleges is represented than in the other high schools. Many of the faculty have advanced training and have been involved in programs for inner-city teachers sponsored by the National Science Foundation and foundations at two neighboring universities. Given the composition of the student body, the school's location, and the stress placed by universities on inner-city teaching, Franklin has been a popular placement for student teachers, who receive supervision from an assistant principal as well as from their university. Student teachers are expected to prepare fully for their classes, just as do regular teachers, and must check their plans with the assistant principal. An effort has been made to recruit high quality instructors, and the principal works personally on staff evaluation.

Mr. Noyes' administrative style is exemplified by the delegation of responsibility to his four assistant principals for separate areas of school functions. We interviewed two of them who were involved with curriculum, student teachers, and substitutes. The administrative style is one of checks and controls. Teachers are required to validate absences for illness with a physician's note. Substitute teachers must go over the day's teaching plans, present student papers, and return plans to the principal at the end of the day in order to be certified for payment. Obtaining substitutes is a problem; while two to three a day report, eight or nine are needed. No reason was given as to why more substitutes are not available. We received an impression of the principal trying to run a tight ship in the face of disorganization in the larger social system. This was particularly clear in the discussion of student attendance and the visits to the classrooms.

Upon direct questioning the principal admitted that classroom attendance had been a great problem when the new school first opened. Between classes, the halls teemed with students who never attended. To cope with this problem, an hourly check of attendance was instituted and a study was made of which classes were better attended. It was found that the best attendance was reported in mathematics, where the teachers made the most demands on the students and where the best classroom preparation was evident. English was the least popular subject, followed closely by social studies. The principal said that daily attendance averaged a little under 90 percent, but we have reason to believe that this figure was produced for purposes of obtaining state aid and retaining teaching staff. Truancy has always been a major problem in this area and every effort has been made to boost attendance. Last year the principal took a group of parents to court in an attempt to enforce better attendance. In the main, his effort was futile, as parents had lost control of their children, several of whom were no longer living at home. "Do whatever you want with them; I can't do anything," was a typical statement made to the judge.

The investigators were given free rein by the principal to visit any classes they wished, with the permission of the teacher. This was the only one of the four schools in which we were refused admission to a classroom. The refusal was based on the grounds that the students did not like visitors looking at them. On the whole, teachers were not as open to our visits, and several were plainly uncomfortable in our presence. After we had observed several classrooms, the reason became clear: there were very few students in attendance, classes ranged from seven to thirteen in size, and a teacher was very uncertain as to whether any students would show up. It was the observers' opinion that attendance on the day of our visit was closer to thirty percent than ninety percent. Our approximation was further substantiated by examination of a teacher's attendance book which showed that, out of a registration of fifty-three, about ten students were in regular attendance. "These students just quit coming to school, especially as the weather warms up," said one teacher. Outside on the playground we noticed a number of hangers-on, including several young girls with babies.

The classes we visited were slow-moving, haphazard, and lacked focus. One teacher said she never gave homework because it was to no avail—students never completed it. Reading levels are very low, and most work is remedial, but little individualization of instruction was in evidence. Students were responsive, but the purpose of the instruction seemed limited—question, answer, and teacher extension of student response. Student achievement gets progressively worse as students move from 9th to 11th grade at Franklin High (Table 15-1). Is this because their life styles become more involved with outside interests so that they attend less as they grow older? We can only hypothesize that this may be one reason. It is fairly obvious that students at Franklin High mirror the problems of the larger social system surrounding the school—lack of employment and low employability. Already they evidence the attitudes and life styles that pervade the surrounding culture and that inhibit economic mobility through engagement in the world of work. Can a school surmount the cultural accouterments that are reactive against the task of the school, especially when these seem to be widespread in a homogeneous population? In Ironton High there seemed to be a spark of potential struck by a core of students. We failed to find that spark at Franklin and believe that therein lies the difference between the two schools in the direction of gains in achievement.

Summary and Conclusions

The four high schools observed were divided by the original study into two categories. In one category, two schools showed increased achievement from grade 9 to grade 11; in the other, two schools showed a decline in achievement from grade 9 to grade 11. What were the similarities and differences between the two categories? Although dissimilar in population mix, the two achieving high schools, Shadyside and Ironton, did have a focus and emphasis on instruction that was lacking in Rider, a low achieving high school. At Rider, the teacher reigned supreme in the classroom in determining the direction of learning activities. To an outside observer, the teaching lacked focus, and the students seemed to have little understanding of what was expected of them. By contrast, the two higher achieving schools had more active programs of instructional leadership. At Shadyside there was concern for maintaining an instructional climate free of disruption where learning could take place. At Ironton, where the majority of students were low achievers, remedial work was emphasized in an atmosphere where students were treated with respect and responded positively to teachers' efforts.

Franklin High seems to pose a different problem than Rider. At Franklin, considerable effort was exerted to improve instruction, and sufficient resources existed to support change. Outside technical assistance for in-service training was available, student teachers supplemented instructional manpower, and special programs were developed for slow learners. All these well-meaning efforts to improve the education of students at Franklin High, however, may be to no avail. Students simply are not present regularly enough to profit from instruction. Unless the problem of attendance is solved, expenditures for instructional resources will not pay dividends.

The data in Table 15-1 indicate that schools mirror the cultural resources that students bring with them. Also, educational literature points out that these cultural resources limit a school's ability to raise achievement as measured by conventional achievement tests. The reader should be encouraged by the fact that two schools in this study were able to shift achievement upward. In their efforts to boost achievement, these schools also bring about good student attitudes toward property and encourage a feeling of personal responsibility toward their environment. The writers believe that this may be of more long-range significance than gains in achievement. The data reported here does not seem to support the romantic critics' notions of the need for individual freedom and determination for students, and we believe that the trend of evidence emphasizing socially desirable attitudes and achievement is strong enough to render questionable programs that fail to stress the schools' mission to increase academic competence. While schools that do so may not revolutionize the social order and create instant equality, they can at least produce citizens who have skills to review intelligently the choices a society presents, to realize the consequences of these choices, and to elect alternatives.

To effect a press that gives promise of achieving these ends, much depends on educational leadership at the building unit level.

The principal cannot induce this press alone; he needs community support and the wherewithal to create a managed social setting if chaos from the surrounding environment is to be avoided. Simple slogans of community control or accountability will not produce the desired press. What is needed is an orchestration of resources and sentiments at the building level by a creative, talented leader whose authority needs to be sustained and whose educational wisdom is valued by those who are not in contact with the day-to-day operation of the school. As long as these policies are ignored by large city school boards, talented leadership will be scarce and the quality of inner-city education limited.

16. WORK ATTITUDES
Robert J. Coughlan
Robert A. Cooke

Educational administrators are continually faced with evidence that their staffs hold various attitudes toward them personally, their schools and communities, their jobs and students, their policies and procedures. Many administrators are intrigued by such questions as: How should they react to these opinions and sentiments? Should they respond as if these perceptions and feelings didn't exist? Or should they try to understand them and put this knowledge to some constructive use? If so, then what attitudes should they attempt to measure? How should they interpret any findings they obtain through systematic surveys? Who should see the results and for what purposes?

Perhaps the most important question is, does information on teacher work attitudes tell administrators and others concerned with schools anything about school performance? For example, are student rates of learning higher in schools where teachers are relatively satisfied with key aspects of their work environment? Or does it make any difference educationally if teachers are happy or dissatisfied with their jobs? Is there any truth in the argument that making people happy in their work only undermines the drive for accountability, promotes excessive group conformity, and militates against the development of outstanding individuals?

Educational administrators and school evaluators seem to be faced with the problem of coming to terms with their *own* attitudes toward the work attitudes of school personnel. The purpose of this chapter is to help them in arriving at an informed judgment. The position we take is that work attitudes are important indicators of school performance. They can serve as one basis for gauging personal and organizational efficiency and effectiveness. They can also provide a framework for diagnosing organization problems and needs, and for designing programs of organizational improvement and staff development in schools. Thus we feel they merit the serious attention and consideration of administrators, evaluators, and commentators on American public education.

In the following sections, we will deal with most of the questions posed at the beginning of this chapter. We will refer to theory and previous research findings on employee attitudes, job satisfaction, and morale. We also will draw on data from an exploratory study conducted with a small sample of "high" and "low" performance schools to show how certain faculty attitudes may be related to productivity. Finally, we will present some guidelines indicating how attitudinal data might be used in the formative and summative evaluation of schools and in programs of school improvement.

Research on Work Attitudes

Prior to the 1930s, most administrators failed to pay much attention to the work attitudes, job satisfaction, or morale of their employees. As sound advocates of "scientific management," their thoughts about employees centered primarily on improving selection procedures so that the most competent persons would be hired. Administrative thinking about employees as people focused mostly on notions of how to increase their stability, industry, and perseverance to meet the necessities of work, supervision, and organization procedures.

This disinterest in more humanistic job attitudes was sharply reversed in the 1930s and 1940s as a result of the classic Hawthorne studies. The work of Mayo (1933) and Roethlisthberger and Dickson (1941) seemed to indicate that productivity was not only a function of the employee's aptitudes, training, and skills. Indeed, in over 20,000 interviews, workers revealed that they did, in fact, bring their thoughts and feelings to the job, reacted differently to various aspects of it, and felt that their sentiments were related to how hard and how well they were willing to work. Both administrators and personnel researchers leaped from these findings to the conclusion that "if we can now only improve employee attitudes, we can thereby improve their job performance."

This discovery led to numerous attempts from the 1930s through the mid-1950s to measure employee attitudes. The question was: Where should managers concentrate their efforts on improving job conditions to upgrade employee performance? Most of the studies focused on determining whether any relationship existed between a single organizational variable, such as pay, and a single or global measure of satisfaction. While this research was in progress, administrators were installing training programs to encourage supervisors to develop better human relations with employees in order to improve work attitudes.

The issue of greatest significance in all these studies was the relationship between job satisfaction and performance. After two decades of intensive study, two scholarly reviews of the literature appeared which seemed to demonstrate that the association between satisfaction and productivity might, in fact, be much weaker than earlier investigators had assumed. These reviews, conducted by Brayfield and Crockett (1955) and Herzberg et al. (1957), concluded that the straightforward "high satisfaction leads to high performance" hypothesis was fundamentally unsupported by the evidence.

These reviews and new theories proved to have a dampening effect on personnel researchers and administrators. By the late 1950s, there was a marked decrease in the reporting of morale studies in both scientific and managerial journals. Having found the simple "satisfaction increases performance" hypothesis unsupported, personnel researchers were quick to join administrators in abandoning much of their interest in this line of investigation.

What lessons can be learned from the rise and fall of interest in research on work attitudes, job satisfaction, and morale? First, we would like to underscore that many well-controlled investigations have found positive relationships between certain work attitudes and job performance, and that the trend of studies of related variables seems to be in this direction. For example, Vroom (1965) reviewed some twenty studies and found that in most instances higher satisfaction *was* related to better job performance. Consistency in the direction of findings indicates that there probably is a moderate positive relationship between satisfaction, performance, and other related variables such as absenteeism and turnover. Even more significantly, it would seem that work attitudes are not in and of themselves inconsequential but that their relationships to performance are more complex than had been previously recognized.

Porter and Lawler (1968) point out that most of the early research on job satisfaction tended to be either conceptually naive or greatly oversimplified in design. The more recent studies and formulations of both Porter and Lawler and Vroom posit a similar but more complex relationship between satisfaction and productivity. They hypothesize that satisfaction comes about when certain employee needs are fulfilled; job satisfaction is generated when the individual receives rewards from his work situation. Some of these rewards are intrinsic to the person and his feelings of accomplishment. In such cases, the individual himself is the source of reward. Other rewards, such as a promotion or increase in pay, are provided the individual by his work environment. However, the amount of reward may be unrelated to how well the person has performed. The issue then becomes: Does the organization actively and visibly provide rewards in proportion to the quality of the job performance? If it does, and if the individual realizes this, then high satisfaction should be more closely related to high performance. On the other hand, failure to provide an association between job satisfaction and productivity may simply mean that employees are not being rewarded differentially for superior performance.

Current thinking on job satisfaction therefore regards performance as a function of the interaction of the organization's reward system and the individual's reward expectations for doing superior work. The more highly a reward is valued by the individual and the greater the expectation he has that superior work will lead to this reward, the greater will be the individual's effort to attain the reward through improved performance. The policy implication for educational administrators is that they should insure that their best teachers are the most satisfied. The goal would be not to maximize satisfaction, but to maximize the *relationship* between satisfaction and productivity.

School Performance

We recently conducted an exploratory research study to investigate the relationship between teacher work attitudes and student performance. Our previous studies had suggested that teachers in relatively high and low performance schools may have different patterns of attitudes with respect to certain factors in their work environment. The target population consisted of twenty elementary schools located in a large metropolitan district. Ten schools had been previously identified as high and ten as low performance organizations. School performance was determined on the basis of residual scores obtained from a standardized reading test (sixth grade) not predicted by four independent variables: fourth grade reading scores, teachers' education, number of years teaching experience, and class size. All public schools in this district were ranked on these criteria, and the schools in the top and bottom twentieth percentiles constituted our original sample. The cooperation of the principals and faculties in each school was solicited; participation in the research was on a strictly voluntary basis. Six of the twenty schools chose finally to cooperate in the study; two of these schools were in the high performance and four were in the low performance groups. The results to be reported below refer only to these six schools and should not be interpreted as definitive or generalizable.

Public schools, particularly those in urban areas, tend to restrict any form of outside evaluation. Work attitude surveys apparently are especially threatening to administrators because they often reveal what seem to be embarrassing school problems that would otherwise remain covert. Such surveys are commonly avoided altogether or the results are viewed as unconstructive criticism, rather than as a source of evaluation for decision making.

The defensiveness exhibited by urban educators to outside investigators probably results from the all-too-frequently improper behavior of the researchers. School personnel have been often "burned" by outside investigators; schools frequently gain nothing by participating in research and the guarantee of anonymity in findings is sometimes broken. Further, neither principals nor teachers feel that it is worth their time responding to questionnaires because the results rarely are used for school improvement. More will be said about these points in the next section which deals with the use of survey findings in school research and improvement.

The work attitudes scale used in the research was the School Survey, a 120-item, self-reporting questionnaire (Coughlan, 1966). The instrument is the product of an on-going research effort aimed at (1) identifying the major dimensions underlying the work attitudes of school personnel, and (2) constructing a reliable and valid inventory for measuring these attitudes.

Factor analysis of data from the third School Survey form (Coughlan, 1970) yielded thirteen factors, each containing from six to ten items and accounting for relatively moderate amounts of the total variance. Kuder-Richardson Formula 20 internal-consistency reliability coefficients for individual factor scores range from .44 to .80, with a median of .67. The revised School Survey form used for this exploratory study measures teachers' attitudes along fourteen dimensions plus their attitudes toward the survey. Because the organization serves as the unit of analysis for evaluation, school rather than individual scores are reported.

To begin our discussion, we expected to find that teachers in the two high performance schools would have more favorable attitudes toward certain work factors than their counterparts in the four low performance schools. Though these differences were not predicted to be great, we anticipated that they would be sufficiently sharp to produce an observable difference in overall attitude means between the two groups of schools.

Our exploratory data suggest that teachers in the high performance schools have more favorable attitudes toward their schools' educational effectiveness, student evaluation practices, community relations, performance and development, and voice in the schools' educational program. On the other hand, teachers in both groups of schools have generally similar attitudes toward administrative practices, professional work load, nonprofessional work load, materials and equipment, buildings and facilities, colleague relations, and financial incentives. The results of our research are presented in Table 16-1.

The "administrative practices" category measures the respondents' evaluation of the work and performance of the system's top echelon. It includes both human relations and administrative aspects of the work at the upper levels. Statements focus on the fairness of top-level decisions, the board's efforts to build an effective educational program, administrative interest in teacher welfare, receptivity to faculty suggestions, board respect for the professional character of the teachers' work, and relations between administrators. Items focus also on the board's emphasis on costs versus quality and administration versus education.

Table 16-1. Mean school survey factor scores: high performance vs. low performance schools

| | Schools | | | | |
| | High Performance | | Low Performance | | |
School Survey Factor	mean	s.d.	mean	s.d.	t
1. Administrative Practices	23.550	10.677	16.575	5.823	1.097
2. Professional Work Load	59.800	3.394	54.850	7.934	.808
3. Nonprofessional Work Load	56.500	14.425	49.550	10.047	.710
4. Materials and Equipment	41.750	18.738	46.350	18.785	−.283
5. Buildings and Facilities	41.350	10.253	38.125	22.500	.185
6. Educational Effectiveness	46.200	2.546	25.900	5.957	4.384***
7. Evaluation of Students	45.950	2.899	27.825	8.799	2.698**
8. Special Services	37.100	11.172	27.600	9.313	1.118
9. School-Community Relations	39.800	12.445	22.925	9.017	1.952*
10. Supervisory Relations	74.400	2.263	52.800	13.722	2.089*
11. Colleague Relations	58.300	1.697	42.575	20.466	1.023
12. Voice in Educational Program	47.150	14.637	31.175	9.124	1.713*
13. Performance and Development	57.650	6.152	36.225	6.973	3.650**
14. Financial Incentives	62.200	18.950	49.350	12.782	1.018
15. Reactions to Survey	51.650	25.951	42.650	27.166	.387
Overall	49.850	8.980	37.175	6.430	2.046*

*p < .10
**p < .05

***p < .01
df = 4

Teachers in the high performance schools provided more favorable scores in the administrative practices category than those in the low performance organizations. Differences, however, were not statistically significant. This finding does not necessarily indicate that teacher attitudes toward the top-level district administration are unrelated to school performance. High quality administration may serve to improve school performance directly through effective management of resources, and indirectly by improving teacher satisfaction. For example, unfavorable attitudes along this dimension may indicate that teachers perceive top-level personnel as having educationally irrelevant goals, little respect for the teaching profession, and minimal concern for the welfare of faculty. Extremely unfavorable (or favorable) attitudes of this type could reasonably affect overall satisfaction and influence motivation.

The observed consistency of teacher attitudes toward the top administration, regardless of school effectiveness level, is probably the result of high centralization in this large urban school system. All schools operate under the same board and superintendent; not unexpectedly, teachers in these schools display similar attitudes toward this administration. It is important to note that interschool attitudes in this category are not only consistent, but are consistently unfavorable. Faculty attitudes toward top level administrative practices in suburban and small urban schools tend to be approximately twice as favorable (Coughlan, Cooke, and Safer, 1972). It is possible that teachers' feelings about central office administrators become less favorable as size, complexity, and stratification of the district increase.

Teachers in the high and low performance schools also have similar attitudes toward their "professional" and "nonprofessional" work loads. Professional work load items focus on class size, fairness of work load, opportunity to deal with individual students, frequency and quality of meetings, and frequency of interruptions. This factor also deals with teacher satisfaction with their students and with their particular work assignments. The nonprofessional work load category assesses teacher opinions of the amount and type of noneducational duties performed. Items focus on amount of administrative paper work, number of nonprofessional duties, adequacy of clerical assistance, fairness of extracurricular duty assignments, and noneducational responsibilities.

Equality of Educational Opportunity Survey (EEOS) data (Coleman, 1966) failed to reveal a strong relationship between class size and student achievement. Jencks (1972) notes that, in comparing schools within the same district, there is often no difference in achievement between those with larger and those with smaller classes. Though class size was considered in our classification of schools as high or low performers, the School Survey focuses on teacher attitudes toward numerous aspects of professional and non-professional work load, including teacher-student ratio. Our findings suggest that, from the faculty's perspective, work load factors are not interfering with effectiveness in the low performance schools to a greater extent than in the high performance schools.

This attitude consistency partially results from standardization of work loads throughout the district. As such, it might be argued that a general reduction in work load could result in better school performance. We note, however, that no relationship between work load attitudes and school performance was observed in an earlier study conducted by Coughlan (Campbell, 1968). Additionally, teachers in small city and suburban areas have reported work load attitudes similar to those found in this study.

It could be argued also that attitudes toward work load indirectly affect school performance by influencing teacher satisfaction. While teachers with moderate work loads are possibly more satisfied than overworked teachers, it is doubtful that this satisfaction strongly affects their motivation to perform. The extent to which satisfaction with a work factor influences motivation might possibly be a function of the degree to which teachers perceive that factor as objectively affecting their performance. Work load factors may be unrelated to motivation if teachers feel that any presently feasible reductions in responsibility would not be sufficiently great to directly improve their work. Furthermore, if work load factors indeed affect motivation, the relationship may not necessarily be positive. Overworked teachers might be motivated to exert greater effort to ensure that their students do not fall behind and become deprived of an adequate education. While this is *not* an argument against work load reductions, we suggest that other factors would be more important in equalizing the performance among these six sample schools.

Two particular professional work load items may be of special interest to educators. One item states, "Generally speaking, I could do far better work with students different from those usually assigned to me." About three-fourths of the teachers in both types of schools disagreed with this statement. Self-fulfilling prophecies, with teacher evaluations of student ability as a key factor in influencing student achievement, do not seem to account for the performance differences among the schools in this sample. The other work load item states, "I would prefer a different work assignment . . . from the one I now have." Comparatively more teachers in the low performance schools disagreed with this statement (90 percent in low performance schools, 75 percent in high performance schools), indicating satisfaction with their work assignment. This finding suggests that unusually favorable attitudes toward work assignments are not positively related to performance in these schools.

The "materials and equipment" category provides information on the respondent's opinion about the selection, quality, and use of instructional materials, aids, and equipment in the school. Specific items focus on quality of instructional materials, adequacy of supplies, quality of supplementary materials, availability of materials and equipment, content of textbooks, adequacy of library, and the introduction of new materials and equipment. The "buildings and facilities" dimension focuses on the physical working conditions within and surrounding the school. Items focus on (1) the adequacy of personal facilities, free period facilities, space and equipment, classrooms and offices; (2) the condition of buildings, grounds, and work place; and (3) the layout of the school plant. Teachers in the high and low performance schools had markedly similar attitudes along these two factors.

There is some evidence that educational facilities are not positively associated with (and may even be negatively related to) school performance. On the basis of EEOS data, Jencks (1972) suggests that "students with greater access to books, and especially new books, do fairly consistently worse on the verbal test than similar students with less access. . . ." (p. 95). He notes that increased access to books may be a response to under-achievement rather than a cause of it. He also concludes that physical facilities are generally not associated with student achievement, except for a slight relationship between pupils per room and achievement. Our data indicate that whether or not such physical conditions are superior in the more successful schools, teacher attitudes toward these factors tend to be the same in both the high and low performance schools.

It is unlikely that favorable attitudes toward buildings, facilities, materials, and equipment produce the type of job satisfaction that improves work performance. Working conditions are rarely cited as important sources of satisfaction or dissatisfaction in studies of teacher satisfaction or morale. The indirect satisfaction effects of physical facilities on school performance are probably as weak as the direct effects. Further, it is conceivable that slightly unfavorable attitudes here have the same positive influence on motivation as do slightly favorable attitudes. Nonetheless, if teachers within a particular building report highly unfavorable attitudes toward these factors, inadequate physical facilities may be accounting for overall poor school performance.

The most significant differences between the high and low performance schools is found along the "educational effectiveness" dimension. This category deals with faculty perceptions of the school's effectiveness in meeting the educational needs of the community and the support given the school by community members. Specific items focus on: student preparation for advancement, educational orientation of the community, parental interest in education, student grade level assignments, learning climate of the school, amount of discipline required, comprehensiveness of the school, parent-faculty relations, relative effectiveness of the school, and the extent to which educational standards are being upheld. The category includes both factors affecting school performance and factors reflecting school achievement.

Teachers in the two types of schools revealed significantly different attitudes concerning community support and parent-teacher relations. The importance of community factors on student achievement has been stressed by Coleman (1966) and reaffirmed by Armor (1972). As such, an obtained high relationship between performance and teacher attitudes toward community support was expected.

Teachers in the high performance schools also revealed more favorable attitudes toward those items which more directly reflect school performance. This same trend was observed in an earlier study conducted by Coughlan on teacher work attitudes (Campbell, 1968). School faculties seem to have a fairly accurate perception of their collective achievement. Shared perceptions of quality performance could serve as a source of satisfaction or as an intrinsic reward. If community backing and support are viewed as a result of this effectiveness, then this support could also increase satisfaction. These satisfactions in turn may encourage continued quality performance (Lawler and Porter, 1967).

The "student evaluation" category assesses the teacher's attitudes toward the process of evaluating and reporting student progress. It also focuses on the school's policy of retention and promotion as well as provisions made for teacher-student consultation following progress reports. Some of the items are concerned with student civility, absences, and emphasis on grades rather than on learning. It is reasonable to assume that teachers are highly sensitive to student evaluation procedures. The evaluation of student progress reflects and potentially affects not only student achievement but also teacher performance. Teachers in the high performance schools reported significantly more favorable attitudes than their counterparts in the low performance schools along this dimension.

This difference in attitudes might indicate that the faculties in the successful schools have developed satisfactory means for evaluating and reporting student progress. In these schools, grades might accurately reflect achievement; students may possibly receive more effective counseling on how and where to improve their performance, and be promoted or retained at grade level for rational reasons. However, student evaluation procedures are somewhat standardized throughout the district. These same procedures could be working more effectively in some schools than in others. Faculty members in the four low performance schools apparently perceive the procedures as unsatisfactory for their particular students. Student evaluation may be doing little to improve pupil achievement and, in fact, could conceivably be interfering with learning.

Accurate and meaningful evaluation may also produce satisfaction and indirectly improve performance. When evaluation accurately reflects achievement, good grades act as an extrinsic reward for performance. This might be satisfying to teachers as well as to students, particularly if faculty members measure their own performance in terms of pupil success. Some theorists have suggested that satisfaction through extrinsic rewards increases motivation and improves future performance. In any case, attitudes toward this factor have been associated with school performance in this and an earlier study.

Evaluation procedures standardized at the district level are possibly too inflexible to handle the demands of the different types of students served in the various schools. The four low performance schools might want to modify and reinforce their procedures for student progress reporting.

The "special services" dimension focuses on the adequacy of special services in relation to the perceived needs of students. Specific items relate to curriculum assistance, specialist-teacher coordination, provisions for exceptional students, remedial help for students, willingness to experiment with curriculum, adequacy of library services, and adequacy of special programs and services. Teacher attitudes toward this factor are approximately the same in the low and high performance schools. Our previous research indicates that teachers tend to have somewhat unfavorable attitudes toward their schools' special services. It seems likely that improved services, and more favorable teacher attitudes toward these services, would increase school effectiveness. At this time, however, we have no data indicating that school performance is associated with different attitudes toward such auxillary services.

Teachers in the high and low performance schools exhibited slightly different attitudes toward "school-community relations." Factor items reflect the board's unity on key issues, the board's delegation of authority, superintendent-board relations, parental influence on education, community influence on education, appropriateness of board policies, and the school as a community asset. Though teachers in high performance schools had more favorable responses along all the items within this factor, certain trends are noticed when the items are analyzed individually.

Teachers in both types of schools had highly unfavorable attitudes toward the school board. Teachers reported that the board (1) was divided on too many issues; (2) should reconsider the amount of authority it has delegated to the top administration; and (3) did not have an effective working relationship with the superintendent. On the average, teachers in the low performance schools generated only 10 percent favorable responses on these items; high performance school faculties reported 20 percent favorable responses. More than twice as many high performance school teachers (35 percent) approved of school board policies than teachers in low performance schools (16 percent). The teachers in the sample schools apparently do not identify with organizational policies and/or do not feel that board policies and programs reflect the educational needs of their students.

In response to the item "The parents of students exert too great an influence on the professional work of the school," 60 percent of the teachers in low performance schools disagreed; 95 percent of the teachers disagreed in high performance schools. In response to "Certain community pressure groups exert too much influence on the professional work of this school," 48 percent disagreed in low performance schools and 80 percent disagreed in high performance schools. These differences may actually reflect real parental and community pressure resulting from poor performance in the four lower schools. It is also possible that teachers in the two high performance schools desire and expect more parental influence or that the parental influence in these situations is more constructive and meaningful.

It is interesting to observe that practically no teachers in either type of school felt that their school was "one big reason why people choose to live in this community." In contrast to other districts surveyed in previous studies, these urban teachers had relatively unfavorable attitudes toward a whole range of items dealing with school-community relations.

Faculties in the sample schools displayed their most favorable attitudes along the "supervisory relations" category. This group of teachers generated higher scores along this dimension than those obtained from most other urban and suburban schools we have surveyed in the past. The factor focuses on the teacher's immediate supervisor (the principal, in most cases) in reference to his: support for the staff, downward communication adequacy, initiative in giving help, fairness, support in parental relations, assistance in discipline matters, influence with superiors, attitude toward suggestions, and knowledge of the teacher work situation.

Attitudes toward the principal had a slight positive relationship with performance. Teachers in the high performance schools in particular had more favorable attitudes toward his initiative in giving help, fairness, and knowledge of their work situation. These supervisory characteristics tend to increase teacher performance both directly and indirectly. Gross and Herriott (1965) have observed that the Executive Professional Leadership (EPL) of principals is positively associated with pupil academic performance when family income is held constant. Their findings reveal "that both teachers' professional performance and morale *may* serve as links in a causal chain between the EPL of principals and the performance of pupils" (p.57). Similarly, the teachers in our high performance schools might be doing a more effective job because (1) their principals directly improve their ability to perform their assignments and (2) they are extremely satisfied with their principals and this satisfaction in turn may increase their motivation or will to work.

The "colleague relations" factor deals with both the friendliness of people and the nature of professional relations within the school. Items refer to faculty interest in overall school welfare, colleague performance, bossiness among colleagues, cooperation, sharing of ideas and materials, and communication climate. There were no significant differences in attitudes toward colleague relations between the high and low performance groups. Within the low group, one school apparently had excellent colleague relations and two others seemed to have highly unfavorable relations. Previous research suggests that good interpersonal relations may increase job satisfaction, but do not necessarily affect productivity and performance. Our findings for this small sample are consistent with this generalization.

The "voice in educational program" factor deals primarily with the respondent's perceived influence over curriculum development, school objectives, and choice of materials. Individual items focus on: voice in curriculum construction, board interest in staff suggestions, voice in textbook selection, influence over school goals, communication of top-level thinking, and overall district evaluation. In contrast to teachers in the four low performance schools, faculties in the high performance organizations had relatively favorable attitudes toward their voice in the educational program.

Principals in the high performance schools possibly afford their staffs an opportunity to participate in the development of the schools' educational programs. Faculty participation could be realized by means of building-level programs for curriculum modification and effective channels for vertical communication on curriculum matters. This participation would tend to increase teacher acceptance of and satisfaction with the school's program. On-going involvement also improves faculty understanding of the educational program and increases the teachers' ability to implement new procedures. Further, faculty participation may facilitate the adjustment of school programs to the needs of students. These consequences would tend to improve school performance.

It could also be argued that there is no actual difference in teachers' voice in educational program matters among these schools. Less favorable attitudes in the low performance schools could be a result of higher faculty expectations concerning control over curriculum development. Dissatisfaction with the present curriculum might account for these unfavorable attitudes; teachers possibly desire more influence over program development if the present curriculum is considered to be ineffective. As such, the unfavorable attitudes here may be the result of poor school performance.

The "performance and development" category assesses the effectiveness of procedures used to evaluate teacher performance and stimulate the professional growth of individuals in the school. Performance items concern frequency of feedback on performance, usefulness of evaluation procedures for improving work, understanding of appraisal procedures, fairness of appraisal, and efforts to evaluate the school program. Other items focus on development and related issues: encouragement of and opportunities for personal growth, inservice education, fairness of promotions, and recommendation of school as a good place to work. Teachers in the two high performance schools exhibited considerably more favorable attitudes toward this factor than did teachers in the four low performance schools.

This significant difference in performance and development attitudes can be explained in terms of direct and indirect effects. Adequate procedures for teacher evaluation are instrumental in guiding teacher behavior and signaling the need for change in instructional styles. Inoperative or invalid evaluation programs may foster the continuation of ineffective teaching techniques or reward poor rather than high quality performance. The continued professional growth and development of teachers can also positively affect school performance. High performance might be the result of meaningful inservice training programs and teacher participation in outside professional conferences and workshops.

The relationship between performance and development attitudes and school effectiveness could also be mediated by teacher satisfaction. Many important personal needs are fulfilled when a school provides realistic teacher appraisal and encourages professional growth. The individuals' needs for self-esteem, recognition, advancement, and self-actualization are directly related to performance and development issues. It has been argued elsewhere that satisfaction of these higher order needs acts to increase the person's motivation to perform.

Teacher attitudes toward the school system's salary and benefit program are assessed in the "financial incentives" category. This factor includes: adequacy of pay, security through pay, years-of-service compensation, incentives for advanced training, rewards for outstanding work, adequacy of benefits, voice in salary matters, adequacy of salary in comparison to other districts, and fairness of salary schedule. Teachers in both groups reported similar and somewhat favorable attitudes toward their financial incentives. Both groups desired a greater opportunity to express their ideas about salary matters, and felt that the salary system fails to reward outstanding work.

Basic similarity in attitudes along this dimension was expected. First, salary and benefit schedules are standardized throughout the district—objectively speaking, there is little variability between schools. Second, previous research (Lawler and Porter, 1967) indicates that financial incentives will be associated with productivity only if they are related to quality of work. The absence of any program throughout the district and its schools to relate pay to performance might reasonably be expected to produce statistically nonsignificant differences between groups on this factor.

Use of Attitude Surveys for the Formative and Summative Evaluation of Schools

Experience in industry and elsewhere has shown that work attitude surveys can be an important addition to administrative procedures for assessing and improving the performance of school personnel. Such surveys also can provide a sound basis for determining the objectives, content, and emphasis of in-service programs for organizational and staff development. In general, there are three types of survey analyses that have considerable use for school district evaluators and administrators:

1. Overall system findings. Survey results provide an indication of the general level of satisfaction of organizational members

throughout the entire school system. Many instruments, including the School Survey (Coughlan, 1966) and The Purdue Teacher Opinionaire (Bentley and Rempel, 1967), can be employed to assess the underlying patterns of attitudes of faculty members in terms of categories of items. Overall findings thus provide a broad diagnosis of the impact of district programs, policies, and procedures on school personnel.

2. Intra- and Inter-School Findings and Analyses. Survey findings pinpoint the most important issues for analysis in various schools and departments within these schools. Miles has noted that survey feedback disconfirms or corroborates individual feelings, generates interest and concern, and stimulates analysis and problem solving (Miles et al., 1969). Through the analysis of specific issues, meaningful suggestions can be obtained from each school staff about innovative programs that would be helpful in solving or alleviating problems and meeting staff needs.

3. Comparative findings and analyses in terms of norms. Survey results, in terms of system-wide, department, or specialist group scores, can be compared with national norms or other available benchmark data. School districts can thus compare their scores on such categories as supervisory relations, educational effectiveness, professional workload, etc., with scores obtained on these dimensions from other similar schools. For example, the Likert School Profile Measurements allows administrators to contrast their own schools' scores with comparative data provided from a centrally maintained and updated data bank (see Siepert and Likert, 1973).

More than two decades ago, Burns (1952) suggested ways in which the survey procedure can contribute to strengthening the efficiency and effectiveness of the school organization. His observations provide the basis for an expanded list today.

1. As a diagnostic procedure. Attitude surveys enable administrators to obtain measured perceptions of a wide range of problems and issues at the school or district level. If anonymity is preserved, the quality and reliability of survey results suffer a minimum of contamination as a result of staff concealment. Diagnoses can be focused on particular schools and departments, as well as on specific topic areas, so that the procedure can analyze both problems and identify specific problem locations. The results will tell the evaluator

what is troubling the staff, locate where problems are most pressing in the system, and indicate where and what types of changes should be made.

2. As an expression of administrative concern for staff welfare. Attitude surveys provide a means for consulting all organization members in the evaluation of school performance. As administrators use surveys for bringing about school improvement, feelings of release and respect for the administration should increase among the survey respondents. These positive feelings, however, are evoked only to the extent that survey findings are applied by administration in organizational decision making. Active involvement of the staff in survey review activities provides a concrete demonstration of the administrator's interest in the staff and should contribute to healthy staff reactions and responses.

3. As a two-way communication procedure. The attitude survey technique strengthens the weakest link of the communication net in large-scale, hierarchically-structured organizations, i.e., the upward flow of suggestions, problem information, and feelings. The anonymous questionnaire is less subject to censorship than regular upward communication and often provides more objective and task-oriented information. The costs are sufficiently low that it is possible to survey all members of the system and thus obtain total system involvement.

4. As a participative procedure. Attitude surveys tend to be employed most frequently in those organizations where administrators practice relatively democratic or nonauthoritarian leadership styles. It seems that such administrations recognize that the technique is a positive means for consulting their faculties and increasing participation in those problems and decisions which directly affect their work lives.

5. As a procedure for decentralization. The contributions of attitude surveys increase as those individuals surveyed participate in the analysis and interpretation of the findings. To insure the program's success, building principals and central office administrators should encourage and support staff involvement in survey feedback and problem solving activities. As organizational members are provided with the facilities, training, and time necessary for problem analysis, they are able to recommend action and influence school decisions. Such decentralization of school decision-making sub-

processes is often associated with an improved sense of individual initiative and group responsibility, and fosters the development of school personnel.

6. As a means for developing organizational teamwork. Attitude survey techniques can improve staff coordination and collaborative action in the school district in several ways. The survey feedback experience, in conjunction with planned follow-up activities, can help to integrate the objectives of the individual and the teacher group with those of the larger organization, develop common interests and consensus within the system, build understanding and acceptance of changes necessary to reach district objectives, and bring about the sharing of responsibility for implementing new programs and making them effective.

7. As a means for facilitating organization development. School consultants can utilize standardized or specially constructed surveys for the improvement of their organization development interventions. Schmuck (1973) suggests that surveys and feedback can be helpful in developing understanding of and agreement with the objectives of the intervention, improving the quality of OD training events, designing follow-up training to meet staff needs, observing and analyzing interaction processes, and perpetuating norms of openness and trust after completion of program activities.

8. As a mechanism for school collective decision making. Collective decision structures serve to increase organizational flexibility and adaptability in schools by providing for problem identification, solution generation, and change initiation and implementation at the faculty level. Though schools can employ both authority and collective processes for decision making, collective decision activities are commonly underdeveloped and unstructured in educational systems. Survey feedback procedures can act to initiate collective processes by providing an objective base for problem and need identification (Coughlan, Cooke, and Safer, 1972).

9. As a means for guiding innovation implementation. Survey data can be used to monitor the implementation of structural or technological changes in schools. Change implementation often creates problems for staff members as new programs or procedures may be inconsistent with other activities and difficult to apply. Staff members can participate in constructing special surveys for the evaluation of change implementation. Such involvement helps reduce

staff resistance and maximizes interest in the evaluative program (Cooke and Duncan, 1972).

If beneficial results are to be realized from the attitude survey procedure, three administrative requirements should be met. First, the purpose of the survey should be clearly stated and understood by all concerned. It should in some specific way improve the efficiency and effectiveness of the school system and make it a better place in which to work. It should be clearly understood that survey findings will not be used to embarrass people in positions of leadership or to undermine individuals or schools that have particular problems. The clear purpose of the survey process must be constructive rather than punitive; otherwise, apprehension and defensiveness will interfere with the identification and solution of problems.

Second, it must be said that few school systems have a tradition of sharing information about problems. Communication is often one-way downward to the teachers, with little upward feedback. The problem solving that does occur is often carried out in an authoritarian or paternalistic atmosphere. The most essential requirement for conducting a successful survey is that of freely sharing and candidly assessing the results with all those who have been involved. This includes all the findings, both favorable and unfavorable. It also means presenting results in an understandable way, allowing for group discussion at the school level, and giving the school staff the resources and encouragement needed to analyze what teachers are saying in their school, why they are saying it, and what can be done about it.

Conference discussion techniques seem most appropriate for sharing findings with the rest of the system. An open climate and an accepting atmosphere are essential in these discussions. Participants must feel free to come to grips with problems in their schools. If this is done effectively, the best ideas and experiences of those closest to problems can be constructively used. People will come to understand the cause of their problems and can plan for their solutions. Having been involved in the identification and analysis of problems, they will then more readily accept responsibility for undertaking action on their own as well as for making recommendations for constructive and corrective measures which lie beyond their own sphere of authority.

Finally, it should be emphasized that the central office must be willing to act upon recommendations from individual schools. If communication between levels of the district organization is to be maintained, top administrators must take the appropriate action or explain why this cannot be done. The dissemination and discussion of survey findings throughout the system will promote free expression of ideas and experience. It will encourage participation in the decision-making process. The survey procedure also can increase improved communication about problems and possible solutions throughout the entire school district. The procedure can therefore establish the climate and conditions for making long-needed changes in our public school systems.

References

Armor, D. J. "School and Family Effects on Black and White Achievement: A Reexamination of the USOE Data." In *On Equality of Educational Opportunity*, edited by F. Mosteller and D. P. Moynihan. New York: Vintage Books, 168-229, 1972.

Bentley, R. R., and Remple, A. M. *Manual for the Purdue Teacher Questionnaire*. West Lafayette, Ind.: The University Bookstore, 360 State Street, 1967.

Brayfield, A. H., and Crockett, W. H. "Employee Attitudes and Employee Performance." *Psychological Bulletin* 52 (1955): 396-424.

Burns, R. K. *Attitude Surveys and the Diagnosis of Organizational Needs*. Personnel Series No. 157. New York: American Management Association, 1952.

Campbell, R. F. *Supplementary Papers: Cincinnati School Survey*. Cincinnati, Ohio: Cincinnatians United for Good Schools, 1968.

Coleman, J. S. *Equality of Educational Opportunity*. Washington, D.C.: U. S. Office of Education, 1966.

Cooke, R. A., and Duncan, R. B. "Evaluative Research as a Component in Organizational Change Strategies." Paper read at American Educational Research Association Annual Meeting, April, 1972.

Coughlan, R. J. "Dimensions of Teacher Morale." *American Educational Research Journal* 7 (1970): 221-35.

————. *The School Survey*. Chicago: Industrial Relations Center, University of Chicago, 1966.

Coughlan, R. J., Cooke, R. A., and Safer, L. A. *An Assessment of a Survey Feedback-Problem Solving-Collective Decision Intervention in Schools.* Evanston, Ill.: Northwestern University, Final Report (Project O-E-105), U. S. Office of Education, 1972.

Gross, N. and Herriott, R. E. *Staff Leadership in Public Schools: A Sociological Inquiry.* New York: Wiley, 1965.

Herzberg, F., et al. *Job Attitudes: Review of Research and Opinion.* Pittsburgh: Psychological Service, 1957.

Jencks, C. D. "The Coleman Report and the Conventional Wisdom." In *On Equality of Educational Opportunity,* edited by F. Mosteller and D. P. Moynihan. New York: Vintage Books, 1972, 69-115.

Lawler, E. E., and Porter, L. W. "The Effect of Performance on Job Satisfaction." *Industrial Relations* 7 (1967): 20-28.

Mayo, E. *The Human Problems of an Industrial Civilization.* New York: Harper, 1933.

Miles, M. B., et al. "The Consequences of Survey Feedback: Theory and Evaluation." In *The Planning of Change,* 2d ed., edited by W. G. Bennis, K. D. Benne, and R. Chin. New York: Holt, Rinehart and Winston, 1969, 457-67.

Porter, L. W., and Lawler, E. E. "What Job Attitudes Tell About Motivation." *Harvard Business Review,* 1968, Jan.-Feb., 118-16.

Roethlisberger, F. J., and Dickson, W. J. *Management and the Worker.* Cambridge, Mass.: Harvard University Press, 1941.

Schmuck, R. A. "Incorporating Survey Feedback in OD Interventions." Paper read at American Educational Research Association Annual Meeting, New Orleans, La., February 1973.

Siepert, A. F. and Likert, R. "The Likert School Profile Measurements of the Human Organization." Paper read at American Educational Research Association Annual Meeting, New Orleans, La., February 1973.

Vroom, V. H. *Work and Motivation.* New York: Wiley, 1964.

17. TREND SURFACE ANALYSIS
Donald N. McIsaac

Today's need for decision-making techniques in urban America calls for parsimonious methods of expressing geographically-related information. Trend surface analysis is such a method. The results of such analysis may be depictions of the information in the form of contour maps, similar to the weather map in the local newspaper, illustrating the gradual change in the value of a given variable as a function of its location on a geographic surface. This technique permits the selection of a limited sample from a given region, and provides a graphic display or mathematical model, so that the urban decision maker is able to base his findings on an approximation of hard data.

In this chapter, the application of trend surface analysis will be briefly explained, and the general methodology outlined. The procedures will then be demonstrated, giving examples of the analysis of math and reading achievement scores. Further examples illustrating applications to community political characteristics and survey data will be given.

The Methods of Trend Surface Analysis

The key to the process of trend surface analysis is the identification of "stations" and "station values." Each station across a surface is the point selected to represent a local geographic region in the

319

overall analysis. These stations are the references used in the modeling process, and may be selected on a random or on a representative basis. In this chapter, the stations are identified as the governmental units under analysis. For example, the analysis of school data employs school averages for achievement as the station value. Achievement is a function of the school average for a given grade level. IQ is an average of all the IQ scores located at a given school. Obviously, the selection of stations on such a basis destroys the notion of random selection. However, the notion of a representative sample is preserved, because all of the available data are included.

A model based on such data may be generalized only with respect to the population of the sample. In the trend analysis of community data, the population and the sample are often the same. Station data may also represent such centers as the voting precincts, census tracts, or schools. For a given analysis, the stations are the points (representing a given local area) that reflect the average of some attribute. Since a variety of station types selected over a given surface represent the same surface, data collected from each may easily be compared. By this method, it is possible to compare the results of a given election with the distribution of student achievement. It is also possible to compare the results of a given election with the attributes represented in the census enumeration. These correlations and comparisons often are difficult to achieve because the different geographic units mean that data are rarely directly comparable.

There are many methods that fall under the general heading of trend surface analysis (Chorley and Haggett, 1965). This discussion is limited to the orthogonal polynomial approach, which offers good promise and is analytical in nature. The method is a multiple curvilinear regression model in which the station coordinates (location of each station from an arbitrary origin) and the station value serve as the independent and dependent variables. Geographic information is often ambiguous. Two sources of the variation in a surface must be considered. It is necessary to separate the smooth regional patterns of variation from the local chance effects (Krumbein, 1956). The researcher then ascribes probable causes to the different components. Thus the regional effect is viewed as a smooth component, called the trend surface. Local effects are the result of local variation; they may be random in nature and are explained by the residual difference between the station and the trend surface values. (Nettleton, 1954) In the case of the trend surface model, the station value is assumed to be some function of its location on the surface. Each station must therefore be identified in terms of its location and of the station value, such as IQ or average achievement.

The basic objective of the trend surface model is to identify some low frequency signal across a broad geographic surface and separate it from local random noise effects. A variety of techniques have been employed for the analysis of surface trends; one of the most promising of these techniques is the least squares fitting of a polynomial surface (Chorley and Haggett, 1965). The output from such a model may be plotted (presented in contour form) to illustrate clearly the trend or broad regional effect. An analysis of the residual may be computed to reveal some measure of the quality of the depiction or model. When plotted, this analysis of residuals may reveal higher level or hidden trends. An expression of R^2, the total sum of squares explained by the regression, provides an assessment of the quality of the overall map. A simple surface may be represented by the quadratic

$$Y' = A + B_1 U + B_2 V + B_3 U^2 + B_4 UV + B_5 V^2,$$

where

U = distance east of origin
V = distance north of origin
Y' = predicted station value
A = Y intercept (predicted value when U and V = 0)
B_i = computed weights of the regression

The application of trend surface analysis can best be illustrated by a specific example. Let us assume that we have a district of 103 elementary schools. We suspect that some trend exists across the city with regard to the ability of students to perform on IQ tests. In other words, we have some reason to believe that the performance in some large regions of the city will be lower than in others. In order to test this hypothesis and to provide a graphic depiction of the data, we would need to have a map of the city with each of the schools identified. We would select the lower left-hand corner of the map as an arbitrary origin.

In the example cited in Figure 17-1, school 1 is located U_1

Figure 17-1. Map of school locations, school and average IQ scores

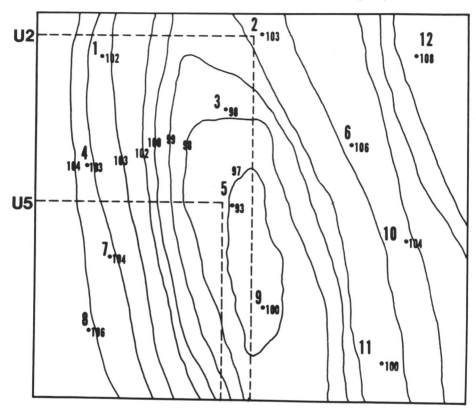

inches west of the origin and V_1 inches north of the origin. The eighth graders in the school station have an average measured IQ of 102. In order to process such information and to produce either a trend analysis or a contour depiction, it is necessary to place the data into a data matrix (Table 17-1).

The result of processing such data through a trend surface analysis program would be a table of the original values, the values predicted from the equation, an analysis of residual differences between the actual and predicted values, and a contour map illustrating the general trend of the change in IQ across the surface of the city. The regional characteristics are explained by the equation, and the R^2 computation provides a quality estimate of the map or an expression of the station variance explained. The residual indicates how each

Table 17-1. Data matrix

School ID	U	V	IQ (Station value)
1	0.9	4.7	102
2	3.0	5.1	103
3	2.6	4.0	98
4	0.7	3.3	103
5	2.7	2.7	93
6	4.4	3.5	106
7	1.0	1.9	107
8	0.7	0.8	106
9	3.2	1.3	100
10	5.0	2.3	104
11	4.7	0.5	100
12	5.3	5.0	108

school varies from the regional trend. High residuals indicate unexpectedly high IQ ratios when compared to the general region. When the station values are achievement data, the high positive residuals may suggest a high-quality program. Negative residuals may suggest a weak or dysfunctional program.

The examples and analyses appearing in this chapter were processed by use of a program developed by the author. The analyses draw heavily on the earlier work of Donald B. McIntyre and his computer programs for the computation of trend surfaces 1 through 8 (McIntyre, 1963).

Computation of higher order equations provides the capability for the depiction of a convoluted or curved surface. When the coefficients have been defined, a grid is produced from which the contour depictions are made. Just as the linear regression equation serves as the descriptive model of a linear relationship, the trend surface model serves as a depiction of a surface. The depiction illustrates the low frequency trends that are too broad in effect to admit to random local occurrence. The trend surface estimates the value of every point on its surface in the same way that a regression line estimates points of a scattergram. In both cases, the method involves a least squares criterion for solution.

The number of schools used for the sample output shown in Table 17-2 is extremely small, and conclusive results are difficult to obtain. However, the output does indicate that school 5 deviates negatively from the established surface. A researcher would be interested in exploring the possible causes. School 7 appears to score considerably above the surface. Further study regarding the causes of this success is also merited.

Table 17-2. Sample trend surface output

School ID	U	V	Y	Predicted	Residual
1	.90	4.70	102.00	101.55	.45
2	3.00	5.10	103.00	103.62	−.62
3	2.60	4.00	98.00	96.06	1.94
4	.70	3.30	103.00	104.66	−1.66
5	2.70	2.70	93.00	97.06	−4.06
6	4.40	3.50	106.00	104.37	1.63
7	1.00	1.90	107.00	103.60	3.40
8	.70	.80	106.00	107.20	−1.20
9	3.20	1.30	100.00	99.06	.94
10	5.00	2.30	104.00	104.53	−.53
11	4.70	.50	100.00	99.99	.01
12	5.30	5.00	108.00	108.30	−.30

Several applications of the trend surface techniques will be discussed. Each offers a unique view of the geographic area surveyed. Trend surface analysis offers the advantage of estimating grid data from randomly spaced points. Many of the natural population centers do not conform to the nice neat grids useful to the production of contour maps. By use of trend surface analysis, it is possible to compare or contrast attributes associated with different data bases, such as response to an election issue based on voting precincts with average income based on census tracts.

Trend Surface for the Depiction of Achievement

The trends of achievement across a large geographic surface can be illustrated by the use of trend surface analysis. The application of such methodology assists in the assessment of specific geographically-related projects over a period of time. Achievement data were collected as part of a student assignment for reading, math, and language in the city of St. Louis, representing the average achievement for the above attributes for the years 1964, 1966, and 1968. (Experienced Teacher Fellowship Program). The results of a testing program were compared across time and across subjects.

The attributes illustrated in the trend surface analysis are the results of the district-standardized citywide testing procedures. Eighth grade data were available for ninety-seven elementary schools (first through eighth grades). The test used was the Iowa Test of Basic Skills, and the results reflect the average eighth-grade achievement score for each school. The station data include the average school achievement score for eighth graders in reading, arithmetic, and language. The results of this analysis are included in Figure 17-2.

The pattern of achievement across the city is characteristically similar for all achievement maps (McIsaac, 1969). The middle east side of the community consistantly reflects the lowest level of achievement. Moving to the north, west, and south, improved achievement is observed. The R^2 for the maps falls around .70, indicating a reasonably good fit. The pattern for reading is quite consistant over the four-year period; the predominant low in the eastern portion of the city moved toward the central part of the city. The change was extremely slight, and little significance could be attached to what might be a spurious local effect.

The maps of language achievement reveal an upward thrust that can be first noticed in the central portion of the 1966 depiction. This plateau is maintained and extended in the 1968 map—perhaps suggesting that purely random effects may not have been the cause of the earlier change. The importance of the trend surface technique applied in this case is that it focuses attention on a part of the community that is possibly undergoing a change.

Mathematics achievement trends demonstrated a deterioriation over the geographic area that experienced improved language tests. The drop is first noticeable in the 1966 mathematics depiction, and is reinforced in 1968. Again, the cause of such a development is not revealed by the analysis. However, the occurrence of this apparent seesaw of language versus mathematics achievement suggests a need for some additional study. A tentative explanation was postulated when similar maps depicted per student expenditure as consistent and class size as decreasing in the central portion of the city. This

Figure 17-2. Achievement results for selected variables; Iowa test of basic skills

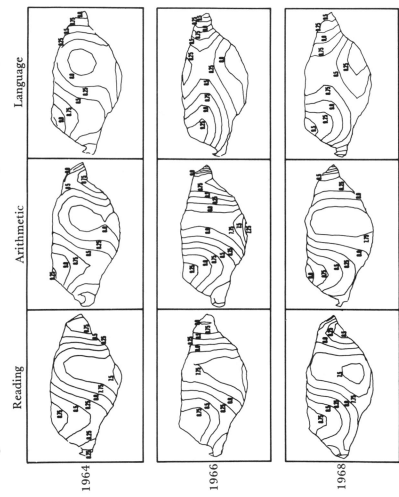

added fact suggests that many new teachers were employed in that portion of the city (the result of lowering class size), and that these new teachers were better trained in the teaching of language skills. Such a tentative hypothesis is highly speculative, but possibly worth following up with additional evaluation.

More Trend Surface Analysis for the Depiction of Achievement

The use of trend surface analysis provides an interesting approach to the assessment of achievement of program goals. In an analysis of the achievement of the goals of a large city right-to-read program, trend surface analysis was applied. The primary objective was one year's growth for one year's effort. Each of the students in the second through sixth grades was administered a complete California Achievement Battery in October, and a second battery the following May. The purpose of administering the battery twice was to assess the amount of change in the district for the subjects of reading and arithmetic during the school year. The trend surface program was used in an attempt to illustrate change equivalent to grade expectations across the entire school district. The tests were administered to every student in the district according to the test publishers' instructions. The results were scored in standard fashion, and reported back to the district personnel. The average score by school was compiled at the time of scoring and recorded on punched cards. A set of cards for each school was thus prepared on which the average achievement was recorded. The school locations were digitized (located by U & V coordinates), and the results of the digitizing were merged with the results of the test scoring, thereby creating a record for each school which contained the school ID, U and V coordinate information, and station values (average achievement scores by grade, expressed in grade equivalent scores).

The results of the analysis revealed that the gradient increased as a function of time (see Figure 17-3). That is to say, the difference between the inner-core and the outer-city children's achievement scores differed by a greater amount in the higher grades. Another way of viewing the same information is that the outer-city children exhibited a faster rate of learning as well as a higher average score. A review of the maps also shows that the inner-core children made remarkable progress during the school year 1970-71. The lowest

Figure 17-3. Illustration of reading achievement

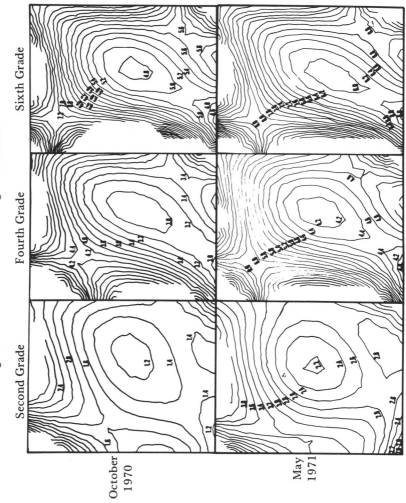

point on the surface for the pre-test period was generally 1.2 grade levels below the post-test period. This means that the children of the inner-core showed an average gain of 1.2 grade equivalents in seven months. This gain is greater than would normally be expected. The expected achievement gain from October to May would ordinarily be .7, since the scores reflect national norms and the period of time is seven months. Specific program implications must be drawn from the analysis of the program plan; the analysis of residuals provides some useful information in this regard. The spring 1970-71 reading scores for fourth grade reveal that six schools achieved at 1.0 grade level, or better than the trend surface (residuals of + 1.0 or better). Table 17-3 illustrates their achievement and residual scores.

Table 17-3. Selected schools performing higher
than trend surface

Fourth Grade Reading, 1970-71

School	Spring 1971 Actual	Spring 1971 Predicted	Spring 1971 Residual	Fall 1970 Residual
A	5.80	4.20	1.60	.14
B	6.30	5.25	1.05	−.19
C	7.30	6.12	1.18	.50
D	6.00	4.90	1.10	.16
E	6.70	5.18	1.52	−.14
F	5.70	4.37	1.33	.03

None of the six schools demonstrated a particularly striking deviation from the fall 1970 (pre-test) trend surface. Each, however, achieved remarkable gains when compared with the general trend for the 1970-71 school year. The components of the reading program as expressed in these schools are worthy of further study. The specific programmatic implications for their gain can be derived from careful and detailed analysis of their programs.

It should be clear to the reader that the results of the trend surface analysis often raise more questions than answers. For example, the observation that students in the outer city generally progress faster than those in the inner core is not a new finding. One must always ask the additional question, "Why?"—a question not answered by trend surface analysis.

The trend surface method provides an opportunity to identify those entities that do not conform to the model. Average achievement for some schools was far greater than expected; careful analysis of the residuals flags these schools, and highlights those situations for which achievement satisfies the model and those for which it does not. The exceptions to the model may be the focus for a more detailed examination.

Trend Surface for the Analysis of Voter Data

Occasionally, the researcher or decision maker in a large urban setting finds it useful to consider the relationship between the known socioeconomic attributes of a community and the known voting patterns of the same group. Such comparisons are often difficult and cumbersome because of the lack of a common data base. The use of trend surface techniques helps to eliminate the difficulty in comparison. Rarely, if ever, do the boundaries of voting precincts coincide with the boundaries of census tracts. Trend surface analysis permits the computation of a map based upon voting precincts that can be easily compared with a map computed from a set of census tracts.

The map in Figure 17-4 illustrates the effect of a multimillion dollar bond election in recent years in the city of Milwaukee. This map was produced from a digitized map in which all of the voting precincts were depicted. The digitized records were then merged with the voting information from each of the precincts and the data processed through the trend surface program. The results clearly indicate that the base of support for the passing of the bond was the central core of the city. Approximately 70 percent of those voting in the core were in favor of the bond. In the more affluent areas to the west, support for the bond diminished. In the near northwest, a saddle developed. This may be explained by the emergence of new housing in a relatively undeveloped area. The area needs schools because few presently exist, and the area is growing.

Again, the analysis of residuals is useful for pinpointing those precincts exhibiting anomalous behavior. Table 17-4 gives some examples. The precincts shown in Table 17-4 reflect those 6 of 319 precincts that supported the bond election at a much lower rate than the surface predicted. These areas and the public relations program associated with the election merit further analysis. The causes for

Figure 17-4. Percent of vote in favor of bond election;
trend surface, 3rd degree

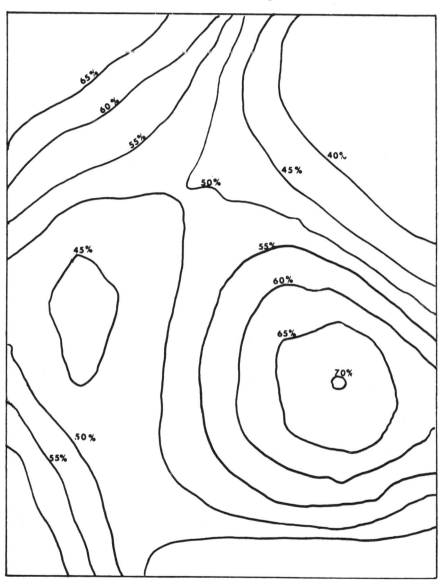

Table 17-4. Residual votes for bond election

Ward	Precinct	Percent for Issue		Residual
		Actual	Predicted	
2	13	31%	52%	−21%
2	20	30%	53%	−23%
2	21	22%	51%	−29%
6	9	37%	63%	−26%
14	1	30%	56%	−26%
18	1	53%	86%	−33%

these surprisingly low results are not inherently explained by the analysis. These are local effects which admit to far greater variation than would be expected.

Trend Surface Analysis of Attitude Surveys

Just as the trends of expenditure, voting response, and school achievement are useful to those who must make decisions or do research, so are the attitudes that people express about a given topic. In 1969, the State Department of Public Instruction in Wisconsin commissioned a study of the perceived needs of education. The results of the study were to be used to guide policy regarding the future distribution of Title III funds.

The study, *Wisconsin Title III Needs Assessment* (Lipham, 1969), involved interviews with more than 1000 people across Wisconsin. The stratified sample from forty districts was carefully selected to represent a cross section of typical respondents in the state. Trend surface analysis was applied to detect the occurrence of regional trends in the state. Since the sampling was done across respondent groups including students, parents, school board members, and school staff, the regional characteristics between groups were of particular interest. Respondents were asked to rank specific educational needs, and a locational average perception was computed for each of the forty districts. The districts were digitized, and the rank data were associated with each of the appropriate U and V coordinates. The results were then processed by use of the standard trend surface program.

Figure 17-5. Need for vocational-technical programs
as perceived by school boards

Low Number = High Need

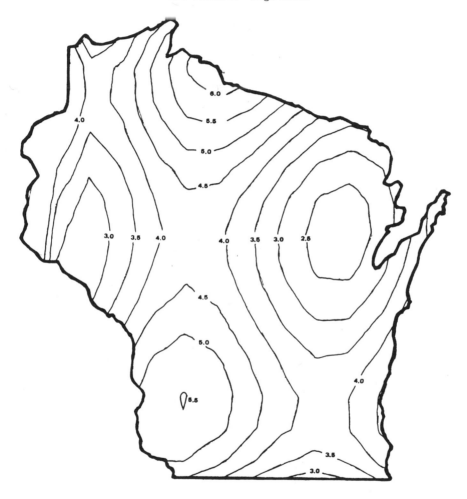

Figure 17-6. Need for vocational-technical programs
as perceived by students

Low Number = High Need

Figure 17-7. Need for vocational-technical programs
as perceived by citizens

Low Number = High Need

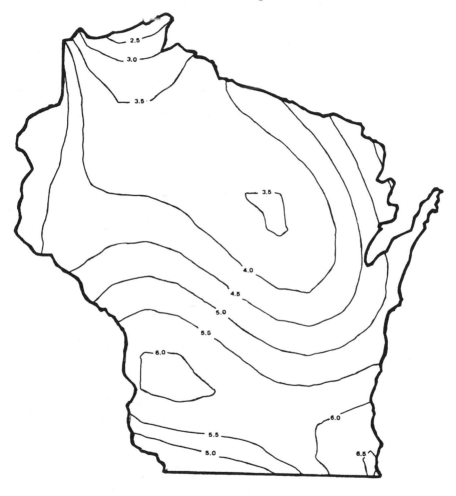

Three trend surface maps that pinpoint the need for additional emphasis on post-secondary vocational-technical education are presented because they highlight differences among three respondent groups: school board members, students, and citizens. Regarding vocational-technical education, Figure 17-5 reveals high concern on the part of school board members in both the northeastern and northwestern parts of the state; Figure 17-6 reveals high concern on the part of students in the south central and extreme northern regions; and Figure 17-7 reveals a high concern on the part of citizens in the northern part of the state along an axis extending from Green Bay diagonally to Superior. The map for educators, which is not reproduced here, revealed no particular regional trends. And, as might be expected, the map for the total sample revealed no particular trends—probably because the regional differences among boards, students, and citizens tended to cancel each other out. To reiterate, school boards and citizens in the northern part of the state generally felt greater need for emphasis on vocational-technical education than did their counterparts in the southern part of the state. For students, the trend was generally opposite (except for a small band of concerned students in the vicinity of Ashland-Superior). These findings might be of special interest to policy makers and planners, particularly in the field of vocational education.

References

Chorley, R. S. and Haggett, P. "Trend Surface Mapping in Geographical Research." *Institute of British Geographers Transaction No. 37.* London: George Philip and Son, 1965, p. 47.

Experienced Teacher Fellowship Program, Grant Number 144-8585, funded by the U.S. Office of Education.

Krumbein, W. C. "Regional and Local Components in Facies Maps." *Bulletin of the American Association of Petroleum Geologists* 40 (1956): 2163-94.

Lipham, J. M. et al. *Wisconsin Educational Needs Assessment Study.* Madison, Wisc.: Wisconsin Department of Public Instruction, 1969.

McIntyre, D. *Program for Computation of Trend Surfaces and Residuals for Degree 1 through 8.* Claremont, Calif.: Pomona College Geology Department, 1963, p. 24.

McIsaac, D. N. *Analysis of St. Louis Achievement Trends.* Unpublished report delivered to St. Louis Schools, 1969, p. 11.

Nettleton, L. L. "Regionals, Residuals and Structures." Geophysics 19 (1954): 22.

18. GEOCODE ANALYSIS
Dennis W. Spuck

School administrators need to have detailed information about the schools in their districts. Of particular importance to educational decision makers is knowledge concerning where students live. The logistics of bus schedules, new school locations, and changing school boundaries, together with such pressing issues as racial and fiscal imbalances, presents an impressive demand for accurate and timely student information. A historical example of geographic information display is the once-familiar "pin map," wherein each school principal positioned pins in a map of the district to locate students. Only the smallest of districts can continue to operate in such a manual mode; most large districts have had little or no geographically-related student data on which to rely. Computers, however, can synthesize information related to students and summarize and graphically display this information on a geographic base. The purpose of this chapter is to describe computer-based techniques and applications of the analysis of geographically-coded student data.

Since the preceding chapter considered another approach to the graphic display of information through trend surface analysis, this chapter will begin by distinguishing between that procedure and geocode analysis. Trend surface analysis produces an analytical model that results in a contour plot. Geocode analysis, too, can result in a contour plot, but different algorithms are used to generate the display. In trend surface analysis, randomly-spaced points across a geographic surface reflecting the distribution of, for example, elementary schools in a large school district, are described by a higher order polynomial model. Usually the data associated with the individual points (schools) are aggregate student data, such as the average reading score for third graders. Once the polynomial has been computed, the contour plot is generated by letting the parameters defining the geographic space range over the specified values, thus predicting the height of the criterion variable (reading achievement) at each point and plotting it at desired contour intervals.

Geocode analysis uses the individual student as the unit of analysis. Since these units are spread finely across the geographic surface, it is possible to aggregate them in any way desired. It is convenient to summarize the information at points dispersed systematically, at constant intervals, on the surface. Connecting four adjacent points will form a square, and each corner will represent the aggregate of student data for the geographic region surrounding it, as shown in Figure 18-1.

If the points a, b, c, and d represent aggregate reading level scores, they might take on the values 3.8, 4.2, 4.1, and 4.3. These points are averaged, to obtain an estimate of the mid-point of the square, and then linear approximations of contour lines through the square are generated. The insert in Figure 18-1 depicts the four reading level scores given above, the estimate of the mid-point (4.1), and two lines of equal achievement (4.0 and 4.25). When this process is completed for all squares covering the surface, contour lines result.

Both trend surface analysis and geocode analysis may yield contour displays of information across a geographic area. In general, trend surface analysis does not have the detail possible in geocode analysis, since it deals with estimated grid data and identifies low frequency trends; on the other hand, geocode analysis costs more to generate than does information summarized through trend surface analysis. Displays other than contour plots are available for use with geocode analysis data, but this procedure has been stressed because it is the point of similarity to trend surface analysis.

If student information is to be displayed on a geographic surface, the information to be plotted and the coordinates specifying the location of the student in the geographic region must be given. This collection of student information, together with the geographic location, is called a geographic data base. The procedures used in geo-

Figure 18-1. Points of aggregate information and contour lines

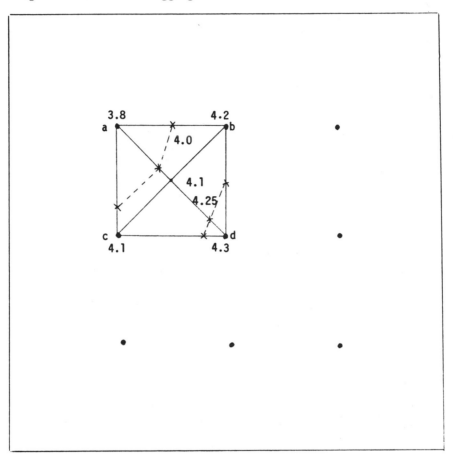

code analysis assume that all students residing within the area of a given block are located at the block's geocenter. The block center is, then, fixed on the two-dimensional surface of a map. Any point on the map may be located by moving to a position a measured distance over from the lower left-hand corner of the map and then moving a measured distance up from that position. This is similar to the street locator on a city map, which overlays the map surface with a grid. The columns of the grid are labeled alphabetically, and the rows of the grid are labeled numerically. To find a street, one must search only within the grid associated with the alphabetic character and the numeral. As the grid size becomes smaller, the location of the street becomes fixed in a smaller and smaller geographic region. The limit of this procedure would be a statement of the exact distance over and up from the lower left corner of the map. In this case, it is easier to use a direct measure of distance—inches on the map, for example—than to use the alphabetic and numeric codes. A student's location, specifically the geocenter of the block on which he resides, may be fixed on a geographic surface such as a map by specifying the distance over and up from a given origin on the surface. It is convenient to choose the origin such that all distances will be positive; this can be accomplished by choosing the lower left-hand corner of the map as the origin.

The formation of a student-oriented geographic data base may be accomplished by merging student data, including the student's home address and the information to be plotted, with geographic data, including an address index and the geographic coordinates of block centers. The collection of student data is called a student data file, and the geographic data is called an address coding guide.

The reasons for developing the student data file and the address coding guide separately and then merging them to form the geographic data base should be explained. First, school districts frequently have collections of student information already on file. Many districts have these records in computer-readable form. Second, much of the information necessary to build the address coding guide is currently available to school districts from the United States Bureau of the Census (United States Department of Commerce, Bureau of the Census, 1970, 1971). This Bureau produces an index of block faces for all cities of fifty thousand or more inhabitants. These cities are known as Standard Metropolitan Statistical Areas. Since an index is available that associates each block face with a block number, the school district need only associate the numbered block centers with the coordinates of the block center to create the required digitized address coding guide. A detailed description of creating and updating the digitized address coding guide, student data file, and geographic data base is given by Spuck (1972) and McIsaac, Spuck and Stofflet (1972). A similar approach to information display appears in the documentation of the *Census Use Study* (United States Department of Commerce, Bureau of the Census, 1970).

Obviously, only that student information included in the student data file can be graphically displayed. Careful consideration and analysis of informational needs should be conducted before the creation of the file. The information specified might include such background and educational variables as birthdate, sex, ethnicity, grade, school, and Aid to Families with Dependent Children (AFDC) status, as well as standardized test score data. It is not the purpose of this chapter to identify the information to be included in the student data file, but rather to provide some examples of the utility of such a file. The content of this file, which may be stored on punched cards or magnetic tape, is critical, since it sets the limits of the application of the geographic data base.

Student information in the geographic data base is aggregated at the center of the blocks on which the students reside. Blocks, even in a fairly small school district, are spread relatively finely across the district. There are too many data points, that is, block centers, to consider individually, and some type of data summary is desirable. The various types of geocode analysis are directed to the summary of information distributed in fine grain across a geographic surface. In geocode analysis, summary begins by selecting the degree of precision required for a particular application; a grid framework of the selected size is imposed over the geographic surface to be displayed. Within this structure, data can be aggregated by combining the desired information from each block center within the grid cell.

A grid count is generated by combining the number of students at each block center possessing a trait of interest to obtain the total number of students within each cell. If, for example, the trait of concern is the number of students entering the third grade, then each grid cell would contain the number of students who lived in the geographic region covered by the grid cell, who are about to enter the third grade. Since the grid cells are of equal size, or represent geographic regions within the school district of equal size, the distribution of counts provides the school district with a population density distribution for the selected student trait.

For some purposes, the grid count is a useful and necessary way to summarize information; for other purposes, the distribution of counts across the surface of a map is confusing, and a more parsimonious means of data portrayal is desirable. The contour plot provides a graphic portrayal of the information presented in a grid cell count. Rather than depicting the cells and counts directly, the contour plot summarizes this information as a series of concentric rings of equal population density. This is similar to the weather map, wherein the contours illustrate lines of equal temperature or barometric pressure, or the geologic survey map, wherein the contours represent lines of equal elevation. The school district may be seen as a graphic representation of these dimensions, with variations in the height above the surface, peaks and valleys, depicting high and low population densities respectively.

A variation of the contour plot is the printer-plot. This procedure displays changes in population density by using shading in the printed output; the darker the shading, the more densely populated the geographic region. This approach offers the advantage of being producible on a standard computer printer, using over-printing to achieve the gradations in shading. Contour plot illustrations require the use of a computer plotter.

The type of information considered so far has been in the form of a count; that is, the number of students possessing a trait falling in a specified geographic region. It is also possible to display aggregated information, such as standardized test means, in a similar way. For this purpose, it is necessary to calculate a measure of central tendency for each grid cell for all students possessing a given trait, rather than merely counting the number of students located in the cell. For example, if it were desired to display the distribution of measured student IQ across the geographic surface of a school district, the average student IQ would first be computed for each nonempty grid cell. The information thus obtained at first appears to be quite similar to that utilized in trend surface analysis. However, two basic differences are apparent. First, the data points, in this case grid cells, are much more numerous than the data points available in trend surface analysis; and second, the information is distributed uniformly, rather than randomly, across the geographic surface. The large number of cells and their equal distribution across the surface allows for a much more direct means of achieving contour display than the polynomial fit of trend surface analysis. Aggregated data of this type should be considered in conjunction with student population density information for the same region, so as to interpret the aggregated data relative to the varying number of students in these regions. Extreme scores in sparsely populated areas can distort the information display.

The remaining discussion will focus on four examples to illustrate the use of a student-oriented geographic data base. These examples, giving profiles of the school attendance area, are derived from actual data. The applications considered display student population density, minority group population density, the location of Aid to Families with Dependent Children (AFDC) support, and student reading achievement levels for grades four and five as grid plots and contour plots.

Redistricting School Attendance Areas

A recurring problem to educational decision makers is that of assessing the impact of school district population growth and redistribution of the boundaries of individual school attendance areas. The limits of school attendance areas are frequently in a state of flux. Timely and accurate information is needed to assist the school administrator in redefining the attendance boundaries of old schools and defining the attendance areas of new schools to be built in the district. School population density information is extremely useful to the educational decision maker.

An example of this information, in the form of a grid plot, is presented in Figure 18-2. Each of the grid cells represents an area of equal size in the school district, and the number of students presently attending grades four through six is identified in the cell center. The actual grid is not depicted on the plot, but it includes a square region surrounding each statistic. The program producing the grid plot is designed so that the size of the grids may be varied to display the information at the desired granularity for the specific application; and the entire plot may be scaled so as to coincide with the boundaries defined by available maps. Generally these plots would be displayed superimposed over district maps to facilitate translation from a location on the plot to a location in the district.

By considering grid plots at regular time intervals, annually or semiannually, the location and magnitude of changes in student population densities for specific grades may be monitored. It is even possible to display this change data in a plot, so that the number associated with a given grid cell represents student population increase or decrease in that geographic region for the grade level(s) under consideration over the given time period.

Figure 18-2. Grid plot, student population density, grades 4-6

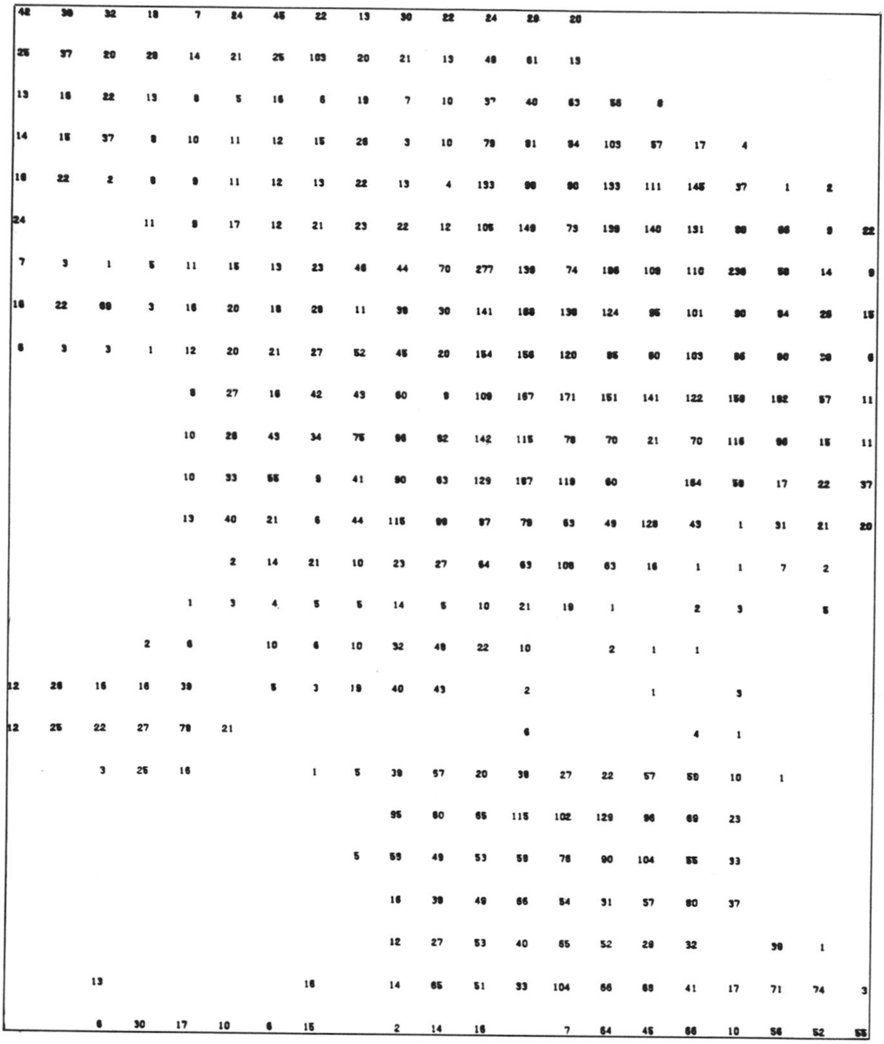

```
42  30  32  18   7  24  45  22  13  30  22  24  29  28
25  37  20  28  14  21  25 103  20  21  13  48  61  13
13  18  22  13   8   5  16   6  18   7  10  37  40  63  56   8
14  15  37   8  10  11  12  15  26   3  10  78  81  84 103  57  17   4
16  22   2   8   8  11  12  13  22  13   4 133  96  90 133 111 145  37   1   2
24          11   8  17  12  21  23  22  12 105 149  73 138 140 131  88  66   9  22
 7   3   1   5  11  15  13  23  46  44  70 277 138  74 186 108 110 238  58  14   9
16  22  68   3  16  20  18  28  11  38  30 141 168 138 124  85 101  90  84  28  15
 8   3   3   1  12  20  21  27  52  45  20 154 156 120  85  80 103  86  80  38   8
                 8  27  16  42  43  60   9 108 167 171 151 141 122 158 182  87  11
                10  28  43  34  76  96  82 142 115  78  70  21  70 116  96  15  11
                10  33  65   8  41  90  63 129 187 119  60     164  58  17  22  37
                13  40  21   6  44 115  90  87  79  63  49 128  43   1  31  21  20
                 2  14  21  10  23  27  64  63 108  63  16   1   1   7   2
                 1   3   4   5   5  14   6  10  21  19   1       2   3       8
                 2   6      10   6  10  32  49  22  10       2   1   1
12  28  16  16  39       5   3  19  40  43       2           1       3
12  25  22  27  78  21                   6               4   1
     3  25  16           1   5  39  57  20  38  27  22  57  59  10   1
                            95  80  65 115 102 129  96  69  23
                     5      59  49  53  58  76  90 104  55  33
                            16  38  49  66  54  31  57  80  37
                            12  27  53  40  65  52  28  32      39   1
     13                 16  14  65  51  33 104  66  68  41  17  71  74   3
     6  30  17  10   6  15   2  14  16       7  64  45  66  10  56  52  55
```

It is clear that the grid plot describes population densities in considerable detail, but it is also evident that it is not presented in a form that makes it easy for the educational decision maker to identify the location of high or low population densities. Figure 18-3 displays the same information presented in Figure 18-2 as a contour plot; the contour interval is 20 students. From the contour plot it is easy to identify the areas of high population density, such as the 277 students located in a given grid in the north-central part of the region.

As with the grid plots, contour plots may be compared for change across time. Either the two contour plots may be compared or the change scores may be plotted. The change data is frequently of most interest to educational planners, since these are the areas that are going to provide schools with changing student populations and that, over time, may suggest redistricting or new building.

Both the grid plot and the contour plot display the same information; however, the grid plot presents the information in more detail than does the contour plot. If general trends are of interest, then the contour plot is desirable; if fine detail is required then the grid plot is useful. The educational decision maker may want to use both in carrying out his responsibilities, while the contour plot alone might be sufficient for presentations to community groups or to the school board.

It might be important to detail the population density for a specific school attendance area, or perhaps for two adjoining attendance areas. By increasing the level of granularity (detail) and increasing the scale, a "blowup" picture of such areas may be achieved. This information could facilitate redistributing at the individual school level. It might also be useful in bus routing and scheduling.

The ethnic balance in district schools is also of great concern to urban educators. Display of population densities of specific minority groups across the geographic surface would greatly facilitate redistricting in such a way as to maximize racial integration, but at the same time minimize student distance from the school building. While mathematical models are available to assist in solving this type of problem, using the information in a student-oriented geographic data base (Van Dusseldorp, 1972), geographic display is useful in that it presents the rationale to the community and allows for "fine tuning" of the mathematical solution. An example of minority population

Figure 18-3. Contour plot, student population density, grades 4-6.
Contour interval: 20 students

densities is presented in Figure 18-4 for students in grades K-12 in the form of a contour plot.

Target Area Schools

School districts desiring or using revenue derived from the Elementary and Secondary Education Act (ESEA) Title I are required to identify these areas and, more specifically, school attendance areas that reflect the greatest density of poverty. Those schools that include areas of extreme economic deprivation are eligible for Title I funds. The data used to identify economically disadvantaged families, as presented in the grid plot of Figure 18-5, was the Aid to Families with Dependent Children (AFDC) status of a student's family. A tally of AFDC families is presented by geographic region for the school district. Attendance areas that include the highest concentration of these families are target area schools and are eligible for Title I support. A contour plot of the same information is given in Figure 18-6. As reported by Costa (1972, p. 8) this type of display is useful not only in identifying target area schools, but in justifying these decisions to school district personnel and community members, such as the Title I Parent Advisory Council. Due to the restrictions on school district use of Title I funds, the classification of a target area school must be rejustified annually, thus stressing the need for a systematic approach to information retrieval and display.

Student Achievement Data

Student achievement varies among attendance areas within a given school district. For assessment purposes, it is useful to display student achievement levels on a geographic surface. Suppose that a standardized reading test is given at grade levels four and five for each student in several school attendance areas. These data may be displayed in the form of a contour plot, as shown in Figure 18-7 for grade four, and variations according to student location or geographic region may be noted. This is useful in suggesting priority needs for supplementary programs in specific areas. Comparison with other plots, such as those depicting AFDC status or ethnic distribution for the same area, can be made. Such comparisons could indicate the availability of federal Title I funds for the programs or perhaps the need for a bilingual approach to the teaching of reading.

Figure 18-4. Minority population density, grades K-12.
Contour interval: 60 students

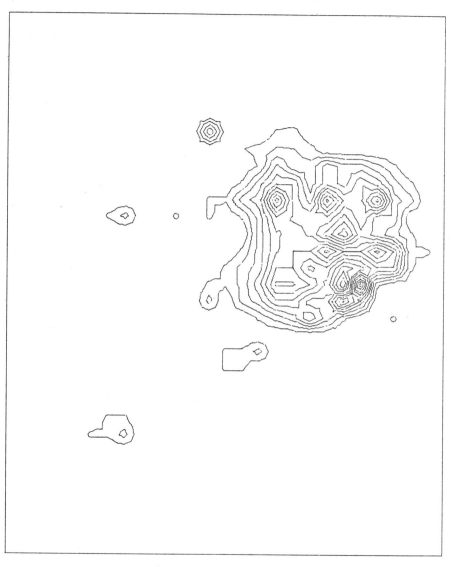

Figure 18-5. Grid plot, Aid to Families with Dependent Children (AFDC)

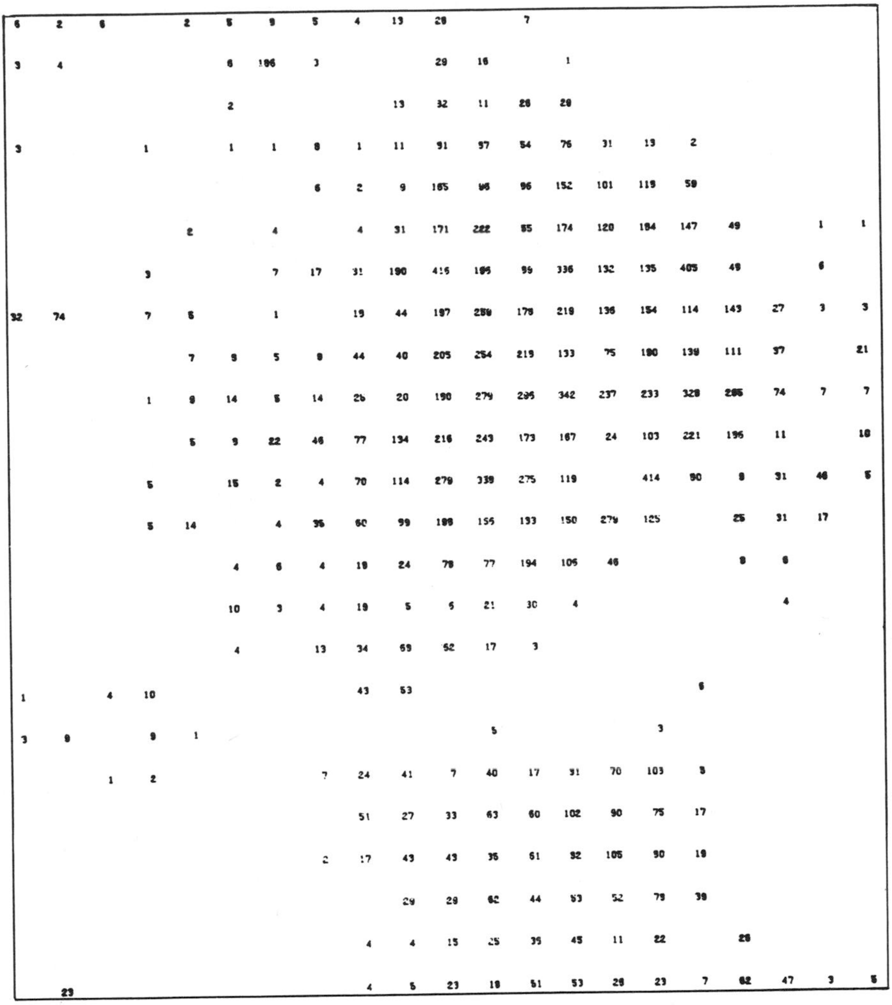

Figure 18-6. Contour plot, Aid to Families with Dependent Children (AFDC). Contour interval: 35 students

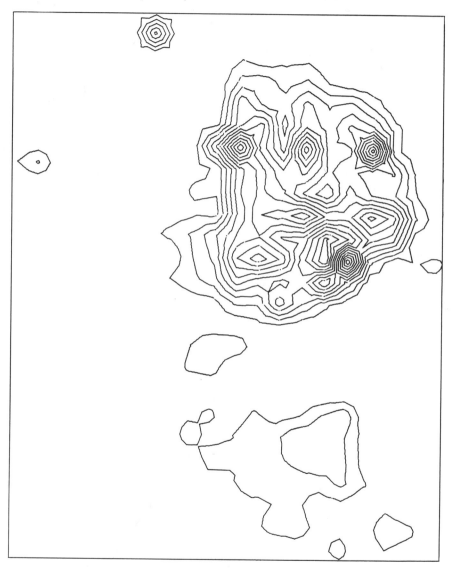

Figure 18-7. Reading level grade 4
Contour interval: 0.2 grade levels

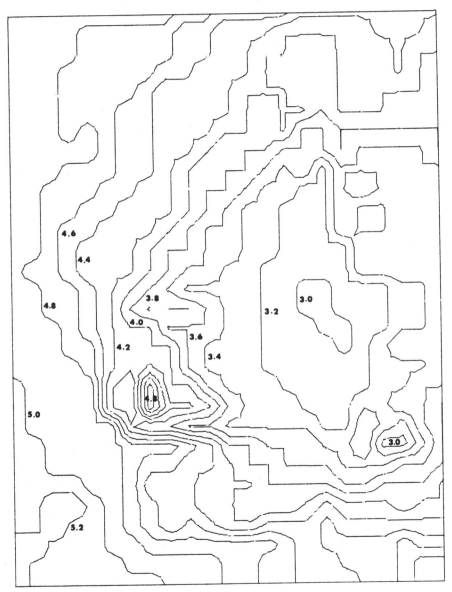

Having implemented a new program in high-priority areas, it is important to monitor differential change. One approach to this informational need would be to plot the reading level scores for the same students a year later, as depicted in Figure 18-8. Change scores between Figures 18-7 and 18-8 substantially less than one indicate little growth in reading between grades four and five, while change scores greater than one indicate that more than a grade level of achievement has been accomplished within the year. Schools or population areas receiving special assistance would be expected to show a differential increase; that is, if starting from a point substantially below the mean, these population areas would move closer to the district mean. This procedure allows for program evaluation in a variety of subject areas on a regular basis. It also provides for curricular program planning on the basis of need in specific subpopulations of the community.

In the example presented in Figures 18-7 and 18-8, a growth of approximately 1.2 grade levels can be seen generally across the attendance areas depicted. Differential growth can, however, be identified in at least three areas of the region. A rather large block of students in Figure 18-7 evidences reading achievement scores at the 3.0 level. Figure 18-8 shows that this "achievement valley" has been substantially reduced in size. Only two small points remain. A similar gain resulted in the target area near the lower right corner. A considerable gain may also be noted in the region of relatively high achievement near the left center of the display. Students in this area changed from a reading level of 4.8 to a level of 6.2. A contour map of the change data could have been plotted directly.

Conclusions

Student-oriented geographic data bases can yield a great quantity of data for the school administrator; but in order for this information to be useful, it must be presented to the educational decision maker in a form that can be readily assimilated. Geocode analysis, as discussed here, is one approach to displaying this information. Grid counts and contour plots, presented on a geographic surface, provide a direct way of relating specific educational information related to student background characteristics or achievement to points on a geographic surface, with the direct result of benefiting educational planning.

Figure 18-8. Reading level grade 5.
Contour interval: 0.2 grade levels

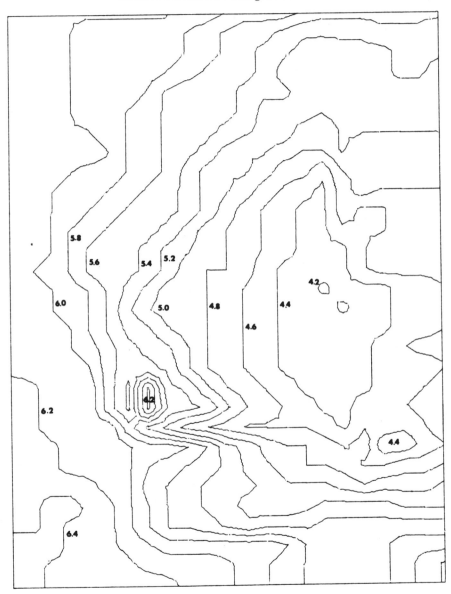

This discussion is not intended to imply that the process of establishing a geocode student file is an easy one, but to suggest that the time, effort, and cost of implementing such a system are justified by the fact that needed information is available in a comprehensible form, more quickly and efficiently, than was previously possible, with the anticipated result that decision making in the district is improved.

References

Costa, C. H. Applications of Geocoding and Mapping. Paper read at Annual Meeting of the American Educational Research Association, 1972, Chicago, Illinois. (ERIC Number ED 064 894)

McIsaac, D. N., Spuck, D. W., and Stofflet, F. P. *A Users Guide to a System of Programs for the Analysis of Geographic Areas.* Madison, Wisconsin: Wisconsin Information Systems for Education, 1972.

Spuck, D. W. Data Base Considerations. Paper read at the Annual Meeting of the American Educational Research Association, 1972, Chicago, Illinois. (ERIC Number ED 064 894)

United States Department of Commerce, Bureau of the Census. *Census Use Study Reports.* Washington, D. C.: U.S. Government Printing Office, 1969-70.

United States Department of Commerce, Bureau of the Census. *Conference Proceedings, November 1970, Wichita, Kansas, on the Use of Address Coding Guides in Geographic Coding—Case Studies.* Washington, D. C.: U.S. Government Printing Office, 1970.

United States Department of Commerce, Bureau of the Census. *Conference Proceedings, April 1-2, 1971, Jacksonville, Florida, on Geographic Base Files—Plans, Progress and Prospects.* Washington, D. C.: U.S. Government Printing Office, 1971.

Van Dusseldorp, R. Linear Programming Possibilities. Paper read at the Annual Meeting of the American Educational Research Association, 1972, Chicago, Illinois. (ERIC Number ED 064 894)

19. URBAN SPATIAL MODELS
Herbert J. Walberg
Mark Bargen

Despite the occasional use of the geographic term "inner city" to characterize the educational situation of the poor, there have been no theoretical or empirical studies of the relationship of location to educational achievement in urban areas. Child and educational psychologists have been concerned with the relations of home and classroom stimulation to achievement; educational sociologists have examined the achievement correlates of socioeconomic and ethnic status; and historians, economists, and other scholars have studied education from their distinctive viewpoints (Walberg, 1972). But none have attempted to analyze and understand educational phenomena in terms of physical space of the city. This is surprising, since the improvement of urban education is one of the most difficult and important challenges facing America, and since geographers have shown that spatial models help to explain variations in such educationally-related variables as family income and migration, crime, delinquency, and physical and mental disease in the city. The purpose of this chapter is to describe a case study of the application of spatial analysis to the educational achievement levels of early grade children in the 389 public elementary schools in Chicago. Though not intended to be comprehensive, the first section reviews some prior theory and findings that suggest the application of the classical concentric, sector, and status models to urban educational achievement.

Some Historical Trends

Until the age of industrialization and the large-scale concentration of population in urban areas, the most desirable residential areas were in the center of the city close to administrative and commercial facilities; the poor lived on the periphery, as they do today in the barrios of the underdeveloped parts of South America, Africa, and Asia. In modern North American cities, however, the affluent, especially those with school-age children, who can afford single family dwellings and commuting have increasingly tended to live farther from the city's center. Though land in the inner city remains more costly than that in outlying areas, the northern poor tend to live in the densely populated fringes of the central business district.

High income families moved from the congestion, noise, and industry of the inner city to newer, more spacious dwellings on the periphery. First streetcars and commuter railroads and later automobiles and thoroughfares enabled breadwinners to commute from pleasant new neighborhoods to central-city occupations. Some homes and apartments near the center were destroyed to make way for factories and businesses, but in many cases they were reoccupied by families of more moderate means, whose own dwellings were inherited by families of still lower incomes. The poorest families closest to the fringe of the central business district were most often immigrants from foreign countries and from rural areas of the United States, especially the South. They lived in subdivided older homes or in hastily constructed apartment buildings.

The magnitude of migration to the northern cities is in some ways unparalleled in human history. The population of Chicago, for example, was 48 percent foriegn-born in 1870 and 36 percent in 1910. Around 1900, large numbers of immigrants came from Ireland, Germany, the United Kingdom, Canada, the Scandinavian countries, Russia, and Italy to the cities of the northeastern and midwestern United States. They were followed by immigrants from Poland, Mexico, and the Carribean. Because of the rapid expansion of industrial employment, especially during wartime, whites and Negroes from the rural south also came in large numbers. Voluntarily or because of discrimination, these immigrant groups found housing close to the central fringe in ethnic areas such as "Little Italy" or "Little Ireland." However, even the largest, most cohesive groups found it difficult to maintain stable ethnic communities in the inner city. They were pushed out by factories, business, and still more recent immigrants; and they or their sons and daughters, as they became educated and enculturated to the mainstream of American society, succeeded in obtaining better housing and amenities away from the old inner districts.

Needless to say, the simultaneous outward and upward social mobility of ethnic groups was not without tension and anguish. Adjacent groups rivaled and feared each other; newcomers felt discrimination; and the displaced felt resentment. The older generation longed for the old country, the farm, or the old neighborhood, and tried to understand how their sons and daughters could marry outside their ethnic group.

The old inner district continued to receive the poorest, most culturally different newcomers, who formed small unstable pockets amid the factories and housing of impoverished, older members of ethnic groups who had not moved out to better locations with their old countrymen and progeny. Often these districts were plagued with social disorganization, population turnover, and residential dispossession. Scholars may have underestimated the strength of the social fabric of some of these districts, particularly the larger, more enduring areas, such as the "Chinatowns" of Chicago and San Francisco, because the purposes and activities of their residents were different from those of the mainstream culture (Gans, 1962; Ward, 1971). However, the population densities and the delinquency, crime, disease, and mortality rates of many of these old inner districts would not seem to lead to high levels of educational achievement. As Wiseman (1964) showed in an ecological study of Manchester, England, district rates of educational retardation are moderately correlated with illegitimacy, infant mortality, and related factors. Poverty, he concluded, is less important in influencing educational achievement than are standards of maternal care and the morale and social organization of the district.

Spatial Models

Although the spatial perspectives mentioned above were developed earlier in this century by insightful, highly inductive urban historians, sociologists, and economists, modern geographers have increasingly attempted to build mathematical and statistical models and to test hypotheses derived from them with large banks of quantified census and field-study data. Three such spatial models have been found to explain a wide variety of social phenomena in cities in various parts of the world. Writings on the development of the models are scattered and voluminous. Only some of the origins, criticism, and synthesis of this work can be mentioned here as it relates to the formulation of the present research.

Stimulated by research on plant ecology, Park, Burgess (1925), and others at the University of Chicago posited a "concentric" model of the city. Population expansion and spatial growth processes were understood as analogous to ecological concepts such as invasion, competition, dominance, and succession. These processes were hypothesized to be ordered by time and distance from the center of the city. The concentric model, however crude and preliminary, provided an explicit explanation of social phenomena in the city that could be put to an empirical test.

Hoyt (1933, 1939), from his studies of land economics beginning in Chicago and later expanding to 142 American cities, derived the "sector" model, an alternative to (or as suggested in the present research, a conditioner of) the concentric model. His studies of land value and the cost of rent showed that the affluent occupied land near radial transportation lines, along water frontage, and on high ground. The costs of housing were not uniformly predictable from the simple distance from the city's center, but depended upon direction. Thus different wedgelike sectors contained housing of relatively homogenous costs.

Firey (1948), in developing the "status" model, rejected the notions that the social ecology of the city resembles a simple polar configuration and that stability and change in land use depend on either radial distance or direction. Firey found that sentiments and prestige determined neighborhood continuity. In Firey's view, districts within cities acquire symbolic or sentimental status among social and ethnic groups, and the prestige or identity of the district outweigh distance and cost in residential choice and retention.

Subsequent research has led to the view that the classic concentric, sector, and status models are useful and complementary working hypotheses in the explanation of spatial variations in socioeconomic factors in the city. Rees (1970, p. 384), from his review of the literature, postulated that:

1. Social rank and economic status indicators vary predominantly by sector of the city.

2. Family size indicators vary principally with distance from the center of the city (concentric).

3. Minority group indicators reveal the tendency for members of such groups to cluster spatially in a few restricted parts of the city.

4. These patterns are independent and additive, in summation, giving rise to the community areas that characterize the city's social geography.

From his analysis of 1960 census data for the Chicago metropolis, that appeared to confirm these postulates in the main, Rees (p. 386) added the following qualifications:

1. The dimensions of social status and family size were independent ("non-colinear") and additive contributors to the variation of residential population groups in the subareas of the metropolis.

2. The principal mode of spatial variation of the social status dimension was sectoral, and that of family size, concentric, but concentric variation was almost as important as sectoral in the case of social status, and sectoral variation was a minor but significant contributor to the spatial variation of family size.

3. A series of independent minority-group dimensions emerged from the analysis, but the most important, that distinguishing the Negro population, was undoubtedly associated with the set of socioeconomic status indicators in a way that clearly revealed the pattern of discrimination along racial lines.

Educational Perspectives

Rees' synthesis of three classic models and his identification of social class, family size, and percent Negro as salient factors in Chicago's social space serve as useful benchmarks for the present research since the three factors predict standard measures of educational ability and achievement. A number of psychological studies of individuals in North America and Europe have shown that social class (as indexed by parental occupation, income, or education) correlates about .4 with standard verbal intelligence measures, and that family size, or more accurately, "sibsize," the number of siblings, correlates about −.3 with these measures.

A recent formulation of these relations shows that class and sibsize interact, and that the inverse of the sibsize provides a better prediction of ability than the simple linear form (Marjoribanks, Walberg, and Bargen, in press). It was reasoned that since children share adult resources of intellectual stimulation in the home, the mathematical relationship between sibsize and parental stimulation is not linear but is of a hyperbolic form involving the term, "one divided by the number of children in the family." That is, the amount of parental attention received by each child decreases as the number of children in the family increases, in such a way that with each additional child the successive decrements in shared attention become smaller. Therefore, the expected percentages of parental attention given children in one-, two-, three-, four-, and five-child families would be 100, 50, 33, 25, and 20 respectively. Thus a single child in a family may score higher on mental ability tests because he receives all available parental stimulation, whereas a child with four siblings may have lower ability scores because he receives an estimated one-fifth of the available stimulation. Moreover, first borns may tend to be brighter either because some of them are single children and receive all available parental attention, or because they receive 100 percent of parental stimulation until the second child is born, whereas later born children usually have to share parental attention.

The apparent impairment effect of sibsize, however, is strongly conditioned by father's occupation: in an Ontario sample of 180 eleven year old boys there was no effect of sibsize from professional-managerial homes but an estimated difference of 40 IQ points between single borns and those from seven-child families with fathers in unskilled occupations (Marjoribanks, Walberg, and Bargen, in press). Social class and family-size impairments in ability and achievement may also be confounded with rural origins and recency of inmigration to inner urban areas. Urbanization was accompanied by declines in family size in Western nations, but many of the urban poor and uneducated are not yet controlling their fertility (United Nations, 1953; Hauser, 1965). Heber (1968), for example, found that one third of the children in classes for the retarded (IQ below 75) came from a part of the Milwaukee area containing only 5 percent of the city population. A sample of mothers from this neighborhood had an average of eight children, and mothers with IQs below 80 accounted for more than 80 percent of the total number of children in the neighborhood sample with IQs below 80. Since Rees found concentric and sectoral patterns of social class and concentric patterns of family size, the level of educational achievement might be hypothesized to exhibit both forms of spatial variation and also, from the reasoning above, an interaction of these forms.

In addition to social class and family size, Rees found that the Negro population percentage in census tracts, along with related variables, constitutes a prominent factor in the analysis of Chicago's social space. This variable, too, has been found to be related to educational achievement measures. For example, the Kerner Commission (1968) reported that Negro students in elementary school in the metropolitan northeast scored an average 1.6 grades below the national norm in reading; by the twelfth grade they scored an average 3.3 grades below. In Harlem, Clark (1965) found 30 percent of the third-grade pupils below grade level in reading, and 77 percent below in sixth grade. Coleman and others (1966) showed that Negro students in the urban north and west are more than three times as likely to drop out of school by age seventeen as are whites. A number of explanations have been put forth to explain these gaps: biased tests, segregation, social discrimination, inexperienced teachers, home environment, family size, inadequate nutrition and health care, heredity, and the confounding of race with social class and recency of migration to the city (Walberg, 1972).

Social class and recency of migration are particularly important in understanding the relation of urban social space to the educational achievement of Negro children. Negroes are by no means homogenous with respect to either of these variables. As Tauber (1972) noted, the first large influx of Negroes from the south was in the period 1919 to 1925. Since successive large waves of Negro inmigrants were mostly of rural origins and of lower socioeconomic status than were resident Negro and white populations, they encountered discrimination and were segregated. As Tauber further noted, the new migrants were often educationally inferior to resident Negroes and were unaccustomed to Northern urban living standards and conduct. Some burdened the schools, police, and welfare agencies; but many sacrificed a great deal for their children, who were upwardly mobile in education, occupation, and income. In Chicago, the new Negro in-migrants, like other ethnic groups before them, found housing near the fringes of the central business district. Unlike other groups, however, they were confined to the west and south sectors of almost exclusively Negro population.

Recent evidence shows a high degree of segregation of Negroes in Chicago and expansion of the Negro areas along their perimeters, rather than random dispersal to white areas (see Figure 12-3, p. 233). Clearly, then, the percentage Negro in the population of a school, though treated here as the indicator variable of the status model, overlaps both the concentric and sector models.

Statistical Models

Though Rees' quantified test of the three classic spatial models is an advance over impressionistic judgments made by earlier workers, his use of analysis of variance, following Anderson and Egeland (1961) does not provide as objective and precise a test as that afforded by regression analysis. For example, Rees divided the Chicago metropolis into six rings and five sectors to yield thirty areas or, in analysis of variance terminology, "cells." The selection of the number of rings and sectors, the angles to form the sectors, and the distances to form the rings is subjective. Some choices could prevent the analysis from detecting significant variation or could favor one model over another. Moreover, the census tracts grouped within the large areas are more heterogeneous than the tracts themselves.

Regression analysis, on the other hand, requires no grouping; it makes full use of the original precision of both the social data (at the tract level or point of observation) and the location coordinates (for example latitude and longitude or angle and distance from the center point). Polynomial functions and products of the coordinates as independent variables can be used to assess nonlinearity and interaction of the models. Regression also provides estimates of variance accounted for by the set or subsets of the independent variables. For example, it was noted earlier that Negroes are distributed in sectors in Chicago (Figure 12-3); regression can be used to determine if the percent Negro in the school can explain variance in school achievement beyond that accounted for by the sector model. Finally, in addition to mapping the fitted models, regression-residual (observed minus predicted values) maps may be computer-drawn to reveal discrepancies and suggest additional variables to account for spatial variation in social phenomena.

Four cautions should be noted regarding the hypothesis formulation above and the statistical analysis of school data presented below. First, school populations are the units. Although the preceding discussion mentions the same relations of social class, family size, and ethnicity to individual measures of IQ and educational achievement, the present analysis deals ecologically with school means on these variables, and the relations would not necessarily be found in aggregate data (Goodman, 1961); indeed, the analysis tests the generality of the propositions to the ecological level using locational variables as proxies for hypothesized social causes. Second, the data are subject to spatial autocorrelation (Berry, 1971); that is, schools closer together are more likely to have more similar mean achievements than are those located at a greater distance from one another. Since inferential statistics assumes independence of units of observation, the analysis is to be regarded as suggestive rather than definitive, and no generalization to other cities or times is warranted. Third, although locational coordinates are used as "independent" variables and may be causally suggestive, they should not be understood as basic "causal" variables. Educational achievement is correctly conceived as a function of psychological factors in the environment and other factors inherent in the individual. To find that educational achievement is systematically distributed in the space of the city does not mean, of course, that it is caused by location. Fourth, many children in Chicago attend private and parochial schools; since these schools are generally selective, systematic bias is introduced that is unaccounted for in the analysis.

Method

School-by-school data were obtained for the 1969-70 academic year on all 389 regular Chicago public elementary schools offering instruction at the first and fourth grade levels. These data included percent of entering first-grade students judged ready for school on the Metropolitan Reading Readiness Test, the median percentile rank of fourth-grade students on the reading subtest of the Metropolitan Achievement Test (Elementary Battery), and the percent Negro students in each school. The fourth-grade median percentile was converted to an equal-interval normal distribution, and that part of the score predictable (by linear regression) from the percent ready for school was subtracted, yielding a residual representing the school's cross-sectional gain between first and fourth grade. In addition to achievement scores, the data for analysis included for each school the distribution of faculty by years of teaching experience. From this distribution the mean years teaching experience for the staff of each school was computed.

The three models described above (concentric, sector, and status) were fitted to the three obtained criteria (first grade achievement, achievement gains, and teacher experience) using ordered stepwise multiple regression. The Negro enrollment in the school (as a percent of the total enrollment) was used to represent the status model. To fit the concentric and sector models to the criteria, the city was viewed as laid out on polar coordinates (rather than the rectangular coordinate system reflected by street numbers). Two coordinates were obtained for each school: its distance from the center of the city (r in polar coordinates), where the intersection of State Street and Madison Avenue was identified as the center; and its direction from the center of the city (θ, the angle from a due west baseline), measured in radians. Thus, a school located four and a half miles northwest of the center of the city received 4.5 as the value of r and .85 radians (45 degrees) as the value of θ.

Three variables were used to represent the concentric model: the linear, quadratic, and cubic forms of r. The sector model was represented by four variables: the linear, quadratic, cubic, and quartic forms of θ, relating only to the direction of the school from the center of the city. Six additional variables were used to assess the interaction of the concentric and sector models, that is, variation in the r gradient associated with θ. These six product terms were: $r\theta$, $r\theta^2$, $r\theta^3$, $r^2\theta$, $r^2\theta^2$, and $r^3\theta$. Although a very slightly better regression fit was obtained with the addition of further polynomial and product terms, the higher terms were found to be nearly linear combinations of the basic terms within the precision of the data and the computer program used. Therefore, they are redundant and unparsimonious and are not discussed further here.

Finally, computer-drawn maps of the observed, regression-fitted, and residual values (Figures 19-1, 19-2, and 19-3) were prepared, with values at points between schools estimated by tringulation from neighboring schools.

Results of the Analysis

The fact that there are three dependent (educational) and fourteen independent (spatial) variables for analysis means that there is a risk of exploiting chance in the forty-two intercorrelations between the sets. It is therefore appropriate to perform a multivariate test, canonical correlation, before examining the individual regression for each dependent variable. This test reveals three canonical correlations (.87, .37, and .32) each significant beyond the .001 level, which implies that the spatial patterns of the educational variables differ, so that each must be examined separately.

The regression statistics are shown in Table 19-1. The first entry of each set of terms in Table 19-1 shows how much variance each set explains by itself; the last entry reveals how much unique variance is explained by each set independent of the other sets. If the sets of terms accounted for completely separate variation in the criteria, first and last entries would account for the same amount of variance; since they do not, the terms are colinear variables. Moreover, the contribution of products of the concentric and sector terms is substantial; this means their effects are not simply additive and that the relation of distance from the center of the city and the educational measures depends upon the angle of the transect (Figures 19-1, 19-2, and 19-3). Thus, contrary to the implications of earlier work cited above that employed analysis of variance, the regression analysis shows definite colinearity and interaction with regard to the educational variables represented here.

Table 19-1 further shows that 66 percent of the variance in first grade reading readiness and the teaching experience of the school staff is accounted for by the four sets of terms. The concentric terms account for the most variance in these variables, followed by the status term, the interaction terms, and the sector model. There is a small difference in the variance distributions for the two variables, which is the reason that there are three canonical correlations: teacher experience in contrast to readiness is less closely associated with concentricity and more closely associated with the percentage of non-Negroes in the school. On the first-to-fourth-grade reading cross-sectional gains, only 17 percent of the variance is explained by all the terms, and the gains exhibit nonsignificant concentricity, but are conditioned most powerfully by the interaction terms, the status model, and the sector model in that order.

The variance accounted for in the gains is relatively small because the covariance common to the spatial terms and readiness has been subtracted, in effect, from the fourth-grade reading achievement scores in calculating the residual gains. Psychological research on individual development also suggests that the gains would be less predictable. Six years elapse between birth and the time of school entry, and the child has been in school for only four years by fourth grade. Moreover, the early childhood years are generally most important for mental development; about half the variance in adult intelligence is predictable by the age of four (Bloom, 1964). The home environment exerts a continuing force in older children, especially on verbal ability (Walberg and Marjoribanks, 1974).

Turning to the maps, it may be noted that the regression-fitted map in Figure 19-1B provides a reasonably good visual approximation of the original observed values plotted in Figure 19-1A. To be sure, some areas are poorly fitted by the spatial models; these are represented in Figure 19-1C. For example, two areas near the southern shoreline of Lake Michigan can be identified as having greater fractions of first-grade children ready for reading then predicted by the regression equation. One is Hyde Park, the location of the University of Chicago, and the other is part of South Shore. Many more well-educated, middle class Negroes and whites live in these neighborhoods than in surrounding areas. Hyde Park schools, however, have relatively high gains, while South Shore schools do not. Also, patches of schools on the north and northwest peripheries of the city, near affluent northern suburbs, have high gains. Another area of interest is South Chicago, also on the shoreline south of Hyde Park and South Shore. Brian Berry's unpublished maps show this area to have high concentrations of Spanish-surnamed students. Figures 19-1C and 19-3C show that schools in this area do poorly on reading readiness but well on reading gains. There are other discrepant areas of the maps, and the authors are now using 1970 census data to investigate their socioeconomic, ethnic, and housing characteristics. It is apparent that the three classic models can be improved upon, especially by adding more terms to the status model. More exquisite regression-fitting of achievement levels and gains can be expected. What interest educators, however, are the characteristics that distinguish the schools that produce larger gains that might be expected from their location, status, and other external factors. As explained in previous chapters, the three teams working with us have made field visits to these and other schools, observed the behavior of the students, interviewed the staff, and administered questionnaires. In our Age of Aquarius and unrest, these schools were found to be more business-

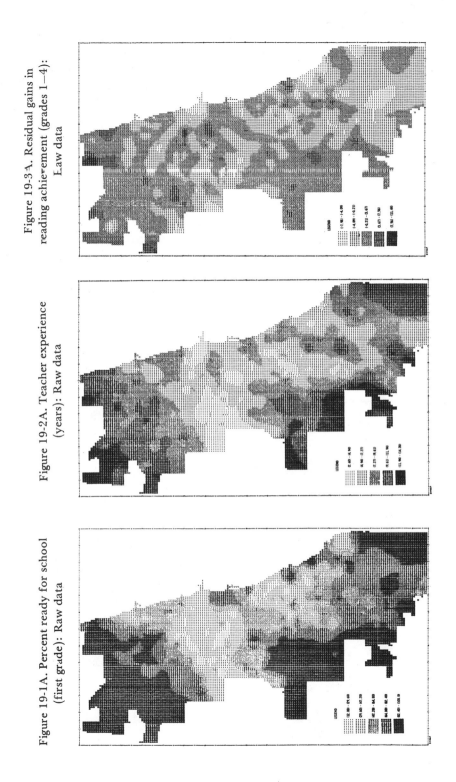

Figure 19-3A. Residual gains in reading achievement (grades 1–4): Raw data

Figure 19-2A. Teacher experience (years): Raw data

Figure 19-1A. Percent ready for school (first grade): Raw data

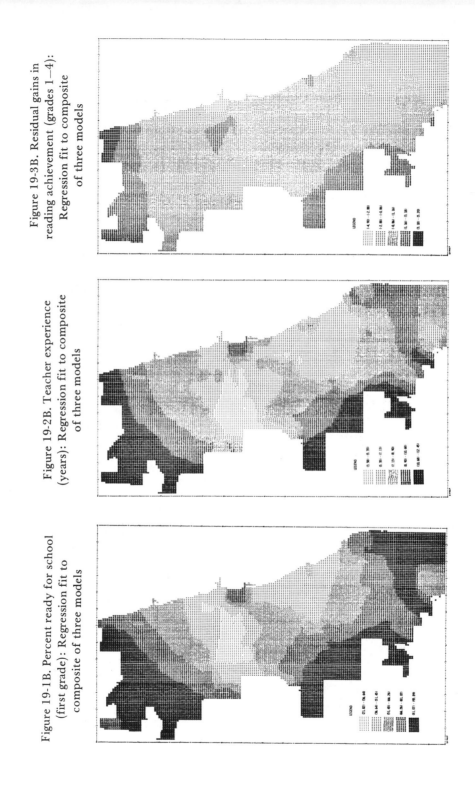

Figure 19-1B. Percent ready for school (first grade): Regression fit to composite of three models

Figure 19-2B. Teacher experience (years): Regression fit to composite of three models

Figure 19-3B. Residual gains in reading achievement (grades 1–4): Regression fit to composite of three models

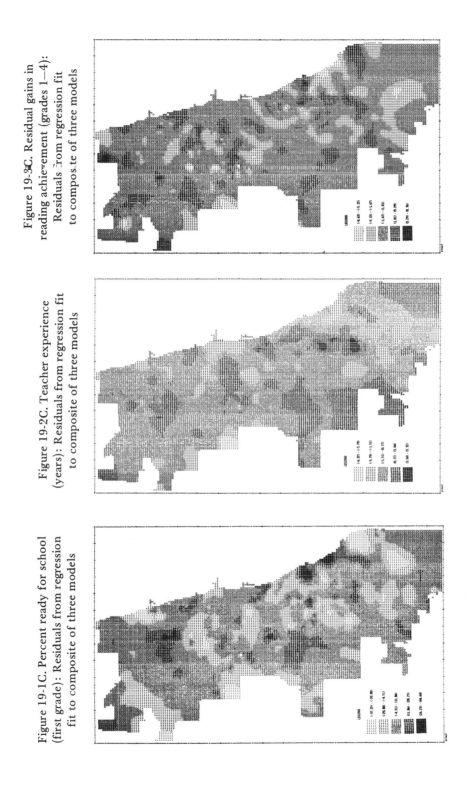

Figure 19-3C. Residual gains in reading achievement (grades 1–4): Residuals from regression fit to composite of three models

Figure 19-2C. Teacher experience (years): Residuals from regression fit to composite of three models

Figure 19-1C. Percent ready for school (first grade): Residuals from regression fit to composite of three models

Table 19-1. Variance explained by four sets of independent variables
when entered first and last in regressions

Criterion	Concentric First/Last	Sector First/Last	Interaction First/Last	Status (% Negro) First/Last	R^2
First Grade Reading Achievement	38.96***/16.32***	9.97***/1.42**	27.37***/3.90***	26.62***/9.78***	66.50***
Teacher Experience	31.62***/13.24***	12.58***/0.83	23.85***/6.80***	29.05***/16.08***	66.18***
First-to-Fourth-Grade Reading Gains	0.58/1.21	5.33***/4.31***	9.14***/7.96***	7.69***/4.30***	17.02***

Note—Increments in variance accounted for significant at the .05, .01, and .001 levels are indicated, respectively, by 1, 2, and 3 asterisks.

like and better organized than ineffective schools. The principals were in command but sought and gained advice and resources from parents. The teachers demanded much of their students and had their respect; their lessons were organized and prepared, and they participated more fully than teachers in other schools in overall curriculum and program planning. If these and the other findings are replicated, they may be taken as suggestions worth trying at other schools.

References

Anderson, T., and Egeland, J. A. "Spatial Aspects on Social Area Analysis." *American Sociological Review* 26 (1961): 392-98.

Berry, B. J. "Problems of Data Organization and Analytical Methods in Geography." *Journal of the American Statistical Association* 66 (1971): 510-23.

Burgess, E. W. "The Growth of the City: An Introduction to a Research Project." In *The City* edited by R. S. Park, E. W. Burgess, and R. D. McKenzie. Chicago: University of Chicago Press, 1925, 47-62.

Bloom, B. S. *Stability and Change in Human Characteristics.* New York: John Wiley, 1964.

Clark, K. B. *Dark Ghetto.* New York: Harper & Row, 1965.

Coleman, J. S. et al. *Equality of Educational Opportunity.* Washington, D.C.: U.S. Office of Education, 1966.

Firey, W. L. *Land Use in Central Boston.* Cambridge, Mass.: Harvard University Press, 1948.

Gans, H. J. *The Urban Villagers.* New York: Viking, 1962.

Goodman, L. "Some Alternatives to Ecological Correlation." *American Journal of Sociology* 64 (1961): 610-25.

Hauser, P. M. "Urbanization: An Overview." In *The Study of Urbanization,* edited by P. Hauser and L. Schnore. New York: Wiley, 1965, 1-48.

Heber, R. *Rehabilitation of Families at Risk for Mental Retardation.* Madison, Wisc.: University of Wisconsin Regional Rehabilitation Center, 1968.

Hoyt, H. *One Hundred Years of Land Values in Chicago.* Chicago: University of Chicago Press, 1933.

Hoyt, H. *The Structure and Growth of Residential Neighborhoods in American Cities.* Washington, D.C.: U.S. Government Printing Office, 1939.

Kerner, O. et al. *Report of the National Advisory Committee on Civil Disorders.* New York: Dutton, 1968.

Marjoribanks, K., Walberg, H. J., and Bargen, M. "Mental Abilities: Family Constellation and Social Class Correlates." *British Journal of Social and Clinical Psychology,* in press.

Rees, P. H. "Concepts of Social Space: Toward an Urban Social Geography." In *Geographic Perspectives on Urban Systems,* edited by B. Berry and F. Horton. Englewood Cliffs, N.J.: Prentice-Hall, 1970, 306-94.

Tauber, K. E. "Demographic Context of Metropolitan Education." In *Human Intelligence,* edited by J. Hunt. New Brunswick, N.J.: Transaction Books, 1972, 77-97.

United Nations. *Determinants and Consequences of Population Trends.* New York: United Nations, 1953, 78.

Walberg, H. J., and Kopan, A. T., eds. *Rethinking Urban Education.* San Francisco: Jossey-Bass, 1972.

Walberg, H. J. and Marjoribanks, K. "Home Environment and Differential Mental Abilities." *Developmental Psychology,* in press.

Ward, D. *Cities and Immigrants.* London: Oxford University Press, 1971.

White, W. F. *Street Corner Society.* Chicago: University of Chicago Press, 1943.

Wiseman, S. *Education and Environment.* Manchester, England: Manchester University Press, 1964.

20. OPTIMIZATION RECONSIDERED
Herbert J. Walberg

A psychologist's reading of contemporary demographic research leads to the belief that trends in population size, education, and their interaction are exceedingly difficult to analyze and forecast. While the number of students and the number of years they attend school has greatly increased during this century (Nam and Folger, 1964), estimation of future trends is best left to demographers. Perhaps psychology can contribute some research and reflections on population quality, and particularly on growing student diversity and its challenge to education at all levels. What is presented here is the viewpoint of one psychologist.

In the last decade, behavioral geneticists have been making increasingly accurate estimates of the roles of heredity, environment, and their interaction in the determination of measured intelligence and other human traits. Nevertheless, it has been difficult for many psychologists, social scientists, and educators to consider the importance of genetics, first because environmental interventionism is their basic professional posture, and second because of the curious history of the nature-nurture controversy.

In the nineteenth century and the first few decades of this century, the influence of religious predestinationism, "instinct" and "faculty" psychology, theories of predetermined stages of human development, explanations of the social order according to evolutionary theory (many were misled into wild speculations by the subtitle of Darwin's famous book, *The Preservation of Favoured Races in the Struggle for Life*), and other ideologies probably led psychologists to overestimate the importance of native endowment in the determination of intelligence and other traits. Such ideologies would have been discredited had they been subjected for a century to the critical scientific scrutiny that has benefited the modern physical sciences. Unfortunately, invidious social comparisons were incautiously derived from them and translated into social policies such as Nazism in Germany and ethnic immigration quotas in England and the United States. Around 1925 in the United States, however, environmentalism, sometimes radical and naive, began its ascendency, partially in revulsion to nativist doctrines. The case was stated audaciously by John B. Watson, who claimed he could train any healthy infant to be a doctor or a thief regardless of his heredity. The sentence following this famous contention—"I am going beyond my facts and I admit it, but so have advocates of the contrary and they have been doing it for many thousands of years." (Watson, 1930, p. 104)—which is seldom quoted, reveals that he was reacting to nativist extremists. Psychologists, after Watson's claim, began positing an "empty organism" whose behavior could be controlled by environmental stimuli; anthropologists explained human diversity in terms of the relative cultural context; and sociologists saw social class and other environmental variables as the main determinants of behavior. In "The Illusion of Personal Individuality," the psychiatrist Harry Stack Sullivan (1950) blended Freud's psychoanalysis with John Dewey's environmentalism, denied individualism as such, and argued that social life is merely a collection of role relationships with others. During the 1960s, environmentalism was translated into social policy: programs were carried out to end the educational disabilities of poor children; bussing was employed to eliminate racial tensions among adolescents; teaching machines were bought to increase learning; and sensitivity training was used to promote self-understanding. Some of these programs apparently failed: the $50 billion spent on school construction during that decade has not transformed educational services; some welfare programs, while rising enormously in cost, may have contributed to the creation of an alienated subculture of broken familites and poverty; and a walk through "model cities" areas often reveals boarded-up abandoned buildings and carries the risk of a mugging. Some of the programs, however, were undoubtedly successful, and the great tragedy is that psychologists and others did not thoroughly evaluate them.

Psychologists are now reexamining the role of heredity and environment in educational and psychological development and in society generally. They will have much to learn from behavioral geneticists. Already it is well established that heredity is a causal agent in many ocular, muscular, neurological, skeletal, blood, and behavioral abnormalties and learning disabilities (Scheinfeld, 1965). A striking example is Huntington's chorea, a disease dramatized in Eugene O'Neill's stage play, *Strange Interlude.*

Other diseases of great concern are inherited polygenetically in a complex fashion that is not well understood. Osborn (1968, p. 54), has estimated that, of the 3 percent of all United States children who die before maturity, more than half die from some genetic defect or anomaly. He also argues that heredity is very likely implicated in schizophrenia, the most common psychosis, which affects about 1 percent of the population. The estimated coincidence of the disease is 14 percent in fraternal twins, 56 percent for identicals reared apart, and 91 percent for identicals reared together (Kallman, 1953, pp. 124-29). Also remarkable are the ways in which human genetic pools change through the centuries of civilization and history by relaxation of natural selection. Human traits that are easily detected, and determined through relatively simple genetic mechanisms, are the best understood. A notable case is color blindness, which is caused by a defect in one or another genetic locus on the X chromosome. In primitive areas where natural selection on this trait has continued to operate until recently, the estimated rate per 1000 in the population is exceedingly low, about .5 percent in Fiji Islanders and 2 percent in Australian aborigines; in modern societies, the rates are several times higher, about 6 percent in Chinese and Japanese samples and as high as 10 percent in European stocks. Unfortunately, far less is known about selection for intelligence and other behavior traits that are transmitted polygenetically and are factorially complex and environmentally confounded in their manifestations. However, to illustrate how genetic explanations can serve as interesting rivals to environmentalistic explanations of individual and cultural development, the little-known work of Weyl and Possony (1963) of Stanford's Hoover Institute can be cited.

Historians and sociologists have made much of Max Weber's

(1930) famous environmental attribution of the Protestant work ethic to the origin and more rapid rise of capitalism and modern economic organization in Northern than in Southern Europe. Weyl and Possony note, however, that Catholicism came far later in Northern Europe, generally was less powerful there, and lost its primacy early in the Reformation; further, that the brightest, most able Catholic boys tended to enter the priesthood and remain celibate, thereby depleting the gene pool of ability that would have led to rapid modernization in Southern Europe. (It could be argued, of course, that priests did not remain celibate, that they were not the more able, or that the prestige of the boy's attainment of the priesthood led his parents to have more children.) Weyl and Possony also attribute the numerous intellectual achievements of Jews, Chinese, and Japanese in the United States relative to their percentages of the population to the prolonged fertility of the religious and intellectual leaders of these groups through the centuries rather than to exposure to distinctive cultural environments during childhood. The point of this example is not to argue the plausibility of the hereditarian explanation—it cannot be scientifically verified—but to illustrate how genetic speculations are novel and foreign to our thinking about social phenomena, while environmental explanations are often taken for granted.

On the other hand, it is possible to illustrate scientific progress in genetic research on intelligence by examining the history of a controversy that has only recently been settled. Environmental psychology never developed as fully or as influentially in England as it did in this country; hereditarian explanations of intelligence were more often espoused.

In the 1920s, English psychologists noted that the number of children in a family is negatively correlated (about −.30) with the average measured intelligence of the children in the family; that is, children from large families tend to score lower on IQ tests. Early studies suggested that parents with lower IQs tend to marry earlier, bear children more rapidly, and continue having them to a later age. The English believed that the national level of measured intelligence was declining 2 points per generation because of genetic selection. Several very large surveys were carried out to test this hypothesis (Royal Commission on Population, 1950). Samples of children in stable population districts of England and in all of Scotland were obtained at two time points more than ten years apart (Cattell, 1950; Emmett, 1950; Scottish Council, 1949; Burt, 1946). The original investigators were astonished to find that the IQ level had remained stable, or increased slightly, but an environmental explanation was soon put forth to defend the hereditarian doctrine: namely, that while the genetic pool was deteriorating, education was improving, and together the two opposing effects maintained the stability of measured IQ or perhaps raised it slightly. In the United States, better and more years of schooling for greater portions of the population appear to have increased IQ during this century: the mean IQ of draftees rose about one standard deviation, or 15 points, between World War I and World War II (Tuddenham, 1948), while the estimated mean rose another half of a standard deviation, or 7 points, between World War II and 1963 (Tupes and Shaycroft, 1964). More than a decade after the new British interpretation, however, American researchers showed that differential fertility may not be eroding gene pools for intelligence.

Correlations between mean sibling IQ and the number of siblings in a family are misleading in the study of genetic change because they fail to account for the noncontribution of barren adults to gene pools (Cole, 1954). Obtaining a record of the IQs of a sample of adults and ascertaining the fertility rates at various levels of IQ can cause completely spurious results (Anastasi, 1956), unless adults both with and without children are included in the original sample. Two research groups recognized this error and avoided it at nearly the same time: Higgens, Reed, and Reed (1962) sampled children and grandchildren of nonepileptic patients in a Minnesota psychiatric hospital; and Bajema (1963) studied the offspring of former public school children in Kalamazoo, Michigan. Both studies agree that adults at the highest level of intelligence (above 130) have the highest average fertility rates, about three offspring, and that feebleminded adults (IQ 55 and below) have very low fertility, perhaps because they are in institutions or do not find mates. These studies suggest that for the populations surveyed, average IQ, insofar as it is genetically determined, has recently been at least stable and probably rising.

Another interesting though unanticipated finding in both the Minnesota and Michigan studies was bi-modal (double peaked) fertility rates across the range of IQ levels. In the larger study of 1,966 individuals (Higgens, Reed, and Reed, 1962), for example, the group with IQs from 56 to 85 had reproductive rates of 2.42; the group from 86 to 115, 2.21; the group above 116, 2.60. Bajema (1966) found bi-modal fertility with respect to the number of years of school completed. The bi-modality of these fertility rates is not sufficient to produce bi-modal IQ distributions in the offspring generation; nevertheless, it is likely to increase the standard deviation (SD); that is, to spread the scores further from the mean, and to make the distribution platykurtic, or flatter than the normal curve. Assortative mating, the tendency for like to mate with like, also increases these tendencies; Warren (1966) found correlation of spouses' years of education to be about .60, and correlation of their socioeconomic statuses (as indexed by father's occupation) to be about .30. Since both these variables are correlated with IQ, assortative mating could also be increasing IQ variation from parent to offspring generations. One study was found that reports IQ SDs for parents and their offspring (Higgens, Reed, and Reed, 1962). My analysis reveals a significant (p less than .05) increase from 14.89 to 15.71; unfortunately, this study concerned a special population, children and grandchildren of mental patients. The three studies that sampled cohorts (not necessarily related) in the same districts at two time points, and reported SDs, were conducted in Britain. The Scottish Council for Research in Education and Population Investigation Committee (1949) found a significant increase from 15.48 to 16.10 in the SD of IQ from 1932 to 1947 in a nearly complete sample of population cohorts in Scotland; Emmet (1950) found a slightly higher increase from 14.21 to 15.00 in a large sample of English districts during the same period. However, in a study of only a few districts in England, using a nonverbal intelligence test, Cattell (1950) found a significant decrease from 1936 to 1949. (Cattell's discrepant finding may be attributable to his less adequate sampling.) At any rate, since it is well established in genetic theory and research that assortative mating and bi-modal fertility produce greater variation in offspring; since these mechanisms operate with respect to IQ, years of education, and social class; and since all three studies of changes in verbal IQ reveal increasing SDs; it appears that, insofar as it is genetically determined, IQ variation is now probably increasing. The following analysis of census data suggests the same conclusion.

Osborn (1968) noted that birth control spread first in the early years of this century among the educated and well-to-do in the United States, which accounts for the negative correlations of family size with measured IQ and educational levels first noted during the 1930s. The widest educational differentials in birth rates occured during the depression years: Osborn's analysis of 1960 census data revealed that for married white mothers born in 1901 through 1905 whose child bearing years were during the depression, offspring per 1,000 mothers were 3,422 for those with less than eight years of education and 1,434 for those with four years of college. However, his data for later years reveal that the differential has subsided because birth control is better understood, more available, and used at all educational levels. Moreover, the recent Bajema (1963) and Higgens, Reed, and Reed (1962) studies mentioned earlier suggest that the differential has reversed, that parents at the highest IQ levels are now having more children than parents with lower IQs. However, birth control is probably not freely available to the less well educated; when married couples were asked whether at least one parent had not wanted their last pregnancy, 33 percent of the couples who had both gone only to elementary school replied affirmatively, as against only 7 percent of college couples (Freedman, Whelpton, and Campbell, 1959). Thus bi-model fertility with respect to IQ and education might be related to a propensity for higher-status groups to want and have more children, for middle groups to neither want nor to have more, and for lower groups to have but not want more children. For adults at the lowest levels of IQ and education, with either genetically- or environmentally-caused mental deficiencies, contraception may be still more difficult to obtain (Osborn, 1968). As Heber (1968) showed, the problems of these individuals are magnified when they are concentrated in a small part of the city. One third of the children in classes for the retarded (IQ below 75) came from a part of the city containing only 5 percent of the city population. A sample of mothers from this neighborhood had an average of eight children, and mothers with IQs below 80 accounted for more than 80 percent of the total number of children in the neighborhood sample with IQs below 80. They might be provided with the same opportunity for birth control that is now freely available to brighter, more affluent parents; they do not generally want more pregnancies and use contraception if given the chance (Osborn, 1968).

Increasing variation in intelligence and other human traits

resulting from bi-modal fertility and assortative mating may be viewed with optimism. A free society does not resignedly accept but celebrates individuality and diversity. In addition, from a biological perspective, genetic diversity can be exceedingly valuable. For example, major agricultural crops, bred to optimize yield per acre during this century, are genetically more uniform, so that a leaf blight wiped out a sizable fraction of the national corn crop in 1971 because a variety of uniformly vulnerable corn was planted by nearly every farmer (National Academy of Sciences, 1972). Analogous mechanisms, although polygenetically complex and little understood, may operate on psychological traits, and it could be dangerous, by genetic or environmental means, to maximize one trait such as verbal intelligence on a mass scale while unknowingly risking the deterioration of others. Aside from the caution suggested by biological analogy, it seems obvious that variety of degrees, types, and combinations of abilities and temperaments in individuals makes for different types of creativity. Society will benefit from their diverse endowments if they are environmentally evoked.

Before turning to environment and education, two unfortunate exaggerations and cases of apparent negligence suggested above should be corrected. First, genetic explanations have been featured not because they are more important for education but because, as noted at the outset, they have been neglected by psychologists and educators for the last few decades. Second, measured intelligence has been emphasized not because it is always more important than other traits but because more is known about its development; it will be argued that this approach has been counterproductively overemphasized in centering educational attention on the narrow verbal abilities it taps. Third, no mention of IQ heritabilities is made; while calculations show that estimated heritability coefficients range from .50 to .93 in sixteen twin studies carried out in England, Finland, France, Germany, Sweden, and United States (Vandenberg, 1971, p. 197), they only indicate how the relative weight of heredity and environment vary in determining IQ in various populations at a certain time, but reveal little about possible changing or changeable causal mechanisms of interest here. Fourth, work on racial and ethnic differences in IQ is not discussed because it is reviewed elsewhere (Scarr-Salapabek, 1971 a,b), because its scientific and social value is dubious (Osborn, 1968; Bloom, 1964; Science, 1972), and because, for educators, differences among individuals are far more important than differences between groups. Fifth, sperm banks, fertilized-egg implantation, cloning, and other methods for controlling heredity (Scheinfeld, 1965) are not discussed because they do not directly concern education at this time, although in the future they may offer a means of promoting learning far more potent and morally challenging than genetic and environmental trends occurring so far in this century.

Consider some recent work on home and community environments as they relate to education. It has long been recognized that socioeconomic status (SES) as indexed by parental income, occupation, or education predicts the child's intelligence. Recent studies of specific aspects of the home learning environment suggest that comprehensive assessments afford a far better prediction. For example, in English homes, the nature of maternal discipline, even though correlationally controlled for SES, predicts IQ; children in demanding homes where rewards depend on achievements tend to score highest (Kent and Davis, 1957). Wolf (1964) and Marjoribanks (1972) showed in Chicago and Toronto that still more accurate predictions of IQ (R's about .80) can be obtained from ratings of the achievement, activeness, intellectual, independence, and language-stimulation in the home obtained from interview with parents; these ratings also predict school achievement, self-esteem, and the need to achieve (Dave, 1963, Weiss, 1969). Moreover, environments other than the family may have beneficial effects on IQ; survey research revealed that the mean IQs of mid-Eastern and European Jews raised in Israeli homes are respectively 86 and 105, while the IQ of both groups when reared in Kibbutzim child centers for four or more years is 115 (Bloom, 1964). Wiseman (1964), working in Manchester, England, found neighborhood rates of educational retardation moderately correlated with illegitimacy, infant mortality, death rates, and other factors, and concluded that poverty is far less important in influencing achievement than low standards of maternal care and the morale and social organization of the neighborhood. Serious delinquency in Chicago is linked to lack of books and stimulation in the home, parental lack of interest in and contact with the adolescent, his or her low educational aspirations and self-esteem, and related attitudinal and environmental factors (Walberg, 1972). None of these correlational studies, of course, assesses genetic factors that may partially determine the environment the parents create in the home in response to the child, or the child's inherited abilities and temperament that influence the way he perceives and shapes his own environment. On the other hand, it is difficult to make a case for any other factors aside from home and community that account for the sizable fraction of IQ variance that is uninherited. It has recently been claimed that highly stimulating environments can raise IQ substantially. Heber (1968), working in a Milwaukee slum with children whose mothers' IQs were below 70, provided intensive tutoring for several hours each day beginning shortly after birth. It was reported in a review by Scarr-Salapatek (1971a) that after four years the mean IQ of the children was 127, or 37 points higher than the mean of an untreated control group. Rynder's similar program for children with Down's syndrome, a genetic mental deficiency, showed a 17 point difference between treated and control group means (85 versus 68; unpublished work described by Scarr-Salapatek, 1971b). Page (1972), however, obtained Heber's reports on his work and has argued that the claims made are unsubstantiated by his research, although they have received wide publicity. Even in the present state of causal uncertainty concerning variation in home environments within the normal range, it can be observed that comprehensive assessments of the child's early rearing probably afford predictions of educational achievement scores and perhaps other attainments as accurate as child IQ tests. As Bloom (1964) observed, educational test performance is already fairly predictable by school entrance.

Indeed, some have doubted that schooling makes a difference in general abilities. In a review of research carried out in Senegal, Nigeria, South Africa, and among canal boat and Gypsy families in England, Vernon (1969) suggests that it does. Generally, groups of pre-school-age children differed little on mental tests, but groups of school-age children who attended school scored higher than comparison groups who attended less or not at all. Selection bias, that is, brighter children more often attending school, may have occurred in these cross-sectional studies; but some longitudinal studies suggest that schooling raises IQ. Lorge (1945) in the United States and Husen (1951) in Sweden retested adults whose childhood IQ scores were on record and found gains during the intervening period associated with years of schooling. These studies are not completely convincing, since children with high endowments and intellectually stimulating out-of-school experiences may attend school longer.

But those who wish to argue that school makes no difference are confronted with the facts cited earlier that during this century in the United States increasingly larger fractions of the school-age population have attended school, while the average IQ of the young adult male population apparently rose an estimated 22 points from World War I to 1963 and, I estimate by extrapolation, 35 points from 1900 to 1970, or an average of half a point a year. Thus, by the standards of a hypothetical IQ test normed in 1900, the typical young American adult would rank at 135, the genius level in measured verbal intelligence. This rapid rise in IQ may account in part for the "generation gap." Better nutrition, child rearing, out-of-school stimulation, and the immigrants' mastery of English probably caused part of this rise, but the probable role of education is difficult to deny. As Vernon's (1969, pp. 76-79) review suggests, schooling seems to prevent measured mental ability from falling off in adolescence. In 1917-18, American Army recruits, many of whom had not gone to high school, scored on the average no better than thirteen-year-old school children on IQ tests; while psychologists at that time believed that IQ reaches a plateau by age fourteen, later research indicated continued increases past the age of twenty among students who stay in school or college. Vernon (1969) found in some ninety thousand British Army recruits, cross-sectionally classified by age and civilian occupation, steady mental ability decrements with age among unskilled workers after age seventeen but stability or slight declines among those in highly skilled, intellectually stimulating jobs. Comparisons at various age levels of the mental abilities of British adolescent males who remained in school and those of imprisoned boys showed large differences between the two groups which favored the older school boys (Vernon, 1969). Thus it appears that more schooling and schoollike experience is causally related to increases in mental abilities from early childhood through adolescence and into the adult years.

Another important issue is the effect of different educational environments on ability and achievement. To estimate environmental effects on psychological growth in natural settings generally, parallel measures on the same individuals at two points in time and indicators of the quality of the environment during the intervening period are required (Bloom, 1964). Correlational studies of educational environments, it may be added, are more valid, accurate, and comprehensive: when multiple measures of students' cognitive and affective states are obtained in parallel at the two time points to guage different varieties of educational growth; when multiple indicators are used to tap various components of the environment and to assess their impact on different kinds of growth among different students; when the indicators are careful judgmental ratings of outside observers or the students themselves rather than "objective" counts of such things as per pupil expenditures, class size, and the incidence of certain teacher behaviors; when molecular rather than molar units, that is, classes rather than schools or districts are analyzed; and when the parallel student measures fairly reflect the educational goal of the contrasted classes; and finally when simultaneous environments other than the classes assessed have minimal effects on the educational growths in question. Twenty-two school-effects studies have been reviewed by Katzman (1971) and in a U.S. Office of Education (1970) report. Although none meet the standards just mentioned, the studies generally show that crude indicators of school quality such as expenditures per student, class size, mean teacher experience and years of education, percentage of university (rather than teachers' college) graduates of the staff, and recency of course work in graduate education are positively, although weakly, related, with student-input characteristics held statistically constant in most cases, to student-output attainments as indicated by general educational achievement and ability tests.

Moreover, Rosenshine's (1971) review of some 50 available classroom instruction studies shows that growth in cognitive achievement appears to be promoted by clarity of presentation; use of variety in the lesson; enthusiasm, task orientation, and businesslike teacher behavior; the avoidance of strong negative criticism; and pupil opportunities to practice criterion tasks. Other classroom studies that meet the standards mentioned above show that increased cognitive, affective, and behavioral learning is associated with student perceptions of high levels of cohesiveness, satisfaction, proper pacing, organization, and instructional materials, and low levels of apathy, favoritism, and friction (Walberg, 1969; Walberg, 1971). Moreover, different environments appear to be more conducive to learning in students of different abilities (Anderson, 1970) and personalities (Bar-Yam, 1969) and those in different courses of instruction (Walberg, 1970, 1971). Interactions of the type mentioned suggest the possibility that components of the social environments that are optimally suited for individual students may be replicated and used to design personalized instructional environments.

It should be emphasized that most of the research mentioned in this chapter concerns the development of currently-tested mental abilities (especially IQ) and, to a lesser extent, educational achievement as measured by standardized tests, because there is very little comparable work published on other educational outcomes of child rearing and schooling. The available corpus of research provides an extremely limited and probably dangerous basis for evaluating schools and formulating educational policies. Standardized ability and achievement tests tap (or are strongly correlated with or often composed of) a narrow group of verbal skills (best exemplified by word recall, fluency, and recognition vocabulary) more than anything else, and while this factor comes into play in many settings, it is far from being the sole criterion of school effectiveness, social progress, or individual worth. Teacher grades largely reflect this limitation; the standardized test scores and grades kept in student records are mainly accounted for by one or two narrow verbal skill factors (Marshall and Lohnes, 1965). To the extent that teachers use a "psychometically-sophisticated" test development and revision procedure (that is, item-total score correlations for item selection), the more their achievement tests become verbal intelligence tests (Gagne, 1970). Use of such tests tends to direct instructional emphasis and energy toward the optimization of a single goal and away from other worthwhile but unmeasured goals; it reinforces the historical tendency of American education since 1890 to evolve into "one best system" that may be unfair to all in varying degrees (Tyack, 1972). Standardized tests do not even reflect the domain of language skills completely; abstract verbal skills do not determine excellence in writing a poem, singing a lullaby, tutoring a child, giving an order in the Chicago stockyards, or teaching. Educational overemphasis on abstract verbal skills can produce glibness, unconcern for concrete realities, and a narrow intellectual elitism in the young; it encourages academics in the worst senses of the term—the equating of knowledge, wisdom, and problem solving with pedantry, verbosity, and eloquence for its own sake. Since measured verbal ability is heritable and also importantly determined by home environment, educational preoccupation with it can produce a hierarchy based on genetic and social inheritance of a single factor, and can encourage invidious comparisons of groups and individuals. To be sure, standardized tests and grades predict how many years of conventional education a student will attain, but for persons with a given number of years in school, these measures do not predict occupational success in the fields where surveys have been conducted, such as medicine, engineering, teaching, scientific research, and business by criteria of professional reputation, income, employee ratings, and on-the-job observations (Hoyt, 1965). More generally, school grades are nearly useless in predicting inventiveness, leadership, good citizenship, personal maturity, family happiness, and workmanship (Pace, 1966). Marks can be helpful; they serve as incentives for learning and help students to guage their own strengths and progress. They should not be lightly abandoned, but they should be placed in perspective and used cautiously and wisely or not at all. In most cases, assessments of specific skills and performance on realistic tasks reflecting the lesson content are more fair and useful to the teacher and student in guiding the learning process than are standardized tests (Ebel, 1969). Standardized achievement tests, and especially aptitude tests including IQ, probably do far more harm than good for the reasons mentioned, and, in my opinion, ought to be questioned. It is presumptuous, misleading, and prejudicial to call what they measure "intelligence" or "aptitude." They might be called "school-mark prediction scales;" but even this term is dangerous because it assumes that marks capture the outcome of schooling. Use of such scales further assumes and reinforces dangerous academic parochialism and discourages concern for individual differences with respect to other human qualities and educational diversity and innovation. A few years ago, a commission sponsored by the College Entrance Examination Board found that college-level examinations such as the Scholastic Aptitude Tests are severely limited. The commission recommended not only that more diversified measures should be developed and used but also that, according to the principle of reciprocity, the Board should provide more information to the student on the type of environments and subenvironments in various colleges and universities (Commission on Tests, 1970). It is time to enact these kinds of recommendations at all levels of education.

In conclusion, the value of individualizing educational environments deserves emphasis. Recall the earlier evidence that genetic changes in the population appear to be raising and causing variation in intelligence and probably in other human traits as well. Other evidence is cited that suggests that more stimulating environments and better and more prolonged schooling are also raising and perhaps spreading American abilities. Educators face a brighter, more diverse student population. A biological analogy may suggest an appropriate course of action: the gene can only express itself in an environment, and the environment can only evoke the genotype if it is present. Environments should evoke genetic potential if we value excellence and diversity in many spheres of life. A wise parent seeks to bring out the best of the individuality inherent in the child.

Similarly, wise educators further evoke and stimulate the unique combination of partially developed capabilities of each student; modify the environment to fit the student rather than vice versa; and, in recognition of individuality, avoid equating student differences with group or individual inferiorities. They hold high but not irresponsible or romantic expectations for the child and create supportive and friendly environments that demand and reward excellence of many kinds. They seek insights not from within the British-American, hereditarian-environmentalistic, Hobbs-Darwin-Hall tradition that evaluates individual and social progress on a single standard such as IQ or gross national product; nor from the biometric-psychometric, Quetelet-Galton-Pearson-Fisher tradition that also tends to emphasize group-mean and individual differences on limited standards; but from the French-Italian-German-Swiss, Rousseau-Pestalozzi-Montessori-Spranger-Piaget tradition that emphasizes qualitative individual standards (Riegel, 1972). In a time of educational gloom and doom, they take pride in their professional ancestors who provided more and better education for a larger fraction of the American population during this century; and look not only toward ways for different students to reach common goals but also toward the development of goals most suitable for different individuals (Walberg, 1971). Finally, in their desire to develop will in addition to intellect and emotion, they encourage students within the social environment of learning to set and attain their own goals with their teacher's and classmate's help. These values are growing in American education today and will be increasingly important for the rest of this century.

Finally, it should be noted that the last decade of the psychological controversy over heredity and environment has produced more smoke and heat than light as far as education is concerned. Extremists and moderates on both sides of the controversy have exaggerated the importance of a limited range of ability and achievement measures; and, to some, it has apparently become acceptable to evaluate schools and individuals on a single criterion, most often verbal aptitude. Hereditarians have given too much attention to ethnic and socioeconomic group differences and underemphasized the comparative size and importance of variation within groups. Environmentalists have generally underestimated the size and difficulty of the task of modifying the child's environment, and have often promised more than they could deliver. The pessimism of both groups about the role of the schools in society is exerting an unconstructive influence on educational theory and practice, not to mention finance and morale.

It is to be hoped that the research undertaken in the next decade will analyze in detail the poorly understood genetic and environmental (including educational) forces that have improved and diversified the abilities and attainments of successive generations of school children. Such research is likely to document our social and educational accomplishments and to lead to further improvements. Perhaps it will also help to reinvigorate the American traditions of optimism and amelioration regarding society and the individual; as deToqueville observed us in 1840:

> They have all a lively faith in the perfectibility of man, they judge that the diffusion of knowledge must necessarily be advantageous, and the consequences of ignorance fatal; they all consider society as a body in a state of improvement, humanity as a changing scene, in which nothing is, or ought to be, permanent; and they admit that what appears to them today to be good, may be superseded by something better tomorrow." (Pp. 409-410)

References

Anastasi, A. "Intelligence and Family Size." *Psychological Bulletin* 53 (1956): 187-209.

Anderson, G. J. "Effects of Classroom Social Climate on Individual Learning." Ph.D. dissertation, Harvard University, 1968.

————. "Effects of Classroom Social Climate on Individual Learning." *American Educational Research Journal* (1970): 135-52.

Averch, H. A. *How Effective is Schooling? A Critical Review and*

Synthesis of Research Findings. Santa Monica, California: Rand Corporation, 1972.

Bajema, C. J. "Estimation of the Direction and Intensity of Natural Selection in Relation to Human Intelligence by Means of the Intrinsic Rate of Natural Increase." *Eugenics Quarterly* 10 (1963): 175 87.

_____ . "Relation of Fertility to Educational Attainment in a Kalamazoo Public School Population: A Follow-Up Study." *Eugenics Quarterly* 13 (1966): 306-15.

Bar-Yam, M. "The Interaction of Student Characteristics and Instructional Strategies." Ph.D. dissertation, Harvard University, 1969.

Bloom, B. S. *Change and Stability in Human Characteristics.* New York: John Wiley, 1964.

Bowles, S., and Levin, H. M. "The Determinants of Scholastic Achievement—Some Recent Evidence." *Journal of Human Resources* 3 (1968): 3-24.

Burt, Sir C. L. *Intelligence and Fertility.* London: Eugenics Society, 1946.

Cancro, R., ed. *Intelligence: Genetic and Environmental Influences.* New York: Grune and Stratton, 1971.

Caspari, E. "Genetic Endowment and Environment in the Determination of Human Behavior: Biological Viewpoint." *American Educational Research Journal* 5 (1968): 43-56.

Cattell, R. B. "The Fate of National Intelligence: Test of a Thirteen-Year Follow-Up." *Eugenics Review* 43 (1950): 136-48.

Cole, L. "The Population Consequences of Life History Phenomena." *Quarterly Review of Biology* 29 (1954): 103-37.

Coleman, J. S. et al. *Equality of Educational Opportunity.* Washington, D.C.: U.S. Office of Education, 1966.

Commission on Tests. *Righting the Balance.* New York: New York College Entrance Examination Board, 1970.

deTocqueville, A. *Democracy in America* Vol. 1. New York: Vintage Books, 1945.

Dave, R. H. "The Identification and Measurement of Home Environmental Process Variables Related to Educational Achievement." Ph.D. dissertation, University of Chicago, 1963.

Ebel, R. L. "Knowledge and Ability in Achievement Testing." In *Toward a Theory of Achievement Measurement,* edited by P. H. DeBois. Princeton, N.J.: Educational Testing Service, 1969, 66-75.

Emmett, W. G. "The Trend of Intelligence in Certain Districts in England." *Population Studies* 3 (1950): 324-37.

Freedman, R., Whelpton, P. K., and Campbell, A. A. *Family Planning, Sterility, and Population Growth.* New York: McGraw-Hill, 1959.

Gagne, R. M. "Policy Implications and Future Research: A Response." In *Do Teachers Make a Difference?*, U.S. Office of Education. Washington, D.C.: U.S. Government Printing Office, 1970, 169-73.

Heber, R. Research on Education and Habilitation of the Mentally Retarded. Paper read at Conference on Socio-Cultural Aspects of Mental Retardation, 1968, at George Peabody College, Nashville, Tennessee.

Higgens, J. V., Reed, E., and Reed, S. C. "Intelligence and Family Size: A Paradox Resolved." *Eugenics Quarterly* 9 (1962): 84-90.

Hoyt, D. P. *The Relationship Between College Grades and Adult Achievement.* Iowa City, Iowa: American College Testing Programs, 1965.

Husen, T. "The Influence of Schooling on IQ." *Theoria* 17 (1951): 61-88.

Jencks, C. et al. *Inequality: A Reassessment of the Effect of Family and Schooling in America.* New York: Basic Books, 1972.

Jensen, A. R. "How Much Can We Boost IQ and Scholastic Achievement?" *Harvard Educational Review* 39 (1969): 1-123.

Kallman, F. J. *Heredity in Health and Mental Disorder.* New York: Norton, 1953.

Katzman, M. T. *The Political Economy of Urban Schools.* Cambridge, Mass.: Harvard University Press, 1971.

Kent, N., and Davis, D. R. "Discipline in the Home and Intellectual Development." *British Journal of Medical Psychology* 30 (1957): 27-33.

Lorge, I. "Schooling Makes A Difference." *Teachers' College Record* 46 (1945): 483-92.

Lowell, K. "A Study of the Problem of Intellectual Deterioration in Adolescents and Young Adults." *British Journal of Psychology* 44 (1955): 199-210.

Majoribanks, K. "Environment, Social Class, and Mental Abilities." *Journal of Educational Psychology* 63 (1972): 103-09.

Marshall, T. O., and Lohnes, P. R. "Redundancy in Student Records." *American Educational Research Journal* 2 (1965): 19-23.

Moynihan, D. P., and Mosteller, F. *On Equality of Educational Opportunity.* New York: Random House, 1972.

Nam, C., and Folger, J. K. "Educational Trends from Census Data." *Demography* 1 (1964): 247-57.

National Academy of Sciences. *Genetic Vulnerability of Major Crops.* Washington, D.C.: U.S. Government Printing Office, 1972.

Nisbet, J. D. "Family Environment and Intelligence." *Eugenics Review* 45 (1953): 31-40.

Osborn, F. *The Future of Human Heredity.* New York: Weybright and Talley, 1968.

Pace, C. R. "Perspectives on the Student and His College." In *The Educational Problem to 1980 and Beyond,* edited by J. I. Goodlad. Washington, D.C.: American Council on Education, 1966, 76-100.

Page, E. B. "Miracle in Milwaukee: Raising the IQ." *Educational Researcher* 1 (1972): 8-16.

Plowden, B. *Children and their Primary Schools.* London: H.M. Stationery Office, 1967.

Riegel, K. F. "Influence of Economic and Political Ideologies on the Development of Developmental Psychology." *Psychological Bulletin* 78 (1972): 129-41.

Rosenshine, B. "The Stability of Teacher Effects upon Student Achievement." *Review of Educational Research* 40 (1970): 647-62.

Royal Commission on Population. *Papers of the Royal Commission on Population.* London: H.M. Stationery Office, 1950.

Scheinfeld, A. *Heredity and Environment.* Philadelphia, Pa.: J. B. Lippincott, 1965.

Science. "IQ: Methodological and Other Issues." In Letters to the Editor, *Science* 178 (1972): 229-39.

Scottish Council for Research in Education and Population Investigation Committee. *The Trend of Scottish Intelligence.* London: University of London Press, 1949.

Scarr-Salapabek, S. "Race, Social Class, and IQ." *Science* 174 (1971a): 1285-95.

————. "Unknowns in the IQ Equation." *Science* 174 (1971b): 1223-28.

Stein, Z., et al. "Nutrition and Mental Performance." *Science* 178 (1972): 708-13.

Sullivan, H. S. "The Illusion of Individuality." *Psychiatry* 13 (1950): 329-40.

Tuddenham, R. D. "Soldier Intelligence in World Wars I and II." *American Psychologist* 3 (1948): 54-56.

Tupes, E., and Shaycroft, M. "Normative Distribution of AQE Aptitude Indexes for High School Age Boys." Lackland, Texas: U.S. Air Force Base (Technical Documentary Reports), 1964.

Tyack, D. B. "The 'One Best System: A Historical Analysis.' " In *Rethinking Urban Education,* edited by H. J. Walberg and A. T. Kopan. San Francisco, Calif.: Jossey-Bass, 1972, 231-46.

U.S. Office of Education. *Do Teachers Make A Difference? A Report on Recent Research on Pupil Achievement.* Washington, D.C.: U.S. Government Printing Office, 1970.

Vandenberg, S. G. "What Do We Know Today about the Inheritance of Intelligence and How Do We Know It? In *Intelligence: Genetic and Environmental Influences,* edited by Robert Canero. New York: Grune and Stratton, 1971, 182-220.

Vernon, P. E. *Intelligence and Cultural Environment.* London: Methuen, 1969.

Walberg, H. J. "Models for Optimizing and Individualizing Learning." *Interchange* 2 (1971): 15-27.

————. "A Model for Research on Instruction." *School Review* 78 (1970): 185-200.

————. "Social Environment as a Mediator of Classroom Learning." *Journal of Educational Psychology* 60 (1969): 443-48.

————. "Urban Schooling and Delinquency: Toward an Intgrative Theory." *American Educational Research Journal* 9 (1972): 285-300.

Warren, B. L. "A Multiple Variable Approach to the Assortative Mating Problem." *Eugenics Quarterly* 13 (1966): 285-90.

Watson, J. B. *Behaviorism.* Chicago: University of Chicago Press, 1930.

Weber, M. *Protestant Ethic and the Spirit of Capitalism.* New York: Scribner, 1930.

Weiss, J. "The Identification and Measurement of Home Environmental Process Variables that are Related to Intelligence." Ph.D. dissertation, University of Chicago, 1969.

Weyl, N. and Possony, S. T. *The Geography of Intellect*. Chicago: Henry Regnery Co., 1963.

Wiseman, S. *Education and Environment*. Manchester, England: Manchester University Press, 1964.

Wolf, R. M. "The Identification and Measurement of Home Environmental Process Variables that Are Related to Intelligence." Ph.D. dissertation, University of Chicago, 1964.